T0250327

Edge Computational Intelligence for AI-Enabled IoT Systems

Edge computational intelligence is an interface between edge computing and artificial intelligence (AI) technologies. This interfacing represents a paradigm shift in the world of work by enabling a broad application areas and customer-friendly solutions. Edge computational intelligence technologies are just in their infancy. *Edge Computational Intelligence for AI-Enabled IoT Systems* looks at the trends and advances in edge computing and edge AI, the services rendered by them, related security and privacy issues, training algorithms, architectures, and sustainable AI-enabled IoT systems.

Together, these technologies benefit from ultra-low latency, faster response times, lower bandwidth costs, and resilience from network failure, and the book explains the advantages of systems and applications using intelligent IoT devices that are at the edge of a network and close to users. It explains how to make the most of edge and cloud computing as complementary technologies or used in isolation for extensive and widespread applications. The advancement in IoT devices, networking facilities, parallel computation and 5G, and robust infrastructure for generalized machine learning have made it possible to employ edge computational intelligence in diverse areas and in diverse ways.

The book begins with chapters that cover edge AI services available as compared to conventional systems. These are followed by chapters that discuss security and privacy issues encountered during the implementation and execution of edge AI and computing services. The book concludes with chapters looking at applications spread across different areas of edge AI and edge computing and also at the role of computational intelligence in AI-driven IoT systems.

Shrikaant Kulkarni, Ph.D., is currently a research and technical advisor at Filantrofia Sarvada CleanTech Pvt. Ltd., Pune, India, and adjunct professor at Padm. Dr. V. B. Kolte College of Engineering, Malkapur, India. He has published over 100+ research papers in national and international journals and conferences of repute. He has authored 50 book chapters and edited 12 books published by Apple Academic Press/CRC Press and Springer Nature. Another ten books are in the offing. He authored four textbooks in engineering chemistry. Dr. Kulkarni possesses M.Sc., M.Phil., and Ph.D. degrees in Chemistry and master's degrees in Economics, Business Management, and Political Science. He has expertise in the fields of green chemistry and engineering, analytical chemistry, and green nanoscience and nanotechnology, wastewater treatment, green and analytical chemistry, and advanced areas in chemical engineering and material science.

Jaiprakash Narain Dwivedi, Ph.D., is currently working as an associate professor, IT Department, Parul Institute of Engineering and Technology, Faculty of Engineering and Technology, Parul University, Vadodara, Gujarat, India. He has published over 20 research papers in international journals and International conferences of repute. He has authored 3 book chapters and 3 competitive books for general aptitude and engineering field. Dr. Dwivedi possesses B.E.(Electronics and Communication Engineering), M.Tech.(Signal Processing), Ph.D.(Machine Learning from Kyutech Japan). His research interest includes artificial neural network, pattern recognition, machine learning, classification, CNN, DNN, deep learning and signal processing. He has expertise in the fields of artificial intelligence, machine learning, ANN and IT software.

Dinda Pramanta received his Bachelor degree from The Telkom University (formerly Telkom Institute of Technology), in 2013, Indonesia, and completed both Master and Doctoral degrees from the Kyushu Institute of Technology, in 2016 and 2020, respectively. He was a post-doctoral fellow in Japan from 2020 to 2021. Currently, he is an assistant professor. His research interests include spiking neural networks, hardware, and AI for educational purposes.

Yuichiro Tanaka, B.Eng., M.Eng., Ph.D., received his degrees from the Kyushu Institute of Technology, in 2016, 2018, and 2021, respectively. He was a research fellow of the Japan Society for the Promotion of Science (JSPS) from 2019 to 2021. Currently, he is an assistant professor with the Research Center for Neuromorphic AI Hardware, Kyushu Institute of Technology. His research interests include soft computing, neural networks, hardware, and home service robots. He is a member of IEEE and JNNS.

Advances in Computational Collective Intelligence
Edited by
Dr. Subhendu Kumar Pani
Principal, Krupajal Group of Institutions, India

Published

Applications of Machine Learning and Deep Learning on Biological Data
By Faheem Syeed Masoodi, Mohammad Tabrez Quasim, Syed Nisar Hussain
Bukhari, Sarvottam Dixit, and Shadab Alam
ISBN: 978-1-032-214375

Artificial Intelligence Techniques in Power Systems Operations and Analysis
By Nagendra Singh, Sitendra Tamrakar, Arvind Mewara, and Sanjeev
Kumar Gupta
ISBN: 978-1-032-294865

Technologies for Sustainable Global Higher Education
By Maria José Sousa, Andreia de Bem Machado, and Gertrudes Aparecida
Dandolini
ISBN: 978-1-032-262895

Forthcoming

Deep Learning for Smart Healthcare: Trends, Challenges and Applications
K. Murugeswari, B.Sundaravadivazhagan, S. Poonkuntran, and Thendral
Puyalnithi
ISBN: 978-1-032-455815

Edge Computational Intelligence for AI-Enabled IoT Systems
By Shrikaant Kulkarni, Jaiprakash Narain Dwivedi, Dinda Pramanta, and
Yuichiro Tanaka
ISBN: 978-1-032-207667

Explainable AI and Cybersecurity
By Mohammad Tabrez Quasim, Abdullah Alharthi, Ali Alqazzaz, Mohammed
Mujib Alshahrani, Ali Falh Alshahrani, and Mohammad Ayoub Khan
ISBN: 978-1-032-422213

Machine Learning in Applied Sciences
By M. A. Jabbar, Shankru Guggari, Kingsley Okoye, and Houneida Sakly
ISBN: 978-1-032-251721

Social Media and Crowdsourcing
By Sujoy Chatterjee, Thipendra P Singh, Sunghoon Lim, and Anirban
Mukhopadhyay
ISBN: 978-1-032-386874

Edge Computational Intelligence for AI-Enabled IoT Systems

Edited by
Shrikaant Kulkarni, Jaiprakash Narain Dwivedi,
Dinda Pramanta, and Yuichiro Tanaka

CRC Press
Taylor & Francis Group
Boca Raton London New York

CRC Press is an imprint of the
Taylor & Francis Group, an **informa** business

First edition published 2024
2385 NW Executive Center Drive, Suite 320, Boca Raton FL 33431

and by CRC Press
4 Park Square, Milton Park, Abingdon, Oxon, OX14 4RN

CRC Press is an imprint of Taylor & Francis Group, LLC

ISBN: 9781032207667 (hbk)
ISBN: 9781032650692 (pbk)
ISBN: 9781032650722 (ebk)

DOI: 10.1201/9781032650722

Typeset in Garamond
by Newgen Publishing UK

Contents

Preface

Edge computational intelligence is an interface between edge computing and edge AI technologies, which are in great demand and their interfacing has resulted in a paradigm shift in the focus of the world of work. These emerging technologies have made inroads in broad application areas and provided customer-friendly solutions. However, these technologies are in their infancy and have a long way to go in reaching every nook and corner of the world in terms of outreach, agility, stability, affordability, robustness, infrastructural facilities, etc. These state-of-the-art technologies have a comparative advantage in terms of ultra-low latency, faster response times, lower bandwidth costs, and resilience from network failure. This is facilitated by data sources and IoT devices closer to users unlike cloud computing, which uses a centralized facility for data storage, analysis, and insight. This book includes chapters that emphasize how we can make the most of both edge and cloud computing as complementary technologies to one another and in isolation for extensive and widespread application areas by leveraging the promising features of both technologies. Advancements in IoT devices, networking facilities, parallel computation and 5G, and robust infrastructure for generalized machine learning have made it become possible to employ edge computational intelligence in diverse areas and different walks of life.

This book sheds light on various aspects of edge computational intelligence in terms of trends and advances in edge computing and edge AI, services rendered by them, security and privacy issues, training algorithms, architectures, sustainable AI-enabled I0T systems, advances in networking, and applications in different frontier areas.

The book is divided into four parts. Part I is devoted to edge AI services on offer as compared to conventional systems. Part II is dedicated to security and privacy issues encountered during the implementation and execution of edge AI and computing services, while part III deals with applications spread across different areas of edge AI and edge computing. Part IV focuses on the role of computational intelligence of AI-driven IoT systems across the board. Part I has three chapters. Chapter 1 introduces edge AI and edge computing and discusses the trends developed over time and some representative applications. Chapter 2 discusses the way IoT services are secured with the help of AI in edge computing. Chapter 3 deliberates on computational-based edge AI services in general and challenges in this area.

Part II of the book has three chapters. Chapter 4 covers security and privacy-related issues when designing, developing, and rendering edge AI services. Chapter 5 gives an overview of contributions of edge computing in the design and development of the Metaverse ecosystem. Chapter 6 sheds light on the way sustainable communication is brought about through robust edge AI systems and algorithms for training machines. Part III includes four topics. Chapter 7 discusses machine learning-based hybrid techniques employed for securing edge computing with efficiency. Chapter 8 deliberates on the use of mobile services in the changing environment created by edge computing. Chapter 9 discusses in detail the novelty in AI-enabled applications in edge computing for IoT-based services. Chapter 10 sheds light on applications of edge AI-related services in the field of medicine in particular.

Part IV is the concluding part of the book with four chapters. Chapter 11 covers AI and soft computing-driven evolutionary computation algorithms for solving unconstrained nonlinear problems. Chapter 12 takes a look at UAV-enabled mobile edge computing for IoT applications. Chapter 13 is dedicated to software-designed networks, which are driven by IoT, and finally Chapter 14 looks at smart and sustainable as well as energy-efficient wireless sensor network design and techniques employed in smart cities for the time-tested IoT services.

MATLAB® is a registered trademark of The Math Works, Inc. For product information, please contact:
The Math Works, Inc.
3 Apple Hill Drive
Natick, MA 01760-2098
Tel: 508-647-7000
Fax: 508-647-7001
E-mail: info@mathworks.com
Web: http://www.mathworks.com

Editors

Dr. Shrikaant Kulkarni, is currently a research and technical advisor at Filantrofia Sarvada Clean Tech Pvt. Ltd., Pune, India, and Adjunct Professor at Padm. Dr. V. B. Kolte College of Engineering, Malkapur, India. Dr. Kulkarni has 40+ years of teaching and research experience. He has published over 100+ research papers in national and international journals and conferences of repute. He has authored 50+ book chapters and edited 12 books published by Apple Academic Press/CRC Press and Springer Nature. Another ten books are in the offing. He authored four textbooks in engineering chemistry. Dr. Kulkarni possesses M.Sc., M.Phil., and Ph.D., degrees in Chemistry and master's degrees in Economics, Business Management, and Political Science. He has expertise in the fields of green chemistry and engineering, analytical chemistry, and green nanoscience and nanotechnology, wastewater treatment, green and analytical chemistry, and advanced areas in chemical Engineering and material science, and industrial organization and management. He was invited by UNESCO to deliver a talk on green education for sustainable development in Bangkok at the International Conference on Green Chemistry. He has conducted many expert sessions as a resource person/session chair in many national and international events. He won many accolades for his institutes and received awards for achieving excellence in education. He is a member of editorial board of many reputed international journals in green and sustainable chemistry, pharmacy and reviewer of high impact factor journals.

Dr. Shrikaant Kulkarni is currently adjunct professor in Science & Technology Department, Vishwakarma University, Pune, India. Kulkarni has been an academician and researcher for 39 years. Kulkarni has delivered lectures and conducted sessions at national and international conferences as well as faculty development programs. He has taught subjects such as edge computing and edge AI, engineering chemistry, green chemistry, nanotechnology, analytical chemistry, catalysis, chemical engineering materials, industrial organization, and management, to name a few. He has published over 100 research papers in national and international journals and conferences. He has authored 36 book chapters in CRC Press, Springer Nature, AAP press, Elsevier, Wiley, and IET books. He has edited six books on green engineering and green nanoscience & nanotechnology published by Apple Academic Press/CRC Press. Another five books are in the offing. He has also co-authored four textbooks and worked as a resource person for many national and international events. Kulkarni holds M.Sc., M.Phil., and Ph.D. degrees in chemistry apart from master degrees in economics, business management, and political science. He has expertise in the field of artificial intelligence and machine learning, material science, green chemistry & engineering, analytical chemistry, and green nanoscience & nanotechnology.

Dr. Jaiprakash Narain Dwivedi received his B.E. (electronics and communication engineering) degree from Rajeev Gandhi Proudyogiki Vishwavidyalaya, Bhopal, India, M. Tech. (signal processing) degree from East Campus NSUT, Delhi, India (formerly AIACTR Delhi, affiliated to Guru Gobind Singh Indraprastha University Delhi), and Ph.D. (artificial neural network) from the Graduate School of Life Science and Systems Engineering, Kyushu Institute of Technology, Japan. He is currently working as associate professor, IT Department, Parul Institute of Engineering and Technology, Parul University, Vadodara, Gujarat, India. He has 14 years of experience in roles such as associate professor, ECE Department, Lingaya's Vidyapeeth, Faridabad, Haryana, India, associate professor, ECE Department, University Institute of Engineering, Chandigarh University, Mohali, Punjab, India, associate professor at Malla Reddy Institute of Technology and Science affiliated to Jawaharlal Nehru Technological University Hyderabad, India, Subject Matter Expert (AI) at Inorbital Solution Ltd. London, research associate at Graduate School of Life Science and Systems Engineering, Kyushu Institute of Technology, Japan for New Energy and Industrial Technology Development Organization (NEDO) Project, Systems Engineer at Polaris Financial Technology Ltd. Mumbai, and lecturer at ACROPOLIS Institute of Technology and Research Bhopal, India. He was also NBA coordinator for three years for the ECE Department at Malla Reddy Institute of Technology and Science, Hyderabad and Internal Quality Assurance Cell (IQAC) coordinator for NAAC accreditation along with team head of the ECE Department for the inspection of JNTUH Fact Finding Committee (FFC). His professional activities include roles as associate editor, editorial board member, and reviewer of various international journals. His research publication includes patents, book chapters, journals, and conference proceedings. He received the Young Scientist Award and lifetime achievement awards. His research interests include machine learning, artificial neural network, pattern recognition, classification, CNN, DNN, deep learning, and signal processing.

Dr. Dinda Pramanta received his bachelor's degree from The Telkom University (formerly Telkom Institute of Technology) in 2013, Indonesia, and completed both master's and doctoral degrees from the Kyushu Institute of Technology, in 2016 and 2020, respectively. He was awarded post-doctoral fellowship of collaborative joint research between Kyushu Institute of Technology and The New Energy and Industrial Technology Development Organization (NEDO), Japan from 2020 to 2021. Currently, he is assistant professor and a committee member of Mathematical-Data Science-AI Educational Program on Kyushu Institute of Information Sciences. His research interests include spiking neural networks, hardware, and AI for educational purposes.

Dr. Yuichiro Tanaka received B.Eng., M.Eng., and Ph.D. degrees from the Kyushu Institute of Technology, in 2016, 2018, and 2021, respectively. He was research fellow of the Japan Society for the Promotion of Science (JSPS) from 2019 to 2021. Currently, he is an assistant professor with at the Research Center for Neuromorphic AI Hardware, Kyushu Institute of Technology. His research interests include soft computing, neural networks, hardware, and home service robots. He is also a member of IEEE and JNNS.

Abbreviations

3D	Three Dimensional
6G	6th Generation
AGI	Artificial general intelligence
AI	Artificial intelligence
AIM	AI in Medicine
ANI	Artificial narrow intelligence
ANN	Artificial neural network
ANOVA	Analysis of Variance
API	Application Programming Interface
APK	Android Package Kit
APU	AI Processing Unit
AQI	Air Quality Index
AR	Augmented reality
AR-VR	Augmented Reality Virtual Reality
ASI	Artificial Super Intelligence
ASIC	Application-Specific Integrated Circuits
C/S	Client Server
CBDLP	Data Leakage Protection Based on Context
CC	Cloud Computing
CCTV	Closed Circuit Television
CDCs	Certified Data centres
CDMA	Code division various accesses
CDN	Content Delivery Network
CH	Cluster Head
CN	Core Networks
CO2	Carbon Dioxide
COD	Cash on Delivery
CPU	Computer Processing Unit
CV	Computer Vision
DBE	Data Box Edge
DBMS	Data Base Management System
DDOS	Distributed Denial of Service
DFL	Decentralized Federated Learning

DL	Deep Learning
DLP	Data Leakage Prevention
DNN	Deep neural network
DP	Differential Privacy
DQN	Deep Q Network
DSN	Distributed Sensing Network
DSRC	Dedicated short-range communication
DWSN	Distributed Wireless Sensor Networks
EA	Evolutionary Algorithms
EC	Edge Computing
ECA	Edge Computing Alliance
EH-WSNs	Energy harvesting-related wireless sensor network
EI	Edge Intelligence
EIN	Edge Intelligence Networks
EMR	Electronic medical records
EN	Edge node
ETSI	European Telecommunications Standards Institute
FC	Fog Computing
FCN	Fog Computing Network
FPGA	Field Programmable Gate Array
FPR	False Positive Rate
GAN	Generative adversarial network
GPU	Graphics Processing Unit
GSA	Gravitational Search Algorithm
GSM	Global System for Mobile Communications
HC	Heterogeneous Computing
HE	Homomorphic Encryption
HFL	Heterogeneous federated learning
HW	Hammeistern Weiner
ICT	Information and communications technology
IDS	Intrusion Detection System
IEEE	Institute of Electrical and Electronics Engineers
IIoTs	Industrial Internet of Things
InfNet	Untrained ObfNet with the trained in-service inference model
IOB	Input-Output Block
IoD	Internet of Drones
IoT	Internet of Things
IoVs	Internet of Vehicles
ISG	Industry Specification Group
ISP	Internet service provider
LAN	Local Area Network
LCA	Logic Cell Array

LED	Light-Emitting Diode
LLC	Logical Link Control
MAC	Media Access Control
MANET	Mobile Ad–hoc Network
MBSs	Mobile Base Stations
MDCs	Micro Data Centres
MEC	Mobile Edge Computing
MEC	Mobile Equipment Consortium
MECs	Mobile or Multi-access Edge Computing
MEDLARS	Medical Literature Analysis and Retrieval System
ML	Machine learning
MN	Mobile Network Operator
MRTD	Maximum Recommended Therapeutic Dose
MSE	Mean Square Error
MVN	Mobile virtual network operator
MVNP	Mobile virtual network provider
NFV	Network Function Virtualization
NGOs	Non-Governmental Organizations
NLP	Natural Language Processing
No SQL	Not Only Structured Query Language
NPU	Neural Processing Unit
NS	Network Slicing
ObfNet	Obfuscation Neural Network
OPC UA	OPC Unified Architecture
PBFT	Protected Byzantine fault-tolerant
PC	Personal computer
PCA	Principle Component Method
PDA	Personal Digital Assistants
PEQ	Periodic, Event-driven, Query-based
PGW	Packet Mobile Gateway
PII	Personally Identifiable Information
PVP	Poly Vinyl Pyrrolidone
PEG	Polyethylene Glycol
QoS	Quality of Service
QSAR	Quantitative structure-activity relationship
QSPR	Quantitative structure-property relationship
RAN	Radio Access Networks
RFID	Radio Frequency Identification
RL	Reinforcement Learning
RNN	Recurrent neural network
ROBLOX	Ro Oders Blox Love On Xan
RPC	Remote Procedure Call

RSU	Road side unit
SA	Security Association
SAS	Synthetic accessibility score
SDA	Secure Data Aggregation
SDN	Software-defined Networking
SIMS	Simulation
SLT	Statistical Learning Theory
SMAC	Sensor Medium Access Control
SMT	Secure Message Transfer
SNPE	Snapdragon Neural Processing Engine
SO2	Sulphur Dioxide
SP	Service Provider
SPs	Smart Parks
SQL	Structured Query Language
SUMEX-AIM	Stanford University Medical Experimental-Artificial Intelligence in Medicine
SVM	Support Vector Machine
TDMA	Time Division Multiple Access
TN	Transmission Networks
TPOT	The Teaching Pyramid Observation Tool
TPR	True Positive Rate
TSN	Time Sensitive Networking
UAV	Unmanned Aerial Vehicle
VANET	Vehicular Ad–hoc network
VM	Virtual Machine
VNFs	Virtualized Network Functions
VR	Virtual Reality
VS	Value Scenarios
WAN	Wide Area Network
WiFi	Wireless Fidelity
WiMAX	Worldwide interoperability for microwave access
WLAN	Wireless Local Area Network
WMN	Wireless mesh network
WSN	Wireless Sensor Network
Z Generation	Zoomers Generation
ZB	Zetabytes

COMPUTATIONAL INTELLIGENCE

I

INTELLIGENCE
Edge AI Services

Chapter 1

Edge Computational Intelligence: Fundamentals, Trends, and Applications

Shrikaant Kulkarni[1]

[1]Faculty of Science & Technology, Vishwakarma University, Pune, India

1.1 Introduction

Computing and storage devices have been proliferating, right from server clusters in the cloud to personal computers and smartphones, apart from a host of Internet of Things (IoT) devices including wearable ones. Information-led computing is witnessed across the board while computational services run from cloud to edge. Cisco [1] reports that internet will connect about 50 billion IoTs till 2020. According to Cisco's estimate 850 zettabytes (ZB) of data need to be managed till 2021, although traffic at global data centers is mere 20.6 ZB [2] the big data sources transition from huge cloud data centers to ever increasing end devices.

Cloud computing (CC) of today is unable to deal with massive but distributed computing capability and data analysis. Many computational tasks are sent to the cloud to process [3], which challenges the network and CC for computing capabilities. Various applications (e.g., automated driving) that demand real-time response and the cloud fail to meet user needs because of distance from users [4].

DOI: 10.1201/9781032650722-2

Hence, edge computing (EC) [5, 6] has come to the fore as a better option, particularly for computational tasks in the vicinity of the sources of data and users. Beyond doubt, EC and CC complement each other [7, 8]. But EC is a complementary and value-added version of CC. EC combined with CC offers the following advantages:

- Edge computing nodes very well handle many computational tasks with no exchange of the concerned data with the cloud and despite network traffic load.
- Edge computing substantially enhances data transmission and has low latency.
- Incredible processing power and huge storage can be used to advantage where the edge is unable to do it.

Cloud to edge transition is a big evolutionary step across the computing model. Evolution in the computing models and equipment are going hand in hand. In the following we discuss the phases in the evolution of computing models.

Edge AI refers to deployment of AI applications in devices cutting across the physical world. It is so called because the AI computation is brought closer to the user at the network's edge, and closer to data sources, instead of centralized and far off as in the case of CC. As the internet has reached out to every nook and corner of the world the edge place such as a device, hospital, industry, virtual machine, phone, streetlights etc.

1.2 Mainframe-Based Computing Model

The earliest computers lacked computing power and required large and expensive equipment for computing, while all computing jobs relied on the centralized parent computer, and other devices were devoid of computing power but were capable of availing the applications and data on the host computer to meet the varying computing needs of users.

1.3 PC File Server-Based Computing Model

With the growth in computing capabilities, computing equipment is getting micronized in volume and price. PCs are the mainstay of the computing model, but lack adequate data storage capacity. Mainframe computers conversely have the capacity to store huge amount of data can be accessed by PCs.

1.4 C/S Architecture-Based Computing Model

Database technology is emerging and gaining popularity given the weaknesses of the old file sharing architecture; thus, the C/S model has substituted conventional ones and is characterized by the use of a database management system (DBMS) that offers users quick access to RPC or SQL.

1.5 Web and B/S Architecture-Based Computing Model

The number of users, computing needs, and quantum of data led to the evolution of the conventional C/S model into bi- or tri-layered C/S models. Similarly, Internet browsers and web servers are developed, popularized, and added as the client and middle layer respectively, leading to the formation of B/S architecture.

1.6 Mobile Devices-Centric Computing Model

Computers today are used in all facets of life resulting in great advancements in computing technologies. However, the computing models need to be before the computer to accomplish tasks. Ubiquitous computing has made inroads in all walks of life using advances in this area.

1.7 Technologies-Based Computing Model

Advances in IT in the form of integration of grid, Peer-to-Peer (P2P) and CC have made it possible to meet the growing and varying needs of users. It demands computing models that have evolved in tune with needs of consumers. Advancement in technology has driven the computing models user friendly, need-based and problem-sentric.

1.8 End–Edge–Cloud Computing Model

IoT and integration of computer technologies with human life is a reality today. It demands not only enhanced computing power and perception, but also the ability to deal with a huge amount of data produced by the innumerable IoT devices. Cloud computing alone is not able to cope with the demands of the current era and thus edge computing is needed to meet the needs of users today.

1.9 EC Trends

Edge computing (EC) has brought to the fore numerous opportunities because of the paradigm shift in technology. Edge computing developed by taking the advantage of emerging technologies to build architectural blueprint for industrial advantage. Similarly, EC technology is matured, standardized and is presenting opportunities to achieve new milestones. Edge computing has the following characteristics:

■ Non-homogeneous computing
■ Intelligence of edge
■ Edge cloud combination
■ 5G + enabled

1.9.1 Heterogeneous Computing

Heterogeneous computing (HC) uses devices with varying performance and config-uration to meet the changing computing needs of users and maximizes performance on heterogeneous platforms with the help of algorithms. This type of computing in EC helps in processing discrete data and proper planning and enhancing utilization of computing machinery.

1.9.2 Edge Intelligence (EI)

Edge intellgience (EI) pushes AI to the edge, and thus applies and expresses AI. It pushes AI to the edge, and uses advancements in the computing power of hardware to advantage in applications. AI deployed on the edge nodes furthers data transmis-sion, and thereby reduces communication costs, lowers latency, and broadens the application horizons. Similarly, EC uses AI to maximize computing resource sched-uling decisions at the edge and supports EC in expanding business scenarios as well as offers users sound services to users. Thus EI will be a key technology in the future.

1.9.3 Edge Cloud Interface

Edge computing is an extended version of CC. They are complementary to one another. On the one hand, CC is centralized and doesn't process and analyze data in real time and has a longer cycle while EC is decentralized and better than localized, real-time and characterized by shorter cycle and therby processes and analyzes data intelligently. Hence, for similar kinds of AI applications the cloud is preferred for computer-intensive tasks, and edge for tasks that demand fast response. Similarly, the edge is responsible for processing the data prior to sending it to the cloud to bring about reduction in network bandwidth consumption. Edge and cloud together can fulfill the computing requirements of users and reduce costs of computing and network bandwidth. Thus, the use of EC and CC together provides an impetus to their further advancement and can be a driver for the furtherance of a host of technologies like EI, IoT, etc.

1.9.4 5G + Edge Computing

It is characterized by:

■ Tremendous speed

- Excellent connectivity
- Abysmally low latency

These objectives are attained by using various frontier technologies including EC. 5G and EC are intricately woven; EC belongs to 5G network and minimizes the big data problem in 5G while 5G presents a sound network facility for the further development of EC. Therefore, both of these technologies complement each other and work in harmony for 5G scenarios and the enhancement of network power.

1.10 EC Applications in Industry

Edge computing is more of a distributed complementary resource-sharing model unlike CC, which is more of a centralized one. Different solutions are proposed by service operators at various levels of "end–edge–cloud."

1.10.1 Cloud Service Provider-Based Model

The edge cloud nodes of Google GKF on-Prem, Microsoft Azure Stack cloud-EC models are aimed at creating hybrid ecosystems where the cloud takes precedence. Greater complex contents are offloaded to the cloud.

1.10.2 Site Facility Edge Service

Vapor has created ecosystems in collaboration with other companies similar to China Tower Corporation presenting numerous edge sites, and connecting through a network with the help of machine rooms and containers.

1.10.3 Fixed Operator-Enabled EC Services

China-based Edge Computing Alliance (ECA) is an example of a fixed network EC launched by Huawei's network and connected extensively with the industry.
 Major areas of focus are:

- Switching equipment for the enterprises
- Edge infrastructure accessed as fixed one

1.10.4 Mobile Operator-Centric EC Services

Edge computing, which was also called "mobile edge computing," until 2014 was so called as it was confined to doing cache at the mobile base station without commercial use because of limitations of base stations in perceiving the distribution as well as management of content. It gave rise to a packet mobile gateway (PGW). In 2017, Huawei's wireless core network recommended the "multi-access EC," connected with the 5G network system.

1.10.5 EC as a Self-Organizing Network

Industry self-built networks combined with computing facilities can be mobile or fixed-operator-based networks using stack protocol. For example, LoRa or Wi-Fi are used in free networking. Application of the cloud, providers of services at sites, the IoT, and end devices result in the protocol stack resembling a self-organizing network.

1.10.6 Near End Computing Services

Near end computing services are used for processing computation in real time and at local level, and are followed by communication with a large network for supporting the upper-level node.

1.11 Intelligent Edge (IE) and Edge Intelligence (EI)

Intelligent edge is primarily and extensively employed in frontier application [9]; many deep learning-enabled intelligent services have brought about significant change in all walks of life by taking advantage of Deep Learning (DL) in areas like Computer Vision (CV) and Natural Language Processing (NLP) [10]. Evolution in AI is instrumental in all these achievements and is intricately woven with growing data and computing capabilities. However, for a host of applications like smart cities, Internet of Vehicles (IoVs), etc., very few intelligent services are available for the following reasons.

1.11.1 Cost

AI algorithms are trained and inferred using huge amounts of data for suitability testing in the cloud, which in turn demands broad network bandwidth and is therefore expensive.

1.11.2 Latency

The delay in response for accessing cloud services is uncertain resulting into inordinate delay in fulfilling the needs of numerous time-based applications namely, autonomous driving [11];

1.11.3 Reliability

CC depends on wireless communications and sound networks for communicating with users, and in industry, intelligent services are characterized by high reliability, in the absence of the network connectivity.

1.11.4 Privacy

AI may require data that carry confidential information, and therefore privacy is vital in applications used in smart homes and cities. Since the edge is in the neighborhood of users unlike the cloud, EC can address a host of the issues such as stability, agility, latency, etc. Edge computing in combination with AI complement one another and realize EI and IE. AI technology in intelligent edge is embodied with EI and optimally utilize resources of EI. Precisely, EI pushes AI computations to the edge to tap its potential to the maximum, thus facilitating many varied, rapidly responsive, and reliable services.

The advantages of edge AI services include:

- Closer to users, and the cloud merely processes surplus data [12], which thereby enhances response and reduces cost of data transmission.
- Demands raw data, stored at the edge or end devices rather than the cloud, which enables enhancement of privacy of users.
- Provides more reliable computation accompanied by large data and distributed application scenarios.
- Promotes the use of AI and provides personalized AI services and organization-centric services across the board [13].
- Diverse and meaningful services and tap the commercial potential of EC and further its use.

Intelligent edge introduces AI for the flexible, adaptive edge for its management. Along with the advancements in the communication technologies, network access methods are getting diversified. Similarly, an EC facility works as a medium, and thus the communication is more reliable between end devices and the cloud [14]. Hence, the end devices, edge, and cloud form a community with all shared resources. However, such a voluminous and complex community is not easy to maintain and manage since it consists of wireless communication, networking, computing, storage etc., a daunting task [15]. Network optimization methods depend on mathematical models that are difficult to model with accuracy in dynamically changing edge environments and computing systems. Deep learning as a key technology of AI deals with the problem of complex edge network environments and works on the basis of its incredible learning and reasoning capabilities to interpret data and make quality decisions and to maintain and manage intelligently.

Five technologies are the most sought after for edge AI:

1. Applications: Technical frameworks for managing EC and AI are essential.
2. Inference: It emphasizes actual implementation and impact of AI on EC architecture to achieve accuracy and ultra-low latency.
3. Edge computing: It involves the use of EC for network architecture, hardware, and software supporting AI.
4. Training: It involves training of AI models needs for EI given the constraints of resources and privacy.
5. Optimizing: It involves employment of AI so as to maintain and manage EC networks (e.g., edge caching [16], computation off-loading [17]).

The current work resembles with the earlier work [18–21] but differs from edge AI, [18] and it emphasizes on the application of ML instead of DL in EI e.g. training algorithms for furtherance of wireless communication at the edge. Apart from this, DL inference and training are very vital contributors [19–21]. Moreover, further focus is on:

■ Holistic deployment of problems of AI in particular DL, by using EC, spanning networking, etc.
■ Comprehensive study of the technical scenarios for combining DL and EC.
■ Support of DL to EC, although deployment alone of DL on the edge is not enough.

1.12 Edge Computing

Edge computing was developed using many frontier technologies and works at the edge of networks with similar principles but differing in focus such as Cloudlet [22], Micro Data Centres (MDCs) [23], Fog Computing (FC) [24, 25], and Mobile [26] or Multi-access Edge Computing (MECs) [27]. The EC community has failed to arrive at a set of uniform standards with regard to definition premises, configurations, and protocols [28]. Edge computing is a term used in general for an array of novel technologies.

1.13 Edge AI & Its Need

Organizations from across industries are enhancing automation of processes to further their efficiency and safety. To bring it about ML-based models are required to recognize patterns and accomplish tasks reproducibly and safely. Given the non-structured nature of the world and the broad spectrum of tasks that people carry out, that are at times difficult to completely describe in the form of programs and rules. Advancements in edge AI have opened up new vistas for machines and devices, for making them intelligent and aligned with human intelligence. AI-driven applications learn to vary repetitive tasks under varying conditions, resembling real life.

The efficacy of deploying AI models at the edge is attributed to the following.

1.14 Maturation of Neural Networks

Neural networks and concerned AI infrastructure have matured and therefore can now provide for machine learning in general. AI models are also successfully trained and deployed in manufacturing at the edge.

1.15 Advancements in Computer Infrastructure

Tremendous distributed computational capability is needed to execute AI at the edge. The latest developments in highly parallel GPUs have been used to run neural networks.

1.15.1 Use of IoT Devices

IoT are extensively adopted, which has led to the generation of big data. Tremendous growth has taken place in the capability to collect data from all aspects of a business such as industrial sensors, smart cameras, robots, etc. We now have the data and devices needed to deploy AI models at the edge. Moreover, 5G is offering IoT with faster and more stable and secure connectivity.

1.15.2 AI at the Edge: Requirement

AI algorithms understand languages, sights, sounds, odors, temperatures, and other analog forms of unstructured information. They find use in instances wherein end users confront practical-life problems. These AI applications are not amenable to be deployed in a centralized cloud because of concerns pertaining to latency, bandwidth, and privacy.

1.15.3 Benefits of Cloud Computing and Edge Computing

AI applications execute in data centers either in the public cloud or out at the edge but nearer to target users. The benefits of both CC and EC can be harnessed for possible deployment of edge AI.

The cloud is characterized by cost of infrastructure, scalability, better use, resilience toward server failure, and collaboration. On the other hand, EC offers rapid response, low bandwidth cost, and resilience toward network failure.

Cloud computing is very handy and complementary to EC and further ensures deployment of edge AI in the following ways:

■ Cloud runs the model during the course of training.
■ Cloud keeps on running and the model gets retrained with data obtained from the edge.
■ Cloud runs AI inference engines, which are supplementary to the models particularly when better computing capabilities supersede response time. For example, a voice assistant responds to its name, but sends complicated requests to the cloud for parsing in return.
■ Cloud supports the latest forms of AI models and applications.
■ Edge AI at times works across an array of devices in practice accompanied by software in the cloud. Hybrids of cloud and edge have emerged in varying edge architectural forms.

1.16 Working of Edge AI

Machines these days perform functions like object, voice detection, drive cars, learn languages, speak, walk, or emulate human cognitive skills, and in other words work as replica of human intelligence.

AI uses a data structure called a deep neural network (DNN) to emulate human cognition. These DNNs are trained to answer typical kinds of questions with the help of numerous examples with right answers.

Machine learning algorithms are trained at a data center or the cloud because of the big data needed to train models to ensure accuracy, and data scientists are required to design these models. After training, the model it is called an "inference engine" that has the ability to answer practical-world questions.

In edge-AI, the inference is deployed on either a computer or device at far-off places such as retail outlets, clinics, cars, satellites, houses, etc. However, when AI is unable to address a problem, the complex data is offloaded to the cloud for retraining of the parent AI model, which at a certain stage substitutes the inference engine at the edge. This feedback loop keeps on going in order to enhance the performance of the model; once edge AI models are deployed, they become more and more intelligent or smarter than earlier ones. The lifecycle of working of edge AI is shown in Figure 1.1.

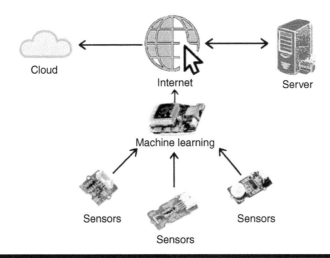

Figure 1.1   Working of edge AI.

Source: www.seeedstudio.com/blog/2020/01/20/what-is-edge-ai-and-what-is-it-used-for/.

1.17 Advantages of Edge AI

Following are the advantages of edge AI.

1.17.1 Intelligence

AI applications are characterized by tremendous power and flexibility compared to traditional ones that respond to inputs anticipated by the programmer. However, an AI neural network is trained to respond to a particular type of question. AI applications have made it possible to process innumerable distinct inputs such as texts, spoken words, or video.

1.17.2 Real-Time

Edge computing technology analyzes data at local level instead of global level (i.e., a cloud is far away and therefore delays the response because of communication over a long distance), and responds in real time to the user's needs.

1.17.3 Inexpensive

Processing power is brought closer to the edge, thus applications require lower internet bandwidth and networking costs.

1.17.4 Improved Privacy

AI analyzes real-world information preventing exposure of a human being and enhances privacy for anyone whose personal details require analysis such as voice, image, etc. Edge AI furthers privacy by storing data at local level, while uploading to the cloud for analysis and insights. Some data is used for training, while protecting the identity of users. Edge AI by way of preserving privacy of user eases the burden regarding data regulatory compliance.

1.17.5 Abundancy

Edge AI is characterized by decentralization, and is offline and robust since it does not require internet access for processing data. It leads to better availability and reliability for mission-centric, production-enabled AI applications.

1.17.6 Persistency

AI models are getting more and more accurate as they are trained using enough data. Edge AI applications learn from failures by processing data and trends developed. So the longer a model is in production at the edge, the more accurate it will be.

1.17.7 Edge AI Future

Over time neural networks are maturing commercially, IoT devices are proliferating, and parallel computing and 5G are advancing. Similarly, machine learning is personalized to make the infrastructure more robust. All these unprecedented changes have made it possible for organizations to reap the maximum potential in availing the tremendous opportunity to incorporate AI into all aspects of businesses and work for real-time insights, at affordable costs and improved privacy.

Edge AI is still in its infancy, but the sky is the limit given its scope and potential in all walks of life.

1.18 Representative Applications of Edge AI

Edge AI has emerged as a powerful technology for the future. It has brought about revolutionary changes in the industrial world and is now used in manufacturing across different areas such as healthcare, financial services, communication, energy, etc. Some of the applications are discussed as follows.

1.18.1 Smart Energy Forecasting

In the energy sector edge, AI models can collectively and intelligently use previous data, track climate change patterns, and create a health grid of pertinent factors to simulate complex correlations that predict highly efficient energy production, distribution, and optimal utilization of energy resources to users.

1.18.2 Predictive Analysis and Maintenance

Sensors-enabled data is used to detect defects at an early stage and predict when a machine will have to be serviced for maintenance or prior to failure. Sensors scan equipment for flaws if any and alert management if a machine requires a repair so that the problem can be dealt with beforehand, preventing costly downtime.

1.18.3 AI-Driven Devices in Healthcare

Advanced and sophisticated medical instruments at the edge are driven by AI with devices that use ultra-low-latency streaming of surgical video to minimize invasive surgeries and provide on-demand insights.

1.18.4 Intelligent Virtual Assistants

Retailers are working to enhance the digital customer experience by incorporating voice ordering instead of text-driven searches using voice commands. Voice ordering helps shoppers search for items easily, find product information, and place online orders with the help of smart speakers or other intelligent mobile devices.

1.18.5 Cloudlet and Micro-Data Centers

Cloudlet is an application derived from EC. Cloudlet is a network architecture that brings together mobile and CC. It comprises an intermediate layer of the three-tier architecture consisting of mobile devices, micro-cloud, and cloud.

The micro-cloud:

- Defines the system and develops algorithms for edge–CC systems characterized by low-latency
- Incorporates the necessary functionality in open source code for Open Stack cloud management software.

Cloudlet is a data center in a box and brings the cloud closer to users. Cloudlet presents real-time data to end devices via a WLAN with the help of virtual machines on devices. Cloudlet comprises many multi-core computers with fast connectivity and larger bandwidth wireless LANs. Cloudlets are secured by packaging them in a box resistant to tampering to ensure the security of areas that are not monitored.

Micro Data Centres (MDCs) were conceived for the first time by Microsoft Research. MDCs are aimed at supporting the cloud like Cloudlet. This is a composite term encompassing all the computing, storage, and networking apparatus required to execute user low-latency applications as a single package, in an isolated secure computing environment, but with constrained computing capabilities. Moreover, MDCs are dynamic and scalable in terms of capability and latency and vary in size in line with the network bandwidth as well as customer requirements.

1.19 Fog Computing

Cisco coined this term in 2012 as a derived product of CC and one that extends from the center to the edge of a network. According to the Open Fog Consortium [8], Fog is a horizontal system-based system used to distribute compute, store, control, and network with users.

Fog computing (FC) is a distributed multi-layered CC system with large number of devices and large CDCs. The fog computing nodes (FCN) connect the end devices with the cloud data centers. FCN are non-homogeneous, cover routers, set-top boxes, switches, IoT gateways, etc. FCN support end devices through various protocol layers and non-IP access technologies. Similarly, the abstraction layer in fog hides the heterogeneity of the nodes, and is responsible for managing data and connecting end devices to the cloud. In spite of this, FC runs with CC and not in isolation. Cloud and FC have many services in common. However, the application of fog is typically geographically confined to an area. Moreover, fog is deployed when real-time response is asked for in the applications unlike Cloudlet, MDCs, MeC, FC.

1.20 Mobile Edge Computing

Mobile edge computing (MEC) is standardized, and The European Telecommunications Standards Institute (ETSI) was instrumental in making this happen. Since needs are ever-changing, ETSI further developed the MEC concept to Multi-access EC, which furthered EC from cellular to other wireless networks.

MEC offers computing power and sound environment conducive to edge mobile networks. It provides low latency, contextual, site awareness, and larger bandwidth. Deploying edge servers on Mobile Base Stations (BSs) helps in incorporating innovative, fast, flexible applications and services. ETSI extended further the MEC terminology by introducing better wireless communication technologies, like Wi-Fi. Multi-access EC incorporates application and content developers with a similar kind of environment toward services and computing capabilities for meeting the varied needs of users. The advancements in MEC involve fulfilling the needs of non-cellular networks that are aligned with present-day application scenarios and the bright future of it.

1.21 EC Terminologies

Edge devices work at the interface of edge nodes and end devices. End devices refer to cellular edge devices that include smartphones, smart vehicles, etc.) and IoT, while the edge nodes include cloudlets, road-side units (RSUs), fog nodes, edge servers, MEC servers, etc., and all servers at the edge.

1.22 End–Edge–Cloud Computing

Cloud computing processes tasks that are purely computational, like DL, but without any guarantee about the latency needs regarding generation through transfer to implementation of data. Further, there are limitations when using end or edge devices such as their computing power, power requirements, and price. Therefore, end–edge–CC [29] is a frontier trend. The tasks with less computational capability requirements generated and executed at end devices are offloaded to the edge, thereby checking the latency due to data sent to the cloud. For tasks involving complex computations Will be decentralized and assigned to end, edge and cloud, thereby lowering the delay in response to the task without compromising the quality of service [29–31]. Emphasis here is not on merely the accomplishment of tasks but also striking the right balance between power consumed by the equipment, server loads, transmission, and latency in implementation.

1.23 Hardware for EC

The advent of EC is attributed to advancements in hardware over the years and it is certain that further advancement in hardware will bring about advancements in EI too. The EI is developing on both software and hardware front by taking cues from AI and EC. Therefore, the edge device hardware of today will pave the way for future EI. Thus, hardware such as AI chips that are customized for edge devices and nodes is of paramount importance.

1.24 AI Hardware for EC

AI hardware for EC is categorized as follows based on technical configuration as shown in Figure 1.2.

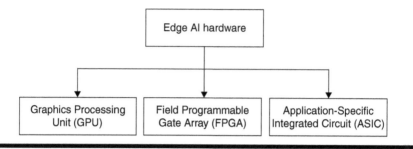

Figure 1.2   Classification of edge AI hardware.

1.24.1 GPU-Enabled Hardware

CPUs have strong common purpose features, while GPUs are primarily configured for processing innumerable similar tasks. GPUs have different arithmetic and logic units (ALU) and fewer caches aimed at improving the services for threads instead of saving the data expected to be accessed at some later stage. GPU-enabled hardware is the prominent architecture in AI hardware due to its incredible computational capabilities as well as compatibility and efficiency, although it requires more power (e.g., NVIDIA' GPUs rely on Turing configuration [32]).

1.24.2 Field Programmable Gate Array (FPGA) — Enabled Hardware [33, 34]

Logic cell array (LCA) in FPGA covers:

- Logic Block (CLB) that can be configured
- Input–Output Block (IOB)
- Interconnect

FPGA is a programmable device used to configure ASIC circuits and is characterized by low production cost, and power consumption, shorter design cycle, can be reused, and easier to understand and employ. FPGA-led hardware is instrumental in bettering EI because of features such as power saving and requiring minimal resources for computation, although it is weakly compatible and programmable.

1.24.3 Integrated Circuit (ASIC)-Based Hardware

The common characteristic of ASIC is that it is specific and need-based, but is not comparable in terms of its advantages against other hardware in particular scenarios. Therefore, ASIC-led hardware supports EI in accomplishing better and stable outcomes in terms of performance and energy use because of the customized design in typical scenarios like Google's TPU [35] and HiSilicon's Ascend series [36].

Smartphones are extensively used edge devices and chips for such devices have developed rapidly and their capabilities are responsible for advancing AI computing. For example, Qualcomm uses advanced AI hardware [37] in Snapdragon Neural Processing Engine (SNPE) SDK. Qualcomm, HiSilicon's 600 and 900 series chips [38], do not rely on GPUs. Rather, Qualcomm introduces one more Neural Processing Unit (NPU) for achieving rapid computation of vectors and matrices, which further enhances the performance of DL. MediaTek's Helio P60 employs GPUs and incorporates an AI processing unit (APU) to exacerbate neural network computing [39]. Various customized chips in edge devices can be compared for their performance in DL [40].

1.24.4 Potential of Integrated Commodities for Edge Nodes

Edge nodes (ENs) possess computing and caching power and offer qualitative connectivity of network and computing facilities near end devices. ENs have far better computing power to achieve tasks than the majority of end devices. Moreover, ENs respond quicker with end devices than cloud. ENs perform the computation-intensive tasks at a faster pace without compromising accuracy. Further, ENs possess the ability to catch popular contents, which lowers the response delay. ENs are capable of processing DL inference and then transferring it to the cloud for analysis and insights.

Examples of edge devices include Data Box Edge (DBE) [41], Jetson, and Atlas [42]. Microsoft developed DBE device by using AI-based EC power. DBE is instrumental in storing and connecting between user sites and Azure storage, which ensures data transmission to and from Azure through the local network. Similarly, DBE is a technology used through IoT Edge that supports users to employ Azure services to the edge. Jetson is an embedded system and basically an AI platform developed by NVIDIA for ensuing generation automated machines, high-end sensors, and video analysis. Jetson series products with varied positioning to meet varying industrial needs right from face recognition to driverless vehicles. Atlas series developed by Huawei is an intelligent cloud-based system that possesses major characteristics such as resource pooling, non-homogeneous computing, etc. Atlas has a module for accelerating the end side, a card for the acceleration of the data center side, a smart station for the edge side, and a single-stop AI platform stationed in the enterprise field. Therefore, Atlas is an AI solution package for improving quality of the product.

1.25 EC Frameworks

A host of solutions are coming to the fore for EC-related issues. DL services having complex configurations, demanding resources intensively, require EC systems with sophisticated and outstanding micro-service architectures that set the tone for futuristic challenges. Edge computing and end devices will create a huge amount of heterogeneous data that will have to be processed by need-based and devices catering to numerous applications. Hence, it is quite challenging to configure an EC framework that ensures feasibility of computing tasks, reliability of applications, and optimization of resource use. However, EC frameworks are application-specific, and due to differences in demand in varied scenarios, EC platforms depend on the following.

1.25.1 Design Goals

Edge computing frameworks have goals related to the problems they aim to address.

1.25.2 End Users

The demands of the end users of the EC framework drive the design and in setting design goals. Few frameworks are available to network operators, without much restrictions, which implies any user can deploy it on the edge device.

1.25.3 Up-Scaling

Frameworks should be scalable so as to align with the demands of the target users. Thus, many target users opt for a framework that is scalable.

1.25.4 System Characteristics

The framework as a system should reflect on the design goals, such that the users can make use of the framework in typical situations based on the system attributes.

1.25.5 Application Environments

Application environments are those wherein EC systems create value and sound application scenarios harness the potential of computing platforms. Presently, Kubernetes is a container-centric system, which is at the center stage for deploying, maintaining, and extending applications of CC [43]. Huawei designed indigenous solution "KubeEdge" based on EC [44] for the purpose of networking, deploying applications, and synchronizing metadata to and from the cloud and the edge [24]). "OpenEdge" [45] is instrumental in shielding the computing frameworks and easing the application creation. Azure IoT Edge [46] and EdgeX [47] are aimed at transferring cloud intelligence to the edge by employing and executing AI with IoT devices on cross-platforms.

1.26 Edge Virtualization

Edge virtualization technology is a key driver for the rapid advancement of CC. However, edge visualization makes a significant impact on the fusion of AI and EC which will pave the way for achieving new milestones in the future.

The integration of AI and EC has considerations like:

- EC is constrained, and does not provide resources for AI applications unlike the cloud. Virtualization should provide for utilization of resources given the availability of constrained resources.
- AI services depend largely on complex software libraries. Virtualization aligned with edge AI services should take into account variations in services. The upgradation shutdown, crashing, and resource intensiveness of a service should not influence scenarios of other services.
- Ultra-low latency is a key to edge AI. Edge AI demands the computing capabilities of edge devices and prompt response in services and that is offered by the sound architecture of EC. Edge computing and AI combined produce highly performing edge AI that offers services that demand cohesion of resources for the purpose of computation, networking, and communication. In fact, virtualization of computation, network, and management of technologies are essential.

1.26.1 *Virtualization Strategies*

There are two types of virtualization strategies: Virtual machine (VM) and container. Normally, VMs are good at sorting and containers make it easy to deploy tasks that are repetitive [42]. The VM strategy involves the use of VM hypervisor, which divides a physical server into single or multiple digital ones, and manages each readily to achieve tasks independently. Moreover, VM hypervisor can assign and utilize unused resources of computing to a greater extent by generating a system that is scalable and contains many isolated digital devices. For example, VM-enabled cloudlets serve consumers by using edge services as convenient, and consumers employ VM technology for availing customized computing services on an edge server close by, and further use the service for an instant response to the local needs.

Unlike VM, virtualization of containers is a relatively dynamic tool offering for applications of various kinds. Container virtualization effectively reduces task achievement time with better performance and makes available numerous scaled-up services in a simplified manner [48]. A container contains a file that is provided with an application and an environment to execute it independently as a sound service provider in congruence with the mobility of users [49]. The container executes the applications without requiring further virtualization layers unlike VM. The processor and memory used to work the application is substantially minimized.

1.26.2 Virtualizing Network

Conventional networking works with necessary hardware and is rigid to a certain extent unlike edge networking, which works in tandem with the needs of users. To ensure consolidation of network devices as a part of servers for industry, networking function virtualization (NFV) provides for virtualized network functions (VNFs) to run software for sorting networking functions and services from hardware dedicated to networking. Moreover, services provided by edge AI typically demand large bandwidth but ultra-low latency and dynamic networking architectures, while software-defined networking (SDN) provides for rapid execution of services, programmable networking, and poly-tenancy help through vital innovations such as [50]:

- Control and data plane isolation
- Control planes that are centralized and programmed
- Standardization of interface between application and programming

Due to these advantages, it has emerged as a network strategy that is extensively customized and thereby caters to the needs of the large bandwidth variations in edge-enabled AI applications.

Virtualized networks and EC complement one another. NFV/SDN promotes functioning of EC architectures. For example, NFV/SDN supports ENs and works symbiotically with CDCs [46], while VNFs and edge AI together [51] to ensure reuse of NFV to the maximum [52].

1.26.3 Network Slicing

Network slicing (NS) is an agile networking system, abstracted from a network that provides for many network scenarios over a shared physical infrastructure meant for selective services. The growing variations in the services and QoS needs, NS, executed using NFV/SDN, align with varied scenarios of EC. To fulfill such needs, NS is combined with resources of communication for optimization of EC networks [53]. Network slicing relies on edge virtualization. For customizing services in NS, virtualized technologies and SDN should go hand in hand for proper resource planning and flexible service delivery at edge nodes. Network slicing on customization and optimization resources are made available to edge AI, which lowers the latency attributed to dense network access to all services [54].

1.26.4 Value Scenarios (VS)

Edge computing is a frontier technology quite useful to industry, and is integrated with industrial production depending on application area. Therefore, there are some advantages of EC that are of paramount importance and cover smart parks, video monitoring, and IIoT.

1.26.5 Smart Parks

Smart parks (SPs) make use of advancements in AI and technologies in communication for detecting, monitoring, analyzing, controlling, and integrating resources, followed by real-time implementation and proper response to the different needs of users. Thus, SPs have the capability of operating, organizing, and optimizing independently.

Edge computing in such scenarios plays the following roles:

- Connectivity and management of network, operation, and maintenance governed by the SDN.
- Collecting and processing data in real-time. For example, face recognition and security alarms that demand ultra-low latency accompanied by real-time data collection or end-to-edge processing in collaboration.
- Localized business autonomy. For example, intelligent buildings with automated control on interruption of network connection while preserving business autonomy at local level with their own logic.

1.27 Video Surveillance

Video surveillance has transitioned from "seeing clearly" to "understanding." Some of it creates some storage and computing needs, while certain monitoring tasks have real-time demands. Hence, the way the network collaborates with EC determines the way it depends on CC such that performance of video surveillance is enhanced. In this respect, EC performs the following functions:

- Image and video analysis at edge nodes
- Intelligent storage at edge node
- Edge–cloud coupling

1.28 Industrial Internet of Things (IIoT)

The application of IIoT is a comparatively vexed issue. Industries differ in their needs with regard to the intelligence of their machines and equipment and application of IIoT with various requirements:

- Heterogeneous data from varied sources bereft of uniformity
- Different on-site network protocols result in difficulty in interconnectivity
- Inadequate security toward data related to production processes

1.29 Conclusion

Advancements in technology and the tremendous rise in data from the internet has led to commensurate sound growth scenarios in EC. Similarly, the advent of EC has brought about a revolutionized change in computing models and network infrastructure. Therefore, EC is a technology instrumental in addressing the problems of users, which can be very well integrated with any incumbent technology and further its efficiency. Hence, EC plays a pivotal role across areas such as industrial manufacturing, recreation, or DL, and perform sexceedingly well.

Edge computing helps in solving issues confronted by IIoT scenarios with the help of numerous technologies. End nodes homogenize heterogeneity in the data by means of pre-processing. A uniform industrial network relying on OPC UA over TSN is deployed to attain interconnectivity and interoperability of data. Security measures in EC and solutions discussed in this chapter are aligned with manufacturing scenarios.

References

1. Fog Computing and the Internet of Things: Extend the Cloud to Where the Things Are. www.cisco.com/c/dam/en_us/solutions/trends/iot/docs/computing-overview.pdf.
2. Cisco Global Cloud Index: Forecast and Methodology. www.cisco.com/c/en/us/solutions/collateral/service-provider/global-cloud-index-gci/white-paper-c11-738085.html.
3. M.V. Barbera, S. Kosta, A. Mei et al., To offload or not to offload? The bandwidth and energy costs of mobile cloud computing, in 2013 IEEE Conference on Computer Communications (INFOCOM 2013) (2013), pp. 1285–1293.
4. W. Hu, Y. Gao, K. Ha et al., Quantifying the impact of edge computing on mobile applications, in Proceedings of the Seventh ACM SIGOPS Asia-Pacific Workshop System (APSys 2016) (2016), pp. 1–8.
5. Mobile-Edge Computing—Introductory Technical White Paper, ETSI. https://portal.etsi.org/ Portals/0/TBpages/MEC/Docs/Mobile-edge_Computing_-_Introductory_Technical_White_ Paper_V1%2018-09-14.pdf.
6. W. Shi, J. Cao et al., Edge computing: vision and challenges. IEEE Internet Things J. 3(5), 637–646 (2016).
7. B.A. Mudassar, J.H. Ko, S.Mukhopadhyay, Edge-cloud collaborative processing for intelligent internet of things, in Proceedings of the 55th Annual Design Automation Conference (DAC 2018) (2018), pp. 1–6.
8. A. Yousefpour, C. Fung, T. Nguyen et al., All one needs to know about fog computing and related edge computing paradigms: a complete survey. J. Syst. Architect. 98, 289–330 (2019).
9. J. Redmon, S. Divvala et al., You only look once: unified, real-time object detection, in Proceedings of the 2016 IEEE Conference on Computer Vision and Pattern Recognition (CVPR 2016) (2016), pp. 779–788.

10. J. Schmidhuber, Deep learning in neural networks: an overview. Neural Netw. 61, 85–117 (2015).
11. H. Khelifi, S. Luo, B. Nour et al., Bringing deep learning at the edge of information-centric internet of things. IEEE Commun. Lett. 23(1), 52–55 (2019) References 13.
12. Y. Kang, J. Hauswald, C. Gao et al., Neurosurgeon: collaborative intelligence between the cloud and mobile edge, in Proceedings of the 22nd International Conference on Architectural Support for Programming Languages and Operating Systems (ASPLOS 2017) (2017), pp. 615–629.
13. Democratizing AI. https://news.microsoft.com/features/democratizing-ai/.
14. Y. Yang, Multi-tier computing networks for intelligent IoT. Nat. Electron. 2(1), 4–5 (2019).
15. C. Li, Y. Xue, J. Wang et al., Edge-oriented computing paradigms: a survey on architecture design and system management. ACM Comput. Surv. 51(2), 1–34 (2018).
16. S. Wang, X. Zhang, Y. Zhang et al., A survey on mobile edge networks: convergence of computing, caching and communications. IEEE Access (5), 6757–6779 (2017).
17. T.X. Tran, A. Hajisami et al., Collaborative mobile edge computing in 5G networks: new paradigms, scenarios, and challenges. IEEE Commun. Mag. 55(4), 54–61 (2017).
18. J. Park, S. Samarakoon, M. Bennis, M. Debbah, Wireless network intelligence at the edge. Proc. IEEE 107(11), 2204–2239 (2019).
19. Z. Zhou, X. Chen, E. Li, L. Zeng, K. Luo, J. Zhang, Edge intelligence: paving the last mile of artificial intelligence with edge computing. Proc. IEEE 107(8), 1738–1762 (2019).
20. J. Chen, X. Ran, Deep learning with edge computing: a review. Proc. IEEE 107(8), 1655–1674 (2019).
21. W.Y.B. Lim, N.C. Luong, D.T. Hoang, Y. Jiao, Y.-C. Liang, Q. Yang, D. Niyato et al., Federated learning in mobile edge networks: a comprehensive survey (2019). arXiv:1909.11875.
22. M. Satyanarayanan, P. Bahl, R. Cáceres, N. Davies, The case for VM-based cloudlets in mobile computing. IEEE Pervasive Comput. **8**(4), 14–23 (2009).
23. M. Aazam, E. Huh, Fog computing micro datacenter based dynamic resource estimation and pricing model for IoT, in *Proceedings of the IEEE 29th International Conference on Advanced Information Networking and Applications (AINA 2019)* (2015), pp. 687–694.
24. F. Bonomi, R.Milito, J. Zhu, S. Addepalli, Fog computing and its role in the Internet of Things, in *Proceedings of the First Edition of the MCC Workshop on Mobile Cloud Computing* (2012), pp. 13–16.
25. F. Bonomi, R. Milito, P. Natarajan, J. Zhu, *Fog Computing: A Platform for Internet of Things and Analytics* (Springer, Cham, 2014), pp. 169–186.
26. Mobile-Edge Computing—Introductory Technical White Paper, ETSI. https://portal.etsi.org/Portals/0/TBpages/MEC/Docs/Mobile-edge_Computing IntroductoryTechnicalWhitePaperV1%2018-09-14.pdf.
27. Multi-access Edge Computing. www.etsi.org/technologies-clusters/technologies/multiaccess-edge-computing.
28. K. Bilal, O. Khalid, A. Erbad, S.U. Khan, Potentials, trends, and prospects in edge technologies: Fog, cloudlet, mobile edge, and micro data centers. Comput. Netw. **130**(2018), 94–120 (2018).

29. Openfog reference architecture for fog computing. www.openfogconsortium.org/ra/.
30. Y. Kang, J. Hauswald, C. Gao et al., Neurosurgeon: collaborative intelligence between the cloud and mobile edge, in *Proceedings of the 22nd International Conference on Architectural Support for Programming Languages and Operating Systems (ASPLOS 2017)* (2017), pp. 615–629.
31. G. Li, L. Liu, X. Wang et al., Auto-tuning neural network quantization framework for collaborative inference between the cloud and edge, in *Proceedings of the International Conference on Artificial Neural Networks (ICANN 2018)* (2018), pp. 402–411.
32. Y. Huang, Y. Zhu, X. Fan et al., Task scheduling with optimized transmission time in collaborative cloud-edge learning, in *Proceedings of the 27th International Conference on Computer Communication and Networks (ICCCN 2018)* (2018), pp. 1–9.
33. What is Azure Data Box Edge? https://docs.microsoft.com/zh-cn/azure/databox-onl ine/databox- edge-overview.
34. An all-scenario AI infrastructure solution that bridges 'device, edge, and cloud' and delivers unrivaled compute power to lead you towards an AI-fueled future. https:// e.huawei.com/en/solutions/business-needs/data-center/atlas.
35. Snapdragon 8 Series Mobile Platforms. www.qualcomm.com/products/snapdragon-8-series-mobile-platforms.
36. Kirin. www.hisilicon.com/en/Products/ProductList/Kirin.
37. The World's First Full-Stack All-Scenario AI Chip. www.hisilicon.com/en/Products/ ProductList/Ascend.
38. MediaTek Helio P60. www.mediatek.com/products/smartphones/mediatek-helio-p60.
39. NVIDIA Turing GPU Architecture. www.nvidia.com/en-us/geforce/turing/.
40. N.P. Jouppi, A. Borchers, R. Boyle, P.L. Cantin, B. Nan, In-datacenter performance analysis of a tensor processing unit, in *Proceedings of the 44th International Symposium on Computer Architecture (ISCA 2017)* (2017), pp. 1–12.
41. Y. Xiong, Y. Sun, L. Xing, Y. Huang, Extend cloud to edge with KubeEdge, in *Proceedings of the 2018 IEEE/ACM Symposium on Edge Computing (SEC 2018)* (2018), pp. 373–377.
42. OpenEdge, extend cloud computing, data and service seamlessly to edge devices. https:// github.com/baidu/openedge.
43. Azure IoT Edge, extend cloud intelligence and analytics to edge devices. https://git hub.com/Azure/iotedge.
44. EdgeX, the Open Platform for the IoT Edge. www.edgexfoundry.org/.
45. Akraino Edge Stack. www.lfedge.org/projects/akraino/.
46. E. Nurvitadhi, G. Venkatesh, J. Sim et al., Can FPGAs beat GPUs in accelerating nextgeneration deep neural networks? in *Proceedings of the ACM/SIGDA International Symposium on Field-Programmable Gate Arrays (FPGA 2017)* (2017), pp. 5–14.
47. S. Jiang, D. He, C. Yang et al., Accelerating mobile applications at the network edge with software-programmable FPGAs, in *2018 IEEE Conference on Computer Communications (INFOCOM 2018)* (2018), pp. 55–62.
48. A. Ignatov, R. Timofte, W. Chou et al., AI benchmark: running deep neural networks on android smartphones (2018). arXiv:1810.01109.

49. D. Bernstein, Containers and cloud: from LXC to Docker to Kubernetes. IEEE Cloud Comput. **1**(3), 81–84 (2014).

50. Microsoft Cognitive Toolkit (CNTK), an open source deep-learning toolkit. https://github.com/microsoft/CNTK.

51. S. Tokui, K. Oono et al., Chainer: a next-generation open source framework for deep learning, in *Proceedings of the Workshop on Machine Learning Systems (LearningSys) in the Twenty-Ninth Annual Conference on Neural Information Processing Systems (NeurIPS 2015)* (2015), pp. 1–6.

52. M. Abadi, P. Barham et al., TensorFlow: a system for large-scale machine learning, in *Proceedings of the 12th USENIX Conference on Operating Systems Design and Implementation (OSDI 2016)* (2016), pp. 265–283.

53. Deeplearning4j: Open-source distributed deep learning for the JVM, Apache Software Foundation License 2.0. https://deeplearning4j.org.

54. Deploy machine learning models on mobile and IoT devices. www.tensorflow.org/lite.

Chapter 2

Securing IoT Services Using Artificial Intelligence in Edge Computing

P. William[1], Siddhartha Choubey[2], Abha Choubey[2], and Gurpreet Singh Chhabra[3]

[1]Department of Information Technology,
Sanjivani College of Engineering, SPPU, Pune, India

[2]Department of Computer Science and Engineering,
Shri Shankaracharya Technical Campus, Bhilai, India

[3]Department of CSE, GITAM Institute of Technology,
GITAM (Deemed to be University), Visakhapatnam, India

2.1 Introduction

More and more physical objects are being connected through sensors as the usage of sensors in the real world grows. Currently, Internet of Things (IoT) technology is widely applied in a range of fields, including smart cities, smart homes, wearable medical devices, and environmental perception applications [1–3]. Sensors and devices must transfer data to cloud servers for processing as part of basic IoT services. The IoT devices will get the processed data when the tasks are completed. Sensor and device compute loads are reduced thanks to the cloud; nevertheless, the massive

DOI: 10.1201/9781032650722-3

transmission overhead of the data must not be disregarded. According to a recent report, there were 11.2 billion IoT-enabled devices globally in 2018, and that figure is likely to rise to 20 billion by 2020 [4]. Network capacity expansion of data growth is far behind and latency reduction is very challenging due to the complex network environment that exists. Typical IoT services are constrained by network capacity. A whole new computer paradigm called edge computing (EC) is garnering a lot of attention in an effort to overcome the aforementioned hurdle. Computing tasks are being moved to the network's edge through EC [5, 6]. End-user privacy, reduced data transfer latency, reduced network capacity restrictions, and lower energy consumption are just a few of the advantages that EC has over cloud computing. EC allows IoT device data to be processed, stored, and transported at the edge nodes (ENs) rather than being uploaded to a centralized cloud platform. This reduces latency by eliminating the need for duplicate data transmission. For IoT and mobile computing applications requiring rapid response times, EC will offer expanded support. However, EC isn't a cure-all. To put it another way, IoT devices under the EU's EC have considerably improved their capabilities in several areas. According to the security experts, there are three ways in which EC might be a security risk and increase a system's attack surface [7–8]:

1. Distributed layout
2. Sources of limited computing
3. Different environment

Numerous security procedures and algorithms have been created to address the safety hazards connected with EC's characteristics [9, 10]. The bulk of today's security solutions are based on algorithms and models that employ a single pattern to detect breaches, protect privacy, or limit access. Traditional defense mechanisms are frequently promptly abandoned when attack techniques and methods are improved. What's exciting is that the introduction and evolution of artificial intelligence (AI) allow the creation of creative solutions to security and privacy problems as follows:

1. Detection of Intrusion: DDoS refers to the management of the various hacked ENs used to attack the server, while DoS assaults the server with frequent requests, increasing the server's strain and decreasing the server's response time to regular requests. Attacks from the hijacked ENs may be identified and blocked by an intrusion detection system (IDS), which keeps an eye out for unusual network activity. Intrusion detection systems (IDS) may more quickly and accurately detect intrusions using IDS thanks to machine learning (ML), which uses historical data to determine dangerous access patterns [11, 12].
2. Privacy preservation: Our lives are replete with IoT gadgets that store and transmit vast amounts of personally identifiable information (PII) [13]. Privacy preservation techniques including anonymization, cryptographic

procedures, and data obfuscation all encrypt transmitted data in order to protect it from security breaches. In spite of this, many of the methods discussed above are computationally intensive, making them difficult to implement on resource-limited ENs. A key advantage of Data Manipulation Language over standard encryption approaches is that it requires ENs to share parameters for cooperative learning with other ENs after each training session, rather than sending the actual material directly [14].

3. Access control: When several IoT devices coexist in the same area, access management becomes critical. Each authenticated node is limited to accessing nodes and data within their access authority and is not permitted to do any additional actions [15, 16]. ENs must be divided into several groups based on their permissions, which correspond to the classification process used in ML [17]. Algorithms categorize ENs connected to the network as low- or high-privileged IoT devices.

To avoid possible threats, access to such highly privileged devices is rigorously monitored. As AI research advances, it is progressively being used in a variety of sectors of edge security [18, 19]. There are, however, a number of challenges to applying comparable principles on ENs. It is important to have large amounts of clean data [20]. It is important to remember that attacks on the training set may degrade the model's performance by interfering with its parameters [21–25]. It is also necessary to use lightweight AI techniques since ENs have limited computing and storage resources. However, this will reduce the accuracy. There has been various research on the integration of AI with EC, but AI's function in IoT security based on EC is now under dispute and scrutiny only .Consequently, a comprehensive evaluation is provided that concentrates on the most recent advancements in the aforementioned field. IoT and EC are introduced in Section 2. EC and AI provide IoT privacy protection as discussed in Section 4, which begins with a look at the architecture of IoT services in Section 3. EC-enabled IoT blockchains may benefit from the usage of AI, which is discussed later in Section 5. AI-based IoT security is still plagued by unsolved issues and challenges, which are addressed in Section 6.

2.2 Conception and Depictions

2.2.1 IoT Service

When it comes to the IoT, everything is connected through the Internet, making it possible for all devices to communicate with one another and work together without the need for human intervention. Sensors may be integrated into a wide range of items, such as medical equipment, home appliances, and automobiles, allowing the IoT to be used in a number of applications. Sensor technology, RFID (Radio Frequency IDentification), and wireless communication technology are only a few of the technologies that make up the perceptual layer. It is important to note that this layer relies heavily on a cloud platform, which enables the storage and processing of vast volumes of data. The IoT architecture's top layer is called the application layer. Customer-specific services are provided by this layer based on data that has been processed and examined. As a result of these three tiers, IoT devices are able to better meet the needs of their users and hence improve their overall quality of life.

1. Remote control and monitoring: The IoT enables users to remotely operate equipment linked to the Internet and monitor a real-time situation, which adds a layer of convenience to our lives. Users may monitor their newborns' health from any location thanks to sensors put in their homes. Additionally, cameras may transmit footage of a newborn to people in real time. When it comes to logistics, clients can simply track the status of their items while they are en route. Regardless of the time of day, consumers may inquire about the quality and present location of items bought online.

2. Smart house: There is nothing new about the concept of a "smart house" [26–30] now that it has grown through the years. Smart home products, however, have the potential to become more intelligent and flexible, and hence better serve consumers, thanks to the IoT. Say your room's air conditioner automatically kicks on as you go up the steps from the hallway outside. There are many more gadgets, such as sweeping robots, that will take care of domestic duties, and even lights may be switched on and off without the need for a person. As a result, the smart home is a prime illustration of how IoT services improve the quality of our lives [31–33].

3. Natural disaster prediction: The IoT is essential for predicting natural disasters, such as earthquakes, floods, droughts, and tsunamis. It is possible that data gathered by outside sensors may provide important information about an impending natural disaster, enabling us to evacuate people and minimize property damage as much as possible.

We've just scratched the surface of IoT's potential benefits thus far. The IoT has unquestionably been a driving force in the transformation of many traditional off-line enterprises [34–35].

2.2.2 Edge Computing

Mobile devices and users at the network's edge may benefit from EC. There are two ways to look at the idea of EC. Data created by IoT devices has grown exponentially in recent years, as mobile devices have become larger and more powerful [35–37]. It is not a good idea to move all of your data to the cloud, because of the high bandwidth and power needs. There is also an issue with latency and response times due to the inability of typical cloud computing to adequately handle such a vast amount of data [38, 39].

The following are three major advantages of EC:

1. Low latency: The network's edge, which is closer to mobile devices, is where computations are executed instead of in the cloud, improving response time and minimizing latency [40].
2. Security and Privacy concern: If you don't need to send your private information over the internet, you may keep your data on your own computer or on a local area network (LAN).
3. Decrease energy consumption in cloud center: Offloading certain computing tasks to multiple ENs not only alleviates bandwidth restrictions but also adds to the energy efficiency of the cloud center in EC [29, 30].

2.3 Framework of IoT Service with EC

The device layer, the network layer, the edge layer, and the cloud layer make up the architecture for IoT services using EC. Figure 2.1 depicts the EC-based IoT service architecture in its most basic form.

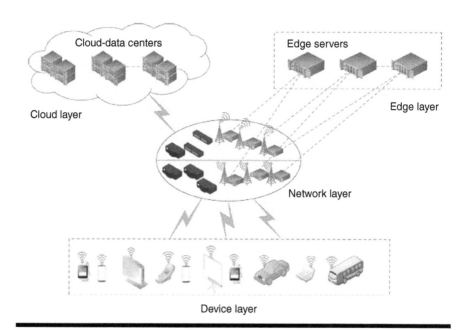

Figure 2.1 Edge computing based IoT service framework.

2.3.1 Layer of Device

Many mobile and computers devices are equipped with a variety of sensing devices, in addition to their other electronic components. Context-sensitive information about the devices themselves or their surroundings may be provided by "things" in the IoT, providing an enormous amount of real-time data [41–43]. The processing requirements of this data are very different, yet the vast majority of them are immediate, immediate, and frequent.

2.3.2 Layer of Network

Clouds can not get to the finish without this layer. This is a transitional layer that acts as a bridge between device and edge layers. In the IoT service architecture, it serves as the brain, connecting sensors all across the network and handling data transmissions. A variety of communication technologies, including cellular networks, WiFi, ZigBee, and Bluetooth are used to transmit the data collected by sensing devices. These technologies all adhere to a variety of IoT protocols or data transmission protocols but also act as a link between the data centers of the edge layer and the clouds themselves. The edge layer's structured or completed data is sent to the cloud layer, and the cloud layer sends instructions or feedback to the edge layer.

2.3.3 Layer of Edge

EC's IoT service framework has a lower bandwidth need and a higher delivery delay than the normal IoT service framework, that is why this layer is so important. An edge server deployment that must fulfil user needs while running. Close proximity to cellular base stations is common for edge servers. Rather than multi-tenant setups, they are often employed in single tenant setups [44–47].

2.3.4 Layer of Cloud

The layer acts as the platform's central processing unit. Massive IoT services with EC commonly utilize the cloud layer to analyze and store data from the edge layer, as well as to do sophisticated deployments. When it comes to collaborating between the cloud and edge, the two entities are seen as a single entity that can be dynamically scheduled and reinforced. Using virtual machines and containers, the cloud layer may be able to aid the edge layer when its computing resources are in short supply. An enhanced cloud security policy may identify and halt potentially hazardous traffic as it emerges at an edge layer. This prevents it from spreading further. In the wake of cloud-edge collaboration, multiple processes are concerned. There are a few cloud-edge collaboration solutions that are promoting cloud-edge collaboration's success. The use of IoT services in combination with EC is on the rise.

2.4 Privacy Maintenance with AI for Edge-Enabled IoT Services

Training schemes and inference schemes are two major classifications of ML privacy protection solutions proposed in Ref. [48]. When transmitting sensitive information, the privacy-preserving training programs utilize encryption methods to protect it. Private-preserving inference systems put a high value on protecting private data throughout the inference phase of the process.

Typically, in order to preserve inference schemes, an EN sends unclassified data for inference to a well-trained model [49–50]. The most commonly used encryption techniques are anonymization, cryptography, and data obfuscation. However, each of the aforementioned encryption algorithms incurs a distinct amount of computation and transmission overhead. This makes it more difficult to apply encryption algorithms on ENs with low resources. As seen in Figure 2.2, the subsequent sections of this section will examine current fundamental encryption techniques first, and then adequate solutions as per privacy preserving [51–53].

2.4.1 Traditional Encryption Methods

2.4.1.1 Anonymization

In order to protect the anonymity of a group of persons, anonymization techniques are employed to remove some easily recognizable features. As long as the missing data is linked to a specific user, the most important information should remain intact throughout the transfer process. In the literature, there have been several privacy-preserving models based on anonymization technologies. If there are more than k elements in an attribute set that share the same quasiidentifier, then that attribute set is generalized to remove the explicit identifiers before the data is made public. However, the k-anonymity strategy is flawed. There are a number of ways in

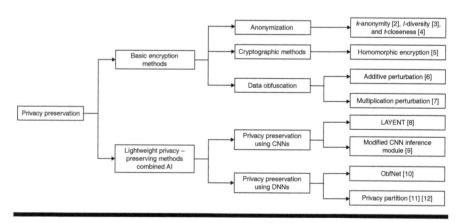

Figure 2.2   Section's structure.

which an attacker might find out more about an individual's identity based on their previously provided information.

2.4.1.2 Cryptographic Method

Encryption methods are used before transferring data to cloud servers to protect the data's context. A reliable and resilient key management is required for cryptographic approaches because of their high computational cost (millions of times more than the multiplicative projection). Others, such as many cloud computing programs, can process data without divulging the contents thanks to homomorphic encryption (HE). The HE method is secure because it creates a key pair by solving complex mathematical problems. The encrypted data is subsequently decoded only by the private key of the third parties, ensuring that the privacy is maintained throughout the process. Techniques such as RSA and ECC are widely used in homomorphic encryption. The latter is less expensive in terms of computing.

2.4.1.3 Data Obfuscation

Samples of data needed to train a global module are contaminated by obfuscation tactics. There are two types of perturbation: additive and multiplicative. It is impossible to talk about differential privacy (DP) without mentioning additive perturbation, a method for aggregating data without revealing any particular items. The DP approach ensures the safety of unique records from close datasets by making it impossible for the adversary to distinguish between the outputs of nearby datasets. A number of noise-introducing processes are used by DP to conceal data. The Laplacian method uses a Laplacian distribution to add random noise to the exact query results in order to ensure DP protection. It is common practice in data mining to obfuscate data in order for protection of data privacy.

2.4.2 AI-Based Privacy-Preserving Methods in ENs

Here, the focus has been on privacy concerns not just during module training but also during work offloading methods. Anonymization, encryption, and data obfuscation have all been used in cloud centers, where processing capacity is at a premium. Since ENs are resource-constrained, traditional encryption algorithms have a hard time running efficiently. Recent studies have focused on the development of privacy-preserving lightweight approaches that use AI technology.

2.4.2.1 CNN-Based Privacy Preservation

Modified CNN and LAYENT inference modules are presented in the following. An improved module's foundation is used in the first approach, whereas the latter method relies on the already-trained module to protect users' personal information.

1. *LAYNET.* LAYENT is a new ML system that protects user privacy. Comparing LAYRNT's accuracy (up to 91 percent) with other similar algorithms that employ cloud computing's processing capability, we see that it does both while incurring minimum computer costs. Before it is sent to the third party, which may be harmful, the data is disrupted. To do this, the procedure is as follows: LAYENT adds an additional layer between the convolutional and fully connected layers—the randomization layer—to augment the fundamental CNN structure. A unique unary encoding approach is also included in the randomization layer to boost the layer's flexibility while encoding the context.

2. *Inference Module-based modified CNN.* Theft detection based on an energy system has been developed to spot anomalous behavior in a smart grid's smart meters. CNNs are used in the framework, although they have been changed. The current module is used to train the CNN module, which can then detect anomalous data by making logical assumptions based on the smart meters' data. The technique paired with the updated CNN module demonstrates great performance in experimental analysis, with an inference accuracy of up to 92.67 percent.

2.4.2.2 Privacy Preservation Using DNNs

These networks have been used widely in a range of domains, including language understanding, audio recognition, and image identification. DNN modules need a lot of processing power to be trained. Two lightweight systems are described in the following:

1. *ObfNet.* Using an obfuscation neural network (ObfNet) technique, the inference data is obscured before it is sent to the backend. There are a number of techniques that may be used to obscure data for the sake of inference, but ObfNet is one of the most effective and least intrusive. These two adjectives suggest that ENs just need to build a simple neural network, and they do not even need that ENs indicate if the input they are processing has been veiled. The implementation of edge-enabled IoT presents two issues. Both data sources and processing resources must be separated, and the privacy of inference models must be safeguarded. Remote inference may be utilized to get over the issues outlined above. When using remote inference, information is sent to the backend for analysis, and the results are then returned. Because of its tiny size, the ObfNet neural network is well-suited for use in ENs. The training process is outlined in the following steps. ObfNet and InfNet are linked together in the backend, creating a DNN module that is trained in-service and ready to use. In the DNN module, the ObfNet output is used as the input for InfNet. As with InfNet, ObfNet is trained in the backend using the same random data as InfNet. There will only be weights from ObfNet

until convergence. Repeating the process may provide a collection of ObfNets. Each ObfNet is unique due to the unpredictability of the data sources and the randomness of the starting weights. ObfNets are selected dynamically and at random by EN in the final step.

2. *Privacy Partition.* A realistic solution dubbed privacy partition is described for preserving privacy in ML. Privacy partition is a method for preserving privacy in deep neural networks. Deep network architecture is divided into two parts: a trusted local computing environment and an untrustworthy remote one. The outcome of the preceding transformation is processed in a trustworthy local computing environment by a learning module. Afterwards, in the context of remote computing, the processed data is sent to the first transformation layer. Certain centralized deep learning frameworks may use privacy partitioning as an optional feature on the edge network. Access to sensitive data streams may be restricted by users in order to ensure privacy. When ENs need distant services and compute, the interactive adversarial network offers a realistic option.

2.5 Edge-Enabled IoT Services with AI and Blockchain

For many contemporary technologies, the blockchain is already a distributed processing and storage architecture. The distributed consensus algorithm generates and updates data, enables peer-to-peer networks to exchange data, and uses a distributed ledger to maintain the stored data unchangeable. Additionally, it implements upper-layer application logic through automated script code or smart contracts. In summary, blockchain enables a new method of preserving and transmitting data that is resistant to attack and creates a decentralized ecosystem. The blockchain may be utilized to solve some of the most significant security concerns in IoT services, as discussed in Part 1 of this section. Second, we will take a look at how various mechanical devices communicate and share data resources. Part 3 focuses on enhancing environmental efficiency via the use of IoT networks. Additionally, Figure 2.3 depicts the section's hierarchical taxonomy.

2.5.1 Blockchain for IoT Services' Security

An IoT network is built using massive terminal devices, and any device linked to the network will have full access to the network's data. In light of the sheer number of gadgets, it is difficult to guarantee the safety of a single device. Compromise of an IoT device may lead to the exposure of vast volumes of data, with potentially disastrous results. As a consequence, it is vital to improve the security of IoT services. The security of IoT devices is compromised because of the enormous number of connected gadgets. As a result, bad actors have an easy time stealing data sent back and forth between devices.

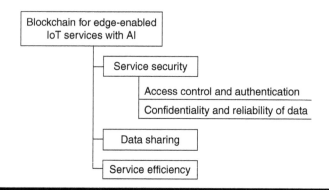

Figure 2.3   Edge-enabled IoT services using blockchain with AI as per taxonomy.

2.5.1.1 Authentication Management and Access Control

All system processes, data, and user interfaces are organized and identified via the use of access control methods, which are designed to provide a simple and distinct user interface. Authentication is the process of identifying the user's access using verification techniques such as passwords and deciding whether to provide access to the system's interface. In a standard IoT service that does not use AI or blockchain, identity verification is accomplished by verifying the user name and password combination for each device. Because of the high-power consumption and difficulty in scaling this approach, it is inappropriate for use with IP cameras. However, if a user's account is hacked or a device malfunctions, this will have a detrimental influence on the whole IoT system. A literature review suggests a unique design to overcome these concerns. To use the system, users must first verify their identity on a blockchain. To authenticate the package, the IoT service receives a package including the user's public key, IP address, and token from the smart contact during identity validation. Additionally, blockchain technology may be used to complete the collecting, storage, and verification of fingerprint information, therefore resolving the current falsification issue in access authentication technology.

2.5.1.2 Reliability and Confidentiality of Data

Health care, finance, and agriculture are just few of the areas where the IoT is having a positive impact. Many kinds of physical sensors are being utilized in the medical field to gather information on a patient's body functions, which may be used by doctors to improve their treatment methods. It is imperative that this sensitive personal data be protected. Byzantine fault-tolerant consensus method (PBFT) for safe storage of IoT data has been optimized to achieve distributed storage and tamper resistant data in data blockchains.

2.5.2 Blockchain for Edge-Enabled IoT Data Sharing

More accurate research and application development is possible because of the IoT network's base in data. Isolating data incurs significant energy and time expenses due to the repeated nature of the data collection. Data from IoT services may be stored in a database to facilitate resource allocation and cost-cutting. However, enormous data, diverse devices, a lack of trust, security concerns, and a variety of other issues act as impediments to secure data exchange. To create a platform capable of securely sharing data, blockchain technology becomes an attractive option. By using blockchain technology, we can create a decentralized network that is trustworthy without relying on a central authority. Zheng et al. propose the Microthings Chain architecture. This is what they came up with: an untamable and traceable EC network built on the blockchain. Additional data is sent to the blockchain's back end through Sash, so that the blockchain can defend against malicious behavior by itself. A smart contact is used to incorporate policy decision points into the blockchain and analyze requests for data sharing, which helps both the owners and consumers by enabling data sharing. DRL (Data Retrieval Language) is used in private blockchain networks to capture distributed data in the Industrial IoT (IIoT). In addition, IoT networks allow for the safe and equitable flow of knowledge, such as data. Using smart contracts and consortium blockchains, knowledge, such as data, is transferred fairly, quickly, and securely. Proof-of-Trading, a new consensus method, has the potential to dramatically reduce the costs of computing resources.

2.5.3 Blockchain for Edge-Enabled IoT Services' Efficiency

Parts 1 and 2 of this section discussed how blockchain may be used to IoT to ensure data security. However, solving the basic issue by simply increasing the computational capability of IoT devices is impractical at the moment. We'll take a look at a few studies from a variety of angles that help IoT services run more smoothly. In order to maximize the overall system efficiency, a balance must be struck between cache capacity and processing capabilities. Each data point in IoT networks may exchange data to disperse the cache of a single device, therefore Geometric Programming-based solution is implemented. This solution proposes a three-level cache and a cooperative computing approach that virtualizes data point servers into computation-intensive virtual machines. Blockchain IoT applications may benefit from the method by addressing multi-hop computation offloading concerns associated with ordinary and mining workloads by leveraging blockchain ledgers and a non-dominated sorting genetic algorithms.

2.6 Challenges and Issues

IoT security in EC is expected to be improved by AI, but numerous important concerns need to be fixed before AI is used to protect IoT.

2.6.1 Schemes Based on ML Security

Due to its capacity to boost the analytical powers of IoT devices, ML is an excellent option for securing IoT services, and there are already security schemes based on ML. Nevertheless, the vast majority of these approaches have serious problems that preclude their use in IoT systems at this time.

Solutions for Security Backup: Two separate kinds of ML, deep learning (DL) and reinforcement learning (RL), each have their own set of limitations. Over- or under-training may impair DL's ability to correctly assess attacks. In order to attain low error rates, DL requires a large enough training dataset. Let's then talk about real life. It is only possible to use existing techniques of reinforcement learning if the intelligent agent has a precise state and is capable of quickly analyzing the input from each action. Reinforcement learning security approaches, on the other hand, may not be able to withstand attacks of the learning process in beginning times, increasing the risk of IoT being hacked. As a result, in the event that ML-based schemes fails, IoT services established in order to defend further.

2.6.2 Adopt ML in Blockchain Technology

The IoT is expanding fast, and its services are progressively permeating every part of our lives. However, IoT is destined to face cyber-attacks and face a security hazard throughout its development. Additionally, trust issues that impede information flow between various IoT devices pose as roadblocks to the IoT's future progress. ML is crucial in protecting blockchains from attacks, but more work is needed before we can effectively integrate ML with blockchain to improve IoT security. Privacy considerations must be given the highest priority since data stored on the blockchain may be accessed by any blockchain node. It is hard to construct a reasonable model for privacy protection using private blockchains [27] and encryption, despite the fact that these technologies have been utilized to solve privacy problems. When these models are put to use in the real world, they are likely to fall short of our expectations and leave us feeling let down.

2.7 Conclusions

IoT development and the diversity of IoT application ecosystems would benefit greatly from EC, which is a new computing paradigm that tackles cloud computing's limitations. Electronic communications must meet stringent privacy and security standards if the IoT is to function properly. The usage of AI and EC in IoT security was discussed in this chapter. To get things started, some basic concepts and terminology were introduced. EC serves as a basis for IoT services. These two methods to edge-based IoT privacy preservation were then compared, and a third was devised using AI.

References

[1] F. X. Ming, R. A. A. Habeeb, F. H. B. Md Nasaruddin, and A. B. Gani, "Real-time carbon dioxide monitoring based on IoT & cloud technologies," in Proceedings of the 2019 8th International Conference on Software and Computer Applications, pp. 517–521, Cairo, Egypt, April 2019.

[2] S. Moin, A. Karim, Z. Safdar, K. Safdar, E. Ahmed, and M. Imran, "Securing IoTs in distributed blockchain: analysis, requirements and open issues," Future Generation Computer Systems, vol. 100, pp. 325–343, 2019.

[3] F. Chu, S. Yuan, and Z. Peng, "Using machine learning techniques to identify botnet traffic," Encyclopedia of Structural Health Monitoring, pp. 967–974, Wiley, Hoboken, NJ, USA, 2006.

[4] Y. Xiao, Y. Jia, C. Liu, X. Cheng, J. Yu, and W. Lv, "Edge computing security: state of the art and challenges," Proceedings of the IEEE, vol. 107, no. 8, pp. 1608–1631, 2019.

[5] X. Xia, F. Chen, Q. He, J. Grundy, M. Abdelrazek, and H. Jin, "Cost-effective app data distribution in edge computing," IEEE Transactions on Parallel and Distributed Systems, vol. 32, no. 1, pp. 31–44, 2020.

[6] P. K. Manadhata and J. M. Wing, "A formal model for a system's attack surface," in Moving Target Defense, pp. 1–28, Springer, Berlin, Germany, 2011.

[7] S. M. Tahsien, H. Karimipour, and P. Spachos, "Machine learning based solutions for security of Internet of Things (IoT): a survey," Journal of Network and Computer Applications, vol. 161, Article ID 102630, 2020.

[8] F. Liang, W. G. Hatcher, W. Liao, W. Gao, and W. Yu, "Machine learning for security and the internet of things: the good, the bad, and the ugly," IEEE Access, vol. 7, pp. 158126–158147, 2019.

[9] H. Haddadpajouh, R. Khayami, A. Dehghantanha, K. R. Choo, and R. M. Parizi, "AI4SAFE-IoT: an AI-powered secure archi-tecture for edge layer of internet of things," Neural Comput-Ing and Applications, 2020.

[10] A. Jonathan, M. Ryden, K. Oh, A. Chandra, and J. Weissman, "Nebula: distributed edge cloud for data intensive computing," IEEE Transactions on Parallel and Distributed Systems, vol. 28, no. 11, pp. 3229–3242, 2017.

[11] Prashant Madhukar Yawalkar, Deepak Narayan Paithankar, Abhijeet Rajendra Pabale, Rushikesh Vilas Kolhe, P. William, Integrated identity and auditing man-agement using blockchain mechanism, Measurement: Sensors, 2023, 100732, ISSN 2665-9174, https://doi.org/10.1016/j.measen.2023.100732.

[12] P. William et al., "Divination of air quality assessment using ensembling machine learning approach," 2023 International Conference on Artificial Intelligence and Knowledge Discovery in Concurrent Engineering (ICECONF), Chennai, India, 2023, pp. 1–10, doi: 10.1109/ICECONF57129.2023.10083751.

[13] P. S. Chobe, D. B. Padale, D. B. Pardeshi, N. M. Borawake and P. William, "Deployment of framework for charging electric vehicle based on various topolo-gies," 2023 International Conference on Artificial Intelligence and Knowledge Discovery in Concurrent Engineering (ICECONF), Chennai, India, 2023, pp. 1–4, doi: 10.1109/ICECONF57129.2023.10084062.

[14] D. B. Pardeshi, A. K. Chaudhari, P. Thokal, R. S. Dighe and P. William, "Framework for deployment of smart motor starter using android automation tool," 2023 International Conference on Artificial Intelligence and Knowledge Discovery in Concurrent Engineering (ICECONF), Chennai, India, 2023, pp. 1–6, doi: 10.1109/ICECONF57129.2023.10083946.

[15] H. P. Varade, S. C. Bhangale, S. R. Thorat, P. B. Khatkale, S. K. Sharma and P. William, "Framework of air pollution assessment in smart cities using IoT with machine learning approach," 2023 2nd International Conference on Applied Artificial Intelligence and Computing (ICAAIC), Salem, India, 2023, pp. 1436–1441, doi: 10.1109/ICAAIC56838.2023.10140834.

[16] Dhanabal, S., William, P., Vengatesan, K., Harshini, R., Kumar, V.D.A., Yuvaraj, S. (2023). Implementation and Comparative Analysis of Various Energy-Efficient Clustering Schemes in AODV. In: Venkataraman, N., Wang, L., Fernando, X., Zobaa, A.F. (eds) Big Data and Cloud Computing. ICBCC 2022. Lecture Notes in Electrical Engineering, vol 1021. Springer, Singapore. https://doi.org/10.1007/978-981-99-1051-9_19.

[17] Rushikesh Vilas Kolhe, P. William, Prashant Madhukar Yawalkar, Deepak Narayan Paithankar, Abhijeet Rajendra Pabale, Smart city implementation based on Internet of Things integrated with optimization technology, Measurement: Sensors, Vol. 27, 2023, 100789, ISSN 2665-9174, https://doi.org/10.1016/j.measen.2023.100789.

[18] M.A. Jawale, P. William, A.B. Pawar, Nikhil Marriwala, Implementation of number plate detection system for vehicle registration using IOT and recognition using CNN, Measurement: Sensors, Volume 27, 2023, 100761, ISSN 2665–9174, https://doi.org/10.1016/j.measen.2023.100761.

[19] P. William, G. R. Lanke, D. Bordoloi, A. Shrivastava, A. P. Srivastavaa and S. V. Deshmukh, "Assessment of human activity recognition based on impact of feature extraction prediction accuracy," 2023 4th International Conference on Intelligent Engineering and Management (ICIEM), London, United Kingdom, 2023, pp. 1–6, doi: 10.1109/ICIEM59379.2023.10166247.

[20] P. William, G. R. Lanke, V. N. R. Inukollu, P. Singh, A. Shrivastava and R. Kumar, "Framework for design and implementation of chat support system using natural language processing," 2023 4th International Conference on Intelligent Engineering and Management (ICIEM), London, United Kingdom, 2023, pp. 1–7, doi: 10.1109/ICIEM59379.2023.10166939.

[21] P. William, A. Shrivastava, U. S. Aswal, I. Kumar, M. Gupta and A. K. Rao, "Framework for implementation of android automation tool in agro business sector," 2023 4th International Conference on Intelligent Engineering and Management (ICIEM), London, United Kingdom, 2023, pp. 1–6, doi: 10.1109/ICIEM59379.2023.10167328.

[22] P. William, G. R. Lanke, S. Pundir, I. Kumar, M. Gupta and S. Shaw, "Implementation of hand written based signature verification technology using deep learning approach," 2023 4th International Conference on Intelligent Engineering and Management (ICIEM), London, United Kingdom, 2023, pp. 1–6, doi: 10.1109/ICIEM59379.2023.10167195.

[23] P. William, V. N. R. Inukollu, V. Ramasamy, P. Madan, A. Shrivastava and A. Srivastava, "Implementation of machine learning classification techniques for

intrusion detection system," 2023 4th International Conference on Intelligent Engineering and Management (ICIEM), London, United Kingdom, 2023, pp. 1–7, doi: 10.1109/ICIEM59379.2023.10167390.

[24] Korde, S. K., Rakshe, D. S., William, P., Jawale, M. A., & Pawar, A. B. (2023). Experimental investigations on copper-based nanoparticles for energy storage applications. *Journal of Nano-and Electronic Physics*, 15(3).

[25] Rakshe, D. S., William, P., Jawale, M. A., Pawar, A. B., Korde, S. K., & Deshpande, N. (2023). Synthesis and characterization of graphene based nanomaterials for energy applications. *Journal of Nano-and Electronic Physics*, 15(3).

[26] Jawale, M. A., Pawar, A. B., Korde, S. K., Rakshe, D. S., William, P., & Deshpande, N. (2023). Energy management in electric vehicles using improved swarm optimized deep reinforcement learning algorithm. *Journal of Nano-and Electronic Physics*, 15(3).

[27] Rashmi, M., William, P., Yogeesh, N., Girija, D.K. (2023). Blockchain-based cloud storage using secure and decentralised solution. In: Chaki, N., Roy, N.D., Debnath, P., Saeed, K. (eds) Proceedings of International Conference on Data Analytics and Insights, ICDAI 2023. ICDAI 2023. Lecture Notes in Networks and Systems, vol 727. Springer, Singapore. https://doi.org/10.1007/978-981-99-3878-0_23.

[28] Girija, D.K., Rashmi, M., William, P., Yogeesh, N. (2023). Framework for integrating the synergies of blockchain with AI and IoT for secure distributed systems. In: Chaki, N., Roy, N.D., Debnath, P., Saeed, K. (eds) Proceedings of International Conference on Data Analytics and Insights, ICDAI 2023. ICDAI 2023. Lecture Notes in Networks and Systems, vol 727. Springer, Singapore. https://doi.org/10.1007/978-981-99-3878-0_22.

[29] S. Yi, Z. Hao, Q. Zhang, Q. Zhang, W. Shi, and Q. Li, "Lavea: latency-aware video analytics on edge computing platform," in Proceedings of the Second ACM/IEEE Symposium on Edge Computing, pp. 1–13, San Jose, CA, USA, October 2017.

[30] L. Wang, X. Zhang, R. Wang, C. Yan, H. Kou, and L. Qi, "Diversified service recommendation with high accuracy and efficiency," Knowledge-Based Systems, vol. 204, Article ID 106196, 2020.

[31] Z. Ziming, L. Fang, C. Zhiping, and X. Nong, "Edge computing: platforms, applications and challenges," Journal of Computer Research and Development, vol. 55, no. 2, p. 327, 2018.

[32] C. Avasalcai, C. Tsigkanos, and S. Dustdar, "Decentralized resource auctioning for latency-sensitive edge computing," in Proceedings of the IEEE International Conference on Edge Computing (EDGE), pp. 72–76, IEEE, Milan, Italy, July 2019.

[33] Q. He, G. Cui, X. Zhang et al., "A game-theoretical approach for user allocation in edge computing environment," IEEE Transactions on Parallel and Distributed Systems, vol. 31, no. 3, pp. 515–529, 2019.

[34] P. William, D. Jadhav, P. Cholke, M. A. Jawale and A. B. Pawar, "Framework for product anti-counterfeiting using blockchain technology," 2022 International Conference on Sustainable Computing and Data Communication Systems (ICSCDS), 2022, pp. 1254–1258, doi: 10.1109/ICSCDS53736.2022.9760916.

[35] R. Jadhav, A. Shaikh, M. A. Jawale, A. B. Pawar and P. William, "System for identifying fake product using blockchain technology," 2022 7th International Conference

on Communication and Electronics Systems (ICCES), 2022, pp. 851–854, doi: 10.1109/ICCES54183.2022.9835866.

[36] P. William, Y. N., S. Vimala, P. Gite and S. K. S, "Blockchain technology for data privacy using contract mechanism for 5G networks," 2022 3rd International Conference on Intelligent Engineering and Management (ICIEM), 2022, pp. 461–465, doi: 10.1109/ICIEM54221.2022.9853118.

[37] A.B. Pawar, M.A. Jawale, P. William, G.S. Chhabra, Dhananjay S. Rakshe, Sachin K. Korde, Nikhil Marriwala, Implementation of blockchain technology using extended CNN for lung cancer prediction, Measurement: Sensors, 2022, 100530, ISSN 2665-9174, https://doi.org/10.1016/j.measen.2022.100530.

[38] P. William, A. Shrivastava, H. Chauhan, P. Nagpal, V. K. T. N and P. Singh, "Framework for intelligent smart city deployment via artificial intelligence software networking," 2022 3rd International Conference on Intelligent Engineering and Management (ICIEM), 2022, pp. 455–460, doi: 10.1109/ICIEM54221.2022.9853119.

[39] S. S. Gondkar, D. B. Pardeshi and P. William, "Innovative system for water level management using IoT to prevent water wastage," 2022 International Conference on Applied Artificial Intelligence and Computing (ICAAIC), 2022, pp. 1555–1558, doi: 10.1109/ICAAIC53929.2022.9792746.

[40] S. S. Gondkar, P. William and D. B. Pardeshi, "Design of a novel IoT framework for home automation using google assistant," 2022 6th International Conference on Intelligent Computing and Control Systems (ICICCS), 2022, pp. 451–454, doi: 10.1109/ICICCS53718.2022.9788284.

[41] S. Choubey, P. William, A. B. Pawar, M. A. Jawale, K. Gupta and V. Parganiha, "Intelligent water level monitoring and water pump controlling system using IOT," 2022 3rd International Conference on Electronics and Sustainable Communication Systems (ICESC), 2022, pp. 423–427, doi: 10.1109/ICESC54411.2022.9885358.

[42] Deepak Narayan Paithankar, Abhijeet Rajendra Pabale, Rushikesh Vilas Kolhe, P. William, Prashant Madhukar Yawalkar, Framework for implementing air quality monitoring system using LPWA-based IoT technique, Measurement: Sensors,2023,100709,ISSN 2665-9174, https://doi.org/10.1016/j.measen.2023.100709.

[43] K. Gupta, S. Choubey, Y. N, P. William, V. T. N and C. P. Kale, "Implementation of motorist weariness detection system using a conventional object recognition technique," 2023 International Conference on Intelligent Data Communication Technologies and Internet of Things (IDCIoT), Bengaluru, India, 2023, pp. 640–646, doi: 10.1109/IDCIoT56793.2023.10052783.

[44] P. William, Y. N, V. M. Tidake, S. Sumit Gondkar, C. R and K. Vengatesan, "Framework for implementation of personality inventory model on natural language processing with personality traits analysis," 2023 International Conference on Intelligent Data Communication Technologies and Internet of Things (IDCIoT), Bengaluru, India, 2023, pp. 625–628, doi: 10.1109/IDCIoT56793.2023.10053501.

[45] M. Zheng, D. Xu, L. Jiang, C. Gu, R. Tan, and P. Cheng, "Challenges of privacy-preserving machine learning in IoT," in Proceedings of the First International Workshop on Challenges in Artificial Intelligence and Machine Learning for Internet of Things, pp. 1–7, New York, NY, USA, November 2019.

[46] B. Zhou and J. Pei, "*e k-anonymity and l-diversity approaches for privacy preservation in social networks against neighborhood attacks," Knowledge and Information Systems, vol. 28, no. 1, pp. 47–77, 2011.

[47] P. C. M. Arachchige, P. Bertok, I. Khalil, D. Liu, S. Camtepe, and M. Atiquzzaman, "Local diffierential privacy for deep learn-ing," IEEE Internet of Things Journal, vol. 7, pp. 5827–5842, 2020.

[48] Y. Donghuan, M. Wen, X. Liang, Z. Fu, K. Zhang, and B. Yang, "Energy theft detection with energy privacy preservation in the smart grid," IEEE Internet of >ings Journal, vol. 6, no. 5, pp. 7659–7669, 2019.

[49] D. Xu, M. Zheng, L. Jiang, C. Gu, R. Tan, and P. Cheng, "Lightweight and unobtrusive privacy preservation for remote inference via edge data obfuscation," 2019, https://arxiv.org/ abs/1912.09859.

[50] X. Xu, X. Liu, X. Yin, S. Wang, Q. Qi, and L. Qi, "Privacyaware offloading for training tasks of generative adversarial network in edge computing," Information Sciences, vol. 532, pp. 1–15, 2020.

[51] J. Chi, E. Owusu, X. Yin et al., "Privacy partition: a privacy preserving framework for deep neural networks in edge networks," in Proceedings of the IEEE/ACM Symposium on Edge Computing (SEC), IEEE, Seattle, WA, USA, pp. 378–380, October, 2018.

[52] A.B. Pawar, P. Gawali, M. Gite, M. A. Jawale and P. William, "Challenges for hate speech recognition system: approach based on solution," 2022 International Conference on Sustainable Computing and Data Communication Systems (ICSCDS), 2022, pp. 699–704, doi: 10.1109/ICSCDS53736.2022.9760739.

[53] P. William, D. Jadhav, P. Cholke, M. A. Jawale and A. B. Pawar, "Framework for product anti-counterfeiting using blockchain technology," 2022 International Conference on Sustainable Computing and Data Communication Systems (ICSCDS), 2022, pp. 1254–1258, doi: 10.1109/ICSCDS53736.2022.9760916.

Chapter 3

Computational-Based Edge AI Services and Challenges

Bharati Ainapure[1]

[1]*Department of Computer Engineering, Vishwakarma University, Pune, Maharashtra, India*

3.1 Introduction

The Internet of Things (IoT) vision has evolved over the past few years from a theoretical idea to a practical priority for many organizations. Companies are searching for innovative methods to use and manage the data they collect as they integrate IoT devices into their network infrastructures. Depending on applications and domain, such as smart transportation, retail business, smart healthcare, self-driven cars, etc., data collected from various IoT devices must be processed to yield insightful information and actionable decisions. In these cases, data needs to be sent to a centralized server such as the cloud to process the data and get insightful information to make future decisions. However, this process involves delay, which will make the application's intended use unattainable. The latency at which data is transferred to the cloud or central server becomes a concern when organizations try to push huge amounts of data to the software. It becomes less cost-effective to manage everything centrally as the volume of data increases. Not only the data, but some applications like self-driving cars

DOI: 10.1201/9781032650722-4

need quick data processing and decision-making for further actions in critical situations. Edge computing (EC) has evolved because cloud computing or data centers are insufficient to meet the varied requirements of data analysis of today's intelligent society. By moving storage, applications, and processing capacity from the cloud or data center to edge devices, EC has brought data processing to the point of acquisition.

Massive amounts of data must be moved to the cloud for analysis in order to use centralized processing. This involves intensive network bandwidth and latency. As a result, this process has severe latency, bandwidth-related problems, and high transmission energy, all of which are intolerable in applications like augmented reality, video conferences, streaming software, etc. However, in reality networks have limited bandwidth. Additionally, real-time data analysis is practically impossible when data are transferred to the cloud. However, many real-time applications need data analysis very fast. For example, in smart home systems in which every corner of the home is monitored to maintain safety and security. Instead of sending data to the cloud server to which smart home users are connected, upon receiving the data, the system will take action by seeking help from others. The monitoring system itself will be equipped with the capability to process the data so that it can produce actionable decisions without delay. In addition, it itself will direct the required action like sending information to emergency professionals and preventing the transfer of data to a centralized infrastructure. In situations where data analysis at the edge is required, it should be carried out at the edge device rather than through cloud or data centers.

Cloud computing offers low-cost hardware and services that encourage organizations to build AI-enabled business models to train on massive data. Even though the cloud is highly suitable to train AI models, real difficulty arises when there is a need for response to user queries in real time, which require some inference from the data using AI models. The following are some of the challenges in predicting data using AI over the cloud:

■ To get real-time response from AI applications, the data from edge devices need to be sent to cloud, and then the cloud must send the answer back to the edge device.
■ User experience is degraded due to high latency network requirement over the cloud for data prediction.
■ Cloud AI-based prediction becomes difficult when there is no internet connection or for internet connection issues. Even if the device has internet access, it might not have enough bandwidth to send the necessary quantity of data in a specified time period.

Edge AI enables AI models to run locally on a device without latency or network access. This facilitates much quicker prediction and the support of real-time applications. However, edge AI also has a few challenges as edge devices need to learn continuously from real-time data.

- It is difficult to process the huge amount of data at the edge, because edge devices are computationally weak.
- Handling of huge amounts of data in less time without delay needs to be adapted at edge devices using AI algorithms.
- AI model building, training, and execution of applications in real time need significant processing power, storage, and a huge amount of data for learning at edge.
- Advanced AI algorithms like deep neural networks need huge processing power and storage to build inference model.

AI algorithms have the potential for massive carbon footprints. AI algorithms could leave significant carbon footprints. A steady stream of improvements in hardware, software, and data usage must be made in order to get them to infer the real-time data. Architectures for AI in combination with IoT are required to be established. The cooperation of specialized hardware designs, suitable architecture selection, and model optimization is required for the training and inference stages of AI models.

In this context, this chapter discusses various edge AI services in real time and their challenges. The chapter is organized into four sections. In section 3.2, a literature review is presented. Current real-time edge AI services are discussed in section 3.3. Section 3.3 talks about the challenges of implementing EC, followed by the conclusion.

3.2 Background

A discussion of the previous work done by many researchers related to various applications using EC is presented in the literature section. As this chapter focuses on computational-based edge AI services and challenges, around fifty recently published papers related to edge AI were found and analyzed. We obtained articles from journals and conferences indexed by the Scopus database and excluded non-referred articles. Top databases this work used include MDPI, IEEE, Springer, ScienceDirect, and PubMed. Distribution of papers among these databases is shown in Figure 3.1. The literature was made more comprehensive from these databases using Boolean search and was carried out using keywords [1] "Edge Computing" AND "AI", "Deep Learning" AND "Challenges" AND "Computations" AND "Applications" as shown in Tables 3.1 and 3.2.

Literature overview considering the scope of the proposed chapter is shown in Table 3.2.

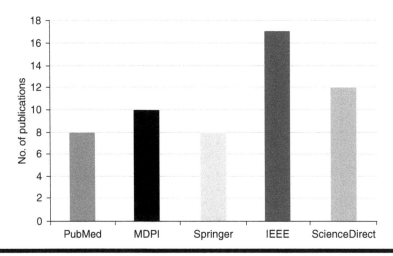

Figure 3.1 **Chapter relevant literature based on keywords.**

Table 3.1 **Keyword Search on Scopus Indexed Sources**

Time Period	Keyword used
Jan 2012 to Feb. 2023	Edge Computing, AL, and DL
	Challenges and Computations
	Applications

3.3 Edge AI Services

This section discusses the edge AI services in different domains. Edge AI is the fusion of EC and AI. In EC the AI models are initially trained and tested on the cloud to overcome the resource problem at edge devices. The tested model can be then deployed on edge devices for future prediction of real-time data. Inference updates can be then sent back to cloud servers to keep the models updated. This will eliminate the huge data transfer from edge device to cloud and back to edge device and also provide solutions to the latency, scalability, and privacy challenges of cloud computing. Edge computing facilitates computational abilities to compute resources that are placed very near to edge devices. An edge compute node, for instance, might be situated on a premise network or next to an IoT gateway and a cellular base station. The high-level architecture of edge AI is shown in Figure 3.2. This expands to three layers: Cloud or data centers, edge nodes, which are located very close to end user devices, and edge devices. These layers are explained below:

■ Cloud or data centers: This refers to actual cloud or data center storages, where abundant computational resources are available to train the AI models. In

Table 3.2 Historical Perspective

References	Edge AI category	Research Focus
[2]–[5]	Based on survey	• Need of edge AI • Edge devices requirements to process huge data • Different edge AI use cases • Challenges in implementing edge AI
[6]–[8],[9]	Edge in Healthcare	• Health monitoring using smart devices • Human fall detection • Alarming system in case of emergency • Recommender systems for personalized health care • Precision medicine in disease detection, prediction and prognosis.
[4], [10]–[13],[14]	Role of AI ML algorithms.	• Traditional machine learning algorithms and accuracy • Deep learning algorithms in health care and manufacturing industry • Genetic and evolutionary algorithms for task optimization on edge
[15]–[18]	Process/task optimization	• Well know optimization techniques and methods • Heuristic techniques for computational offloading of task • Minimizing power consumption, resources latency etc. • Device performance improvement
[19]–[23]	Resource allocation	• Decision making for offloading computational task on edge devices • Maximizing the user utility • Price-based resource allocation • computational efficiency analysis toward user • Resource allocation based on task priority

addition to its powerful computing and storage capabilities, the cloud also has the ability to macro-control the entire EC architecture.

■ Edge nodes: These comprise certain computation resources and storages. These nodes use AI algorithms to draw inference from real-time data that is coming from edge devices. These nodes are meant to share the work of the cloud so as to reduce delay of data transfer over the network. Therefore, they are located very close to edge devices. Generally, the edge nodes comprise control units, gateways, storage, and computing units.

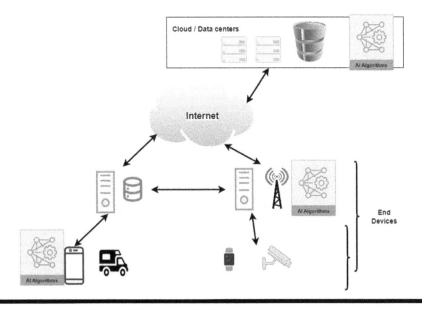

Figure 3.2   High-level architecture of edge AI.

- Edge devices: This layer contains devices like sensors, smartphones, etc. These devices have limited storage and computing capabilities, and are supposed to observe and receive data from the physical world. If required they also have to make intelligent decisions. The other task these devices do is to receive data or information from the edge node or cloud and perform corresponding tasks.

Numerous AI algorithms are best suited for the edge due to high-level computational resources available at edge devices. Different edge AI services in practice such as self-driving cars, smart hospitals, surveillance and security, energy, etc., are shown in Figure 3.3. These examples highlight how edge AI is positively impacting the world today. They showcase some of the most important innovations and inventiveness edge AI can offer users at home and work.

3.3.1 Edge AI Services in Healthcare

The quantity of patient data collected from devices, sensors, and other medical equipment has dramatically increased in the healthcare sector. This huge amount of data requires EC and AI algorithms to identify critical data so that health workers working in hospitals can take quick action to help patients in case of health incidents in real time.

One of the edge AI services is the smart hospital. Adaptation of edge AI will enhance the operational efficiency in patient care. As shown in Figure 3.4 the

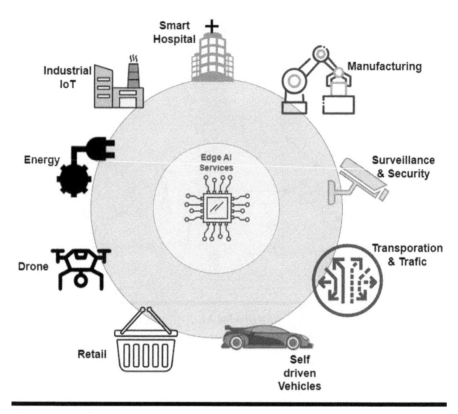

Figure 3.3   Edge AI services in practice.

real-time data collected from wearable and health monitoring devices can be analyzed on edge devices that are located on premise. This will help clinicians and other medical staff to take better care of patients in critical situations. Here, in this situation, data is not required to be sent to the cloud for analysis. This prevents the sensitive patient data to be transmitted over the public network, which provides data security.

In today's world it is necessary for smart hospitals to incorporate AI and EC into technologies like patient monitoring, heart rate monitoring, CT scanners, interactive AI, etc. These advances in technology can assist in identifying patients who are in danger of falling out of the bed in hospital and sending messages to medical staff. One of the known computer vision applications is estimation of human pose, which captures the key positions of human body parts such as legs, arms, eyes, etc., and classifies them into different categories. These categories may be walking, standing, sitting, or lying down on the bed. Such range of applications can be used in the healthcare industry for patient monitoring. This will help patients who need medical assistance by sending alerts to medical staff.

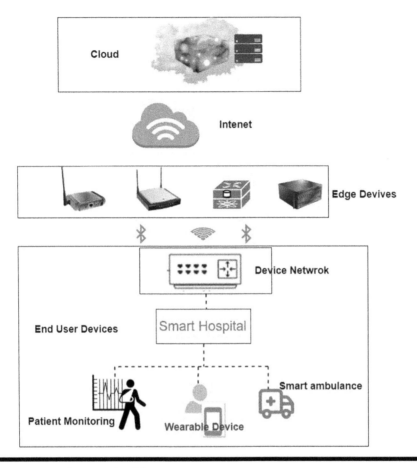

Figure 3.4   Edge AI in healthcare.

The abovementioned application is more suitable for monitoring elderly people. Per the literature, the elder population is expected to increase and will reach 1.4 billion by 2030 and 2.1 billion by 2050 [24]. As people get older, their eyesight, balance, and cognitive abilities deteriorate more, which raises their risk of falling. More than 30% of people over 65 years of age fall frequently, which can result in serious or even fatal injuries. But it has been observed that in such situations only one-third of such people get medical assistance [6].

In conventional fall detection systems, the movements of elderly people is captured using cameras and sensors. This data is sent to the cloud servers for analysis [7], [8], [25]. If any fall data is noticed during analysis by the server, immediately this is notified to the hospitals to which people are connected or else notified to the relatives. In this case the analysis of data is highly accurate and the cloud has more computational resources. The primary drawback of uploading a lot of data to a cloud server is the high cost of network bandwidth that results, as well as the high latency and privacy issues that arise. The network bandwidth and loading of cloud computing may become problematic with too many people using the system [26]. With advancement in technology, the real-time data can be processed locally without sending it to the cloud. For fall monitoring systems, EC-based systems have the potential to perform better in real-time than in cloud-based systems [27].

Other edge AI services in healthcare systems include:

- Cardiovascular abnormalities
- Radiology
- Patient monitoring at home
- Measurement of vital parameters
- Video consulting sessions
- Patient geolocation
- Administration of pharmacological treatment
- Medicinal product procurement requests

3.3.2 Edge AI in Retail Industry

In today's digital era, integration of edge AI into the retail market is becoming necessary and important. The retail market comprises goods, sales, and services both offline in physical stores and online. Edge AI in the retail market deals with data collection, processing, and analysis on servers near edge devices. In retail business, edge AI can enhance customer experiences, streamline store operations, and support cutting-edge technologies like self-checkout and virtual reality systems. As a result, real-time data analysis becomes necessary, enabling customers to experience cost reduction and more personalized shopping. This will also increase the revenue of retail businesses.

Figure 3.5 shows different edge AI services in retail. Live video stream feeds generated by multiple devices in retail shops has many challenges in sending data to the cloud such as delay in contactless checkout if the network latency is high. Rather, in edge AI the data is processed at the edge device, which may be the server on campus, on which alters and insights are generated on demand. This provides real-time data analytics to respond faster to customers and assures robust and faulty tolerant capabilities.

In inventory and fraud management, the edge AI will collect the data from cameras and hand-held Radio Frequency Identification (RFID) devices. Analytics of such data will help stores to enhance security against theft. This will also help store staff to make demand-based inventory decisions on receipt of alert message regarding inventory stock. For instance, Walmart in the United States uses edge AI. Here, day-to day forecasts for millions of items are done at edge across tens of thousands of locations [28]. This helps Walmart more effectively deliver the right

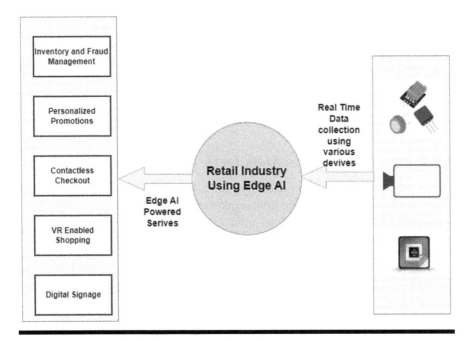

Figure 3.5   Scenario of edge AI in retail market.

goods to the right stores, respond in real-time to consumer trends, and achieve large-scale inventory cost savings [29].

Personalized promotions can be adapted using edge AI to attract more customers and increase their loyalty both online and offline. Personalization may impact customer behavior, lower acquisition costs, boost revenue, and improve marketing effectiveness [30]. Personalized shopping can also promote the recommender system. Very powerful algorithms like machine learning and deep learning, which are part AI, are used to create recommender system. These algorithms help retailers to identify customer details, their likes and dislikes, and what they are most likely to purchase. The edge AI in the recommender system can produce accurate and comprehensive results, and thus attract more customers [31].

Consumers want to save time and have everything at their fingertips. Before COVID-19, use contactless payment was less common. Currently, many retailers have adapted mobile and contactless payment systems. There are two different ways retailers can provide contactless payment options: 1. Customers can have smartphones with retailer application running through which items can be added and deleted. Final bill will be generated and application can show different payment options for users like card payment. 2. Customers can go with smart cart in malls. This cart will add and deleted the items that are added and taken out from the cart. Finally this cart will can send the final bill to customers and to retailers [32], [33].

Other edge AI services in retail business include [34]:

- Real-time brand promotions
- VR-enabled shopping
- Digital signage
- Inventory management
- Temperature monitoring in cold storage

3.3.3 Role of Edge AI in Manufacturing Industry

Recent years have resulted in a revolution in the manufacturing industry with the introduction of sensors. With the growing demands for products, it is necessary for industries to maintain, monitor, and automate industrial processes, environments, assets, and systems. Industries are automating processes in order to fulfill the growing demands for products using IoT sensors as shown in Figure 3.6. Manufacturers can increase operational efficacy using insightful information generated using IoT sensor data and AI algorithms. The vast amount of data collected from sensor-enabled devices can be collected and processed using edge AI locally on manufacturing premises without having communicated with the cloud. AI algorithms deployed on edge devices can help to get insights on the real-time data. This will help factory management make decisions fast in the case of product defects on the assembly line, for example. This will also help to identify factory floor risks.

Condition monitoring and predictive maintenance is one of the services in edge AI that can be used for better results. Predictive maintenance is a technique in which machine maintenance can be scheduled ahead of the actual breakdown. It detects anomalies in equipment before they turn into system critical failures. Predictive maintenance reduces maintenance costs and increases equipment uptime. Condition monitoring is used know the health of various assets or equipment in the factory [35]. The data collected from sensors can be used to find patterns in critical parameters such as current flow, vibrations, sound variation, etc. Such data can help management to make more valuable and precise decisions [36]. The enormous amount of raw data generated by machines can overload central servers and also create data access problems. Using EC a huge amount of raw data can be cleaned and only useful data can be sent to the cloud server to avoid access delay. The other way in edge AI is that, first train the models using cloud server and then push the trained models on edge to predict critical conditions of the machine in real time. This will speed up the whole process of condition monitoring. Manufacturers have the opportunity to generate additional revenue streams by employing remote asset monitoring and providing maintenance services on a "pay-per-use" basis, allowing customers to pay for services only when their equipment requires attention. Other edge AI services in the manufacturing industry include:

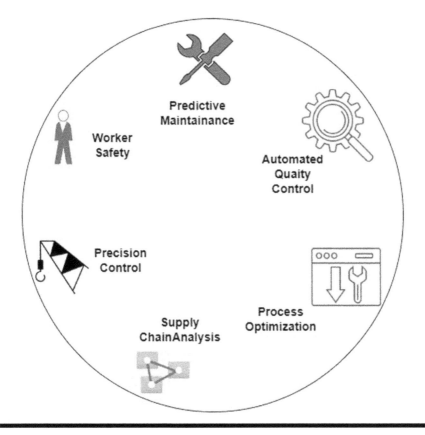

Figure 3.6 Edge AI services in industry IoT.

- Worker safety on sight
- Supply chain analysis to increase sales and productivity
- Defect detection and quality control
- Yield optimization in food industry

3.3.4 Role of Edge AI in Transportation and Traffic Management

The autonomous vehicle is one of the innovative AI applications of smart transportation. Traffic management and safety have become more important to urban residents and transportation agencies as more vehicles have entered roadways [37]. A survey released by statista.com reported that worldwide car sales in 2022 was 66.1 million and increased to 66.9 million in the year 2023 [38]. More vehicles on the road can cause traffic congestion, which leads to more fuel consumption, air pollution, and traffic rule violations. Using edge AI sensors deployed in vehicles, smart stations, and smart cameras installed across urban infrastructures can collect and process information gathered in real time.

Traffic lights can also be automated using edge AI, and can be used to measure vehicle behavior, expand road network capacity, and resolve conflicts in vehicle movement. An edge system, a backend tracking system, and a self-adaptive traffic light system can be part of the integrated setup for efficient traffic control. The data collected in the form of videos from cameras can be transmitted to an edge AI system to produce inferences so that inferred data can be sent to backend monitoring. To create proper traffic flow, pre-trained AI models can immediately send the processed data back to the self-adaptive traffic lights. Moreover, road vehicle movement can be regulated by traffic light timing that automatically changes by the second with the help of a real-time traffic light. Through interoperable communication, the changing traffic situation and the timing at intersections can be shared, enabling all connections to be ready to optimize the flow of upcoming traffic. In Delhi, the capital city of India, sensors from over 7,500 Closed Circuit Television (CCTV) cameras, 1,000 Light Emitting Diode (LED) signs, and programmed traffic lights gather real-time data that AI transforms into instantaneous insights that are then used by authorities for better traffic management [39].

3.4 Edge Computing and AI Algorithms

Machine learning (ML) and deep learning (DL) algorithms are part AI, which are frequently used to train the model bring the intelligence in devices. The other categories of AI algorithms are reinforcement learning and deep reinforcement learning. This chapter focuses on AI algorithms, especially those used on edge devices to make intelligent decisions.

3.4.1 Traditional Machine Learning

ML algorithms can be trained in a number of ways, each with its own set of benefits and drawbacks. Before we can understand the advantages and disadvantages, we must know the type of data used by ML algorithms. These are unlabeled data and labelled data [40]. Labelled data are presented in machine-readable form and consist of both inputs as features and outputs as labels, whereas unlabeled data don't have output labels. Whatever the form of data used by ML, algorithms are classified into three major categories [41] as shown in Figure 3.7:

- Supervised Learning
- Unsupervised Learning
- Reinforcement Learning

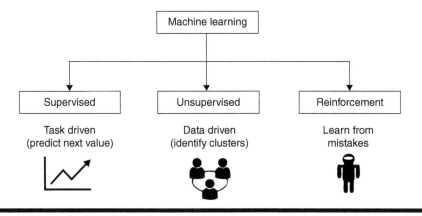

Figure 3.7 Types of machine learning.

Supervised learning algorithms include K-Nearest Neighbor (KNN), Support Vector Machine (SVM), Naive Bayes, Decision Tree, Logistic regression, Artificial Neural Network (ANN), etc. Prediction of statistically likely future events with the use of historical data is a common way of supervised learning. Anticipation of future fluctuations in stock market information is one of the use cases of historical data in supervised learning.

In unsupervised learning, the model is trained based on input features. The model really does not know what the output label is for a given data point. In this learning, the model is created by feeding a large amount of data to the model to know the properties of the data. Once the properties of the data are understood by the model, then it groups the data into different clusters depending on pattern, similarities, and differences. Feature learning, reduction of dimensionality, forming association rules, clustering, etc., are some of the tasks of unsupervised learning. Unsupervised learning is said to be data driven, because learning is based on data and its properties [42]. Grouping of user choices in retail markets and recommender systems, etc., are fewer applications of unsupervised learning. Unsupervised algorithms include: Fuzzy clustering, K-Means clustering, and Hierarchical clustering [42].

There are some drawbacks of traditional AI learning. For example, they require complex artificial feature engineering, are sensitive to data sets, and become less effective when the data set is sufficiently big. Despite these drawbacks, traditional ML is simpler to deploy than DL and reinforcement learning and consumes less energy and computing capacity. Because of the distributed nature of EC, deployment of traditional ML algorithms on edge devices will be of benefit considering the resource and task requirement.

3.4.2 *Deep Learning Algorithms*

DL models based on ANN have led to cutting-edge innovations in computer vision, voice recognition, and health science. DL, a form of ML, is inspired by the working

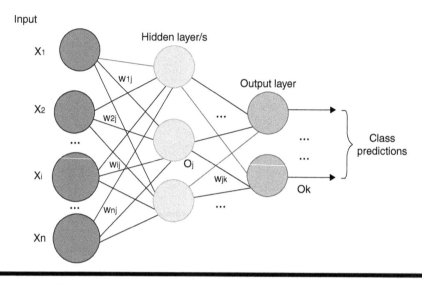

Figure 3.8 Deep neural networks.

of biological neural networks. DL is a multi-layer network of computing units called neurons operating in parallel to simulate certain cognitive tasks of humans. As shown in Figure 3.8, the network comprises input layer, one or multiple hidden layers, and an output layer.

The input layer is fed with the independent variables or inputs. The neural network consists of a multiple number of hidden layers. The neurons in a layer are connected with neurons in the adjacent layer [43].

Performance of the DL algorithm is better compared to traditional ML algorithms in the case of huge datasets. DL algorithms perform well in different domains like computer vision, natural language processing, etc. [11]. In EC data collected from different devices is processed locally, which meets the requirements of DL algorithms. DL algorithms can also be used for optimal resource allocation, customer data security, anomaly detection [10], etc.

3.4.3 Reinforcement and Deep Reinforcement Learning

Reinforcement learning (RL) is different from that of supervised and unsupervised learning [44]. Models in reinforcement learning learn from mistakes. This type of learning consists of two components, an environment and an agent. Both need to be connected to the feedback loop as shown in Figure 3.9. A set of actions is needed by the agent to get connected to the environment. Such a set of actions affects the environment. Similarly, the environment needs connection with the agent continuously by issuing two signals: State and Reward [45], [46].

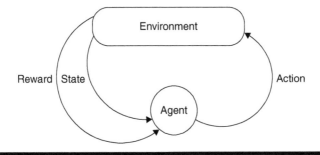

Figure 3.9 Reinforcement learning.

In the initial stage of learning, a model may make many mistakes. We can reinforce the model by preparing to identify good decisions over bad ones. The model is trained by sending some signals that are associated with bad and good decisions. Over time the model will learn to make better decisions than it used to. RL is influenced by psychology and neuroscience and thus is called behavior-driven learning. Q-learning is an example of an RL algorithm. This algorithm calculates cumulative rewards using Q-values based on an action given and current state. As the complexity of the problem increases, the state space and action space will increase, which will require a lot of memory to store values and will reduce the convergence speed of the algorithm [47].

Deep Q Network (DQN) is advanced Q–learning, which overcomes the problem of Q-learning. This algorithm approximates Q-value using deep neural network. This algorithm accepts initial values as input to the network and returns all possible Q-values. Considering EC characteristics, this algorithm is suitable to process huge and complex data at edge nodes. Therefore, these algorithms are more suitable for making optimized controlled decisions for real-time data [23].

3.4.4 Evolutionary Algorithms

Evolutionary algorithms (EAs) use optimization methods to solve complex problems. Natural processes like selection, recombination, mutation, migration, position, and neighborhood are modeled by evolutionary algorithms. The general working of an EA is shown in Figure 3.10. Instead of using a singular solution, EAs operate on populations of individuals. The search is carried out in parallel, which helps in getting a quick response on real-time data. EAs are deployed using the following steps:

1. Population initialization
2. Apply fitness function on population
3. Producing next-level population using crossover and mutation functions
4. Termination

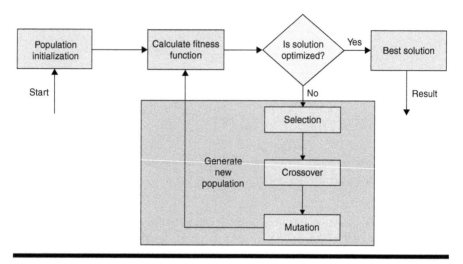

Figure 3.10   General working of EA.

In EC EAs are used for load balancing, optimal resource allocation, and task scheduling [12], [13].

3.5 Challenges in Implementing Edge AI

Despite the fact that executing edge AI is extremely gainful for many industries, it does have its difficulties. There are many parameters that make implementation difficult. For example, computational resource allocation, model training and deployment, framework integration, task optimization, energy consumption, memory storage, etc. Additionally, it is imperative for companies using edge AI to keep up with market advancements.

When a task is small and limited to solving classification problems, the smart device in which ML models have been deployed works efficiently. As model complexity increases, edge AI devices present a serious trade-off between accuracy and resource requirements. For AI applications intended to handle complex issues, the number of parameters that need to be learned and configured on a computing chip can increase exponentially. This shows that the edge devices must have an efficient chip to process large amounts of real-time data, but such chips can consume a huge amount of energy.

Edge AI plays a crucial role where life critical decisions are involved. For example, in the healthcare industry, AI systems must ensure data security, make accurate decisions, and meet safety standards. However, existing AI-ML algorithms that are deployed on edge devices are able to retrieve a limited amount of useful information from the data. The manual labelling of the data for supervised learning may lead to unknown prediction mistakes and less accuracy. Additionally, wearable technology will be the primary platform for data gathering in smart medical systems in the future. The deployment of AI models to these wearable devices is another challenging step in order to quickly analyze and respond to the collected data. Apart from that, the devices' energy supply and memory storage will be a significant challenge. Therefore, wearable devices need lightweight and accurate AI models [5].

In the smart manufacturing industry huge numbers of heterogeneous sensors are deployed to monitor assets, tolls, and shop floors. These sensors generate huge data streams, which have different sizes, formats, and timestamps. Processing such data requires high computational powered devices and intelligent AI algorithms. Therefore, integration of hardware in edge devices is one of the major problems in edge AI. For example, autonomous vehicles require data processing in real time to make future decisions. Such applications need AI-based deep neural network algorithms to run on edge. These algorithms are efficient in processing images. But deployment of such algorithms on edge has some constraints. Optimization of algorithm behavior on real-time data will affect the model accuracy. Hence, it is important to optimize the algorithm on edge devices without compromising the performance accuracy. Another challenge is optimization is hardware specific, so if you change hardware the model needs to be optimized again for that hardware.

Other challenges include:

■ Lack of human experts
■ Cost and time involved in development
■ Hardware standardization
■ AI integration with various devices

3.6 Conclusion

This chapter identified and demonstrated both potential and proven services in EC. In summary based on present research outcomes on combining AI and EC, this chapter concludes that: 1. Conventional non-AI methods are constrained in their ability to deal with the complex and dynamic nature of EC, and further AI can enhance and optimize the performance of EC. 2. Integration of AI algorithms in edge devices can bring quick response in real-time applications. 3. Huge data transmission over a slow network to the server for further processing can be avoided. 4. Edge AI can serve better in life critical applications such as autonomous vehicles. The methods for overcoming the challenges and concerns related to the implementation of edge AI in the form of AI algorithms were also covered in this chapter.

References

[1] R. Cioffi, M. Travaglioni, G. Piscitelli, A. Petrillo, and F. De Felice, "Artificial intelligence and machine learning applications in smart production: Progress, trends, and directions," *Sustain.*, vol. 12, no. 2, 2020.

[2] S. Iftikhar *et al.*, "AI-based fog and edge computing: A systematic review, taxonomy and future directions," *Internet of Things (Netherlands)*, vol. 21, no. November 2022, p. 100674, 2023.

[3] R. Singh and S. S. Gill, "Edge AI: A survey," *Internet of Things and Cyber-Physical Systems*, vol. 3. Elsevier, pp. 71–92, 01-Jan-2023.

[4] M. Merenda, C. Porcaro, and D. Iero, "Edge machine learning for AI-enabled IoT devices: A review," *Sensors (Switzerland)*, vol. 20, no. 9, pp. 1–34, 2020.

[5] J. Zhang and D. Tao, "Empowering things with intelligence: A survey of the progress, challenges, and opportunities in artificial intelligence of things," *IEEE Internet of Things Journal*, vol. 8, no. 10. pp. 7789–7817, 2021.

[6] B. S. Lin *et al.*, "Fall detection system with artificial intelligence-based edge computing," *IEEE Access*, vol. 10, pp. 4328–4339, 2022.

[7] S. Usmani, A. Saboor, M. Haris, M. A. Khan, and H. Park, "Latest research trends in fall detection and prevention using machine learning: A systematic review," *Sensors*, vol. 21, no. 15, pp. 1–23, 2021.

[8] B. H. Wang, J. Yu, K. Wang, X. Y. Bao, and K. M. Mao, "Fall detection based on dual-channel feature integration," *IEEE Access*, vol. 8, pp. 103443–103453, 2020.

[9] P. C. Lin, Y. S. Tsai, Y. M. Yeh, and M. R. Shen, "Cutting-edge AI technologies meet precision medicine to improve cancer care," *Biomolecules*, vol. 12, no. 8. Biomolecules, 01-Aug-2022.

[10] R. Dong, C. She, W. Hardjawana, Y. Li, and B. Vucetic, "Deep learning for hybrid 5G services in mobile edge computing systems: Learn from a dgital twin," *IEEE Trans. Wirel. Commun.*, vol. 18, no. 10, pp. 4692–4707, 2019.

[11] Y. Lecun, Y. Bengio, and G. Hinton, "Deep learning," *Nature*, vol. 521, no. 7553. Nature, pp. 436–444, 27-May-2015.

[12] Z. Li and Q. Zhu, "Genetic algorithm-based optimization of offloading and resource allocation in mobile-edge computing," *Inf.*, vol. 11, no. 2, p. 83, Feb. 2020.

[13] B. M. Nguyen, H. T. T. Binh, T. T. Anh, and D. B. Son, "Evolutionary algorithms to optimize task scheduling problem for the IoT based Bag-of-Tasks application in Cloud-Fog computing environment," *Appl. Sci.*, vol. 9, no. 9, p. 1730, Apr. 2019.

[14] H. Hua, Y. Li, T. Wang, N. Dong, W. Li, and J. Cao, "Edge computing with artificial intelligence: A machine learning perspective," *ACM Comput. Surv.*, vol. 55, no. 9, pp. 1–35, 2023.

[15] K. Sadatdiynov, L. Cui, L. Zhang, J. Z. Huang, S. Salloum, and M. S. Mahmud, "A review of optimization methods for computation offloading in edge computing networks," *Digit. Commun. Networks*, Mar. 2022.

[16] Y. Liu, Q. He, D. Zheng, M. Zhang, F. Chen, and B. Zhang, "Data caching optimization in the edge computing environment," in *Proceedings–2019 IEEE International Conference on Web Services, ICWS 2019–Part of the 2019 IEEE World Congress on Services*, 2019, pp. 99–106.

[17] H. Feng, Z. Cui, and T. Yang, "Cache optimization strategy for mobile edge computing in maritime IoT," in *5th Conference on Cloud and Internet of Things, CIoT 2022*, 2022, pp. 213–219.

[18] K. Toczé and S. Nadjm-Tehrani, "A taxonomy for management and optimization of multiple resources in edge computing," *Wireless Communications and Mobile Computing*, vol. 2018. Hindawi Limited, 2018.

[19] X. Liu, Z. Qin, and Y. Gao, "Resource allocation for edge computing in IoT networks via reinforcement learning," in *IEEE International Conference on Communications*, 2019, vol. 2019-May.

[20] H. Liu, S. Li, and W. Sun, "Resource allocation for edge computing without using cloud center in smart home environment: A pricing approach," *Sensors (Switzerland)*, vol. 20, no. 22, pp. 1–28, Nov. 2020.

[21] J. Liu, T. Yang, J. Bai, and B. Sun, "Resource allocation and scheduling in the intelligent edge computing context," *Futur. Gener. Comput. Syst.*, vol. 121, pp. 48–53, Aug. 2021.

[22] Z. Sharif, L. Tang Jung, M. Ayaz, and M. Yahya, "Priority-based task scheduling and resource allocation in edge computing for health monitoring system," *J. King Saud Univ.–Comput. Inf. Sci.*, vol. 35, no. 2, pp. 544–559, Feb. 2023.

[23] D. Zeng, L. Gu, S. Pan, J. Cai, and S. Guo, "Resource management at the network edge: A deep reinforcement learning approach," *IEEE Netw.*, vol. 33, no. 3, pp. 26–33, May 2019.

[24] S. Naja, M. M. El Din Makhlouf, and M. A. H. Chehab, "An ageing world of the 21st century: A literature review," *Int. J. Community Med. Public Heal.*, vol. 4, no. 12, p. 4363, 2017.

[25] F. Harrou, N. Zerrouki, Y. Sun, and A. Houacine, "An integrated vision-based approach for efficient human fall detection in a home environment," *IEEE Access*, vol. 7, pp. 114966–114974, 2019.

[26] C. Guleria, K. Das, and A. Sahu, "A survey on mobile edge computing: Efficient energy management system," in *2021 Innovations in Energy Management and Renewable Resources(52042)*, 2021, pp. 9–12.

[27] Y. Liu, M. Peng, G. Shou, Y. Chen, and S. Chen, "Toward edge intelligence: Multiaccess edge computing for 5G and internet of things," *IEEE Internet Things J.*, vol. 7, no. 8, pp. 6722–6747, 2020.

[28] "Walmart Innovates at the Retail Edge with AI–insideBIGDATA." [Online]. Available: https://insidebigdata.com/2021/05/24/walmart-innovates-at-the-retail-edge-with-ai/. [Accessed: 20-Mar-2023].

[29] K. R. Kanjula, V. V. Reddy, J. K. P, J. S. Abraham, and T. K, "People counting system for retail analytics using edge AI," *arXiv:2205.13020 [cs.LG]*, 2022.

[30] I. O. Pappas, "User experience in personalized online shopping: A fuzzy-set analysis," *Eur. J. Mark.*, vol. 52, no. 7–8, pp. 1679–1703, 2018.

[31] C. Countouris, "Top 3 Pillars of AI Enabled Edge Computing in Retail," *NVIDIA*, 2021. [Online]. Available: https://developer.nvidia.com/blog/top-3-pillars-of-ai-enabled-edge-computing-in-retail/. [Accessed: 21-Mar-2023].

[32] "Enabling the next stage in retail checkout convenience with AI-powered autonomous shopping with AI-driven, autonomous," *Dell Tchnology*, 2021.

[33] H. Kim, H. Hong, G. Ryu, and D. Kim, "A study on the automated payment system for artificial intelligence-bsed product recognition in the age of contactless services," *Int. J. Adv. Cult. Technol.*, vol. 9, no. 2, pp. 100–105, 2021.

[34] V. Anand, "How the retail industry can benefit from EDGE IoT | Capgemini," *Capgemini*, 2022. [Online]. Available: www.capgemini.com/insights/expert-perspectives/retail-industry-edge-iot/. [Accessed: 22-Mar-2023].

[35] J. Wójcickia, M. Leonesioa, and Giacomo Bianchia, "Potential for smart spindles adoption as edge computing nodes in Industry 4.0," in *ScienceDirect Procedia CIRP*, 2020, no. July.

[36] M. Werner, "[White Paper] APM 4.0 with Predictive and Prescriptive Analytics," *Mocrosoft*, 22AD. [Online]. Available: https://discover.aveva.com/paid-search-iar/whitepaper-apm-predictive-and-prescriptive-analytics-10-22?utm_term=artificial intelligence in manufacturing&utm_campaign=G_S_A_APAC_All_Campaign_Solution_Operations_Increase+Asset+Reliability&utm_source=adwords&. [Accessed: 22-Mar-2023].

[37] A. C. Chen Liu, O. M. K. Law, J. Liao, J. Y. C. Chen, A. J. En Hsieh, and C. H. Hsieh, "Traffic safety system edge AI computing," *6th ACM/IEEE Symp. Edge Comput. SEC 2021*, pp. 468–469, 2021.

[38] "International car sales 2022," 2022. [Online]. Available: www.statista.com/statistics/200002/international-car-sales-since-1990/. [Accessed: 22-Mar-2023].

[39] V. Bijlani, "5G and Edge AI: Tackling Traffic Management." [Online]. Available: www.iotforall.com/busting-traffic-woes-with-5g-and-edge-ai. [Accessed: 22-Mar-2023].

[40] V. Nasteski, "An overview of the supervised machine learning methods," *Horizons.B*, vol. 4, no. December 2017, pp. 51–62, 2017.

[41] T. Oladipupo, "Types of machine learning algorithms," *New Adv. Mach. Learn.*, no. February 2010, 2010.

[42] I. H. Sarker, "Machine learning: Algorithms, real-world applications and research directions," *SN Comput. Sci.*, vol. 2, no. 3, pp. 1–21, 2021.

[43] I. H. Sarker, "Machine learning: Algorithms, real-world applications and research directions," *SN Comput. Sci.*, vol. 2, no. 3, pp. 1–21, May 2021.

[44] C. Szepesvári, "Algorithms for reinforcement learning", *Synthesis Lectures on Artificial Intelligence and Machine Learning*, 2010, Springer Nature

[45] H. nan Wang *et al.*, "Reinforcement learning: A survey," *Front. Inf. Technol. Electron. Eng.*, vol. 21, no. 12, pp. 1726–1744, 2020.

[46] T. Collett and R. O. Reilly, *Spatial Learning Related papers*. 2007.

[47] A. H. Y. Boren Guo, Xin Zhang, Yaxin Wang, "Deep-Q-Network-Based Multimedia Multi-Service QoS optimization for mobile edge computing systems," *IEEE Access*, pp. 1343–1348, 2019.

COMPUTATIONAL INTELLIGENCE

II

INTELLIGENCE

Edge AI Security and Privacy

Chapter 4

Security and Privacy in Edge AI: Challenges and Concerns

Ritu Sachdeva[1] and Shilpa Bhatia[1]

[1]Manav Rachna International Institute of Research & Studies, Faridabad, Haryana, India

4.1 Introduction

The concept of Internet of Things (IoT) refers to connecting any device with an on/off switch to the internet and other devices. It depends on a number of technologies like software, sensors, cloud computing, software and communication protocols to enable data exchange and analysis. Thus, several physical items are connected to one another via sensors in the actual world. IoT aims to link an increasing number of physical objects in order to share information. Smart cities, wearable medical devices, smart homes, and environmental perception are just a few sectors that have embraced IoT technology [1],[2].

4.1.1 IoT Service

The primary goal of IoT is to create a comprehensive network of objects where everything is currently connected to the internet, allowing all devices to be interconnected using internet technology. Devices can communicate with one another using IoT technology, and without the need for human intervention, numerous devices can work together to perform a task. Sensors can be integrated into things such as medical equipment, household equipment, and transportation. IoT applications can be found in a wide range of industries, integrating human civilization with the natural environment.

To perform computational activities in traditional IoT devices, IoT-connected services and sensors must submit data to cloud servers. The processed data is sent to the IoT devices once the task is finished. Although the cloud reduces the computing load on sensors and devices, there is still a considerable data transmission overhead to consider. Globally, there were 35.82 billion IoT-connected devices as of 2021; by 2025, that number is expected to rise to 75.44 billion, creating a huge explosion in data. However, network bandwidth expansion is currently outpacing data growth, and the complicated network environment makes latency reduction difficult. For typical IoT services, network bandwidth has become a critical barrier that must be addressed. In order to overcome the aforementioned difficulty, edge computing (EC), a new computer paradigm, has recently been invented and is gaining momentum.

4.1.2 IoT Architecture

4.1.2.1 Components of IoT Architecture

Four essential components—the application and analytics component, the integration component, the security and administration component, and the infrastructure component—are included in an IoT architecture. The description is as follows:

- **The applications and analytics component**: This component analyzes and presents the data gathered through IoT. Various tools for analysis, AI, and machine learning, as well as visualization competencies, are all included. R, IBM SPSS, and SAS are few traditional as well as visualization tools used by this component. Amazon, Google, Microsoft, Oracle, and IBM are few specialized IoT tools.
- **The integration component**: This component ensures that the infrastructure, security, and tools all work well with the company's current ERP and other management systems.
- **The security and management component**: In addition to typical security vendors like Forescout, Symantec, and others, IoT security also includes protecting the system's physical components using various security providers (firmware and embedded such as LynxOS, Azure Sphere, etc.).
- **The infrastructure component**: This includes actual hardware such as IoT sensors that record information and actuators that regulate the environment. The network the sensors or actuators are connected to is also included. The components of IoT architecture are shown in Figure 4.1.

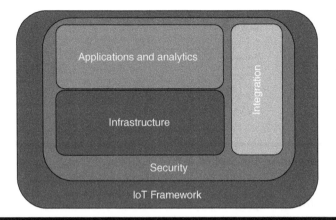

Figure 4.1   Components of IoT architecture.

Different components establish a relationship with one another via their communication patterns and the information that is transferred. This may involve information flow, metadata flow, control information, or even a lack of information. Each component has embedded layers. A layer is a group of related functions that, to other parts of the system, can be seen as a single transparent entity. Network layer components often communicate with one another through network protocols, while software components frequently do so through APIs. The network layer, which carries traffic as required by the applications, is made up of all network hardware. All network hardware is comprised of the network layer, which transports traffic as needed by the applications. The application layer in IoT architecture is not required to be aware of the kind of physical network used to transport data.

4.1.2.2 Layers of IoT Architecture

In a complex architecture like of IoT, the architecture includes layers that are further divided into sublayers. The three-layer architecture has been the preeminent design for IoT applications ever since the first studies on IoT were conducted. The three layers are Perception (or Devices), Network, and Application. Although an excellent approach to define an IoT project, the three-layer architecture has several limitations. Thus, many suggested additional or different layers. A popular one is called the five-layer architecture, which includes Physical layer, Network layer, data layer, Analytic layer, Application layer, and Security layer. Each layer has a distinct purpose [3]. These layers are ordered from bottom to top, much like the Open Systems Interconnection model that served as the foundation for the layering idea. The layered architecture of IoT is as shown in Figure 4.2 and as follows:

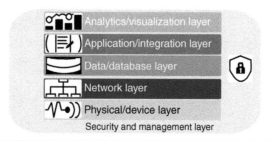

Figure 4.2 Layered architecture of IoT.

- **Physical/device layer:** The physical or device layer includes sensors, actuators, and other intelligent and linked devices. Actuators are designed to conduct action, whereas sensors are intended to collect data. Sometimes both devices are needed to carry out both tasks, such as collecting data and taking action.
- **Network layer:** This layer transmits data to the application layer from the perceptual layer. The cloud platform is an important component of the network layer. As a result, this cloud platform is used to store and analyze a lot of data. The network and communications devices as well as required protocols are included in this layer, along with protocols like 5G, Wi-Fi, Bluetooth, etc., that are necessary for communications and network devices. Dedicated IoT-specific networks are increasingly becoming the norm, despite the fact that a lot of IoT architectures still use general-purpose network layers.
- **Data/database layer:** Moreover, the database platform layer is included in this. There are numerous different databases that may be utilized for IoT architectures, and many businesses take some time to choose and architect the best IoT databases.
- **Analytics/visualization layer:** This layer consists of the analytics layer, visualization layer, and perception layer. A few technologies like wireless communication technology, RFID, and sensor technology are used to sense the environment and gather data through the perceptual layer, which serves as the IoT's necessary foundation. In essence, the goal of this layer is to analyze IoT data and deliver it to users and applications for further analysis.
- **Application/integration layer:** Based on gathered and analyzed data, this layer offers users personalized services. The platforms and applications of this layer interact with one another to bring functionality from the IoT infrastructure to the business. In other words, the application layer, platform layer, and integration layer give the IoT infrastructure's commercial value. The bigger application/integration layer includes both the processing layer and the business layer.
- **Security and management layer:** Both the administrative layer and the security layer are included in this layer. This isn't strictly a layer because it

works with all the other layers to provide security and administration. Yet it's an important factor that needs to be considered at every level.

4.1.2.3 IoT Services

Three common IoT services are remote monitoring and control, smart homes, and natural catastrophe prediction. The following are three IoT services along with their application consequences:

- **Remote monitoring and control**: IoT makes our lives easier by enabling users to remotely manage and keep an eye on linked objects. To monitor the health of the baby from anywhere, sensors can be put in the home to capture data all the time. Additionally, cameras have the ability to deliver video of a baby to consumers in a timely manner. Customers can quickly learn about the present situation in case of logistics. Moreover, customers can always enquire to the whereabouts of online purchases.
- **Smart homes:** Smart home goods that employ IoT have a big competency to grow high-level intelligence (decision-making capability) and multifaceted, allowing them to serve the users in a better way. Many other items, such as sweeping robots, are completely automated. In short, the smart home is the best example of an IoT service since it makes our lives easier.
- **Prediction of natural disaster**: The Internet of Things can help foresee calamities like earthquakes, floods, droughts, and tsunamis. Sensors placed outside are tasked with collecting data from the surrounding environment, and the resulting information could be useful in predicting impending natural disasters. This could result in evacuating people in time and reducing property loss to the greatest extent possible.

4.2 Edge Computing (EC)

Edge computing (EC) is a technique that moves computer workload towards the edge of the network [4]. Compared to cloud computing, it has a number of benefits, including protecting end-user privacy, reducing latency during data transfer, conserving network bandwidth, and using less energy in data centers. Under the scenario of EC, the raw data from IoT devices does not have to be sent to a centralized cloud platform; instead, ENs can compute, store, and transfer data, lowering latency by eliminating duplicate data transmission. EC will boost support for IoT and mobile computing applications with strict reaction time requirements.

Edge computing is a novel approach to computing that processes and stores data at the edge of the network. It is also a technique for bringing computing resources closer to the sources of data, such as mobile devices and customers. The volume of mobile devices has increased since the IoT era began, and terminal devices produce vast amounts of data every day [5]. Consequently, High bandwidth demand from increased cloud and networking utilization results in increased energy use. Furthermore, standard cloud computing is incapable of efficiently processing such a large amount of data, resulting in increased latency and slower reaction times [6]. Similar to this, certain emerging technologies like augmented reality and virtual reality have more stringent requirements for latency and response time. To balance between the increasing demand for increased processing efficiency and privacy security, as well as the inadequacies of cloud computing, the requirement for a decentralized computing method in addition to cloud computing has arisen.

The following are three noteworthy advantages of EC:

- **Low latency**: Data calculations are done at the network's edge, closer to mobile devices, in place of transferring all data to a cloud data center, resulting in faster reaction times and lower latency [7].
- **Privacy and security**: As EC allows for the local or edge node storage of data, data can be held locally or in ENs. As a result, there is less risk of privacy violations because personal data does not need to be sent to the cloud center [7].
- **Lower energy utilization in cloud center**: A fraction of computing work in EC is split among several ENs. This results in fewer bandwidth constraints as well as lower energy usage at the cloud center [8].

4.3 EC in Consonance with IoT Devices

The EC has dramatically enlarged the possibilities of IoT devices in several sectors (computation delegating, accurate positioning, real-time processing, and so on) andenabled data processing with minimal latency close to end-users. Although EC has many pros like enhanced performance, bandwidth consumption, and increased security, still EC raises additional security risks and broadens the system's attack surface in three different aspects. These aspects are:

- **Distributed layout**: Because the ENs are dispersed around the network's edge [8,] it is impossible to bring all of the equipment together for centralized control. The adversary can target ENs with security defects and attack the comprehensive structure using the seized nodes as a base of operations.
- **Restricted computing source**: In contrast to cloud computing, ENs have restricted processing capabilities due to their physical structure, ineffective heavyweight security approaches, and catastrophic large-scale centralized strikes like distributed denial of service attack (DDoS).

■ **Heterogeneous environment**: EC employs a variety of technologies, including grid computing, mobile data collection, and wireless sensor networks. In this diverse context, it is challenging to develop a single security mechanism and to achieve consistency of security rules across many security domains.

4.4 Edge AI

4.4.1 Definition

Edge AI is the term used to describe the placement of AI software on hardware in the physical world. It is denoted as edge AI. It is so called because AI computation is done at the edge of the network where the data is located, whereas generally, computation is done centrally in a cloud computing facility or private data center. Any location can be considered as the network's edge due to accessibility of the internet everywhere. It might be a department shop, factory, hospital, or one of the gadgets we see every day, like traffic lights, robots, and phones.

4.4.2 Traditional Intelligence vs. Edge Intelligence

Unlike edge intelligence, which performs intelligent application operations at the edge using locally generated data in a distributed manner, traditional intelligence requires that all data be uploaded to a single central cloud server. Figure 4.3 illustrates implementation of centralized intelligence and edge intelligence.

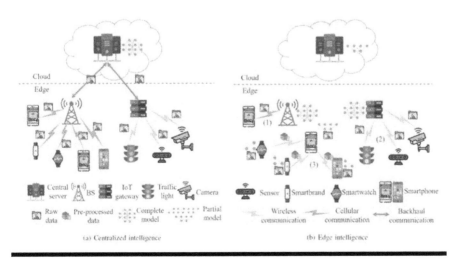

Figure 4.3   Representation of implementation of centralized intelligence and edge intelligence.

4.4.3 Need of Edge AI

Every industry is working to increase automation in order to improve efficiency, production, and security. In order to help people, computer programmes must be able to recognize patterns and conduct tasks reliably and securely. As the world is not organized, the variety of tasks that people perform covers countless circumstances that are impossible to fully explain in codes and rules. Robots and devices may now operate anywhere with the "intelligence" of human cognition due to advancements in edge AI. Intelligent software with AI capabilities can learn to perform the same tasks under different circumstances, just like in real life. The effectiveness of applying AI models at the edge is explained by the following recent advancements:

- **Maturation of neural networks**: Generalized machine learning is now feasible due to advancements in neural networks and related AI technology. Companies are gathering information on how to efficiently train AI models and apply them in production at the edge.
- **Advancements in computing infrastructure**: Strong distributed computing power is required to implement AI at the edge. Recent advancements in massively parallel GPUs have made neural network processing viable.
- **Adoption of IoT devices**: Big data has exploded as a result of the widespread adoption of IoT, with the sudden volume to gather data from industrial sensors, smart cameras, robotics, and more in every part of a business. We currently have the tools and data required to implement AI models at the edge. Furthermore, 5G is improving IoT by enabling faster, more dependable, and secure connections.

4.4.4 Reasons for Deploying AI at the Edge

AI algorithms are capable enough to understand each and every input either structured or unstructured such as sounds, language, sights, scents, faces, temperature, etc. However, they are particularly useful in situations where end users are actually having issues. Due to problems with latency, bandwidth, and privacy, it would be impractical or perhaps impossible to implement many AI applications in a central data center or cloud.

4.4.5 Pros of Edge AI

There are a number of advantages of edge AI:

- **Intelligence**: Unlike conventional programmes, which are only capable of responding to inputs that the programmer had foreseen, AI applications are more powerful and versatile. An AI neural network, on the other hand, is trained to respond to a particular type of question rather than a specific one, even if the question itself is novel. Applications would be unable to process inputs as varied as texts, spoken speech, and video without AI.

▪ **Real-time insights**: Edge technology responds to user requirements instantly since it analyzes data locally rather than in a distant cloud where it is delayed by long-distance connectivity.

▪ **Reduced cost**: Applications require less internet bandwidth as a result of moving computing power closer to the edge, which significantly lowers networking expenses.

▪ **Increased privacy**: Any person whose look, voice, medical image, or other personal information has to be studied can considerably increase their privacy thanks to AI's ability to assess real-world data without ever exposing it to a human. By keeping the data on-site and only uploading the analysis and insights to the cloud, edge AI further improves privacy. Even if some of the data is uploaded for training, user identities can still be protected. Edge AI makes data regulatory compliance concerns easier to handle by protecting privacy.

▪ **High availability**: Edge AI is more reliable since it is decentralized and has offline capabilities, which eliminates the need for internet connectivity when processing data. As a result, production-grade AI applications that are mission-critical are more available and reliable.

▪ **Persistent improvement**: AI models learn from more data and their accuracy increases. Often, an edge AI application will upload encountered data that cannot be processed precisely or confidently to the cloud so the AI algorithm can retrain and learn from it. Hence, a model is more accurate the longer it is produced near the edge.

4.4.6 Working of Edge AI Technology

Machines need to effectively mimic human intelligence in order to perceive, identify objects, drive automobiles, understand speech, speak, walk, or execute other human-like functions. To mimic human cognition, AI uses a deep neural network data structure. By being shown several samples of that sort of inquiry and the appropriate responses, these DNNs are trained to respond to particular question types. The lifecycle of an edge AI application is depicted in Figure 4.4.

Due to the huge quantity of data needed to train an appropriate model and the requirement for data scientists to work together on model configuration, this training process, known as "deep learning," frequently takes place in a data center or the cloud. The model advances through training to become an "inference engine" that can respond to inquiries in the actual world.

The inference engine in edge AI deployments operates on some sort of computer or device in remote areas including factories, hospitals, automobiles, satellites, and residences. The problematic data is frequently sent to the cloud when the AI runs

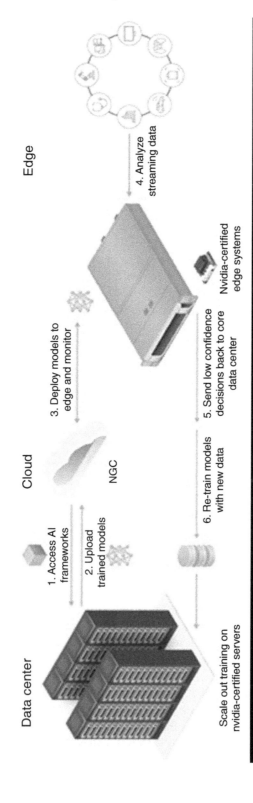

Figure 4.4   Lifecycle of an edge AI application.

into a difficulty so that the original AI model can be further trained before it eventually takes the place of the inference engine at the edge. As edge AI models are implemented, they continue to get more and more intelligent thanks to this feedback loop, which significantly improves model performance.

Many security solutions and algorithms have emerged to mitigate the security threats provided by EC's properties [9]. Widely held modern security systems that detect intrusion, preserve privacy, or regulate access are based on models and algorithms with a predetermined structure. When attack strategies and techniques are continuously improved, conventional security solutions are frequently abandoned. However, AI is gaining traction, which opens up new avenues for addressing security as well as privacy concerns as follows:

- **Intrusion detection**: Common intrusive attacks are denial of service (DoS) and distributed denial of service (DDoS). DDoS refers to the use of numerous exploited ENs to assault a server, causing the server to become overburdened and slow to respond to normal requests. DoS refers to bombarding a server with requests, causing the server to become overburdened and slow to respond to normal queries. By monitoring unusual network behavior, intrusion detection system (IDS) detects and blocks the attacks from seized ENs. Machine learning (ML) derives harmful access patterns from earlier data sets, allowing IDS to detect intrusions faster and more accurately than traditional recognition algorithms, resulting in a considerable increase in detection efficiency [10],[11].

- **Preserving privacy**: IoT devices have infiltrated all facets of our lives, and they hold a great deal of personally identifiable information. Most known privacy preservation solutions, like data obfuscation, cryptographic methods, and anonymization, encrypt sent data to protect data security. Nonetheless, the approaches described above have a substantial computational overhead, making them challenging to implement on ENs with limited resources. Instead of passing the actual data immediately, cooperative learning is performed after each training by passing parameters from one EN to other ENs. During transmission, distributed machine learning (DML) reduces the possibility of data leakage and network load.

- **Access control**: Access control becomes a major concern when several IoT devices are used in the same location. Each authorized node has access to only the nodes and data that fall within their access authority and they are unable to perform any additional operations [12],[13]. ENs must be divided into distinct categories based on permissions, which correspond to the classification process used by ML. According to the algorithm, ENs linked to the network can be classified as either highly privileged IoT devices or low privileged IoT devices. Access to highly privileged devices is tightly regulated to eliminate any risks.

Many domains of edge security have gradually adopted AI [14]. However, there are still significant difficulties in putting related theories on ENs into practice. For ML training to be effective, significant amounts of clean data are required. On the other hand, the premise of abundant data is that the system has experienced massive attacks and can reliably discern between them [15]. Thus, strikes on the training set must be watchful, as tampering with the parameters will lower the model's performance [16]. Because of the limited processing resources and storage at ENs, a lightweight AI algorithm is also required; however, its use will result in a decrease in accuracy.

4.5 Edge AI Compared to Edge Computing

The application of AI to devices at the edge of the network is known as edge AI. The great researcher Deng et al. divided edge AI into two categories: edge AI and AI on the edge.

The first category "AI for edge" is also called intelligence-enabled EC. It is concerned with "carry[ing] out complete process of constructing [and operating] AI models on the edge" while the second category "AI on edge" is focused on "optimizing the allocation of resources employed at the edge." An example of AI on the edge is a smart thermostat. It updates the ML algorithm, develops inferences, and determines what actions should be taken to shape the behavior of the heating, ventilation, and air-conditioning system [17]. The data required for algorithm refining is the data across the edges, which is one of the advantages of edge AI technology. The ability to analyze data and make decisions close to the data source is another benefit. Edge AI can eliminate attack vectors by limiting or eliminating data transit between edge devices and their data centers from a security and privacy standpoint.

4.6 Security and Privacy Concerns for Edge AI

EC has become a prominent reckoning exemplar aimed at reducing the time between end users and the cloud. EC's reduced latency benefits a wide range of AI applications, including driverless automobiles, smart homing, and so on. On the contrary, EC faces the capacity constraints of edge devices, therefore, AI applications are computationally expensive [18]. The edge cloud computing paradigm allows for a trade-off between AI applications, computer resource requirements, and low latency to overcome these drawbacks. In the edge cloud computing context, there are no security solutions or privacy protection measures specifically intended for AI applications allowed by the edge cloud computing paradigm, unlike the centralized cloud. AI applications are vulnerable to a radius of security vulnerabilities in the edge cloud context, including data privacy disclosure, adversarial attacks, confidential assaults, and so on.

4.6.1 AI and Edge Computing Security

Over the past few years, EC and gadgets have grown in popularity. As of 2018, there were about 22 billion connected IoT devices as well as billions more devices like computers, phones, cameras, printers, etc. Anything at the edge of a network is referred to as EC, including smart TVs, cars, cameras, IoT devices, and mobile devices. Edge computing enables data to be handled at or nearer to the device, reducing latency, as opposed to having to be sent to a data center.

These edge devices are increasingly using AI to raise the level of sophistication in their capabilities. In order to combat new security concerns, experts caution that data security will also need to be increased.

4.6.2 Integration of Edge Computing with AI

Almost all of the technology we use now incorporates AI. Cellphones, security cameras, and other IoT devices will soon be standard IoT devices with AI capabilities. These devices may incorporate a variety of ML-enabled features, such as those for image identification, natural language processing, pattern recognition, and anomaly detection. By lowering their influence on the network and extending battery life, AI is also utilized to manage the devices themselves. AI will make data processing almost instantaneous. The best part is that by eliminating the need for files to be transported across a network in order to be examined, AI can be implemented on these devices to boost security.

Uniquely better equipped to gain from AI use are wearable devices. Data collection, analysis, and transmission are all made considerably simpler when these devices are connected. With the use of AI on a phone or other device, these wearable gadgets can detect health problems or any other anomalies that may require a medical professional.

Autonomous vehicles are also powered in part by edge technology. Vehicles can have a network connecting all of their onboard sensors and equipment thanks to AI at the edge. The edge network's decreased latency enables real-time data about traffic and the surroundings of the automobile. Also, it enables prompt communication between moving autonomous vehicles. For instance, your automobile might get warnings of problems further down the road and recommend alternate routes or warn you to avoid potentially hazardous circumstances.

4.6.3 Security Risks of Edge Computing

The installation of computing resources outside of the data center is referred to as EC. It is similar to the activity of connecting the edge device to consumers or applications through a chain of linked devices, such as IoT elements. Therefore, Edge computing resources are now free of the protective physical, access, and network security umbrella provided by the data center due to this change in deployment practices.

Edge applications also represent a significant transition in the IT architecture for most enterprises, moving away from human oversight and toward a machine-to-machine (M2M) model. As a result, edge security threats can be particularly dangerous. It is crucial to know what they are and how to deal with them if you want your business to run well.

4.6.3.1 Security in Edge Computing

The procedure of bringing the security of EC up to data center as well as compliance standards involves installing whatever extra protection is required. This entails safeguarding edge device access in a sense that is functionally equivalent to data center technologies in use today, both physically and through a user interface, but that can be deployed outside of the data center. Edge security is difficult to achieve for edge elements like EC devices and any local access interface, portals, or terminals without at least some control over physical access. Therefore, it is necessary to have close alignment of edge network, application, and data security procedures with the data center.

4.6.3.2 Advantages of Security in Edge Computing

However, EC is not always fraught with danger. The vast majority of edge applications are M2M or IoT variations that rely on low-cost devices with insufficient security. By terminating connections to these devices locally, EC reduces the attack surface of programmes. It also secures the link between the edge and the data center or cloud or with more standard encryption and access security safeguards.

Although the edge supports powerful laptops, desktops, or mobile devices with robust security capabilities as well as consolidates their traffic to a single connection to a company VPN or data center, security watching and control is improved. Local devices can also be protected against denial-of-service attacks by using the EC capability as a security barrier between them and the VPN or the internet.

4.6.3.3 Security Strategies for Edge Computing

1. To strengthen physical security at the edge, use access control and surveillance.
2. From central IT operations, manage edge configuration and actions.
3. Set up auditing processes to keep track of data as well as application hosting changes at the edge.
4. Between devices/users and edge facilities, utilize the greatest level of network security available.
5. Monitoring and logging of all edge activities like operations, computations, etc.

1. Navigating the Horizon: Unveiling Common Edge Computing Security Risks
Edge computing comes with its own set of security issues. Access controls and audit procedures are just two elements that can help secure the edge. In many ways, EC is a form of minimized data center. Reduced security measures are used in order to keep costs at a minimum for the cutting-edge facility [19], which is one of the most significant sources of additional security risk in EC.

■ **Data storage, backup, and protection risks**

Physical security measures are different for data held at the edge and data kept in data centers. The whole database can be stolen by simply removing the disc from the EC source or inserting a memory stick to copy data. As there are often restricted local storage options in EC facilities, it is difficult or impossible to store key files. As a result, there may be no backup copy accessible to restore the database if an incident occurs.

■ **Password and authentication risks**

Local IT operation staff that are concerned about security rarely support EC services. Maintaining edge systems is often a shared part-time job. This environment fosters poor discipline of password sharing, such as taking default passwords into consideration, choosing uncomplicated, easy-to-remember passwords, posting passwords for vital apps on sticky notes, and failing to change passwords frequently. For the sake of user and administrator convenience, edge systems may not use sophisticated security mechanisms like multifactor or two-stage authentication.

■ **Perimeter security risks**

Due to the expansion of the IT perimeter, EC typically concedes perimeter security. At the edge, credentials are commonly kept, and edge systems are sometimes asked to verify their apps with partner apps from the data center. As a result, a breach in edge security could lead to the disclosure of login information for data center assets, greatly expanding the extent of the security incident. It is thus more challenging to deal with perimeter threats due to hosting architecture differences at the edge limit security capabilities.

■ **Edge and IoT security risks**

Development of IoT devices meant for low cost and power consumption as well as deployment are not always conducive to complicated environments with temperature and humidity, dust, or vibration. They are often not ideal for complex technology. IoT edge apps come with their own set of security concerns. Following are these security risks:

■ Usage of specific M2M protocols that are typically devoid of advanced security features such as encryption.
■ Due to easy access to the region where Wi-Fi hubs are situated, wireless interfaces such as Wi-Fi could be hacked or hijacked.
■ Consumers rely on specialist IoT or industrial controllers as EC resources, even if updating these specialized devices with appropriate security software is difficult.

4.6.3.4 Edge Security Best Practices

There are six basic rules for EC security, as follows [20]:

1. To improve physical security at the edge, use access control and surveillance.
2. Control the configuration and functioning of the edge from the IT operations center.
3. Set up auditing processes to keep track of data and application hosting changes at the edge.
4. Between devices/users and edge facilities, utilize the greatest level of network security available.
5. Treat the edge as an autonomous and distinct aspect of your public cloud IT business that requires its own set of tools and processes to be addressed and secured.
6. All edge activity, particularly activity related to operations and configuration, should be monitored and logged.

Because all edge information, operations practices, and messages pass through the network connection to the edge, it is vital that it is entirely secure. This entails employing high-quality encryption and avoiding the insecure practice of storing keys on the edge system. For all network, application, and operation access, multifactor authentication or a properly regulated physical security dongle should be required. Furthermore, Wi-Fi-enabled EC resources should be on their own independent Wi-Fi network, with safeguards in place to prevent outsiders from gaining access to the password and logging in.

Every event related to EC operations must be reported and audited, including all deployments, configuration changes, and access to any supervisory modes via a local keyboard/screen or remotely. However, before implementing any modifications, IT operations and security staff should be alerted, and an acceleration system should be put in place to alert administration if anything unexpected is discovered.

4.6.3.5 Edge Security Vendors and Products

■ Although edge security supports secure communications from any edge, computation at the edge still needs firewalls, secure communication (all software-defined WAN) vendors and products as well as tunneling. Security and firewall products from big firms like Palo Alto Network, Cisco, and Juniper can also protect the edge.

■ To control and secure applications at the edge, IT operations tools such as Puppet, Ansible, DevOps Chef, and container and container orchestration tools like Kubernetes should be employed. These technologies are sold by firms such as HPE, IBM, Red Hat, and VMware, to name a few.

■ Detection of threat at the edge might be considered as a characteristic of a certain application set or as a result of network and system monitoring. Argus, Nagios, and Splunk are examples of popular monitoring software. Tools such as OSSEC, SolarWinds Security Event Manager, Suricata, and Snort provide specific support for intrusion detection and prevention.

■ EC requires a solid problem-tracking and management system, especially if there are many of these facilities or if they are geographically dispersed. Security protections are put into practice by the software or hardware that resides there, and popular systems include OSSEC, Tripwire, and Wazuh.

All of these technologies should be utilized in conjunction with a well-planned and documented edge security practices policy. These security policies should be updated on a regular basis to reflect any changes in practices or tools.

4.7 IoT Service Architecture with Edge Computing

There are four essential layers in the IoT service framework with EC. These layers are edge layer, device layer, cloud layer, and network layer. The basic diagram of the IoT service architecture utilizing EC is shown in Figure 4.5 [21].

4.7.1 Device Layer

Many products and electronic equipment, including cellphones, computers, autos, and even individuals, have sensing devices like RFID, intelligent sensors, and QR codes (in IoMT). They can be used by "things" in the IoT to deliver context-based information in real time about themselves or their surroundings, resulting in a significant volume of real-time data. Because of the various processing needs, these data vary widely, but the majority are quick, immediate, and frequent [1].

4.7.2 Network Layer

The edge, cloud, and endpoints are all connected via this layer. This layer connects the bottom-up edge layer to the top-down device layer. It connects sensing devices throughout the IoT and performs transmission operations. It is the brain of the IoT service framework. A number of communication technologies, including cellular networks with base stations, WiFi, ZigBee, Bluetooth, and other data

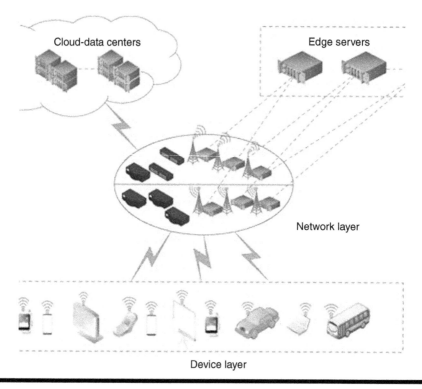

Figure 4.5 IoT service framework with EC.

transfer protocols or IoT protocols, like Message Queuing Telemetry Transport, and Hypertext Transfer Protocol (HTTP), are used to transmit data from sensing devices [22].

A named data network is one in which data and services are named and addressed. To adapt to the new computing model of EC, this networking is used in the context of EC and to support the dynamic implementation of computing services, data transit, and computing channels. Apart from that, SDN is a programmable network in which the control plane and data plane are separated and basic network management is feasible. Consequently, it is possible to effectively combine data migration and transmission and service organizations. In the context of EC, these service organizations enable the network layer to meet the demands of service discovery and rapid creation. This layer, on the other hand, connects the edge layer to the cloud layer, which consists of cloud-data centers. It primarily conveys data the edge layer has structured or finalized, as well as receives instructions or comments from the cloud layer.

Furthermore, security of the network layer can't be overlooked. A layer can be secured two basic ways: logical security design and physical isolation design. Air Gap, which isolates the interior and outside networks using high-strength protocol analysis, physical isolation technology, denial-of-service protection design, and routing attack protection design are commonly used.

4.7.3 Edge Layer

The edge layer is the primary distinctive aspect in the framework of IoT service with EC in comparison to a regular IoT service framework, since it partially resolves issues such as low bandwidth and long delivery times. Parts of computing resources are relocated from the cloud to the edge, which is much closer to data sources. These computing resources are used efficiently and precisely handle enormous amounts of data from IoT devices.

As a fundamental component of the edge layer, edge servers are the primary data processors, managers, and archivists. The results are sent to the necessary devices via the network layer, or they are stored or transferred to the cloud layer for further analysis. The impact of edge server deployment on compute efficiency and resource consumption is significant. It must match the needs of the user while working with restricted resources.

Typically, edge servers are located near cellular base stations. Furthermore, rather than being multitenant, they are frequently implemented in a single entity [23]. Zhao et al. (2018) developed a new three-phase deployment technique [24] for large-scale IoT that considers traffic diversity and wireless IoT variation and reduces EN significantly.

The key technologies accelerating the development of the edge layer to ensure that computing operations run smoothly and efficiently include solation mechanisms and edge operating and data processing platforms. These technologies speed up the development of the edge layer in order to ensure that computing activities function smoothly and efficiently.

4.7.4 Cloud Layer

The cloud layer along with EC plays the role of brain in the IoT service framework. Large cloud-data centers with loads of computational capacity are often used. In an IoT service framework with EC, the cloud layer is frequently utilized for advanced deployment, data processing from the edge layer, and storing or updating key data.

Nevertheless, the value of cloud-edge collaboration is emphasized in a few specific instances such as management collaboration, safety collaboration, resource collaboration, etc., which considers the edge and cloud as one to strengthen and schedule dynamically. This layer is an advantage in the case of computation. It can make available assistance for computation via virtual machines and containers in the case of the inefficiency of computing resources at the edge layer. When malicious traffic arrives on a certain edge layer, a cloud layer with higher security policy can detect and stop it, preventing it from propagating further. A few platforms for cloud-edge collaboration like KubeEdge, Edge Tunnel, and AWS Wavelength can be adopted to accelerate this growth.

4.8 AI-Assisted Privacy Preservation for Edge-Enabled IoT Services

In Ref. [25], ML techniques meant to protect the privacy are divided into training schemes as well as inference schemes. Encryption techniques are used in the privacy-preserving training programmes to ensure the secrecy of sensitive personal data during transmission. Schemes for privacy-preserving inference are inference approaches that protect confidential data throughout the inference phase. In most preservation inference systems, the EN provides unclassified data for inference to a well-trained model. Anonymization, cryptographic procedures, data obfuscation, and other encryption technologies are popular. Each of the following encryption techniques, however, necessitates various stages of computing and transmission expenditures. It makes it difficult to adopt encryption algorithms on ENs with low resources. Figure 4.6 shows the hierarchical structure of different privacy preservation methods.

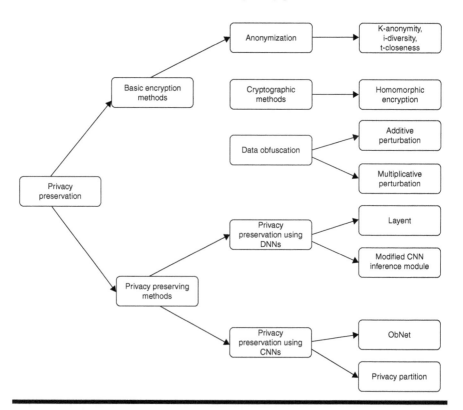

Figure 4.6 Different privacy preservation methods.

4.8.1 Traditional Encryption Methods

4.8.1.1 Anonymization

Anonymization is a technique used to mask the identity of participants in a group of people by deleting some evident attributes like name of the user, gender, and identification number. Some anonymization technologies using anonymization technology such as l-diversity, k-anonymity, and t-closeness are suggested [26, 27]. In K-anonymity model, the attributes related to participants are divided into three categories. These categories are explicit identifiers, sensitive attributes, and a set of quasi-identifier attributes. Among these traits, explicit IDs are removed before the data is provided but, on the other hand, the data in the quasi-identifier attribute set is generalized so that at least k items have the same quasi-identifier. The main drawback of this technique is that the invader can spot the victim via observing unique features found in the disclosed data. Another flaw with this concept is that the attacker can identify the victim by linking or comparing the data to other information. The t-closeness models and l-diversity models protect against the preceding attacks. These models are based on the method of k-anonymity. In each quasi-identifier class, the multiplicity of sensitive traits should not be less than I, according to the l-diversity model. This results in lowering the likelihood of sensitive traits and their owners matching. On the other hand, according to the t-closeness module, the gap between the distribution of sensitive features in each equivalence class and the distribution of sensitive characteristics as a whole should not be greater than the upper limit t.

4.8.1.2 Cryptographic Method

Before uploading data to cloud servers, data is encrypted by cryptographic methods. Due to this, there is high computation overhead but necessitates reliability as well as effective key management [28]. Homomorphic encryption, a secure encryption approach, may entrust diverse cloud computing apps (third parties) to process data without disclosing the content. This encryption method generates a key pair using a set of mathematical problems that are difficult for a computer to solve. A public and a private key are included in this key pair. Third parties are given access to the public key and some operational measures. Third parties gain access to the encrypted data and conduct all activities on it before returning the results. These findings can only be decrypted using the private key, keeping the information private throughout the process. The Rivest-Shamir-Adleman (RSA) and Elliptic Curve Cryptography (ECC) are two widely used homomorphic encryption methods. In comparison to RSA, ECC has a lower computational cost.

4.8.1.3 Data Obfuscation

Data samples needed to train a global module are disrupted by obfuscation tactics. Additive and multiplicative perturbation are two of the approaches used. Differential privacy (DP) is a technique for aggregating data without revealing individual items, and it is always associated with additive perturbation [29]. Because it ensures the safety of separate records from surrounding datasets, the attacker is unable to distinguish between the results of adjacent datasets. The process of obfuscating the data is done using noise-generating methods such as the median, Laplacian, and exponential mechanisms. The DP protection is achieved via the Laplacian approach, where random noise is added to the exact query outputs using a Laplacian distribution. Using a mechanism that works on exponential scale, the best output is chosen on the basis of likelihood after each query that was missing in Laplacian mechanism. A type of multiplicative perturbation is one of the randomize multiplicative data perturbation approaches. By randomizing multiplicative matrices, the random projection method seeks to construct a new data representation with fewer measurements. To safeguard consumers' privacy while acquiring high-quality data, data obfuscation is a common practice in data mining.

4.8.2 ENs with Lightweight AI Privacy-Preserving Methods

EC makes use of the computing and storage capabilities of device nodes positioned between the cloud center and the terminal devices. EC, in comparison to traditional cloud computing, moves the data processing closer to sources of data and reduces the quantity of data that must be sent to the data center in the first place. It provides low-latency real-time services while reducing transmission bandwidth utilization [29]. As a result, traditional encryption approaches struggle to perform successfully on ENs with limited resources. Anonymization, cryptographic procedures, and data obfuscation are examples of traditional encryption methods. Recently, emphasis has been put on lightweight privacy preservation approaches that improve existing encryption methods by utilizing ML technologies as well as AI technologies like deep neural networks (DNNs) and convolutional neural networks (CNNs).

4.8.2.1 Role of CNNs in Privacy Preservation

Privacy preservation using CNNs is performed via two techniques: Modified CNN inference module and LAYENT. LAYENT makes the module privacy-aware by improving the fundamental framework, while modified CNN inference module is used to protect privacy.

■ **LAYNET:** This is an algorithm to preserve the privacy in ML. A new layer called the randomization layer is inserted between the convolution layer and fully connected layers and extends the basic framework of the CNN algorithm. To boost randomization's flexibility while encoding the context, this randomization layer employs a new unary encoding approach. In comparison with the most related algorithms in terms of processing capacity of cloud computing, this algorithm not only offers a very above average accurateness up to 91% but also maintains anonymity while incurring minimal computational overhead [29]. Before being sent to a potentially harmful third party, the data is disrupted.

■ **Modified CNN inference module:** To identify the odd behavior of the smart meters in the smart grid, an energy theft detection technique was developed. In this technique, a modified CNN module is incorporated in the framework of the module. It identifies unusual smart meter behavior in the smart grid. The data generated by the smart meter is used to train the CNN module. After training, this trained module can detect aberrant data by forming acceptable assumptions.

4.8.2.2 Role of DNNs in Privacy Preservation

DNN is a deep learning framework that has been extensively employed in areas including image and audio recognition, as well as natural language understanding. To train the DNNs modules, a significant amount of processing resources are required. Two lightweight schemes come under this category:

■ **ObfNet:** ObfNet is a lightweight and unobtrusive data obfuscation method for remote inference. Using this approach, ENs need to construct a tiny neural network and are not required to alert users when data is hidden. Inference data is concealed before being sent to the backend [30].

There are two obstacles to overcome in order to establish edge-enabled IoT. Maintaining the privacy of inference models while separating data sources and processing resources is a challenge. In remote inference, the data is delivered to the backend, which then returns the conclusions of the inference.

■ **Privacy partition:** A bipartite deep network topological network and an interactive adversarial network serve as the foundation of the DNN privacy-preservation system. Due to its design, the edge network can serve as a competitive alternative to many centralized deep learning systems [31]. Consequently, a bipartite deep network topology is made up of two neural network partitions: a trusted local computing environment and an unreliable remote computing context. The output of the prior transformation is processed by a learning module in a secure local computing setting. The processed data is fed into the first transformation layer in the case of remote computing. Users may restrict access to the sensitive data stream for privacy concerns. An attacker's capacity to learn privacy-sensitive input is limited if an attacker has access to the deep network intermediate state.

4.9 Edge-Enabled IoT Services by AI-Powered Blockchain

Blockchain is a technology that integrates multiple technologies to create a decentralized computer and storage system. In a peer-to-peer network, data is generated, updated, and transported between nodes using the distributed consensus mechanism. This data is maintained by keeping it immutable with a distributed ledger [32]. In a nutshell, blockchain is a cutting-edge method of storing and sending data that offers a decentralized environment that is secure against attack or bug.

4.9.1 Role of Blockchain for Maintaining the Security of IoT Services

To set up an IoT grid, enormous terminal devices are associated in a way that each and every device connected to the network has access to data from the IoT network as a whole. The enormous number of devices makes it impossible to get around a single device's defect. Large amounts of data from IoT services are exposed in the event of device hacking, with disastrous consequences. It is therefore necessary to increase the security of IoT services.

Due to the numerous devices, connecting these IoT devices is risky. Hence, data transferred between devices can easily be stolen by malicious parties. This threat can be overcome by using CAPTCHAs but there are still limitations in terms of data security. To overcome this limitation, blockchain technology is integrated with AI. Data confidentiality and dependability as well as access control and authentication management are two related aspects explained below.

4.9.1.1 Access Control and Authentication Management

A set of mechanisms is defined as access control for identifying, organizing, and hosting all system operations, as well as systematizing and distinguishing all data and providing an uncomplicated and distinctive interface [33]. Authentication is a process of determining whether or not to grant access to a system using verification techniques such as passwords.

In traditional approach of IoT services (without AI or blockchain), an authentication is set for the user by combining the user name and password. Although this technique is ineffective and challenging to scale, IP cameras can employ it. By enabling a trusted third-party organization to offer a user access to several devices by confirming their identity for only one, single sign-on approaches facilitate identity identification. Despite the fact that it can speed up authentication, the IoT system as a whole suffers catastrophic repercussions when one device fails or a user loses access to their account.

To overcome this drawback, a design [34] has been proposed in which users just need to verify their identity once on a blockchain like Ethereum before gaining access to the system by means of the smart contract token. During the identification of the authentication, the Ethereum address as well as the token are both communicated using smart contact. Thus, the IoT service will get a package containing a public key for the user, IP address, and token, which is used to authenticate the package. Moreover, fingerprint data may be collected, stored, and verified using blockchain, eliminating the falsification issue with the present access authentication technique.

4.9.1.2 Confidentiality and Reliability of Data

The IoT is mostly used in sectors including banking, agriculture, and healthcare. Several physical sensor types are utilized in conjunction with IoT applications in the healthcare industry to gather biological data. This collected data is used to help doctors provide improved medical treatment to patients. These sensitive details must be kept secure.

For storing IoT data securely, Rui et al. [35] suggested a technique for establishing distributed data storage and tamper resistance in data blockchains. The author also proposed a Byzantine fault-tolerant (PBFT) consensus algorithm with little improvement. A crowdsourcing technique based on blockchain technology was proposed by Xu et al. The researchers created mobile crowdsourcing architecture based on blockchain technology to maintain the accuracy and security of high-profile data. By combining more effective dynamic programming with geographical categorization of apps based on density and noise, they produced service limits. They also employed basic additive weighting and various criterion decision-making to evaluate the policies.

4.9.2 Blockchain's Role in Edge-Enabled IoT Data Sharing

An IoT network's foundation is data. The larger the data, the more accurate the research results as well as more precise the application enhancement. IoT data is currently collected in a variety of methods in a variety of fields including healthcare, agriculture, industry, and automated driving. This highlights the diversity of sensors used to collect various sorts of data, as well as the fact that the database is held by a number of companies, organizations, or governments. Data isolation is costly because of collecting repeating data as it costs a lot of energy and time. Consequently, the resource can be properly allotted and needless costs can be avoided by storing data from IoT services in a database.

But there are certain roadblocks in secure data exchange including massive amounts of data, lack of confidence, heterogeneous devices, security as well as other issues. The best possible solution is blockchain for creating a platform that can securely transfer data. Moreover, blockchain technology is also used to create a distributed platform with a trust-based approach that does not require central support.

MicrothingsChain is an architecture proposed by Zheng et al. [36]. They demonstrated a blockchain-based EC network with traceable and untamable data at each node. Data can be shared properly by constructing a Proof-of-Edge computing node on the basis of Proof-of-Authority. Furthermore, Truong et al. [43] proposed a Sash design in which more data is sent to the blockchain's back end to prevent malicious activity through its own resistance. Smart contact can also be used to set policy decision points on the blockchain and analyze requests with access control, which benefits both owners and customers by allowing data to be shared. Liu et al. [37] proposed architecture for the Industry Internet of Things (IIoT) that uses blockchain and deep reinforcement learning to collect and distribute data. It divides private blockchain networks into compute and sharing zones and collects dispersed data in the IIoT using DRL.

Knowledge, like data, may also be safely and equally shared via IoT networks. Lin et al. [38] proposed a blockchain-based market based on edge-connected IoT and AI. To keep knowledge such as data trade fair, efficient, and secure, smart contracts from blockchain as well as consortium blockchain are used. They create Proof-of-Trading, a new consensus technique that can lower the cost of computer sources.

4.9.3 Enhancing Efficiency of Edge-Enabled IoT Services with Blockchain

Earlier it was described that security of data of IoT services can be assured by using blockchain for IoT. But as IoT services expand, the exigency for computational resources will effortlessly surpass the limited resources that the internet can provide. It then results in affecting the efficiency of IoT services. Data overflow, service delays, and other issues have occurred. This type of situation can lead to data overflow, service delays, and other issues. However, solving the basic problem by simply increasing the computational capabilities of IoT devices is currently impractical. The following are several ways to help increase the efficacy of IoT services from various perspectives.

To enhance the overall efficiency of the system, Khanji et al. [39] looked into the balance of cache capacity and processing ability. They created a Geometric Programming technique for combining each data point in IoT networks and sharing data. This technique allows the cache of a single device to be disseminated to other devices. Fu et al. [40] presented a cooperative computing system in which data point servers are virtualized into high-performance virtual machines as well as a three-level cache designed to correctly allocate processing. Chen et al. [41] proposed a game theory-based solution for solving multihop compute offloading difficulties in blockchain IoT services with normal and mining jobs.

Xu et al. [42] proposed the BeCome algorithm for the offloading problem in edge IoT. This approach monitors EC device resources by allocating computing resources using a non-dominated sorting genetic algorithm III (NSGA-III) and blockchain ledgers.

4.10 Challenges and Concerns

Despite the fact that edge AI is intended to improve the security of IoT services in the EC, there are a number of hurdles to secure IoT using edge AI.

4.10.1 Security Schemes Based on ML

Machine learning is a great option for safeguarding IoT services since it may increase the analytical capabilities of IoT devices. While a number of security methods based on ML do exist due to severe flaws it is impractical to use them in IoT systems.

4.10.1.1 High Cost of Communication and Computation

In order to construct a viable model that can handle real-world threats, many ML-based security systems have the obvious setback of requiring a huge amount of training data. The process of extracting feature process is also moderately hard. The cost of calculation and communication is also extremely expensive. Consequently, a new security method based on ML can help to reduce transmission as well as computation cost.

4.10.1.2 Security Techniques for Backup

Two ML techniques called deep learning (DL) and reinforcement learning (RL) are used as backup security solutions. Each technique has its own set of disdavantages. Due to overfitting or insufficient training data, DL may fail to detect incursions accurately. As a result, for DL to reduce error rates, a good training dataset is required. Existing RL-based systems are only practical if the intelligent agent can assess the feedback of each action in a timely manner and understand the exact condition. In practice, the vulnerability of RL-based security solutions makes it more likely that IoT is attacked during the early stages of learning.

4.10.2 Integration of ML and Blockchain Technology

With the rapid expansion of IoT, its services are gradually affecting every aspect of daily life. However, IoT is doomed to be subjected to cyberattacks and confront a security risk as it develops. Furthermore, trust issues that obstruct information transmission across different IoT devices obstruct IoT's future progress. Trust issues can be resolved via using blockchain technology because this technology has a decentralized nature. In addition, blockchain technology can be employed in IoT to improve security and optimize IoT services.

Furthermore, the usage of blockchain raises fresh security concerns such as majority attack and double spending [28]. As a result, ML technologies can help prevent basic attacks on blockchains, but much more research is still needed to improve IoT security by fusing ML with blockchain.

Privacy issues arise because every blockchain node can access the data that is stored there. Encryption and private blockchains [27] have both been used to address privacy issues, but in the case of insufficiency, this will inevitably result in limited ML training data, resulting in developing a good model for privacy protection at an impractical level [28]. When utilized in real-world circumstances, the performance of these model is likely to fall short of our expectations.

4.11 Conclusion

EC will contribute significantly to the expansion of the IoT business as well as application ecosystems. For high-quality IoT services, reliable privacy protection and security measures are required, increasing expectations for EC privacy and security. IoT security is improved by the use of blockchain and AI. Moreover, difficulties and issues for protecting IoT services in the EC will also need to be considered.

References

[1] Z. Xu, W. Liu, J. Huang, C. Yang, J. Lu, and H. Tan, "Artificial intelligence for securing IoT services in edge computing: A survey," *Secur. Commun. Networks*, vol. 2020, 2020, doi: 10.1155/2020/8872586.

[2] S. Moin, A. Karim, Z. Safdar, K. Safdar, E. Ahmed, and M. Imran, "Securing IoTs in distributed blockchain: Analysis, requirements and open issues," *Futur. Gener. Comput. Syst.*, vol. 100, pp. 325–343, 2019, doi: 10.1016/j.future.2019.05.023.

[3] H. HaddadPajouh, R. Khayami, A. Dehghantanha, K. K. R. Choo, and R. M. Parizi, "AI4SAFE-IoT: An AI-powered secure architecture for edge layer of Internet of things," *Neural Comput. Appl.*, vol. 32, no. 20, pp. 16119–16133, 2020, doi: 10.1007/s00521-020-04772-3.

[4] W. Shi and S. Dustdar, "The promise of edge computing," *Cloud Cover*, no. 0018, pp. 78–81, 2016.

[5] J. Li, T. Cai, K. Deng, X. Wang, T. Sellis, and F. Xia, "Community-diversified influence maximization in social networks," *Inf. Syst.*, vol. 92, p. 101522, 2020, doi: 10.1016/ j.is. 2020.101522.

[6] L. Wang, X. Zhang, R. Wang, C. Yan, H. Kou, and L. Qi, "Diversified service recommendation with high accuracy and efficiency," *Knowledge-Based Syst.*, vol. 204, p. 106196, 2020, doi: 10.1016/j.knosys.2020.106196.

[7] Z. Ziming, L. Fang, C. Zhiping, and N. Xiao, "Edge computing: Platforms, applications and challenges," *J. Comput. Res. Dev.*, vol. 55, no. 2, pp. 1–11, 2018.

[8] C. Avasalcai, C. Tsigkanos, and S. Dustdar, "Decentralized resource auctioning for latency-sensitive edge computing," *Proc.–2019 IEEE Int. Conf. Edge Comput. EDGE 2019–Part 2019 IEEE World Congr. Serv.*, pp. 72–76, 2019, doi: 10.1109/EDGE.2019.00027.

[9] L. Santos, C. Rabadao, and R. Goncalves, "Intrusion detection systems in Internet of Things: A literature review," in *Iberian Conference on Information Systems and Technologies, CISTI*, 2018, pp. 1–7. doi: 10.23919/CISTI.2018.8399291.

[10] M. A. Amanullah *et al.*, "Deep learning and big data technologies for IoT security," *Comput. Commun.*, vol. 151, no. December 2019, pp. 495–517, 2020, doi: 10.1016/j.comcom.2020.01.016.

[11] X. Chi, C. Yan, H. Wang, W. Rafique, and L. Qi, "Amplified locality-sensitive hashing-based recommender systems with privacy protection," *Concurr. Comput.*, no. February, 2020, doi: 10.1002/cpe.5681.

[12] H. A. Khattak, M. A. Shah, S. Khan, I. Ali, and M. Imran, "Perception layer security in Internet of Things," *Futur. Gener. Comput. Syst.*, vol. 100, pp. 144–164, 2019, doi: 10.1016/j.future.2019.04.038.

[13] M. M. Hossain, M. Fotouhi, and R. Hasan, "Towards an analysis of security issues, challenges, and open problems in the Internet of Things," *Proc.–2015 IEEE World Congr. Serv. Serv. 2015*, no. June, pp. 21–28, 2015, doi: 10.1109/SERVICES.2015.12.

[14] X. Xu, X. Liu, Z. Xu, F. Dai, X. Zhang, and L. Qi, "Trust-oriented IoT service placement for smart cities in edge computing," *IEEE Internet Things J.*, vol. 7, no. 5, pp. 4084–4091, 2020, doi: 10.1109/JIOT.2019.2959124.

[15] S. M. Tahsien, H. Karimipour, and P. Spachos, "Machine learning based solutions for security of Internet of Things (IoT): A survey," *J. Netw. Comput. Appl.*, vol. 161, no. April, 2020, doi: 10.1016/j.jnca.2020.102630.

[16] F. Liang, W. G. Hatcher, W. Liao, W. Gao, and W. Yu, "Machine learning for security and the Internet of Things: The good, the bad, and the ugly," *IEEE Access*, vol. 7, pp. 158126–158147, 2019, doi: 10.1109/ACCESS.2019.2948912.

[17] Z. Zhou, X. Chen, E. Li, L. Zeng, K. Luo, and J. Zhang, "Edge intelligence: Paving the last mile of artificial intelligence with edge computing," *Proc. IEEE*, vol. 107, no. 8, 2019, doi: 10.1109/JPROC.2019.2918951.

[18] L. Qi, J. Li, N. Antonopoulos, and H. Wang, "Security and privacy issues for artificial intelligence in edge-cloud computing," *J. Cloud Comput.*, 2020, [Online]. Available: https://journalofcloudcomputing.springeropen.com/securityprivacyaiedgecloud

[19] Y. Xiao, Y. Jia, C. Liu, X. Cheng, J. Yu, and W. Lv, "Edge computing security: State of the art and challenges," *Proc. IEEE*, vol. 107, no. 8, 2019, doi: 10.1109/JPROC.2019.2918437.

[20] C. Risi, "Best Practices for Edge Security," in *Security*, 2021, p. file:///E:/book chapters/RP/EC-IoT.pdf.

[21] E. Dalipi, F. Van Den Abeele, I. Ishaq, I. Moerman, and J. Hoebeke, "EC-IoT: An easy configuration framework for constrained IoT devices," *2016 IEEE 3rd World Forum Internet Things, WF-IoT 2016*, pp. 159–164, 2017, doi: 10.1109/WF-IoT.2016.7845483.

[22] M. Capra, R. Peloso, G. Masera, M. R. Roch, and M. Martina, "Edge computing: A survey on the hardware requirements in the Internet of Things world," *Futur. Internet*, vol. 11, no. 4, pp. 1–25, 2019, doi: 10.3390/fi11040100.

[23] R. D. Agencies, "The Emerging Landscape of Regional Governance," no. May, 2005.

[24] W. Z. Khan, E. Ahmed, S. Hakak, I. Yaqoob, and A. Ahmed, "Edge computing: A survey," *Futur. Gener. Comput. Syst.*, vol. 97, pp. 219–235, 2019, doi: 10.1016/j.future.2019.02.050.

[25] M. Zheng, D. Xu, L. Jiang, C. Gu, R. Tan, and P. Cheng, "Challenges of privacy-preserving machine learning in IoT," *ACM ISBN 978-1-4503-7013-4/19/11*, pp. 1–7, 2019, [Online]. Available: https://doi.org/10.1145/3363347.

[26] B. Zhou and J. Pei, "The k-anonymity and l-diversity approaches for privacy preservation in social networks against neighborhood attacks," *Knowl. Inf. Syst.*, vol. 28, no. 1, pp. 47–77, 2011, doi: 10.1007/s10115-010-0311-2.

[27] L. Ninghui, L. Tiancheng, and S. Venkatasubramanian, "t-Closeness: Privacy beyond k-anonymity and ℓ-diversity," in *Proceedings–file:///E:/book chapters/RP/ECG-IJS key agreement.pdf International Conference on Data Engineering*, 2007, no. 3, pp. 106–115. doi: 10.1109/ICDE.2007.367856.

[28] I. Techology, "Additive Gaussian noise based data perturbation in multi-level trust privacy preserving data mining," *Int. J. Data Mining& Knowl. Manag. Process*, vol. 4, no. 3, pp. 21–29, 2014.

[29] D. Xu, M. Zheng, L. Jiang, C. Gu, R. Tan, and P. Cheng, "Lightweight and unobtrusive data obfuscation at IoT edge for remote inference," *IEEE Internet Things J.*, vol. 7, no. 10, pp. 9540–9551, 2020, doi: 10.1109/JIOT.2020.2983278.

[30] A. Boulemtafes, A. Derhab, and Y. Challal, "A review of privacy-preserving techniques for deep learning," *Neurocomputing*, vol. 384, pp. 21–45, 2020, doi: 10.1016/j.neucom.2019.11.041.

[31] H. T. M. Gamage, H. D. Weerasinghe, and N. G. J. Dias, "A survey on blockchain technology concepts, applications, and issues," *SN Comput. Sci.*, vol. 1, no. 2, pp. 1–15, 2020, doi: 10.1007/s42979-020-00123-0.

[32] S. N. Mohanty *et al.*, "An efficient lightweight integrated blockchain (ELIB) model for IoT security and privacy," *Futur. Gener. Comput. Syst.*, vol. 102, pp. 1027–1037, 2020, doi: 10.1016/j.future.2019.09.050.

[33] A. Z. Ourad, B. Belgacem, and K. Salah, *Using blockchain for IOT access control and authentication management*, vol. 10972 LNCS. Springer International Publishing, 2018. doi: 10.1007/978-3-319-94370-1_11.

[34] H. Rui, L. Huan, H. Yang, and Z. YunHao, "Research on secure transmission and storage of energy IoT information based on Blockchain," *Peer-to-Peer Netw. Appl.*, vol. 13, no. 4, pp. 1225–1235, 2020, doi: 10.1007/s12083-019-00856-7.

[35] J. Zheng, X. Dong, T. Zhang, J. Chen, W. Tong, and X. Yang, "MicrothingsChain: Edge computing and decentralized IoT architecture based on blockchain for cross-domain data shareing," *Proc.–2018 Int. Conf. Netw. Netw. Appl. NaNA 2018*, pp. 350–355, 2019, doi: 10.1109/NANA.2018.8648780.

[36] C. H. Liu, Q. Lin, and S. Wen, "Blockchain-enabled data collection and sharing for industrial iot with deep reinforcement learning," *IEEE Trans. Ind. Informatics*, vol. 15, no. 6, pp. 3516–3526, 2019, doi: 10.1109/TII.2018.2890203.

[37] X. chapters/RP/blockchain mechanisms for I. security. pd. Lin, J. Li, J. Wu, H. Liang, and W. Yang, "Making knowledge tradable in edge-AI enabled IoT: A consortium blockchain-based efficient and incentive approach," *IEEE Trans. Ind. Informatics*, vol. 15, no. 12, pp. 6367–6378, 2019, doi: 10.1109/TII.2019.2917307.

[38] D. Minoli and B. Occhiogrosso, "Blockchain mechanisms for IoT security," *Internet of Things (Netherlands)*, vol. 1–2, pp. 1–13, 2018, doi: 10.1016/j.iot.2018.05.002.

[39] S. Fu, L. Zhao, X. Ling, and H. Zhang, "Maximizing the system energy efficiency in the blockchain based Internet of Things," *IEEE Int. Conf. Commun.*, vol. 2019-May, pp. 1–6, 2019, doi: 10.1109/ICC.2019.8761539.

[40] W. Chen *et al.*, "Cooperative and distributed computation offloading for blockchain-empowered industrial Internet of Things," *IEEE Internet Things J.*, vol. 6, no. 5, pp. 8433–8446, 2019, doi: 10.1109/JIOT.2019.2918296.

[41] X. Xu, X. Zhang, H. Gao, Y. Xue, L. Qi, and W. Dou, "BeCome: Blockchain-enabled computation offloading for IoT in mobile edge computing," *IEEE Trans. Ind. Informatics*, vol. 16, no. 6, pp. 4187–4195, 2020, doi: 10.1109/TII.2019.2936869.

[42] L. Xiao, X. Wan, X. Lu, Y. Zhang, and D. Wu, "IoT Security Techniques Based on Machine Learning," no. January 2018, 2018, [Online]. Available: http://arxiv.org/abs/1801.06275.

[43] H. T. T. Truong, M. Almeida, G. Karame, and C. Soriente, "Towards secure and decentralized sharing of IoT data," in *Proceedings – 2019 2nd IEEE International Conference on Blockchain, Blockchain 2019*, 2019, pp. 176–183. doi: 10.1109/Blockchain.2019.00031.

Chapter 5

A Study of an Edge Computing-Enabled Metaverse Ecosystem

Pooja Kulkarni[1], Ashish Kulkarni[2], and Shriprada Chaturbhuj[1]

[1]Vishwakarma University, Pune, India
[2]Universal AI University, Karjat, India

5.1 Introduction

5.1.1 Metaverse

The metaverse is a virtual world where people can interact with each other and with their digital avatar. The world is just replica of what real world is in this they will perform all the activity like social activity, playing game, attending, or conducting event, business meetings, etc. The metaverse can be possible due to massive data generation and dependency on computer system through latest technology. The mixer of all latest technologies like extended reality, blockchain, cloud computing and semi structured data storge its possible to fill the experience of virtual reality through metaverse due to metaverse many organizations try to put their footprint on virtual platform and provide experience before buying product like one of the major Spakes organizations allow user to upload photograph and provide 3D angle viewing of Spake with our own photograph more organization like real estate, gold will make

DOI: 10.1201/9781032650722-7

their impact on virtual platform as they already transiting few occurrences on paper-based system.

The few more area where metaverse can make impact are as follows.

Social interaction: People are using the metaverse to connect with friends and family from all over the world. As they are meeting personally with them.

Entertainment and gaming: the metaverse already running the games and generating massive response from the young crowd. As well as entertainment coming with this platform one of the singers made his show form virtual universe.

Education and training: Educational institutions are using the metaverse for virtual classrooms, training simulations etc.

Business and commerce: Companies are using the metaverse to create virtual storefronts where users can browse products, try virtual samples, and make purchases in a digital environment.

Virtual real estate: The concept of virtual real estate is emerging, where users can buy, sell, and develop virtual properties.

Creative expression: Artists, musicians, and designers are using the metaverse as a canvas for creative expression. They are building immersive art installations and interactive experience.

5.1.2 Edge Computing

Edge computing is a new way to process and store data that is closer to where it is generated. This can make applications run faster and more reliably. The metaverse is a virtual world where people can interact with each other. Edge computing is important for the metaverse because it can improve the performance, reliability, and scalability of metaverse applications. It can also reduce the cost of operating the metaverse.

5.1.3 Edge Computing and Metaverse

Low latency: Edge computing can reduce the delay, between a user's action and the response by computer. This is important for the Metaverse, where real-time interactions are crucial. Low latency makes the Metaverse more reactive.

Scalability: Edge computing can help the Metaverse to support more parallel people. Required to generate the metaverse.

Bandwidth optimization: Edge computing can reduce the amount of data that needs to be sent over the network.

Privacy and security: Edge computing can enhance privacy and security in the Metaverse. By processing sensitive data locally, user information and interactions can be safeguarded more effectively.

Offline functionality: Edge computing allows certain functionalities to be available offline.

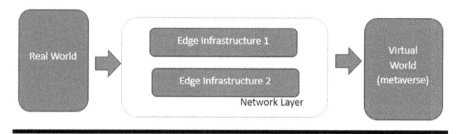

Figure 5.1 Working of edge computing.

Edge computing is a key technology that can help to enable and improve the Metaverse. It offers several advantages over other computing architectures, making it a highly effective solution for delivering seamless and immersive virtual experiences.

Few examples are as follows.

Edge computing is gaming for giving gaming experience specially for player setting on longer distance edge computing is used which allow user to fill that they are closer to each other can play the game effectively.

Another example is IoT devises used in homes to make smart home, especially the consumer electronic devises connected around the home operated from anywhere using mobile applications even it feels like we are operating from our home and not to worry about any device in terms of its working. Working on IoT always required full support and proper installation of required hardware which can be fit using Edge Computing and with minimal hardware and utilization of same hardware for many devices.

The above examples related with only gaming and home industry but there are many areas where expensive use of IoT devises going on such as Hospital, Factories, and retail location where data is much sensitive and required support of huge devises may not all devices procure by each department of each organization, but they believe of sharing the infrastructure as well as optimizing the resources for making effective utilization helped by edge computing. Edge computing allow the feel of working over internet as working on desktop-based computer which required in the Metaverse ecosystem.

The working and definition of edge computing referencing to bringing cloud and data centres closer to us and which is a basic requirement of Metaverse. The layers metaverse many focus on security and privacy, bringing devices closer so Avatar of us can easily navigator at multiple place and AR-VR devices which provide us real time and be there experienced particular to have gaming experience where multiple players can feel they are closer to each other.

There are some issues which may focus while using metaverse like Financial Frauds, privacy Issue cyber thread, extended reality thread social engineering, and many more traditional attacks which can be handled by effective utilization of edge computing.

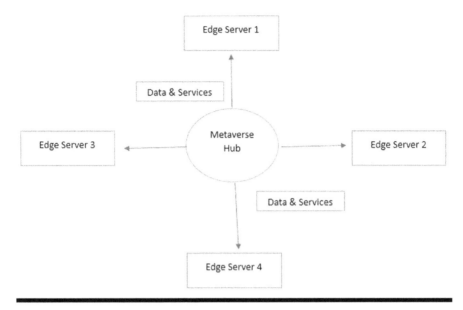

Figure 5.2   Prospective use of edge computing in Metaverse.

In this chapter we will discus, the integration of edge computing in the Metaverse is essential for its sustainable growth and its ability to meet the evolving needs of users and business.

5.1.3 Metaverse and Traditional Cloud-Based Platform

Latency: Data traveling between user and server may take time depending upon the traffic on web portal as well as the complexity of the request which can lead to delay in processing the request and hence, they may be buffering or other delay due to which live activity get interrupted.

Scalability: the number of users connected to the centre server are quite more and parallel there are many different requests occurred simultaneously which can lead to performance and scalability issue.

Security: the security is always the major concern of any data same with metaverse as well. If hacker crack the data server stored on cloud all information can be stolen and we even didn't have backup of same as well as its big data set.

Bandwidth: the images, audio, video, special characters, high resolution required bandwidth to reach to the user. If the bandwidth is not sufficient the user may face issue some time users drop the application and move out to different one.

Personalization: Cloud-based platforms may struggle to personalize experiences for individual users.

Reliability: Cloud-based servers are vulnerable to outages and downtime, which can disrupt user experiences and discourage them from using the platform.

Addressing these challenges is essential for the Metaverse need reliable and secure eco system particular to data storage and share.

5.1.4 Edge Computing in the Metaverse

Edge computing can help to solve the problems that cloud-based Metaverse platforms.

Reduced latency: Edge computing reduces the distance between user and server hence data reach to closer to the user due to which the travel time get reduced, and user makes real time interaction with server or metaverse eco system.

Improved scalability: Edge computing used distributed server system hence load on server is balanced among multiple servers and finally it stores in cloud storage device hence edge computing can handle multiple users at a time.

Enhanced security: the data is closer to user and dedicated edge server only accessing the data from cloud hence even hacker hack the edge server he or she can't steal the entire data and copy of data being intact on cloud storage. Which increase the security to the data.

Reduced bandwidth usage: Edge computing can help to reduce bandwidth usage by processing data closer to the user. Because of this less data needs to be broadcast over the network.

More personalized experiences: Edge computing can be used to personalize the Metaverse experience for each user. This can be done by analysing user data, such as preferences and behaviour. This can make the Metaverse more engaging and enjoyable for users.

Improved reliability: Edge computing can help to improve the reliability of the Metaverse by distributing the load among distributed system. This means that the Metaverse is less likely to go down if one server goes down.

Overall, edge computing can help to make the Metaverse a better experience for everyone. It can reduce latency, improve scalability, enhance security, reduce bandwidth usage, create more personalized experiences, and improve reliability.

5.1.5 Use of Edge Computing by Prominent Leaders in Gaming Market

Microsoft Azure Edge Zones: Microsoft Azure Edge Zones are used to improve online gaming experiences by reducing latency.

Google Stadia: Google Stadia uses edge computing to process game data and stream high-quality graphics directly to players' devices.

Niantic's Pokémon GO: Niantic uses edge computing to distribute the computational load during large-scale events. This ensures that millions of players can participate simultaneously without over burdening the servers.

AWS Wavelength: AWS Wavelength integrates edge computing with 5G networks to provide ultra-low latency for applications, including online gaming.

Alibaba Cloud's Mobile Edge Computing (MEC) for Gaming: Alibaba Cloud's MEC technology improves the delivery of game content and processes user inputs at the edge of the network.

5.2 Relevance

Luyi Chang, Z. Z. (2022) focused on challenges in Metaverse such as privacy, delay, and resource allocation and suggested a mixture of 6G-oriented edge intelligence into Metaverse. Challenges with privacy were suggested to be handled by integrating learning into secure user data and creating user replacement avatars to confuse users' real location. The author suggests implementing a silent auction using deep support learning to improve communication efficiency, as well as employing a blockchain-driven spontaneous method to motivate workers to actively execute system tasks. Resource allocation was found to be increased by shared technology creating partitions based on actual user requirements and documenting the needs of users to select relevant model training result by edge nodes [2].

Vesal Ahsani proposed a Fog-Edge computing architecture for Metaverse implementation to make use of edge devices to attain the required computations for heavy tasks such as collision detection in virtual universe and computation of 3D physics. Simulation results revealed that the given architecture could minimize the visualization latency by half compared to traditional cloud based Metaverse applications [3].

In Lik-Hang Lee's conference paper future challenges of MEC-based Metaverse are discussed such as computer resource allocation, user experience, data, mobility management, delay, and privacy. Offloading of computation-intensive job to the edge of the network can be done by using mobile edge computing as a distributed computing model [4].

Luyi Chang in his paper focused on an edge-enabled Metaverse concept. They also scrutinized the significance of networking and blockchain challenges. Challenges discussed include shared Metaverse, implementation of Metaverse at mobile edge computing network from interoperability, communication, heterogeneity and computation point of view. The proposed solution is digital replication of real-world entities in Metaverse, physical virtual synchronization, and leverage computing capacity of mobile edge networks [5].

In Yitong Wang's article the author proposes an architectural design of Metaverse and edge intelligence operated infrastructure. Convergence of Metaverse and edge intelligence is depicted using a smart city development case study [6].

Sahraoui Dhelim's paper compares various modern mobile computing paradigms of mobile edge computing. It also illustrates development of MEC with AI and blockchain. It gives MEC application in area of vehicles and smart city or homes [7].

Xu's paper empowers the Metaverse by combining primary components into a 6th generation mobile edge framework. It also elaborates on novel communication paradigms to meet user needs in Metaverse. Integrating heterogeneous technologies, improving user experience, and addressing privacy and security are some of the challenges faced in Metaverse while deploying the 6G framework [8].

Metaverse is a 3D virtual space where people can learn, play, work, live, and interact with others. Mobile edge computing provides advantages such as low latency, bandwidth utilization, and the ability to perform intensive computations at the edge of the network. This paper discusses the potential applications of Mobile Edge Computing (MEC) in enabling a Metaverse. Additionally, it addresses future challenges that might arise when implementing a large-scale system in the context of varying and diverse traffic patterns [8].

In their work, Yu delves into the development of digital replicas of physical objects within the Metaverse. The paper outlines the essential components necessary for creating digital twins and emphasizes the challenges associated with twin synchronization and divergence [13].

Yang stated that AI and blockchain play important role in Metaverse. This work discusses the use of AI technology such as support vector machine, neural network, and reinforcement learning. Challenges such as AI issues, blockchain-related issues, digital economy in Metaverse, governance in Metaverse, and security and privacy for Metaverse are also discussed [14].

5.3 Architectural Framework of an Edge Computing-Enabled

The edge computing plays vital role in metaverse ecosystem by allowing user uninterrupted, reliable and scalable experience. As well as edge node provide the high quality of graphics due to which user UI-UX experience increases. In addition the edge node can process the data from IoT / AR-VR devices to create a realistic environment which increase the attenuation span of user on the metaverse platform.

In the Architectural Framework of an Edge Computing-Enabled Metaverse the Metaverse layer is responsible for creating and managing the virtual world. It hosts the Metaverse's content and applications, such as virtual games, social spaces, and e-commerce platforms. The Metaverse layer also provides users with avatars and other tools to interact with the virtual world.

The cloud layer provides additional computing resources and storage capacity to the Metaverse. It also hosts centralized services such as user authentication and billing.

The Edge Computing is used as mediator between user and cloud storage where the work of edge node is to fetch the data from cloud and bring closer to the user its used for as synchronization to get the feel to user as well as getting data from

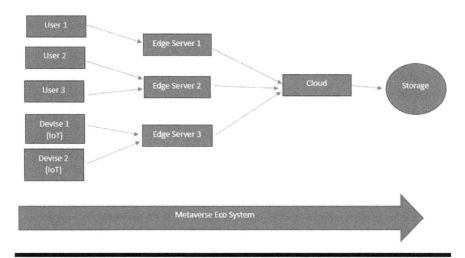

Figure 5.3   Involvement of edge computing in Metaverse.

user devices so they can get uninterrupted services. Due to implantation of edge computing the metaverse ecosystem will be benefited by Reduced latency, Improved scalability, Enhanced security and privacy, Reduced bandwidth usage etc.

5.4 Edge Computing Case Studies in the Metaverse

Edge computing is transforming the Metaverse, making it more immersive, interactive, and scalable.

Roblox: Roblox uses edge computing to process in-game interactions. This reduces latency and ensures real-time gameplay for millions of concurrent users.

Magic Leap: Magic Leap uses edge computing to enhance X-R experiences. By processing complex AR data at the edge, Magic Leap devices deliver high-quality, real-time visuals without overwhelming device hardware.

Decentral: Decentral and is a blockchain-based virtual reality platform that uses edge computing to manage in-game transactions and asset exchanges.

AltspaceVR: AltspaceVR is a social virtual reality platform that uses edge computing to synchronize user interactions in real time provide experience of social gathering.

Viveport Infinity: Viveport Infinity is a virtual reality subscription service that uses edge computing to optimize game streaming. This allows users to stream high-quality games directly to their VR headsets without the need for high-end hardware.

These case studies show how edge computing is being used to create a more seamless, immersive, and secure Metaverse. As edge computing technologies continue to develop, we can expect to see even more innovative and groundbreaking applications in the years to come.

5.5 Challenges for Edge Computing-Enabled Metaverse

5.5.1 Synchronization Challenges

The edge node working near to the user hence they need to synchronise the data with cloud server for getting recent transactions which can be implemented using synchronization protocol and timestamp mechanism can help to overcome synchronization challenge.

5.5.2 Load Balancing

The load on edge node can be uneven hence the performance can be tossed up particular at the peak time this can be handled by using the load balancing algorithm and dynamic resource allocation even the threading can be used in such kind of issues.

5.5.3 Network Complexities

The edge node is decentralised and handling diverse network which can lead to configuration issue, can be handled by implementing standardized communication protocols and security measures across nodes simplifies network complexities.

5.5.4 Data Privacy and Security

Although edge node working closer the user still, they may raise the issue of security and privacy and its mandatory to safeguard the user's data. This can be handled by introducing the encrypted data transfer algorithm as well as by doing regular security audit and compliance.

5.5.5 Interoperability

Confirming sharing between various edge devices, platforms, and Metaverse applications is challenging due to the integration of multiple technology which can be taken care by adopting standardized interfaces and APIs and seamless integration with different edge computing devices and software platforms is key.

5.5.6 Resource Constraints

Edge nodes often have limited computational resources compared to centralized servers can be solve by Implementing lightweight algorithms, edge-native applications, and efficient code optimization techniques.

5.5.7 Scalability

Ensuring that edge computing infrastructure scales efficiently with the growing demands of the Metaverse. Designing a scalable architecture that allows seamless addition of edge nodes based on demand is essential. Implementing auto-scaling mechanisms and predictive analytics for capacity planning ensures scalability.

In addressing these challenges and probable solution, the integration of edge computing in the Metaverse can be optimized for superior performance, enhanced user experiences, and seamless interactions. A balance of technological solutions, best practices, and ongoing optimizations is necessary to overcome these challenges and unlock the full potential of edge computing in shaping the future of the Metaverse.

5.6 Conclusion

Edge computing in metaverse is extremely important for synchronization, reducing latency, Edge AI allows for real-time data analysis and intelligent decision-making directly within edge devices. This can be used to personalize the Metaverse experience for each user. Decentralized identity solutions, such as Self-Sovereign Identity (SSI), empower users to own and control their digital identities. This can be integrated with edge computing to ensure secure, user-owned data in the Metaverse. Blockchain technology can be used to provide secure, transparent, and tamper-proof transactions in decentralized edge environments. This can be used to implement secure transactions, such as virtual asset exchanges, and enhance smart contract functionalities in the Metaverse. Fog computing is an extension of edge computing that focuses on collaborative intelligence among edge devices. This can be used to create dynamic and interactive virtual worlds in the Metaverse. Seamless orchestration between edge and cloud resources is essential for efficient resource utilization and scalability in the Metaverse. 5G networks provide ultra-low latency and high bandwidth, making them ideal for edge computing applications. This can be used to ensure unparalleled responsiveness and immersive virtual reality experiences in the Metaverse.

Edge computing is transforming the way we interact with the Metaverse, making it more real-time, scalable, secure, and immersive. Edge computing reduces latency, bringing users closer to the virtual experience. Edge computing enables the Metaverse to accommodate large numbers of users without slowing down. Edge computing decentralizes data processing, making it more difficult for hackers to steal sensitive user information. Edge computing powers innovative Metaverse experiences, such as AI-driven personalization and dynamic environment adjustments.

These advancements are tiling the way for a Metaverse that is not just a digital extension, but a seamless blend of our physical and virtual realities. It is a Metaverse that adapts, learns, and evolves, tailoring experiences in real-time and ensuring users are active co-creators of their virtual journeys.

The integration of edge computing in the Metaverse represents more than just technological progress. It indicates a pattern shift towards a more connected, intelligent, and user-centric digital arena.

As we embrace this digital revolution, the Metaverse, empowered by edge computing, is poised to redefine human interaction, creativity, and expression. It offers a canvas where the limits of our imagination are stretched, enabling us to paint vibrant, immersive, and endlessly evolving digital worlds.

References

[1] Z. X. D. N. Wei Yang Bryan Lim, Realizing the Metaverse with edge inelligence.

[2] J. Z. Yitong Wang, A Survey of Mobile Edge Computing for the, IEEE.

[3] A. R. M. L. H. K. Vesal Ahsani, Unlocking Metaverse-as-a-Service, IEEE.

[4] T. B. P. Z. L. W. D. X. Z. L. A. K. B. P. H. Lik-Hang Lee, All One Needs to Know about Metaverse: A Complete Survey on Technological Singularity,Virtual Ecosystem, and Research Agenda.

[5] Z. Z. P. L. S. X. W. G. Y. S. Z. X. J. K. D. N. X. Q. Y. W. Luyi Chang, "6G-Enabled Edge AI for Metaverse: Challenges, Methods, and Future Research Directions," *Communications and Information Networks*, vol. 7, pp. 107–121, 2022.

[6] J. Z. Yitong Wang, "A Survey of Mobile Edge Computing for theMetaverse: Architectures, Applications, and Challenges," in *8th International Conference on Collaboration and Internet Computing (CIC)*, 2022.

[7] T. K. L. C. N. A. H. N. a. L. A. Sahraoui Dhelim, "Edge-enabled Metaverse: The Convergence of Metaverse and Mobile Edge Computing," *LATEX CLASS FILES*, pp. 1–8, 2015.

[8] M. W. C. N. W. Y. B. L. J. K. Z. X. D. N. Q. Y. X. S. S. a. C. M. Xu, "A full dive into realizing the edge-enabled Metaverse: Visions, enabling technologies, and challenges," *IEEE Communications Surveys & Tutorials*, pp. 1–44, 2022.

[9] W. Y. B. Z. X. D. N. X. C. C. M. S. S. a. Q. Y. Lim, "Realizing the Metaverse with edge intelligence: A match made in heaven.," *IEEE Wireless Communications*, pp. 1–9, 2022.

[10] J. Z. Yitong Wang, "Mobile Edge Computing, Metaverse, 6G Wireless Communications, Artificial Intelligence, and Blockchain: Survey and Their Convergence," in *8th World Forum on Internet of Things (WF-IoT)*, 2022.

[11] A, A. P. H. D. H. T. Jiadong Yu, "6G Mobile-Edge Empowered Metaverse: Requirements, Technologies, Challenges and Research Directions," *arXiv e-prints*, p. arXiv:2211.04854, 2022.

[12] A. Y. W. a. J. Z. Liu, "Mobile Edge Computing for the Metaverse," *arXiv preprint*, pp. 1–7, 2022.

[13] J. A. A. P. H. a. D. H. T. Yu, "Bi-directional Digital Twin and Edge Computing in the Metaverse," *arXiv preprint*, p. arXiv:2211.08700, 2022.

[14] Q. Y. Z. H. H. Z. X. J. K. a. Z. Z. Yang, "Fusing blockchain and AI with Metaverse: A survey," *IEEE Open Journal of the Computer Society*, pp. 122–136, 2022.

Chapter 6

Sustainable Communication-Efficient Edge AI: Algorithms and Systems

Pradnya S. Mehta[1], Dattatray G. Takale[1],
Sachin R. Sakhare[2], Parishit N. Mahalle[3],
Sarita D. Sapkal[4], and Gopal B. Deshmukh[1]

[1]*Department of Computer Engineering, Vishwakarma Institute
of Information Technology, SPPU Pune, India*

[2]*Department of Computer Engineering, Vishwakarma Institute
of Information Technology, SPPU Pune, India*

[3]*Department of Artificial Intelligence and Data Science, Vishwakarma
Institute of Information Technology, SPPU Pune, India*

[4]*Department of Computer Engineering, MMCOE, SPPU Pune, India*

6.1 Introduction

Sustainability is becoming an increasingly essential concept in a variety of fields, including the natural sciences, architecture, and the constructed environment, in particular. The goal of sustainable science, engineering, and the built environment is to provide solutions that satisfy current needs without endangering the

DOI: 10.1201/9781032650722-8

capacity of future generations to satisfy their own needs. This can be accomplished by minimizing the impact of human activity on the natural and built environments [1].

With environmental science, investigative methods are used to reduce environmental effects and increase community benefits. This may entail creating emerging technologies that use renewable energy sources or are more energy efficient. It may also entail creating procedures that use fewer resources, result in minimal waste, and are more morally upright.

Sustainable engineering aims to minimize the negative effects on the environment and optimize resource consumption when building, constructing, and improving infrastructure, structures, and systems. This can entail constructing transportation systems that cut emissions, designing buildings that utilize ecofriendly materials and are energy efficient, as well as devising water and waste management systems that consume the least amount of resources available.

Sustainability can be attained in the built environment through urban planning, architecture, and landscape design. Sustainable urban planning entails developing livable, walkable, and accessible to public transportation neighborhoods. Sustainable architecture entails creating structures that are comfortable for inhabitants, employ recycled material, and are energy efficient. Establishing green zones that are advantageous to the environment and for societal health is a key part of environmentally friendly design concept.

Creating approaches that are environmentally, commercially, and ecologically sound is the overarching goal of environmentally friendly science, technology, and the built environment. We can build a more prosperous future for coming generations by adopting sustainability behaviors and values into science, innovation, and implementation.

6.1.1 Edge Devices

Smart objects are computational units that analyze information remotely, such as at the data source, as opposed to globally, like in a data center. The "edge" of the connection, which might be a LAN, WAN, or the internet, is where these devices are quite often positioned.

Smartphones, ipad, laptops, home automation gadgets (including voice assistants and thermostats), advanced manufacturing sensors and controllers, video surveillance, and driverless vehicles are just a few examples of edge devices. In comparison to conventional computer devices, these devices frequently have less processing, memory, and storage, but they are made to do a limited set of tasks with high dependability and minimal latency [2].

Since more and more data is produced at the edge of networks, especially in the context of the internet of things (IoT) and smart cities, edge computing has grown in significance. Devices can make quicker judgments, minimize latency, and increase the system's overall efficacy and efficiency by processing data at the edge.

6.1.2 Cloud Computing

The widespread adoption of cloud computing has had a significant impact on the day-to-day activities and routines of individuals. Google, Amazon, and Microsoft are just three examples of the many major corporations that have introduced their very own cloud computing services in recent years (Google Cloud, Amazon Web Services, and Microsoft Azure, respectively). Cloud computing is able to intelligently supply customers with compute, storage, and communications networks in a prompt fashion based on their particular requirements thanks to its extensive network of dispersed servers [2]. Cloud computing can do this because its servers are located in a variety of locations.

As a direct result of the proliferation of the IoT, an enormous diversity of physical devices and sensors have been produced, and they are now finding ubiquitous application all over the world. These mechanical components and apparatuses have the capability to understand the conditions that are external to them and to transform that comprehension into data. Even though enormous quantities of data are being transferred to the cloud for processing or storage, customers can still gain access to the data that is housed there in compliance with the particular needs that they have.

However, because the IoT is used by so many people and is continuing to develop, cloud computing has started to demonstrate an increasing number of problems. For instance, if the data that is produced by terminal devices all over the world is computed and stored in a centralized cloud, this will result in a number of issues, such as the lowest throughput possible, high latency, bandwidth bottlenecks, violation of privacy laws, centralized flaws, and additional costs (such as transmission cost, energy cost, storage cost, and calculation cost). In point of fact, a significant number of use cases involving the IoT, particularly those involving the Internet of Vehicles (IoV), call for the expedient processing of data, the comprehensive analysis of data, and the expedient distribution of results.

6.1.3 Challenges to Cloud Computing

Several more advantages, including cost reductions, scalability, and adaptability, have been brought about by cloud computing. Yet, there are a number of difficulties associated with cloud computing. Some of the main obstacles to cloud computing include:

- **Security:** One of the main difficulties with cloud computing is security. Data that is kept on the cloud is subject to a number of threats, including hacking, information leakage, and cyberattacks. To protect data in the cloud, it is crucial to put in place strong security measures including cryptographic protocols and access management.
- **Compliance:** Businesses that operate in regulated sectors like financing or medical are subjected to stringent rules concerning data security and privacy. These guidelines must also be followed by cloud computing companies, which can be difficult.
- **Data governance:** It can be challenging to manage and oversee the amount and complexity of data processed in the cloud. To guarantee data accuracy, confidentiality, and integrity, it's critical to have a clear data governance strategy in place.
- **Vendor lock-in:** Whenever the business uses a cloud computing environment, that provider may come to dominate its business. In the future, switching suppliers or shifting to a new system may be difficult as a result.
- **Reliability:** Due to their dependence on broadband connections, cloud services may experience outages or service interruptions at any time. To maintain business continuity, backup and disaster recovery procedures must be in place.
- **Cost management:** Although cloud computing can lower infrastructure costs, if not properly managed, it might also result in unforeseen costs. For cloud expenditures to be as efficient as possible, it's critical to monitor consumption and prices.
- **Performance:** If cloud services are not set up properly, efficiency problems may arise. As a result, users may encounter delayed response times. For cloud services to function at their best, configuration and performance must be optimized.

Because of the issues that have been discussed, cloud computing has attracted a lot of attention in the shape of a new approach for computers known as edge computing (EC) [3]. The essential concept that underpins the EC model is the concept of relocating the computing, data processing, and storing functions that were initially required by the cloud to the periphery of the network, which is in close proximity to the endpoint devices. This is conducive to decentralization as it shortens the amount of time necessary for data to travel between devices and networks, speeds up device reactions, and reduces the expense of data communication.

6.1.4 Challenges before Cloud Computing for Building Edge Computing

EC is a design that incorporates data processing and carrying out calculations nearer the area where the information is originated, at the network's edge. The obstacles of stacking distributed computing on the upper edge of cloud computing include:

- **Connectivity:** The cloud serves as the processing, storage, and administrative platform for EC. Connectivity between the edge devices and the cloud must be dependable and fast. The user experience may suffer as a result of latency problems and slower reaction times caused by poor connectivity.
- **Security:** Edge devices might not offer the same level of safeguarding as the cloud, and it could result in weaknesses that criminals could take advantage of. To stop unauthorized access and data breaches, it is crucial to secure edge devices and their connections to the cloud.
- **Scalability:** The need for processing power and storage space at the edge may rise as edge devices create more data. Scalability can be aided by cloud computing, but this requires adequate deployment and execution to make sure edge devices can make the most of cloud resources.
- **Complexity:** A complicated architecture is needed to interconnect machine learning and artificial intelligence (AI) with cloud computing, and controlling and maintaining the system may present issues. The system must be managed by IT staff, who must also assure that it is configured correctly and is performing at its best.
- **Cost:** It can be costly to build cloud technology on top of virtualization, especially if the system calls for a substantial investment in new technology and software. The company must assess the benefits and drawbacks of deploying the system to make sure it fits their objectives and budget.

Consequently, adding EC on top of cloud computing poses a number of difficulties, but these difficulties may be surmounted with careful design and execution to produce a resilient, secure system that delivers great performance and a satisfying user experience.

6.1.5 Edge Computing

An alternative to centralized data centers, EC is a distributed computing architecture in which data processing and storage are carried out closer to the data source, frequently at the network's edge. As a result, data processing can be done more rapidly and effectively, with much less network traffic and delay.

On what are known as edge devices, which can range from smartphones to IoT devices, information is processed remotely when using EC. As a result, there is no longer a requirement for data to be transferred to a centralized information facility for processing, which can create delays and use up a lot of bandwidth.

In situations where real-time data processing is necessary, such as in the case of self-driving vehicles, automation systems, and smart cities, EC is very useful. These technologies can support speedier, more informed judgments, minimize response times, and provide better system performance by processing data at the edge. Ultimately, EC offers a more decentralized and distributed computing model that enhances traditional cloud computing and can assist in meeting the rising demand for real-time data processing in today's linked world. Figure 6.1 shows how EC device management works.

Figure 6.1   Edge Computing Device Management.

6.1.6 Artificial Intelligence

The term "artificial intelligence" refers to the process of developing computer systems that are capable of performing tasks that would normally require the intelligence of a human being. Some examples of these tasks include speech recognition, decision-making, visual perception, and the ability to understand natural language. In AI, algorithms and machine learning techniques are used to analyze data, learn from it, and then make projections or judgments based on the acquired knowledge. This process is known as "data mining."

Depending on the degree of intelligence displayed by the system, multiple categories of AI can be created. These groups consist of:

- **Reactive machines:** Some AI systems can only respond to specific inputs; they lack the capacity to remember prior events or draw conclusions from them in the present.
- **Limited memory:** Such systems have a limited capacity for using past experiences to guide present choices.
- **Theory of mind:** These technologies can comprehend the thoughts and feelings of human beings, which enables them to communicate with people more successfully.
- **Self-aware:** These technologies are cognitive, aware of their surroundings, and aware of their own identity.

Robotics, autonomous cars, natural language processing, picture and audio recognition, language translation, and recommendation systems are just a few of the many useful uses of AI. It has the power to transform a number of industries and alter how we live and work. But as the technology advances, there are also concerns about how AI will affect jobs, privacy, and ethics, which need to be addressed.

6.1.7 Edge Computing with AI

The use of AI algorithms and models at the edge of a network, near to where data is generated, gathered, and processed, is known as EC with AI. Using this method, real-time monitoring and judgment calls are made possible while latency is decreased and data transmission is rendered more effective.

There are several uses for EC with AI, including:

- **Smart manufacturing:** By evaluating information obtained from sensors and machines on the manufacturing floor, EC with AI can provide preventative maintenance and in-the-moment quality standards.
- **Autonomous vehicles:** By evaluating information from sensors and anticipating potential pitfalls, EC with AI can assist autonomous vehicles in making conclusions in real-time.

- **Smart cities:** By analyzing information captured by sensors and cameras positioned around the city, EC with AI can help cities strengthen public safety, streamline flows of traffic, and consume less energy.
- **Healthcare:** By examining data from medical equipment and sensors, EC with AI can enable distant monitoring of patients and genuine diagnosis.

Unfortunately, implementing AI at the edge can also come with number cognitive obstacles, such as constrained resources, safety concerns, and the needs for efficient data handling. To assure the productivity and reliability of EC with AI systems, it is crucial to carefully develop and deploy them.

6.1.8 Edge AI

In contrast to using cloud-based computing, edge AI refers to the application of AI algorithms and systems on edge devices like smartphones, smart speakers, and sensors. Due to its rapid data processing, capacity to conserve power and storage, and ability to ensure privacy, edge AI is becoming more and more widely used. The restricted connection capacity and high latency that exist between edge devices and cloud servers, however, provide a significant obstacle to the implementation of edge AI [4].

The development of edge AI algorithms and systems with effective communication has received increasing attention as a solution to this problem. Following are some regularly utilized methods and techniques:

- **Model compression:** In order to transfer less data, this entails shrinking the size of the AI model by eliminating extraneous parts like redundant parameters.
- **Quantization:** In order to limit the quantity of data that needs to be conveyed, this includes decreasing the precision of model parameters, such as weights and activations.
- **Federated Learning:** This method of dispersed intelligence uses several edge devices to cooperatively train a single model without transferring the raw data to the cloud. By using this strategy, privacy can be maintained while reducing communication overhead.
- **Edge intelligence:** This entails analyzing the information on the edge device and delivering the cloud with only the pertinent data. As a result, less data must be delivered and the reaction time is shortened [4].
- **Offloading strategies:** Choosing which components of the AI algorithm should operate on the edge device and which components should run in the cloud is involved in this. The edge device's resources and communication costs may be taken into consideration while making this choice.
- **Network Optimization:** To do this, the entire network and communication interface must be optimized to cut down on latency and expense. For instance, applying compression algorithms or giving crucial data packets priority can help to increase communication efficiency.

In summary, effective communication is crucial for the success of edge AI algorithms and systems. These methods can raise the effectiveness, efficiency, and dependability of edge AI systems by lowering transmission cost and latency.

Edge AI refers to the deployment of AI software on hardware across the real world. The term "edge AI" refers to the practice of performing artificial intelligence simulations close to the user, at the network's periphery, rather than centrally, at a cloud computing facility or private data center [5]. The edge of the networking can relate to any region since this internet is reachable everywhere. It might be a commercial shop, workplace, hospital, or one of the gadgets we routinely encounter, like signalized intersections, robotics, and smartphones.

6.2.1 Need of Edge AI

Due to a number of factors, edge AI, or AI that would be processed on local machine as contrast to on the cloud, has grown in importance.

Computer programmes must really be capable of detecting trends and carrying out tasks routinely and safely in order to assist people. The variety of jobs that people conduct, nevertheless, encompasses limitless situations that are unattainable to explain precisely in codes and rules since the world is chaotic.

To name a few:

- **Reduced latency decreased latency:** By processing data locally instead of sending it to the cloud, edge AI cuts down on the delay. This is crucial in time-sensitive situations like driverless vehicles, during which a computing lag can have negative effects.
- **Enhanced privacy:** Edge AI makes it possible for data processing to take place locally on the device, eliminating the necessity to send confidential data to the cloud. When confidential material may be stored locally and properly secured, this can help with confidentiality.
- **Enhanced efficiency:** As local devices may process data on their own, edge AI can minimize the requirement for ongoing cloud access. Both the workload on cloud servers and device energy consumption may be reduced as a result.
- **Increased reliability:** Edge AI can increase system resilience by lowering reliance on the cloud. This seems to be crucial in circumstances whereby accessibility to the cloud may be hindered, as in rural areas or after natural catastrophes.

6.2.2 Advantages of Edge AI

The use of AI algorithms on edge devices, such as smartphones, sensors, and cameras, as opposed to a centralized cloud server, is referred to as edge AI, also known as edge computing or edge analytics. Edge AI has many advantages, some of which are as follows:

- **Lower bandwidth:** By lowering the quantity of data that must be sent via the network, edge AI may potentially use less bandwidth and save money.
- **Increased reliability:** Edge AI can improve the robustness by making sure that crucial operations keep running even if network connectivity is lost.
- **Lower costs:** Edge AI can lower costs by doing away with the requirement for centralized server architecture, reducing the amount of data sent over the network, and maybe reducing the amount of electricity needed to analyze the data.
- **Smart:** AI applications are more robust and adaptable than traditional programs, which can only respond to inputs that the programmer has predicted. An AI neural network, on the other hand, is trained to respond to a particular type of question rather than a specific one, even if the question itself is novel. Applications would be unable to process inputs as varied as textual, voiced words, and video without AI.
- **Legitimate discoveries:** This is possible because edge technology examines data locally rather than in a remote cloud where responses are delayed by protracted transmission.
- **Improved data protection:** Because confidential information is dealt with locally, there is less chance that it will be stored in the cloud or captured while being transferred.
- **Lower power consumption:** Numerous AI operations can be carried out on a device with less power than would be needed to transport the information to a cloud, thus prolonging battery life.

6.2.3 How Does Edge AI Technology Work?

Edge AI is the term used to describe the AI technique that is implemented directly on edge devices, such as smartphones, wearables, IoT devices, and other connected devices, with no requirement for connectivity to a central cloud or server. Edge AI enables real-time data analytics and judgment by bringing machine learning algorithms and other AI capabilities nearer to the data being processed [6].

Here are the steps involved in edge AI technology:

- **Data collection:** Sensors, cameras, and other data-generating devices are used by edge AI technology to gather data.
- **Preprocessing:** Raw data collected from devices is preprocessed to clean and normalize the data for further processing.

- **Model deployment:** Machine learning models are deployed directly on the edge device, which includes a combination of neural networks and other deep learning algorithms.
- **Inference:** The edge device runs the deployed model to generate insights and predictions from the preprocessed data.
- **Decision-making:** The predictions generated by the deployed model are used to make decisions on the edge device itself, without the need for sending data to a central server or cloud.
- **Feedback:** The decision made on the edge device is then used to provide feedback to the user or other connected devices, enabling the device to take action.

6.2.4 Edge AI Architecture

AI models that can operate locally on edge devices, such as smartphones, IoT devices, and embedded systems, without the requirement for a constant connection to the internet or cloud computing infrastructure are known as edge AI architecture. Software as well as hardware components including sensing devices, CPU, memories, heuristics, and software platforms are frequently combined in edge AI architectures. The following are some typical elements of edge AI architecture:

- **Sensor(s):** Physical devices that capture data from the environment.
- **Edge device:** Computing device located close to or on the sensor that runs edge AI applications.
- **Edge AI framework**: A software framework that enables building and running edge AI applications.
- **Preprocessing:** A set of operations performed on the raw sensor data before feature extraction.
- **Feature extraction:** A process that identifies and extracts relevant features from preprocessed data.
- **Inference:** A process that uses machine learning models to predict outcomes based on extracted features.

The many elements of edge AI are represented in this architecture diagram, including the sensors that collect environmental data, the edge device that executes edge AI applications, and the software framework that enables the creation and execution of edge AI applications. Preprocessing, feature extraction, and inference make up the three key parts of the edge AI application. Prior to feature extraction, actions are conducted on the raw sensor data as part of preprocessing. Feature extraction finds and extracts pertinent features from the preprocessed data, while inference makes predictions based on the extracted features using machine learning models. Figure 6.2 depicts the architecture of edge AI.

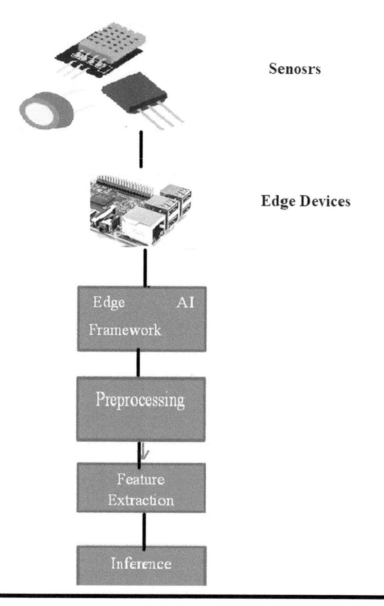

Figure 6.2   Architecture of edge AI.

6.3 Communication-Efficient Edge AI: Algorithms and Systems

When AI algorithms and models are implemented on edge devices like smartphones, smart cameras, and sensors, this is referred to as edge AI. Because it reduces latency and minimizes data transfer to the cloud, edge AI is becoming more and more popular. It enables real-time processing and analysis of data near the source. Running complicated AI algorithms on edge devices, however, is difficult since they frequently have low computing and storage capacity.

Effective communication is one of the main issues with edge AI. Since edge devices frequently have constrained bandwidth and battery life, it can be expensive to send data to the cloud for processing. In order to reduce communication and energy use, edge AI algorithms and systems must be created.

To help create edge AI that is effective at communication, consider the following algorithms and systems:

- **Federated learning:** A distributed machine learning method known as federated learning enables edge devices to cooperatively build a global model without disclosing their raw information. The edge devices reduce the quantity of data that needs to be communicated by training local models on their data and sending only the model updates to the cloud. When compared to centralized training, federated learning can save communication costs by up to 100 times [7].
- **Quantization:** Quantization is a technique that reduces the precision of model parameters and activations from floating-point to fixed-point, reducing the model size and communication overhead. Recent studies have shown that 8-bit quantized models can achieve similar accuracy as full-precision models with a fraction of the communication cost.
- **Pruning:** With the pruning process, unimportant weights are taken out of the model, resulting in a smaller model and less communication required. Pruning can cut the cost of transmission by up to 90% without greatly reducing accuracy.
- **Edge Intelligence Networks (EINs):** These are a particular class of neural network that are intended to be compact and effective for edge devices. In order to decrease the number of parameters and calculations needed while retaining accuracy, EINs use techniques like depth-wise separable convolution and knowledge distillation. Comparing EINs to conventional neural networks, it is possible to reduce model size by up to 10 times and computation by 100 times.
- **Edge-to-Edge Communication:** Edge-to-edge communication is a method that lets edge devices talk to one other directly instead of through the cloud. In addition to improving privacy and security, this can lower communication costs and latency. Technologies like Bluetooth, WI-Fi Direct, and peer-to-peer networks can be used to achieve edge-to-edge communication.

In summary, optimizations at both the algorithmic and system levels are necessary for communication-efficient edge AI. Edge AI systems can be made effective and scalable by using techniques like federated learning, quantization, pruning, EINs, and edge-to-edge communication. These methods can also assist reduce communication and energy usage.

6.3.1 Communications-Efficient Algorithms for Edge AI

6.3.1.1 Federated Learning

A technique for machine learning known as federated learning is one in which multiple devices work together to build a model without sharing their local data with a centralized computer. Federated learning is an example of distributed learning. In distributed learning, the model is brought to the data rather than the data being transmitted to a centralized computer.

In the process of distributed learning, each device receives the most current version of the model from a centralized server, then trains the model using the device's own data, and finally sends the updated model back to the server for storage. By compiling the most recent information from each of the connected devices, the computer generates an updated version of the global model. After that, the global model is sent back to the hardware so that it can undergo additional training. The model is put through this process over and over again until it either converges on the correct answer or reaches an appropriate level of precision.

Federated learning has a number of benefits over conventional centralized machine learning.

As local data is not forwarded to a central server, it first aids in the preservation of data privacy. The model's resilience and generalization can be enhanced by allowing training on a variety of devices, which is the second benefit. Third, federated learning is helpful when data is dispersed across numerous devices and centralization is impossible or expensive.

Several applications, including image classification, natural language processing, and healthcare, use federated learning. It also presents a number of difficulties, including preserving model consistency across devices, coping with heterogeneity in local data, and guaranteeing data confidentiality and privacy.

In order to address significant challenges such as data privacy, data security, data access rights, and access to heterogeneous data, federated learning enables multiple players to develop a single, powerful machine learning model without sharing data. This makes it possible to address these important challenges. It has applications in a variety of fields, including the military, telecommunications, the IoT, and the pharmaceutical industry, to name just a few. A significant question that still needs to be answered is whether or not the models that are learned from shared data are superior to those that are developed from distributed data. Another question that hasn't been addressed is whether or not the peripheral devices are reliable, as well as how antagonistic players might influence the learned model.

6.3.1.2 Centralized Federated Learning

Federated learning that is "centralized" means that a single server manages the learning activities of numerous clients or devices. The central server in centralized federated learning is in charge of gathering the updates from the participating clients, which are often mobile or IoT devices [6].

Each client device receives a copy of the model during training from the central server, and the clients update the model locally using their own data and computations. The central server then transmits these updates back, where they are combined to update the world model. The model is iterated via this process several times until it achieves the necessary degree of accuracy.

The ability to efficiently coordinate and communicate between clients and the central server is one benefit of centralized federated learning, which can be helpful in situations when network access is constrained or inconsistent. Additionally, the training procedure is completely under the control of the central server, enabling more effective model optimization.

Once client data is sent to the central server, however, centralized federated learning may also cause issues with privacy and data security. Researchers have put forth a number of strategies, such safe aggregation and differential privacy, to allay these worries and guarantee that client data is kept private during the learning process.

6.3.1.3 Centralized Federated Learning Design

The coordination and optimization of the learning process are made possible by the architecture of centralized federated learning, which includes a number of important components. Some of the main design components are as follows [7]:

- **Central server:** The main building block of the centralized federated learning system is the central server. It is in charge of bringing together the updates received from the participating clients and organizing the learning process among them.
- **Model architecture:** The neural network's design, or "model architecture," is what will be used to facilitate learning. Based on the particular use case and the kind of data that will be utilized for training, the architecture should be chosen.
- **Client selection:** An essential component of centralized federated learning is client selection. To guarantee that they represent a varied range of data and that they can consistently participate in the learning process, customers should be carefully selected.
- **Data partitioning:** The process of distributing the data across customers is known as data partitioning. Each client should have access to enough data to

facilitate effective learning, and the data should be dispersed in a manner that accurately represents the population's underlying distribution.

■ **Communication protocol:** The collection of guidelines that control communication between the clients and the central server is known as the communication protocol. The protocol should be created to guarantee that the information is transferred securely and effectively, and that the changes are compiled in a timely and precise manner.

■ **Optimization algorithm:** The technique used to update the model in response to client updates is known as the optimization algorithm. To efficiently optimize the model while simultaneously having the least amount of negative influence on client privacy, the algorithm should be carefully selected [8].

In order to enable efficient and effective learning while protecting privacy and security, the design of centralized federated learning needs careful consideration of the fundamental components and how they interact with one another.

6.4 Centralized Federated Learning Pseudo Code

// Initialization

■ Initialize a global model with random weights
■ Set the number of iterations (epochs) and the learning rate
■ Divide the dataset into multiple subsets, one for each client

// Federated learning loop

for epoch in range(num_iterations):

// Client updates

■ Select a subset of clients to participate in this round
■ For each client in the subset:
■ Send the current global model to the client
■ The client trains the model on its local dataset for a few epochs
■ The client sends the updated model weights to the server

// Server updates

■ Aggregate the updated weights from all clients to form a new global model
■ Update the global model with the aggregated weights
■ Broadcast the new global model to all clients

// evaluate the global model

■ Compute the loss and accuracy of the global model on a validation set

The server maintains a global model in this straightforward federated learning process, while the clients train their local models using their own data. After that, a new global model is created by averaging the modified weights from all clients. The resulting global model is assessed on a validation set after being repeated for a predetermined number of iterations. Be aware that there are numerous varieties of federated learning; the pseudocode presented above is but one of them.

The central server in this design is in charge of directing the learning procedure and combining the updates gathered from the involved clients. Devices 1, 2, and 3 serve as the clients, which each have a local copy of the model and carry out local training on their individual datasets. Each device generates local model changes, which are subsequently transmitted to the central server, which combines them to update the global model. Up until the model converges to the appropriate level of accuracy, this process is repeated repeatedly over several rounds [9].

6.4.1 Decentralized Federated Learning

A machine learning method called Decentralized Federated Learning (DFL) combines federated learning and decentralized computing. In DFL, the participating devices communicate directly with one another to cooperatively train a shared model rather than depending on a central server to manage the learning process.

The following traits apply to DFL:

■ **Decentralized architecture:** DFL manages learning without the use of a centralized server. Instead, to train a shared model, the participating devices speak with one another directly.
■ **Data protection:** DFL protects data privacy by conserving it on the devices and only sharing model updates. This technique guarantees that sensitive and confidential data are not sent over the network.
■ **Error sensitivity:** DFL is fault-tolerant, thus even if some of the networked nodes are down, learning can still proceed normally.
■ **Scalability:** DFL is very scalable since it allows for the distribution of learning over hundreds or even millions of devices.
■ **Concord framework:** To agree on the model updates, DFL follows a consensus protocol. The proposed protocol guarantees that the collaborating units concur on the model updates and guard against rogue devices impairing the learning process.

Applications for DFL include personalized recommendation systems, natural language processing, and healthcare, all of which place a high priority on data privacy.

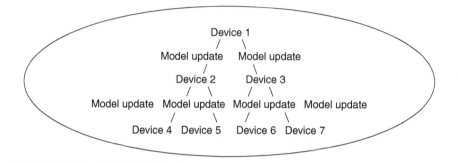

Figure 6.3 Decentralized federated architecture.

The significant computational overhead and communication costs connected with transferring model updates amongst the participating devices are two issues that DFL, however, faces.

As seen in the Figure 6.3 a number of devices (Devices 1–7) take part in the federated learning process. Direct communication between the devices allows them to jointly train a single model.

The model is trained on each device's local data, and the revised model is subsequently sent to other devices for additional training. Up until they agree on the final model, the devices communicate with each other to trade model updates. Until the model achieves an acceptable degree of accuracy, this process is repeated.

DFL protects data privacy by keeping the information on the devices and only sharing model updates. This method makes sure that private information is not transmitted over the network and that sensitive information is not.

The final aggregated parameters of the trained model are represented by this output. It is calculated by combining the local models' parameters from all customers. The centralized federated learning algorithm's weights and bias parameters have the same definitions. On the basis of fresh data, predictions can be made using these parameters. Be aware that the precise method of parameter aggregation can vary based on the algorithm and may also depend on the network architecture or the clients' chosen communication protocol.

6.4.2 Heterogeneous Dederated Learning

A form of federated learning known as Heterogeneous Federated Learning (HFL) involves the participation of devices with appropriate characteristics, including processor speed, memory, and network connectivity. The objective of HFL is to enable heterogeneous device collaboration to build a shared machine learning model without sacrificing security.

- **Design of heterogeneous federated learning:** In heterogeneous federated learning, machine learning models are trained utilizing data from many sources that vary in some way, such as the way the data is distributed, the range of features, or the available hardware. Several important factors must be taken into account while designing a successful HFL system.

- **Preprocessing and data representation:** An essential component of federated learning, particularly heterogeneous federated learning, is data representation. The representation of data on all participating devices must adhere to a uniform format. This can be done by preprocessing the data and putting it in a common format that the federated learning system can use.

- **Architectural models:** Another important factor in HFL is selecting the right model architecture. The model architecture should be adaptable enough to take into account variations in the feature space and data distribution of the participating devices. It should also be capable of handling the computational and memory restrictions placed on the participating devices.

- **Consolidation and information exchange:** Two essential elements of federated learning are aggregation and communication. To address the heterogeneity of the participating devices in heterogeneous federated learning, the communication and aggregation techniques must be carefully constructed. For instance, devices with constrained resources could need to communicate less frequently or transmit the server only a portion of an update.

- **Device selection:** The choice of devices to take part in the federated learning process is another important factor. Devices may vary in their hardware capabilities, network capacity, and data dissemination in heterogeneous federated learning. Because of this, it is critical to choose gadgets that can aid in learning without materially impairing the functionality of the other gadgets.

- **Safety and confidentiality:** Furthermore, security and privacy are crucial factors in HFL as well as other federated learning systems. The data sent between the devices and the server should be safe and shielded from unauthorized access, thus appropriate precautions should be taken to ensure this. Privacy-preserving methods, such as differential privacy or safe multi-party computation, are other ways to ensure data privacy [10].

In conclusion, careful consideration of data representation, model architecture, communication and aggregation protocols, device selection, and security and privacy are essential components of developing a successful heterogeneous federated learning system.

Following 6.4 shows several clients (represented by Clients 1, 2, and 3) presented in this design, each of which has a local dataset and processor. Clients create their own local model updates based on local datasets, train those changes, and then encrypt them before transmitting them to one or more aggregator nodes [11].

The clients' encrypted model updates are received by the aggregator nodes, which then decode them and aggregate them to produce a fresh global model update. The clients receive this global model update after it has been encrypted, decrypted, and utilized to update their local models.

Its architecture enables the construction of a global model that is more accurate and robust than any single client's local model [12], while also facilitating privacy-preserving collaboration amongst clients with various local datasets and processing capabilities. Figure 6.4 is meant for heterogeneous federated architecture.

Managing the variety of the devices is one of HFL's key challenges. Different processing capabilities, network bandwidth, and privacy issues may be present in the devices [13]. This may have an impact on the model's convergence, training, and privacy guarantees.

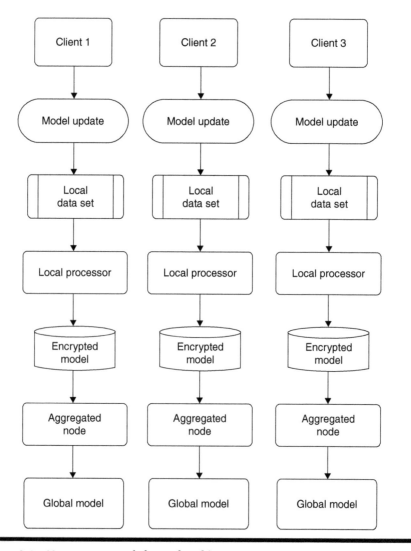

Figure 6.4   Heterogeneous federated architecture.

Researchers have suggested a number of solutions to overcome these issues, including:

- **Resource-adaptive federated learning:** With this method, the training procedure is adjusted to each device's capabilities. For instance, devices with limited processing power can update the model less frequently whereas devices with high processing power can update the model more frequently.
- **Federated learning with effective communication:** By compressing the updates or applying quantization techniques, this method minimizes the quantity of communication between the devices. This may lower the training process's latency and network bandwidth.
- **Privacy differentiation for federated learning:** To safeguard the devices' privacy, this method makes the updates noisier. Depending on each device's privacy needs, the noise level can be changed.
- **Aggregation of models with weight diversity:** This method enables the model to have various weights for various devices, which can enhance the model's performance on devices with various capabilities.

Healthcare, the IoT, and mobile devices are just a few of the many uses for HFL. For instance, HFL in healthcare can let hospitals work together to develop a machine learning model on medical data while protecting patient privacy. HFL in the IoT can make it possible for intelligent devices to work together and share sensor data to train a model more efficiently [14]. HFL in mobile devices can make it possible for multiple cellphones to work together to train a model, saving power and maintaining user privacy.

6.4.3 Quantization

To make neural networks smaller and more effective for use on edge devices with constrained resources, the quantization technique is employed in edge AI. The goal is to represent the neural network's weights and activations using lower precision numbers (such as 8-bit integers) rather than the full-precision floating-point numbers used during training (e.g., 32-bit floating-point numbers).

Depending on the requirements and limitations of the edge AI system, a variety of quantization structures can be applied.

Post-training quantization is a popular quantization design that involves applying quantization to a fully trained neural network [15]. This method is easy to use and can be applied to any pretrained model, although it might not always yield the most accurate and effective outcomes.

Other strategy is "quantization-aware training," which entails training the neural network from the outset with quantization in mind. More accuracy and efficiency may be the consequence of this method, but it uses more processing resources and might not work with all neural network architectures.

Quantization architecture also comes in a variety of forms, including hybrid quantization, which combines post-training and quantization-aware training techniques, and per-channel quantization, which applies various quantization scales to various neural network channels.

There are numerous methods that can be used to optimize the quantization process in addition to the particular quantization architecture that is employed [16]. Examples include dynamic quantization, which modifies the quantization scales during inference based on the data being processed, and symmetric quantization, which maps both positive and negative values to the same range of integers.

Generally, the decision about the quantization architecture will be based on the particular needs and limitations of the edge AI system as well as the acceptable trade-off between accuracy and efficiency for the particular application [17].

The following steps are commonly included in the quantization algorithm:

- **Collect statistics:** The neural network is first tested using a representative dataset, and data is gathered about the weights and activations, including their minimum and maximum values.
- **Quantize encumbrances:** Based on the gathered statistics, the weights are then quantized by being translated into a smaller set of discrete values. For instance, the weights may be quantized to 8-bit integers if they are represented as 32-bit floating-point numbers.
- **Quantize stimulations:** Similar to how the weights are quantized; the activations may also need to be adjusted to take into consideration the data's dynamic range.
- **Fine-tune:** Following quantization, the neural network may be adjusted to make up for any accuracy loss that may have resulted from the quantization procedure.

A neural network that has undergone quantization is faster, smaller, and uses less memory and energy. Deploying on edge devices like smartphones, IoT devices, and embedded systems is made simpler by this. While selecting a quantization scheme, it is crucial to carefully consider the trade-off between accuracy and efficiency as quantization can also result in some accuracy loss. Figure 6.5 presents the steps involved in quantization algorithm.

The neural network in this diagram receives full-precision activations and weights as input and generates full-precision outputs [18]. The weights and activations are then subjected to quantization by the quantization algorithm to decrease their precision, resulting in lower-precision weights and activations. Then, on edge devices with constrained resources, these lower-precision data can be used for inference.

The data has been quantized to 8 bits using uniform quantization, and this output is the result. With quantization to the nearest representable value of 0 or 1, each value is a floating-point number between 0 and 1. Since the quantized information is smaller in size, it may be transmitted more easily or stored more efficiently.

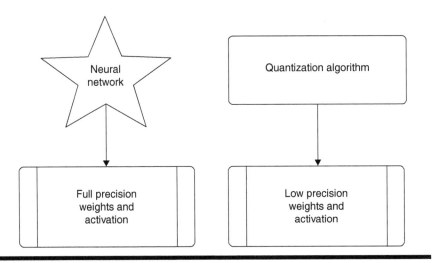

Figure 6.5   Quantization algorithm steps.

Keep in mind that the quantization range and bit depth can be tailored to the needs of the application and the available hardware [19].

6.4.4 Pruning

Pruning, a method for reducing the size and computational complexity of neural networks, is frequently employed in edge AI algorithms. As a result, less memory and processing power are needed to run the algorithm on edge devices. Pruning's fundamental goal is to eliminate small-weighted, insignificant connections from the neural network without significantly compromising the algorithm's performance as a whole.

Both before and after the network has been taught, pruning can be done. Pruning can be used as a regularizer during training to avoid overfitting and enhance the network's generalization capabilities. Pruning can be used to compress the network and lessen its computational complexity after training.

In order to create smaller, more effective neural networks that can be run on low-power edge devices with limited resources [20], pruning is a valuable strategy for edge AI algorithms.

The following is a simplified illustration of how weight pruning works in a neural network.

1. Train a neural network that contains all of the connections between the neurons.
2. Assess and rate the significance of each relationship (often based on the size of its weight).

3. Eliminate a particular portion of the connections that aren't essential (e.g., the connections with the smallest weights).
4. Retrain the pruned network to regain any performance lost as a result of the connections being cut.
5. Up until the appropriate level of pruning is reached, repeat steps 2–4.

The network will be smaller and have fewer connections as a result of pruning, making it easier to use on edge devices with constrained processing power.

6.4.4.1 Design of Pruning

- **Determine the criteria for pruning:** For choosing which connections, neurons, or filters should be pruned as the initial stage in creating a pruning algorithm. This may be based on a number of variables, including the size of the weight, patterns of activation, or other metrics that express the significance of a particular network component.
- **Set the pruning rate:** The percentage of connections, neurons, or filters that will be removed during each iteration is determined by the pruning rate. Usually, the desired level of compression is taken into account while setting this value, with greater pruning rates resulting in more aggressive compression but possibly worse performance [21].
- **Choose the pruning technique:** There are several methods for debugging neural networks, each having pros and cons, such as weight pruning, neuron pruning, and filter pruning. The technique selected will depend on the particular requirements and limitations of the application.
- **Determine the pruning schedule:** When and how frequently pruning is applied to the network is decided by the pruning schedule. To enhance performance and avoid overfitting, pruning can be carried either in a single pass after training or iteratively throughout training.
- **Evaluate the pruned network:** The network must be assessed when pruning is finished to make sure it satisfies the required performance standards. The trimming procedure can be repeated with other parameters if the performance is unsatisfactory until the required level of performance is reached.

In order to establish a network that properly satisfies the demands of the application, pruning algorithms must carefully weigh the trade-offs between compression, performance, and computational economy.

6.4.4.2 Pruning Techniques

The size and complexity of neural networks can be reduced using a variety of pruning approaches. The following are a few of the most popular pruning methods:

- **Weight pruning:** This method entails deleting from the neural network the connections with the least weights. According to the theory, these connections are less crucial to the network's overall performance and can be safely eliminated without significantly compromising accuracy.
- **Neuron pruning:** When a neuron is thought to be insignificant, the entire neuron is removed from the network. This may be determined by a number of factors, including the neuronal activation patterns or their contribution to the network's output.
- **Filter pruning:** Convolutional neural networks (CNNs)-specific filter pruning entails eliminating the entire network's convolutional filters. This can maintain the network's performance while significantly reducing the network's size and computational complexity.
- **Structured pruning:** Pruning that is structured entails the removal of entire subnetworks from the neural network, such as entire layers or collections of neurons. Comparing this to unstructured pruning techniques, it may improve performance while maintaining the network's overall structure.
- **Adversarial pruning:** A more contemporary technique named adversarial pruning means identifying and discarding the most crucial links from the network using adversarial assaults. This may result in compression that is more aggressive without compromising performance.

6.4.4.5 Edge Intelligence Network

A network of intelligent devices, including as sensors, cameras, and other edge devices, are referred to as an edge intelligence network (EIN) and are connected to a central processing unit for real-time analysis and decision-making. The EIN is created to process data locally at the network's edge, reducing latency and enhancing reaction time.

In the EIN, data generation devices at the network's edge can access sophisticated analytics and insights without having to send their data to a centralized place for examination. The EIN can increase system efficiency by processing data at the edge, which can assist lessen network traffic, cut costs, and limit the amount of data that needs to be transferred.

The EIN is especially helpful in real-time decision-making applications like autonomous vehicles, industrial automation, and smart cities. In these and other applications, the ability to process data locally at the network's edge can help to boost productivity, decrease response time, and improve safety.

The design of the EIN algorithm involves several steps. Here are some of the key steps:

- **Pinpoint the problem:** The problem that needs to be solved must be identified as the first step in building an EIN algorithm. This could involve anything from identifying sensor data anomalies to foretelling equipment failures.

■ **Facts assortment:** Data collection from edge devices is the next step after the issue has been located. This information may take the form of sensor readings, pictures, or other kinds of information.

■ **Data preprocessing:** Before being used for analysis, the data gathered from the edge devices may need to be preprocessed. This can entail scaling the data, removing outliers, or filtering out noise.

■ **Algorithm selection:** The preprocessing of the data must be followed by the selection of an appropriate algorithm for analysis. This can entail applying machine learning techniques like support vector machines, neural networks, or decision trees.

■ **Model training:** The preprocessed data must be used to train the chosen algorithm. In order to achieve correct results, the algorithm's parameters must be adjusted once the data is input.

■ **Model deployment:** The model must be deployed to the edge devices after it has been trained. Deploying the model to an edge device or a gateway device that can connect to the edge devices may be necessary.

■ **Real-time analysis:** The established model may now be used to analyze data produced by the edge devices in real time. This could entail spotting abnormalities, making failure predictions, or spotting trends.

■ **Feedback loop:** Lastly, the EIN algorithm can be strengthened using the findings of the real-time analysis. This can entail changing the algorithm's input parameters, gathering more information, or retraining the model.

In short, recognizing the issue, gathering and preparing data, choosing and training an appropriate algorithm, deploying the model to the edge devices, and using the model for real-time analysis are all steps in the creation of an EIN method.

6.4.4.5 Edge-to-Edge Communication

■ **Design edge-to-edge communication:** Edge-to-edge communication is the transfer of data and information between systems or devices at the edge of a network without the need of a cloud-based platform or centralized processing. The devices involved, the network architecture, and the communication protocols employed must all be taken into account when designing an edge-to-edge communication system. In order to create an edge-to-edge communication system, follow these steps:

■ **Define the communication requirements:** Determine the particular use case and the conditions for communication between the network's edge devices.

Take into account the various data types that must be transferred, the communication frequency, and any latency or reliability specifications.

■ **Choose the devices:** Choose the right hardware for your edge-to-edge communication system. They might include data-transmitting and -receiving sensors, controllers, gateways, and other edge devices.

■ **Select the communication protocol:** Choose a protocol for communication that complies with the demands of the edge-to-edge communication system. Take into account elements like data transmission speed, dependability, and security. MQTT, CoAP, and DDS are common edge-to-edge communication protocols.

■ **Plan the network infrastructure:** The network architecture needed to support the edge-to-edge communication system should be determined. Choosing the suitable network topology, network hardware, and network protocols may fall under this category.

■ **Develop the communication interface:** Describe the interface for communication between the devices that allows for data exchange. Depending on the unique needs of the edge-to-edge communication system, this may entail developing software interfaces, APIs, or hardware interfaces.

■ **Test and validate the system:** The edge-to-edge communication system should be extensively tested and validated after it has been created and put into use to make sure it fits all the requirements and performs as intended.

These methods will help you create a successful edge-to-edge communication system that permits seamless and effective communication between devices at the network's edge.

References

1. Shi, Y., Yang, K., Jiang, T., Zhang, J., & Letaief, K. B. (2020). Communication-efficient edge AI: Algorithms and systems. IEEE Communications Surveys & Tutorials, 1–1. doi:10.1109/comst.2020.3007787 10.1109/comst.2020.3007787.

2. Zhou, Z., Chen, X., Li, E., Zeng, L., Luo, K., & Zhang, J. (2019). Edge intelligence: Paving the last mile of artificial intelligence with edge computing. Proceedings of the IEEE, 1–25. doi:10.1109/jproc.2019.2918951 10.1109/jproc.2019.2918951.

3. H Hua, Y Li, T Wang, N Dong, W Li, J Cao–ACM Computing Surveys, 2023–dl.acm.org Edge Computing with Artificial Intelligence: A Machine Learning Perspective, Vol. 55, No. 9, Article 184. Publication date: January 2023.

4. J. Zhang and K. B. Letaief, "Mobile edge intelligence and computing for the internet of vehicles," Proc. IEEE, vol. 108, pp. 246–261, Feb. 2020. Z. Zhou, X. Chen, E. Li, L. Zeng, K. Luo, and J. Zhang, "Edge intelligence: Paving the last mile of artificial intelligence with edge computing," Proc. IEEE, vol. 107, pp. 1738–1762, Aug. 2019.

5. Y. Dong, J. Cheng, M. Hossain, V. Leung, et al., "Secure distributed on-device learning networks with byzantine adversaries," IEEE Netw.,vol. 33, pp. 180–187, Nov. 2019.

6. G. Zhu, D. Liu, Y. Du, C. You, J. Zhang, and K. Huang, "Towards an intelligent edge: Wireless communication meets machine learning," IEEE Commun. Mag., to appear.

7. K. Yang, T. Jiang, Y. Shi, and Z. Ding, "Federated learning via overtheair computation," IEEE Trans. Wireless Commun., 2020.

8. O. Shamir, N. Srebro, and T. Zhang, "Communication-efficient distributed optimization using an approximate newton-type method," in Proc. Int. Conf. Mach. Learn. (ICML), pp. 1000–1008, 2014.

9. V. Smith, C.-K. Chiang, M. Sanjabi, and A. S. Talwalkar, "Federated multi-task learning," in Proc. Neural Inf. Process. Syst. (NeurIPS), pp. 4427–4437, 2017.

10. M. Ye and E. Abbe, "Communication-computation efficient gradient coding," in Proc. Int. Conf. Mach. Learn. (ICML), pp. 5606–5615, 2018.

11. Aijaz Ali Khan, R. M. (2022). A Research on Efficient Spam Detection Technique for Iot Devices Using Machine Learning. NeuroQuantology, 625–631.

12. D.G, M. (2019, January). A review on implementing energy efficient clustering protocol for wireless sensor network. Journal of Emerging Technologies and Innovative Research (JETIR), Volume 6(Issue 1), 310–315.

13. D.G, T. (2019, January). A review on QoS aware routing protocols for wireless sensor networks. International Journal of Emerging Technologies and Innovative Research, Volume 6(Issue 1), 316–320.

14. D.G, T. (2019, January). A review on wireless sensor network: Its applications and challenges. Journal of Emerging Technologies and Innovative Research (JETIR), Volume 6(Issue 1), 222–226.

15. Dattatray G. Takale, R. R. (2022). Skin disease classification using machine learning algorithms. NeuroQuantology, 9624–9629.

16. Dattatray G. Takale, S. D. (2022). Road Accident Prediction Model Using Data Mining Techniques (Vol. 20). India, Maharashtra, India.

17. Dattatray G. Takale, S. S. (2022). Analysis of Students Performance Prediction in Online Courses Using Machine Learning Algorithms. Neuroquantology, 13–18.

18. Dattatray G. Takale, S. U. (2022). Machine Learning Methode for Automatic Potato Disease Detection (Vol. 20). India, Maharashtra, India.

19. Dr. Dattatray G. Takale, P. S. (May 2019). Load balancing energy efficient protocol for wireless sensor network. International Journal of Research and Analytical Reviews (IJRAR), 153–158.

20. Dr.Dattatray G. Takale, M. A. (2014, November). A study of fault management algorithm and recover the faulty node using the FNR algorithms for wireless sensor network. International Journal of Engineering Research and General Science, Volume 2(Issue 6), 590–595.

21. Takale D.G, D. K. (2019, January). A review on data centric routing for wireless sensor network. Journal of Emerging Technologies and Innovative Research (JETIR), Volume 6(Issue 1), 304–309.

COMPUTATIONAL INTELLIGENCE **III**

INTELLIGENCE

Edge Computing and

AI Applications

Chapter 7

Machine Learning- Based Hybrid Technique for Securing Edge Computing

P. William[1], Pravin B. Khatkale[2], and Yogeesh. N[3]

[1]Department of Information Technology, Sanjivani College of Engineering, SPPU, Pune, India

[2]Department of Mechatronics, Sanjivani K.B.P. Polytechnic, Kopargaon, India

[3]Department of Mathematics, Government First Grade College, Tumkur, Karnataka, India

7.1 Introduction

With the help of edge computing and the Internet of Things (IoT), mobile devices like tablets, smartphones, wearables, and personal digital assistants have changed industrial operations (PDAs). These days, mobile devices can provide cloud services that are more trustworthy, flexible, and extensible by using mobile edge computing (MEC) [1]. Many techniques of malware detection [2–4] have been developed to prevent the damage caused by such assaults. Static and dynamic Android security solutions are used to evaluate and analyze Android vulnerabilities and malware. Analyzing application code in this manner is known as "static analysis." It

DOI: 10.1201/9781032650722-10

is a technique that examines apps as they run and their connections with other system modules and networks. A large percentage of today's anti-malware tools don't account for the fact that malicious Android apps may have different permissions and intents. Utilizing various dynamic characteristics may aid in the detection of a number of malicious actions and application security concerns during run-time analysis. At the penalty of increased execution overhead, a thorough dynamic method can identify the majority of vulnerabilities and security threats. As part of this study, we provide an all-encompassing technique that takes into consideration dynamic factors including data leaks, network connection manipulation, and the imposition of certain permissions while also integrating static analysis. The following are the significant contributions of this research.

7.2 Literature Review

7.2.1 Static Analysis Based on Malware Detection

Static examination of permissions may be done by using the manifest file, according to Arora et al. [5]. Using real Android malware samples, a lightweight malware detection method was developed and tested. Permissions were gleaned from the manifest file and matched to a set of predefined keywords. Intentions and API requests were not included in the model since it only considered one aspect of vulnerability. Another study [6-8] looked at the semantically rich features of intentions (both explicit and implicit) to encode the harmful aims of malware, especially when paired with permissions.

An intent-based filtering and permission system was proposed by the author. Almin and Chatterjee [5] utilized the k-means clustering approach to identify programs that misused their authority to engage in destructive behavior. Comparing the study to well-known antivirus solutions revealed that the suggested approach was capable of detecting malware that was previously undetectable by the majority of antivirus software. MalDozer [9–11] is an artificial neural network-based system that accepts raw sequences of API method calls in the same order as they appear in the.dex file for the purpose of detecting and classifying android malware. The raw method call sequences in the assembly code may be examined by MalDozer to find harmful patterns automatically during training. A framework [12–15] has been proposed that uses multiple qualities to show the multidimensional aspects of Android applications that are critical for virus identification. An advanced deep neural network was utilized to identify features with different characteristics. In addition to Opcode, API, permissions, and other static features like permissions, components, as well as environmental and string attributes, they focused their attention on these. The Virus-Share and Malgenome projects' data sets were used for the experiments. It was found that the proposed method has an accuracy rate of up to 98%. In addition to static features [16–18], the authors also looked at dynamic factors that may help identify zero-day threats and malware that has been camouflaged. Multiple aspects of an Android application were reconstructed, and multiple CNNs were used to identify malware effectively. A total of 23,000 Android applications were used in the empirical study, which yielded a precision rate of 99.8%.

7.2.2 Dynamic Analysis Based on Malware Detection

An application's behavior may be observed while it is operating as part of a dynamic analysis. Bouncer, a dynamic analysis-based security architecture created by Wang et al. for Android, was introduced by Google in 2012 [16]. When a new app is submitted to the Google Play store, it is initially tested on Google Cloud infrastructure, according to executives from the company (using software named Bouncer). Malware assaults on the Google Play store may be prevented using the Bouncer. System calls were used by Canfora et al. [8] to design a strategy for identifying malware attacks. System calls may have been used to carry out harmful acts, according to the researchers. There's an Android software called IntelliDroid that may be used to track down hazardous behavior that occurs while an application is running. IntelliDroid was able to track down instances of API calls that were made. Several events were produced by the recommended system's inputs to keep track of how the program was being used. API sequence analysis was offered by the authors of [19–20] as a dynamic technique. The proposed system is compared to a reference database of API call sequences once it has been extracted. If a match is detected, a warning is sent about the potential presence of malware.

7.2.3 Hybrid Malware Analysis Techniques

The proposed method's static component discovers possible assaults and classifies programs as benign or harmful based on this information. The proposed dynamic analysis comprises the application's behavior as a result of numerous code components. Code coverage for the prototype model was sufficient because to the use of attack trees (ordered rules). Rules had to be manually created and dynamic analysis had to be carried out manually. The Application Sandbox (Sandbox) approach, introduced by Blasing et al. [21–25], is capable of detecting malicious applications using hybrid analysis. Decompiling Index files into a human-readable format was done using the proposed analyzer's static component. Anomalies in the coding are also looked for. During the execution of an application in a sandbox environment, the proposed system gathered low-level information on the interactions between the various components of the system. Analysis system security and privacy were ensured through sandboxing in a secure environment. An application may be monitored using the Monkey tool [25] by producing random events, which is the dynamic element of the recommended strategy. Unknown or unique kinds of malware could not be detected by the system, which was one of its flaws. To find malware patterns on a local host, system calls were used to do dynamic analysis. Up to 98 percent of malware may be detected using SAMADroid's trial results. Thus, applications are examined statistically. Only system calls are analyzed in the dynamic analysis done. Code obfuscation is a well-developed area of study, and many malwares are able to bypass system call inspections by using this technique. As a consequence, it is necessary to check out more dynamic elements like network activity, API calls, and actual executable code. [26–29] An approach to detecting all of a program's interesting API's flow paths has been put forward. They preferred static analysis over dynamic analysis since dynamic analysis is not always capable of extracting all important APIs. When using permissions and payloads, the proposed static analysis technique neglects the close relationship between intents and permission. Sometimes, depending on rights alone is not enough to identify malware [30].

Q1: What static characteristics—such as permissions and specific purpose patterns—are most crucial for identifying Android malware?

Q2: Which combination of dynamic elements—including system calls—such as network activity, file access, SMS and phone call activity, external DexClass usage, data leakage, cryptography activity, and run-time permissions—is essential for Android malware identification?

Q3: By integrating hybrid analysis and machine learning-based categorization, how can we increase malware detection rates?

HybriDroid, an Android-based hybrid malware detection system based on machine learning, was created to address these problems.

7.3 Proposed Hybrid Malware Analysis

HybriDroid and cHybriDroid, two machine learning-based hybrid malware analyzers, may be used to gauge the impact of hybridization. Static and dynamic malware are both evaluated by HybriDroid using a hierarchical technique. It is initially analyzed using static characteristics and then the suspicious applications are checked using dynamic attributes. The cHybriDroid framework is also presented to assess the impact of combination analysis on the results (using both static and dynamic characteristics).

7.3.1 HybriDroid Architecture

A framework for analyzing Android malware, HybriDroid, is presented in this section (shown in Figure 7.1). Static and dynamic phases are separated by a hierarchical framework in the hybrid approach proposed in this chapter (as depicted in Figure 7.2). APK files are first broken down into XML and Java files for static analysis. A further step is to examine the application's XML files for permissions and intents. The machine learning-based static analyzer that is recommended is fed with

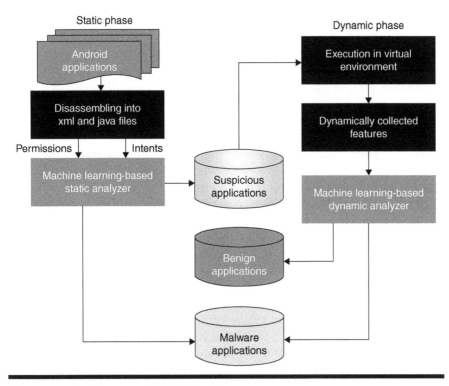

Figure 7.1   Architecture of *HybriDroid*.

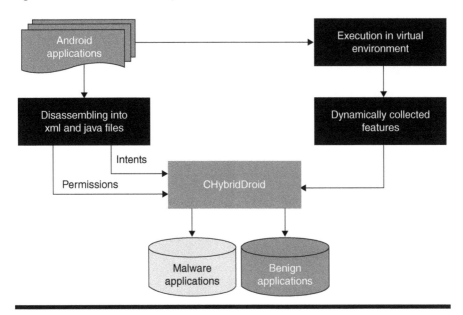

Figure 7.2   Architecture of cHybriDroid.

these properties. In order to determine whether or not a program is malicious or suspicious, the machine learning-based analyzer uses static properties. In order to perform additional investigations into dubious applications, a dynamic analysis phase is triggered. Following this, the dynamic analyzer is used to examine the programs runtime behavior [31–33].

7.3.2 Classifier Training for HybriDroid and cHybriDroid

The entire training procedure for the proposed HybriDroid malware analyzer is shown in Figure 7.3(a). 50 percent of the clean Android apps and 50 percent of the malicious Android apps make up the training data set.

The data set's applications are then compared to these intents and permissions. It is set to 1 if the purpose or permission of an application matches one of the retrieved permissions, and to 0 otherwise. 407 different values are used to build a feature vector [34–35]. The static machine learning analyzer receives these feature vectors and the application's classification or label at the same time (i.e., malicious or benign). Similar to this, half of the training data for the benign and half of the training data for the malware-based dynamic analyzer were completed in a virtual environment during the HybriDroid framework's training (i.e., DroidBox [36]). An application's kind (malware or benign) and a total of 15 distinct dynamic characteristics are sent to the dynamic analyzer (HybriDroid). The hyperparameters may be tuned using a K-fold cross-validation technique and a grid search mechanism A single machine learning-based analyzer is used to educate cHybriDroid simultaneously on static and dynamic properties, as shown in Figure 7.3(b). Android applications have their static and dynamic characteristics retrieved and sent to the cHybrid-combined Droid's analyzer (i.e., benign or malware). Analyzers for both static and dynamic features are trained using 432 unique feature vectors.

7.4 Experimental Results

The tests were conducted using a personal computer. We used five machine learning classifiers to assess the proposed frameworks, HybriDroid and cHybriDroid.

7.4.1 Data Set

There are 5,560 malwares in total in the benchmark Drebin [3] data collection, some of which are included and come from 179 different malware families. Studies on Android virus detection often employ Drebin.

7.4.2 Feature Selection

E-permissions are a critical static element that must be carefully studied to protect against any security issues. Along with permissions, intentions inside Android apps

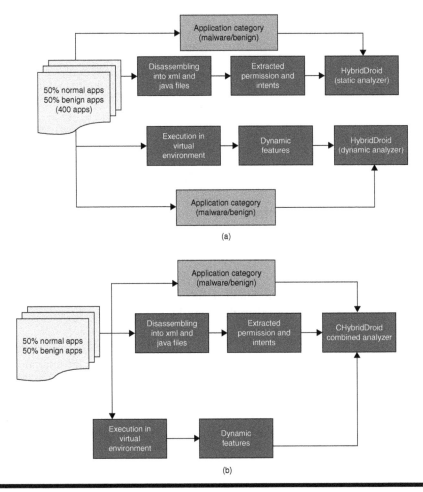

Figure 7.3   Training methodology. (a) Training of static and dynamic machine learning analyzers for *HybriDroid*. (b) Training of the combined analyzer for cHybriDroid.

are another critical feature that requires thorough examination. A component of Android's complex messaging architecture, intents allow a variety of applications, services, and OS operations to be executed. As a result of the use of intent filters, various activities, broadcast receivers, and services might be engaged and their intentions documented in a manifest file. Research shows that malware often abuses the user's intents and rights [10, 37] (e.g., intent spoofing and permission collusion). Because of this, it is imperative that they be thoroughly examined in order to uncover any potentially dangerous activities. The following dataset highlights the details of dataset. Table 7.1 highlights the details of Dataset and Table 7.2 describes the project setup requirements.

Table 7.1   Details of Dataset

Application Type	Number of Applications	Application Categories
Benign	2500	28 different categories
Malware	2500	178 different families

Table 7.2   Experimental Setup Requirements

Processor	Intel Core (TM)
Memory	16GB
Operating System	Ubuntu 16.04LTS
Machine Learning Toolkit	Weka 3.6

7.4.3 Feature Ranking

A reduced feature set is used to eliminate redundant data, minimize overfitting, boost classification accuracy, and cut the algorithm's training time by reducing the number of features that are used [38–40].

Because of the large number of features generated by the dynamic analysis, only the most important ones have to be included in the machine learning model. The information gain technique [41] is used to identify patterns in the attributes employed in the data set's applications. A score is assigned to each property based on how useful it is for categorization. One of the most often used feature selection methods is the well-known InfoGain approach, which tracks entropy changes before and after an observation [42]. To determine how much information has been gained, use the following formula:

$$\text{infoGain}(P, F) = \text{Entropy}(P) - \text{Entropy}(Pv)$$

In this example, C is the class set and Pc is the subset of P that belongs to the c-class. According to some researchers, information gathering is an easy procedure that yields the greatest possible outcome (in our example, virus or benign). More than 400 features may be narrowed down to 172, including permissions and intentions, using InfoGain [43].

7.4.4 Result Discussion

Without choosing any features, TPOT has the highest F-measure (0.91). Naive Bayes achieves accuracy of 0.98 despite TPOT having a recall of 0.91. When features are chosen, TPOT F-measure decreases from 0.91 to 0.87. With an accuracy of 0.88

and an F-measure of 0.88, random forest produced the best outcome. Rough wood-land. The model's poorer performance indicates that the accuracy of the classifiers was only marginally impacted by the deletion of features. Without feature selection, TPO provides the best 0.94 F-measure, which is 0.03 percent superior to the static features offered. This is because TPOT reduced the features from 422 to 20, which resulted in an F-measure loss of up to 0.02.

The extra tree classifier outperforms the other classifier since the random value is utilized for feature consideration. As a probabilistic classifier, Naive Bayes does not need the selection of tuning parameters. Our evolutionary technique was used to achieve hypertuning, which was essential for TPOT. StackedEstimator (LogisticRegression with C=0.1, dual=True, penalty= "l2") and GaussianNB are the TPOT model tuning options. It was because the TPOT technique employed a stack-creation strategy that beat the other classifiers.

7.4.5 Prediction Model Overhead

The cHybriDroid is trained offline. Because a feature is extracted at build time, there is very little cost associated with the cHybriDroid prediction (approximately 1 second overall). The expense of training a prediction model is one-time only. In summary, the prediction model has a tiny overhead, namely two seconds for a single application. We tried with both malicious and benign Android apps using the hybrid analysis technique.

Our research showed that combining static and dynamic application attributes results in an impressive level of malware detection accuracy. We further refined the performance and accuracy of the two suggested hybrid techniques using the fea-ture ranking mechanism. The decreased number of characteristics and the use of just the most critical ones leads to improved detection performance and accuracy. We used two methodologies for hybrid malware analysis: (1) HybriDroid and (2) cHybriDroid. An investigation of hybrid malware utilizing both static and dynamic or run-time properties was often the goal of the HybriDroid approach. It was also used to assess the efficiency of malware detection when both static and dynamic properties were analyzed simultaneously. We found that HybriDroid has a 97% F-measure, which is higher than the 96% F-measure for the Malwarebytes. With the other models tested, we found the TPOT [28] model to be the most successful (for cHybriDroid). False Positive (FPR) and True Positive (TPR) rates were obtained to better understand cHybriDroid classification performance (TPR). Topping the list was the TPOT [28] machine learning model, with a TPR of 96%. Additionally, TPOT's machine learning model's r2 value shows how effective the programme is in spotting malicious code in the wild. It was shown that cHybriDroid, a hierarchical hybrid strategy, was more accurate in detecting malware than the combined hybrid approach (i.e., HybriDroid).

7.4.6 Analysis

We used a huge data set to train the analytical tool and then applied the enhanced machine learning settings. Static examination of the manifest file, which contains permission tags and application intents, is the first step in the proposed security procedure. Preventing malware from executing is the primary goal of static analysis. While it is possible that an incorrect prediction might be made, it is more likely that an incorrect prediction could be made than that an incorrect prediction could be made. Exhaustive testing is required for the dynamic approach, which increases the execution time. The recommended technique may be used to the hybrid model if the model is unknown. Ransomware and antagonistic attacks may benefit from this method. Data sets of any size may benefit from this method. In order to recognize and classify ransomware programs, we can train an ensemble machine learning using the aforementioned characteristics.

7.5 Conclusion and Future Work

Android is currently thought to be the most extensively used smartphone operating system. The Android platform has thus attracted a large number of malware specialists wanting to gain significant financial and societal benefits. To assist in reducing malware activity, many malware detection methods have been presented. On the other hand, our hybrid malware detection system makes use of a variety of crucial static and dynamic features in a cutting-edge machine learning-based methodology. The effect of various machine learning classifiers on the identification of malware was also examined in the study. This study demonstrates the importance of selecting characteristics from the data set for building a machine learning-based malware detection system. The qualities that are chosen are determined by the analytical technique used to extract the data. The trained classifier has an F-measure of 97% and a r2 of 0.91. The FPR is extremely low, at 0.04, but the TPR is also excellent, at 0.96. We wish to give code coverage, memory utilization, and network information for programs that are now operating in the future (for dynamic analysis). The classifiers will also receive guidance on how to categorize the malware into subclasses.

References

[1] P. Calciati, K. Kuznetsov, A. Gorla, and A. Zeller, "Automatically granted permissions in android apps," in *Proceedings of the International Conference on Mining Software Repositories*, pp. 114–124, Montreal, Canada, May 2020.

[2] M. K. Alzaylaee, S. Y. Yerima, and S. S. Dynalog, "An automated dynamic analysis framework for characterizing android applications," 2016, http://arxiv.org/abs/1607.08166.

[3] D. Arp, M. Spreitzenbarth, M. Hubner, H. Gascon, and K. Rieck, "DREBIN: effective and explainable detection of android malware in your pocket," in *Proceedings of the Annual Network and Distributed System Security Symposium*, pp. 1–15, San Diego, CA, USA, March 2014.

[4] M. Y. Wong and D. Lie, "IntelliDroid: a targeted input generator for the dynamic analysis of android malware," in *Proceedings of the Annual Network and Distributed System Security Symposium*, University of Toronto, Toronto, Canada, 2016.

[5] P. William, Y. N, V. M. Tidake, S. Sumit Gondkar, C. R and K. Vengatesan, "Framework for implementation of personality inventory model on natural language processing with personality traits analysis," 2023 International Conference on Intelligent Data Communication Technologies and Internet of Things (IDCIoT), Bengaluru, India, 2023, pp. 625–628, doi: 10.1109/IDCIoT56793.2023.10053501.

[6] Prashant Madhukar Yawalkar, Deepak Narayan Paithankar, Abhijeet Rajendra Pabale, Rushikesh Vilas Kolhe, P. William, Integrated identity and auditing management using blockchain mechanism, Measurement: Sensors, 2023, 100732, ISSN 2665-9174, https://doi.org/10.1016/j.measen.2023.100732.

[7] P. William et al., "Divination of air quality assessment using ensembling machine learning approach," 2023 International Conference on Artificial Intelligence and Knowledge Discovery in Concurrent Engineering (ICECONF), Chennai, India, 2023, pp. 1–10, doi: 10.1109/ICECONF57129.2023.10083751.

[8] P. S. Chobe, D. B. Padale, D. B. Pardeshi, N. M. Borawake and P. William, "Deployment of framework for charging electric vehicle based on various topologies," 2023 International Conference on Artificial Intelligence and Knowledge Discovery in Concurrent Engineering (ICECONF), Chennai, India, 2023, pp. 1–4, doi: 10.1109/ICECONF57129.2023.10084062.

[9] D. B. Pardeshi, A. K. Chaudhari, P. Thokal, R. S. Dighe and P. William, "Framework for deployment ofsSmart motor starter using android automation tool," 2023 International Conference on Artificial Intelligence and Knowledge Discovery in Concurrent Engineering (ICECONF), Chennai, India, 2023, pp. 1–6, doi: 10.1109/ICECONF57129.2023.10083946.

[10] H. P. Varade, S. C. Bhangale, S. R. Thorat, P. B. Khatkale, S. K. Sharma and P. William, "Framework of air pollution assessment in smart cities using IoT with machine learning approach," 2023 2nd International Conference on Applied Artificial Intelligence and Computing (ICAAIC), Salem, India, 2023, pp. 1436–1441, doi: 10.1109/ICAAIC56838.2023.10140834.

[11] Dhanabal, S., William, P., Vengatesan, K., Harshini, R., Kumar, V.D.A., Yuvaraj, S. (2023). Implementation and Comparative Analysis of Various Energy-Efficient Clustering Schemes in AODV. In: Venkataraman, N., Wang, L., Fernando, X., Zobaa, A.F. (eds) Big Data and Cloud Computing. ICBCC 2022. Lecture Notes in Electrical Engineering, vol 1021. Springer, Singapore. https://doi.org/10.1007/978-981-99-1051-9_19.

[12] Rushikesh Vilas Kolhe, P. William, Prashant Madhukar Yawalkar, Deepak Narayan Paithankar, Abhijeet Rajendra Pabale, Smart city implementation based on Internet of Things integrated with optimization technology, Measurement: Sensors, Volume 27, 2023, 100789, ISSN 2665-9174, https://doi.org/10.1016/j.measen.2023.100789.

[13] M.A. Jawale, P. William, A.B. Pawar, Nikhil Marriwala, Implementation of number plate detection system for vehicle registration using IOT and recognition using CNN, Measurement: Sensors, Volume 27, 2023, 100761, ISSN 2665-9174, https://doi.org/10.1016/j.measen.2023.100761.

[14] P. William, G. R. Lanke, D. Bordoloi, A. Shrivastava, A. P. Srivastavaa and S. V. Deshmukh, "Assessment of human activity recognition based on impact of feature extraction prediction accuracy," 2023 4th International Conference on Intelligent Engineering and Management (ICIEM), London, United Kingdom, 2023, pp. 1–6, doi: 10.1109/ICIEM59379.2023.10166247.

[15] P. William, G. R. Lanke, V. N. R. Inukollu, P. Singh, A. Shrivastava and R. Kumar, "Framework for design and implementation of chat support system using natural language processing," 2023 4th International Conference on Intelligent Engineering and Management (ICIEM), London, United Kingdom, 2023, pp. 1–7, doi: 10.1109/ICIEM59379.2023.10166939.

[16] P. William, A. Shrivastava, U. S. Aswal, I. Kumar, M. Gupta and A. K. Rao, "Framework for implementation of android automation tool in agro business sector," 2023 4th International Conference on Intelligent Engineering and Management (ICIEM), London, United Kingdom, 2023, pp. 1–6, doi: 10.1109/ICIEM59379.2023.10167328.

[17] P. William, G. R. Lanke, S. Pundir, I. Kumar, M. Gupta and S. Shaw, "Implementation of hand written based signature verification technology using deep learning approach," 2023 4th International Conference on Intelligent Engineering and Management (ICIEM), London, United Kingdom, 2023, pp. 1–6, doi: 10.1109/ICIEM59379.2023.10167195.

[18] P. William, V. N. R. Inukollu, V. Ramasamy, P. Madan, A. Shrivastava and A. Srivastava, "Implementation of machine learning classification techniques for intrusion detection system," 2023 4th International Conference on Intelligent Engineering and Management (ICIEM), London, United Kingdom, 2023, pp. 1–7, doi: 10.1109/ICIEM59379.2023.10167390.

[19] Korde, S. K., Rakshe, D. S., William, P., Jawale, M. A., & Pawar, A. B. (2023). Experimental investigations on copper-based nanoparticles for energy storage applications. *Journal of Nano-and Electronic Physics*, *15*(3), pp. 03002-1–03002-5.

[20] Rakshe, D. S., William, P., Jawale, M. A., Pawar, A. B., Korde, S. K., & Deshpande, N. (2023). Synthesis and characterization of Graphene based nanomaterials for energy applications. *Journal of Nano-and Electronic Physics*, *15*(3), pp. 03020-1–03020-5.

[21] Jawale, M. A., Pawar, A. B., Korde, S. K., Rakshe, D. S., William, P., & Deshpande, N. (2023). Energy management in electric vehicles using improved Swarm Optimized Deep Reinforcement Learning Algorithm. *Journal of Nano-and Electronic Physics*, *15*(3), pp. 03004-1–03004-6.

[22] Rashmi, M., William, P., Yogeesh, N., Girija, D.K. (2023). Blockchain-Based Cloud Storage Using Secure and Decentralised Solution. In: Chaki, N., Roy, N.D., Debnath, P., Saeed, K. (eds) Proceedings of International Conference on Data Analytics and Insights, ICDAI 2023. ICDAI 2023. Lecture Notes in Networks and Systems, vol 727. Springer, Singapore. https://doi.org/10.1007/978-981-99-3878-0_23.

[23] Girija, D.K., Rashmi, M., William, P., Yogeesh, N. (2023). Framework for Integrating the Synergies of Blockchain with AI and IoT for Secure Distributed

Systems. In: Chaki, N., Roy, N.D., Debnath, P., Saeed, K. (eds) Proceedings of International Conference on Data Analytics and Insights, ICDAI 2023. ICDAI 2023. Lecture Notes in Networks and Systems, vol 727. Springer, Singapore. https://doi.org/10.1007/978-981-99-3878-0_22.

[24] G. Canfora, E. Medvet, F. Mercaldo, and C. A. Visaggio, "Detecting android malware using sequences of system calls," in *Proceedings of the International Workshop on Software Development Lifecycle for Mobile*, pp. 13–20, Bergamo, Italy, August 2015.

[25] S. J. Hussain, U. Ahmed, H. Liaquat, S. Mir, N. Z. Jhanjhi, and M. Humayun, "IMIAD: intelligent malware identification for android platform," in *Proceedings of the International Conference on Computer and Information Sciences*, pp. 1–6,Sakaka, Saudi Arabia, April 2019.

[26] F. Ali, N. B. Anuar, R. Salleh, G. Suarez-Tangil, and S. Furnell, "AndroDialysis: Analysis of android intent effectiveness in malware detection," *Computers & Security*, vol. 65, pp. 121–134, 2017.

[27] E. B. Karbab, M. Debbabi, A. Derhab, and D. M. Maldozer, "Automatic framework for android malware detection using deep learning," *Digital Investigation*, vol. 24, no. S48–S59, 2018.

[28] P. William, D. Jadhav, P. Cholke, M. A. Jawale and A. B. Pawar, "Framework for product anti-counterfeiting using blockchain technology," 2022 International Conference on Sustainable Computing and Data Communication Systems (ICSCDS), 2022, pp. 1254–1258, doi: 10.1109/ICSCDS53736.2022.9760916.

[29] R. Jadhav, A. Shaikh, M. A. Jawale, A. B. Pawar and P. William, "System for identifying fake product using blockchain technology," 2022 7th International Conference on Communication and Electronics Systems (ICCES), 2022, pp. 851–854, doi: 10.1109/ICCES54183.2022.9835866.

[30] P. William, Y. N., S. Vimala, P. Gite and S. K. S, "Blockchain technology for data privacy using contract mechanism for 5G networks," 2022 3rd International Conference on Intelligent Engineering and Management (ICIEM), 2022, pp. 461–465, doi: 10.1109/ICIEM54221.2022.9853118.

[31] A.B. Pawar, M.A. Jawale, P. William, G.S. Chhabra, Dhananjay S. Rakshe, Sachin K. Korde, Nikhil Marriwala, Implementation of blockchain technology using extended CNN for lung cancer prediction, Measurement: Sensors, 2022, 100530, ISSN 2665-9174, https://doi.org/10.1016/j.measen.2022.100530.

[32] P. William, A. Shrivastava, H. Chauhan, P. Nagpal, V. K. T. N and P. Singh, "Framework for intelligent smart city deployment via artificial intelligence software networking," 2022 3rd International Conference on Intelligent Engineering and Management (ICIEM), 2022, pp. 455–460, doi: 10.1109/ICIEM54221.2022.9853119.

[33] S. S. Gondkar, D. B. Pardeshi and P. William, "Innovative system for water level management using IoT to prevent water wastage," 2022 International Conference on Applied Artificial Intelligence and Computing (ICAAIC), 2022, pp. 1555–1558, doi: 10.1109/ICAAIC53929.2022.9792746.

[34] S. S. Gondkar, P. William and D. B. Pardeshi, "Design of a novel IoT framework for home automation using google assistant," 2022 6th International Conference on Intelligent Computing and Control Systems (ICICCS), 2022, pp. 451–454, doi: 10.1109/ICICCS53718.2022.9788284.

[35] S. Choubey, P. William, A. B. Pawar, M. A. Jawale, K. Gupta and V. Parganiha, "Intelligent water level monitoring and water pump controlling system using IOT," 2022 3rd International Conference on Electronics and Sustainable Communication Systems (ICESC), 2022, pp. 423–427, doi: 10.1109/ICESC54411.2022.9885358.

[36] Deepak Narayan Paithankar, Abhijeet Rajendra Pabale, Rushikesh Vilas Kolhe, P. William, Prashant Madhukar Yawalkar, Framework for implementing air quality monitoring system using LPWA-based IoT technique, Measurement: Sensors,2023,100709,ISSN 2665-9174, https://doi.org/10.1016/j.measen.2023.100709.

[37] K. Gupta, S. Choubey, Y. N, P. William, V. T. N and C. P. Kale, "Implementation of motorist weariness detection system using a conventional object recognition technique," 2023 International Conference on Intelligent Data Communication Technologies and Internet of Things (IDCIoT), Bengaluru, India, 2023, pp. 640–646, doi: 10.1109/IDCIoT56793.2023.10052783.

[38] P. William, Y. N, V. M. Tidake, S. Sumit Gondkar, C. R and K. Vengatesan, "Framework for implementation of personality iInventory model on natural language processing with personality traits analysis," 2023 International Conference on Intelligent Data Communication Technologies and Internet of Things (IDCIoT), Bengaluru, India, 2023, pp. 625–628, doi: 10.1109/IDCIoT56793.2023.10053501.

[39] A. B. Pawar, P. Gawali, M. Gite, M. A. Jawale and P. William, "Challenges for hate speech recognition system: Approach based on solution," 2022 International Conference on Sustainable Computing and Data Communication Systems (ICSCDS), 2022, pp. 699–704, doi: 10.1109/ICSCDS53736.2022.9760739.

[40] P. William, D. Jadhav, P. Cholke, M. A. Jawale and A. B. Pawar, "Framework for product anti-counterfeiting using blockchain technology," 2022 International Conference on Sustainable Computing and Data Communication Systems (ICSCDS), 2022, pp. 1254–1258, doi: 10.1109/ICSCDS53736.2022.9760916.

[41] S. Arshad, M. A. Shah, A. Wahid, A. Mehmood, H. Song, and H. Yu, "Samadroid: A novel 3-level hybrid malware detection model for android operating system," *IEEE Access*, vol. 6, pp. 4321–4339, 2018.

[42] S. Hou, A. Saas, L. Chen, and Y. Ye, "Deep4maldroid: A deep learning framework for android malware detection based on linux kernel system call graphs," in *Proceedings of the IEEE/ WIC/ACM International Conference on Web Intelligence–Workshops*, Omaha, NE, USA, October 2016.

[43] A. Pektas and T. Acarman, "Ensemble machine learning approach for android malware classification using hybrid features," in *Proceedings of the International Conference on Computer Recognition Systems*, Wroclaw, Poland, May 2017.

Chapter 8

A Study of Secure Deployment of Mobile Services in Edge Computing

P. William[1], Pravin B. Khatkale[2], and Yogeesh. N[3]

[1]Department of Information Technology,
Sanjivani College of Engineering, SPPU, Pune, India

[2]Department of Mechatronics, Sanjivani K.B.P. Polytechnic, Kopargaon, India

[3]Department of Mathematics, Government First Grade College,
Tumkur, Karnataka, India

8.1 Introduction

The partnership between Nokia Siemens and IBM resulted in the creation of the mobile edge computing (MEC) platform in 2013, which launched in 2013 and enables applications to operate natively on MEC devices. After that, the Mobile Equipment Consortium (MEC) was standardized by the European Telecommunication Standards Institute (ETSI) and the Industry Specification Group (ISG) (ISG). MEC has been identified as a fundamental component of 5G network infrastructure by the European 5G Infrastructure Public Private Partnership [1]. In recent years, there has been a rise in the number of people using Internet of Things (IoT) devices, including wearable technology, sensors, and other types of IoT gadgets [2]. According to projections made by Ericsson, by the year 2030 there will be more than 32 billion mobile devices linked to the network. With the exponential growth of terminal equipment and data, it is easy to understand how online service providers will face substantial hurdles when attempting to offer terminal users with steady and low-latency connections [3–4]. When confronted with the challenges, the scientists came to the conclusion that it would be beneficial to locate processing resources, network management functions, and data caches in close proximity to micro- or macro-basic stations. Computing at the mobile edge is the phrase used to describe this kind of technology [4]. Edge servers often provide service to certain geographic zones inside a network in order to optimize user connections. It is anticipated that there will be many edge servers situated in various parts of the globe. As a direct result of this, resources are squandered as a result of their coverage often overlapping one another. Since MEC's coverage is insufficient, operators are required to charge a premium. It is possible that the edge servers nearest to the user won't be able to handle user requests, and it may be difficult to move such requests to another server [5–6]. Yet, concerns such as the leaking of user data and the security of terminal devices need to be addressed as soon as possible. The challenges that were discussed before are what the author of this chapter refers to as secure edge computing service deployment since they are the outcome of service deployment. There are three approaches used to analyze secure mobile service deployment.

8.1.1 MEC Service Deployment

A flexible and effective MEC service deployment is needed to address future demands for low latency, mission critical, and IoT applications. Furthermore, it must be safe and easy to maintain. The MEC servers must host the services provided to users. So, when designed correctly, a MEC server can appropriately handle user requests. No service is actually deployed on the MEC server receiving the query; instead, the query is sent to the nearest MEC server for execution. The chosen MEC node must also provide Quality of Service for the requested service if there are many nearby MEC nodes providing it. In order to choose the most appropriate final node, we create a model for the RTT between mobile devices and MEC servers. Mobile device processing times may be affected when many mobile devices access the same MEC. Since the MEC has a lot of computing power, the service discovery method needs to take this into consideration. On the other hand, MEC enables applications to operate at the edge of the network, while NFV is more concerned with the operations of the network. On the same platform, infrastructure management that spans from MEC to NFV or services on networks may be repurposed to host virtual network functions and MEC apps [7]. Operators may now perform essential services near to end-devices thanks to the advent of MEC services. Users and content suppliers may also create and administer their own context-aware services using this technology. 5G demands that MEC be implemented in order to meet the tremendous expectations of both users and operators in the future. MEC implementation may also alleviate the problem of inflexibility [8].

8.1.2 Computation Offloading

Offloading may be broken down into three categories: local execution, in which the computation is carried out locally and does not need contact with the MEC [9]. Partial offloading, instead of full offloading, means that just a portion of the computation is offloaded, with the remainder performed locally [10]. Compute offloading may be less stressful if the right service is implemented. Billions of mobile devices are now linked to the Internet. There are significant difficulties in limiting computation to the central cloud due to the common belief among researchers that mobile compute offloading depends on a central cloud [11]. Thus, MEC relies heavily on the offloading of computations [12]. Optimizing only one piece will not ensure a positive user experience, since offloading computation and allocating resources are integral parts of the universal system [13–14].

8.1.3 Data Placement

As a result of the fast expansion of MEC services, prominent service providers are increasingly turning to the deployment of a distributed network of data centers in order to provide their clients with superior levels of service. It is possible to prevent significant data transmission delays by using this method. Using mobile devices generates a lot of data, which is then archived for future use. It is necessary to send data to distant data centers for processing since mobile devices have limited storage space [15]. For the purposes of classification, data placement may be divided into two types: random and purposeful. There is a random distribution of sensors, whereas there is a deliberate installation of sensors [16]. The following conditions must be met in order for a data placement to be successful: Data sets are large and complex, and the organization of the research process is difficult. In order to cut down on the amount of time it takes to transport information between data centers for edge computing and cloud computing, there has to be a strong cohesiveness inside the data centers and little coupling between the data centers. It is recommended that private data be kept in data centers near network edges for data security reasons. Since the storage capacity of edge data centers is limited, transferring some files from one data center to another is necessary. Because of the restricted bandwidth and the stated privacy of the data sets, it might be difficult to install low-latency data sets [17]. According to the chapter's structure, we will first review the basics of mobile devices and MEC, including definitions and nomenclature. Our next step is to examine current frameworks for commercial MEC deployment safety and propose a new framework. A variety of deployment tactics and technologies will also be discussed.

Next, we will have a look at some of the issues with safe deployment. As an added bonus, we provide many solutions for bridging these holes. After that, we will talk about a few unresolved concerns. Mobile service implementation security is also summarized.

8.2 Basic Concepts and Definitions

This section discusses the fundamental principles and terminology of MEC.

8.2.1 Service Deployment

The delivery of services often makes use of technology related to virtualization. A deployed service may be thought of as either a virtual machine (VM) or a group of virtual machines working together as a single entity. The service is comprized of both the functional and nonfunctional requirements for a single deployment target. The network function virtualization (NFV) technologies, software-defined networking (SDN), and cloud computing form the backbone of the MEC deployment. The term "virtualization" refers to a framework that may be used to create and manage network services. The separation of network hardware and software is one of the most important aspects of NFV [18–19]. SDNs are networks controlled by programmes. Logically centralized control programmes that have a global network perspective and are written directly to the switch using a standard API are responsible for keeping track of the status of the network [20].

8.2.2 Mobile Edge Computing

As shown in Figure 8.1, the first step in the process involves the transmission of data to MEC from terminal devices, which may include mobile devices and automobiles among other things. After this step, the majority of the computation is done by MEC, while the remainder is sent to the cloud. With MEC, the central cloud data center operations are "sunk" to the network edge, which is located closer to mobile end users. Operators install MEC close to end users in order to offer essential computing, storage, and other services.

An open cloud platform that depends on some of the end-users and is placed on the mobile edge to conduct vast volumes of real-time storage has been defined as MEC by a variety of academics. These definitions characterize MEC as a mobile edge computing system (rather than being predominantly kept in cloud data centers). MEC can provide a service environment with very low latency, enormous bandwidth, and direct access to real-time network data. Even those who have not paid for the service are unable to access it [21–22]. Most MEC operations are handled locally by network operators, as opposed to cloud-based servers or peer-to-peer mobile

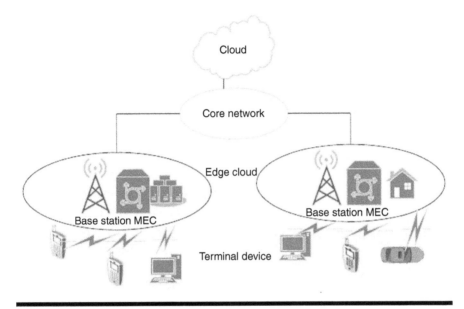

Figure 8.1   The architecture of MEC.

devices. Apps may access the mobile edge hosts' underlying computing resources via virtualization (APIs). User applications may utilize this, as well as operators [23–26].

8.3 Framework for Secure Service Deployment with Commercial MEC

Initially, in this part, we will sift through numerous recommended frameworks for secure service deployment.

8.3.1 Opinions on the Suggested Framework

Deng et al. [27–33] proposed a way to deal with scalability difficulties by offloading calculations. Based on current interference and predicted delays, users' process is to make sequential unloading decisions and adjust the number of unloading users accordingly. Researchers designed a sequential offloading choice game for several users to overcome scale concerns. As a result, users will see a significant reduction in the amount of time and energy they must use. The present interference environment is used to establish the uninstall sequence, and unloading users' times are revised depending on the projected delay. The strategy that they devised is referred to as the Nash method. A noncooperative game is an example of a game that may

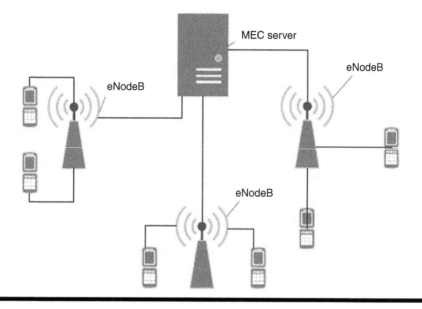

Figure 8.2   The scenario of multicell MEC.

have a Nash equilibrium. This kind of equilibrium describes a condition in which no player's utility can be enhanced by changing their strategy as long as the other players maintain their existing tactics. In a state of equilibrium, mobile device users may agree on a solution that they both find acceptable, and neither one has any incentive to diverge unilaterally. Pure strategy can only be found in dynamic games when all information is available.

Based on the state of equilibrium, according to Nash, the algorithm suggests offloading the selection process as the number of users grows in order to deliver a better user experience. As shown in Figure 8.2, the network is made up of tiny N cells, with nodes on the edge networks serving as the upload points for data from mobile devices. Operators may save money by supporting several terminals using a single MEC server. Due to computing offloading, increased latency, and network load, Verbelen et al. [34] proposed techniques for partitioning a software program made of many components into four cloud-based components with varying capabilities while reducing communication costs between the components. They demonstrated a fast partitioner using a multilevel KL method. Calculations of deployment may be done in real-time thanks to this feature [34–36]. The quality of the solution can be improved by simulated annealing. However, this comes at the sacrifice of the capacity to calculate. When it came time to apportion offloading, they went with a strategy that was known as computing the graph partitioning issue. By completing each of these jobs as quickly as is practically possible, their ultimate objective is to shorten the time required for the node with the worst performance. The term "cooperative offloading" refers to a system that combines the code offloading requests of many applications in order to reduce the amount of power that is required to complete each request. Wrapping code offloading requests in bundles results in a reduction in the amount of time that the network interfaces are required to remain in a high-power state. This leads to an overall savings of energy for mobile devices. When it comes to joint unloading, the challenge can be boiled down to a straightforward issue of joint optimization, with the overarching objective of cutting down on both reaction time and energy usage. The design of middleware helps to reduce inter-action latency [37–39], while other components, such as consumption graph mod-elling and optimum segmentation approaches, dynamic partitioning analysis and prolonged setup, require the processing capabilities of the mobile device. As a conse-quence, the computationally costly nature of the framework causes an increase in the overall execution time of the programme, making it more difficult to achieve smooth application performance [40–43].

8.3.2 A Framework of Commercial MEC

As can be seen in Figure 8.3, in 1998, when the concept of a content delivery net-work (CDN) was being discussed for the first time, there were already a number of proxy servers located closer to users. For instance, as seen in Figure 8.3, each client will keep the material that it first requested from the server/controller, and this

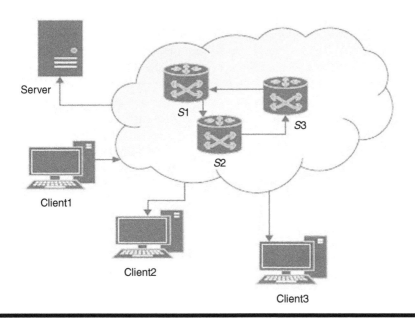

Figure 8.3   A CDN-SDN communication instance.

Table 8.1 Comparison between MEC-Based CDN vs Conventional CDN

Comparison	Traditional CDN	CDN based on MEC
Geographical location	Far from users	Closed to users
Receiving and Sending Resources	Weak ability	Strong ability
Coverage Area	Small Coverage Area	Large coverage area
Kinds of Service	Few Kinds	More Kinds
Cost	Low	High

content will be made available to other clients if they make a request for the same information. The most frequent method of ensuring excellent speed and scalability is to distribute servers across several sites [44]. CDN continues to encounter resource constraints, as servers are unable to keep up with user demand. Server deployment is location-dependent, the installation and deployment of the system necessitates first locating a suitable location with the required capacity [45–48].

The number of people using video clip applications and large video websites has increased over the last several years. As a direct consequence of this, people's viewing habits have shifted. Although many popular video websites have used CDN services, the existing design of the user experience of a mobile communication network still has several fundamental faults. For instance, users located in the same city or county could be interested in downloading the same paper or watching the same movie. All video content must be routed via the provincial core network exits to reach the video website's CDN service nodes on the backbone network, imposing a heavy load on the backhaul link. Popular videos may be kept on edge CDNs, [49] which service providers can install. As seen in Table 8.1, there are significant differences between a standard CDN and a CDN that uses MEC. Requesting hot content from the edge CDN allows users to directly skip the central CDN node and mobile core network and acquire it from the edge. Specification of the caching method or the ability for it to be dynamically altered in response to user requests should be made. There are several instances when data must be sent from the base station to a mobile end device, as shown in Figure 8.4. Thanks to these technologies, devices can process data more quickly with MEC and edge CDNs, compared to a central CDN or cloud. As a result, the speed at which data may be analyzed and sent will be greatly accelerated.

8.4 Secure Service Deployment Challenges

Numerous problems must be overcome in order to ensure the safe deployment of commercial MEC. Table 8.1 offers a comparison between the proposed method and conventional method. Table 8.2 covers some of the difficulties and solutions [38].

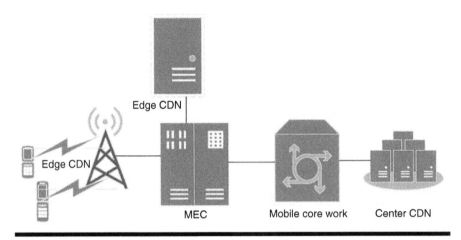

Figure 8.4   An edge CDN framework based on MEC.

Table 8.2   Challenges and Methods of Commercial MEC

Challenges	Reference	Method Used	Contribution
Risk of user data leakage	[42]	VLAN based Security Architecture	Increase protection to prevent data leakage
Secure risk of data transmission	[50]	2D-DWT based Steganography	Enable patients' data as per confidentiality
Security of terminal device	[51]	Lightweight Security Communication Scheme	Support access authentication for massive devices

8.4.1 Risk of User Data Leakage

If you are conducting business with a commercial MEC, you have to share some of your private information with third parties. In light of this, researchers must devise a way to determine whether a distributor's sensitive data has been leaked and fix the problem. Vaidya and Khobragade [39] used Rivest, Shamir, Adleman encryption technology to keep user data safe. The integrity of encoded data may be ensured using RSA's distributed verification. To address the problem of cloud data storage correction, researchers reserved the RSA token properties. Researchers selected to store RSA technology because the key calculation function is a member of the universal hash function family, it shows how to validate the storage's accuracy and detect whether the server is performing abnormally. In their paper, Yu et al. [40]

describe the CBDLP approach for avoiding data leaking. The training phase and the detecting phase of CBDLP are both distinct. The training papers are grouped across the training term. The cluster diagram is compared to the documents during the detection phase. There are many commercial DLP systems that have effectively reduced the risk of most accidental leaks [41].

8.4.2 Secure Risk of Data Transmission

The success of commercial MEC operations is strongly dependent on the confidentiality of information. Hackers that unlawfully obtain IP addresses in order to impersonate real users are a potential threat to the security and stability of data transportation. Sometimes, hackers may transmit an overwhelming quantity of instructions and data to the terminal of the mobile device, which will give the impression that the communication network is down. Due to the data flow that a wireless network makes possible, it is possible for hackers to detect the frequency of a wireless network [42]. If hackers mess with the data used for communication, as they often do in more serious incidents, there is a possibility that data may be lost. In a similar manner, Papadimitratos et al. [43] offered a summary of the secure message transfer (SMT) protocol to address similar challenges. The security association (SA) between the source terminal and the destination terminal may be created with the help of SMT. Because the linked nodes have been selected to interact using a secure communication mechanism, it is vital for the associated nodes to authenticate each other. It is possible to build a trust relationship by knowing the other party's public key, for example; it's not necessary to protect any remaining network nodes with a terminal node. Since these intermediate nodes are unencrypted, SMT does not require encryption. Fog computing-based SGs might benefit from an additional new protocol proposed by Okaya and Ozdemir, called secure data aggregation (SDA) (FCSG). The proposed approach, which uses homomorphic encryption, safeguards user data while reducing the quantity of data stored on cloud servers. As opposed to cloud-based smart grids, linked servers enhance server response time and reduce data traffic [44].

8.4.3 Security of Terminal Device

Many mobile cloud service customers do not have any security protections in place at this time. For example, the cloud platform automatically syncs private data on mobile terminal devices such as contact books, text messages, and notes. User's personal information is securely kept in the cloud, making it available to service providers through the platform. Mobile terminal applications are gaining popularity, and operators now have simple access to the location data that these applications require. This data not only includes the immediate geographic location but also includes the user's potential for privacy in relation to their location. It violates an individual's right to have their privacy protected. The researchers came up with a dynamic route quorum system and a dynamic path quorum-generating technique for mobile ad hoc networks. Both of these were developed by them. For mobile ad-hoc networks, they created a distributed access control approach that is based on quorum, rather than the usual one that relies on a single node for access control. According to this access control mechanism, the ad hoc network's resource sharing and protection level is significantly improved [45] compared to the access control method.

8.5 Open Issues and Challenges

Mobile services in edge computing may be safely deployed as the research and trials indicated in the preceding paragraphs.

8.5.1 Privacy Security

Advocates of MEC sometimes neglect MEC's influence on privacy security, despite the enthusiasm around MEC. Users' location information may be revealed when they utilize MEC's services. When it comes to in-vehicle MEC, for example, this might lead to the abuse of vehicle location information [46]. The user's trajectory may be tracked without authorization from the service provider. As a consequence, commercial MEC's privacy security has to be addressed right now. In spite of earlier research concentrating only on information privacy, we believe there is still a need for more investigation [47].

8.5.2 Data Transfer

New notions, ideas, and paradigms have emerged as a consequence of the explosion of information on the Internet and the creation of new services. In contrast, traditional network architecture is inefficient since it requires several network rules and configuration protocols. In addition, it can handle a large amount of traffic despite its high degree of scalability and severe limitations [48]. MEC is being fueled in large part by the advent of 5G, as is well-known. Thus, in MEC, it is vital that data flow be fast and stable. It is difficult for MEC to deliver a high-quality service due to the diverse geographic locations, receiving and transmitting equipment. That is to say, the ability to share data is critical for commercial MEC collaborative optimization.

5.3. Access Control. Even if the edge computing model is contracted out, a malicious user with an unauthenticated identity has the potential to misuse the services available at the network's periphery. This presents a significant threat to the integrity of access control systems. Devices at the edge, for example, may access and alter virtualized resources in edge server clouds with the right credentials [49–51].

8.6 Conclusion

Commercial MEC will have a huge impact on daily living in the near future. MEC has a bright future in the commercial arena. It has a significant effect on the world around us. Combining different kinds of industrial application scenarios with established 4G networks and more robust 5G networks makes it possible to actively explore MEC deployment and application. When the commercial MEC structure is finally finished, it will significantly affect the cities as a whole as well as the people that live there. Within the scope of this chapter, comprehensive analysis of the risk posed by mobile services at the edge of the network were offered. This chapter discussed the fundamental motivation for conducting the MEC study. Following that, relevant ideas and terminology were discussed. This chapter also discussed frameworks and critical approaches. Finally, numerous unresolved topics were given to help guide future study efforts. In a nutshell, this study aimed to advance commercial MEC.

References

[1] N. Abbas, Y. Zhang, Y. Taherkordi, and T. Skeie, "Mobile edge computing: a survey architecture, applications, approaches and challenges," *IEEE Internet of Things Journal*, vol. 5, pp. 454–455, 2018.

[2] X. Xu, X. Liu, Z. Xu, F. Dai, X. Zhang, and L. Qi, "Trustoriented IoT service placement for smart cities in edge 6 security and communication networks computing," *IEEE Internet of Things Journal*, vol. 7, no. 5, pp. 4084–4091, 2020.

[3] X. Xu, R. Mo, F. Dai, W. Lin, S. Wan, and W. Dou, "Dynamic resource provisioning with fault tolerance for data-intensive meteorological workflows in cloud," *IEEE Transactions on Industrial Informatics*, vol. 16, no. 9, pp. 6172–6181, 2020.

[4] Y. He, J. Ren, G. Yu, and Y. Cai, "D2D communications meet mobile edge computing for enhanced computation capacity in cellular networks," *IEEE Transactions on Wireless Communications*, vol. 18, no. 3, 2019.

[5] T. D. Nguyen, E. N. Huh, and M. Jo, "Decentralized and revised content-centric networking-based service deployment and discovery platform in mobile edge computing for IoT devices," *IEEE Internet of Things Journal*, vol. 6, pp. 6142–6175, 2019.

[6] Y. Hu, M. Patel, D. Sabella, N. Sprecher, and V. Young, "Mobile edge computing: a key technology towards 5G," *ETSI(European Telecommunications Standards Institute)*, vol. 9, pp. 1–16, 2015.

[7] R. Solozabal, "Exploitation of mobile edge computing in 5G distributed mission-critical push-to-talk service deployment," *IEEE Access*, vol. 6, pp. 37665–37675, 2015.

[8] X. Xu, X. Zhang, X. Liu, J. Jiang, L. Qi, and M. Z. A. Bhuiyan, "Adaptive computation offloading with edge for 5G-envisioned Internet of connected vehicles," *IEEE Transactions on Intelligent Transportation Systems*, vol. 1, pp. 5213–5222, 2020.

[9] P. Mach and Z. Becvar, "Mobile edge computing: a survey on architecture and computation offloading," *IEEE Communications Surveys & Tutorials*, vol. 19, pp. 1628–1656, 2017.

[10] Y. Zhu, Y. Hu, and A. Schmeink, "Delay minimization offloading for inter-dependent tasks in energy-aware cooperative MEC networks," *2019 IEEE Wireless Communications and Networking Conference (WCNC)*, vol. 15, pp. 1–6, 2019.

[11] C. You, K. Huang, H. Chae, and B. H. Kim, "IEEE transactions on wireless communications," *IEEE*, vol. 16, pp. 1397–1411, 2017.

[12] C. Wang, C. Liang, F. R. Yu, Q. Chen, and L. Tang, "Computation offloading and resource allocation in wireless cellular networks with mobile edge computing," *IEEE Transactions on Wireless Communications*, vol. 16, pp. 4924–4938, 2017.

[13] S. Agarwal, J. Dunagan, N. Jain, S. Saroiu, and A. WolmanVolley, "Automated data placement for geo-distributed cloud services sharad," *Microsoft Research*, vol. 16, pp. 2910–2918, 2010.

[14] X. Xu, B. Shen, X. Yin et al., "Edge server quantification and placement for offloading social media services in industrial cognitive IoV," *IEEE Transactions on Industrial Informatics*, vol. 16, pp. 2910–2918, 2020.

[15] X. Xu, S. Fu, L. Qi et al., "An IoT-Oriented data placement method with privacy preservation in cloud environment," *Journal of Network and Computer Applications*, vol. 124, pp. 148–157, 2018.

[16] B. Lin, F. Zhu, J. Zhang et al., "A time-driven data placement strategy for a scientific workflow combining edge computing and cloud computing," *IEEE Transactions on Industrial Informatics*, vol. 15, no. 7, pp. 4254–4265, 2019.

[17] R. Mijumbi, J. Serrat, J. L. Gorricho, N. Bouten, F. De Turck, and R. Boutaba, "Network function virtualization: state-of-the–art and research challenges," *IEEE Communications Surveys & Tutorials*, vol. 18, 2015.

[18] E. Ahmed and M. H. Rehmani, "Mobile edge computing: opportunities, solutions, and challenges," *Future Generation Computer Systems*, vol. 23, pp. 59–63, 2016.

[19] H. Li, G. Shou, Y. Hu, and Z. Guo, "Mobile edge computing: progress and challenges," *Future Generation Computer Systems*, vol. 5, p. 3, 2016.

[20] T. Verbelen, P. Simoens, F. De Turck, and B. Dhoedt, "Aiolos: middleware for improving mobile application performance through cyber foraging," *Journal of Systems and Software*, vol. 85, no. 11, pp. 2629–2639, 2012.

[21] P. William, N. Chinthamu, I. Kumar, M. Gupta, A. Shrivastava and A. P. Srivastava, "Schema Design with Intelligent Multi Modelling Edge Computing Techniques for Industrial Applications," 2023 3rd International Conference on Pervasive Computing and Social Networking (ICPCSN), Salem, India, 2023, pp. 1280–1285, doi: 10.1109/ICPCSN58827.2023.00215.

[22] P. William, D. Jadhav, P. Cholke, M. A. Jawale and A. B. Pawar, "Framework for product anti-counterfeiting using blockchain technology," 2022 International Conference on Sustainable Computing and Data Communication Systems (ICSCDS), 2022, pp. 1254–1258, doi: 10.1109/ICSCDS53736.2022.9760916.

[23] R. Jadhav, A. Shaikh, M. A. Jawale, A. B. Pawar and P. William, "System for identi-fying fake product using blockchain technology," 2022 7th International Conference on Communication and Electronics Systems (ICCES), 2022, pp. 851–854, doi: 10.1109/ICCES54183.2022.9835866.

[24] P. William, Y. N., S. Vimala, P. Gite and S. K. S, "Blockchain technology for data privacy using contract mechanism for 5G networks," 2022 3rd International

Conference on Intelligent Engineering and Management (ICIEM), 2022, pp. 461–465, doi: 10.1109/ICIEM54221.2022.9853118.

[25] A.B. Pawar, M.A. Jawale, P. William, G.S. Chhabra, Dhananjay S. Rakshe, Sachin K. Korde, Nikhil Marriwala, Implementation of blockchain technology using extended CNN for lung cancer prediction, Measurement: Sensors, 2022, 100530, ISSN 2665-9174, https://doi.org/10.1016/j.measen.2022.100530.

[26] P. William, A. Shrivastava, H. Chauhan, P. Nagpal, V. K. T. N and P. Singh, "Framework for intelligent smart city deployment via artificial intelligence software networking," 2022 3rd International Conference on Intelligent Engineering and Management (ICIEM), 2022, pp. 455–460, doi: 10.1109/ICIEM54221.2022.9853119.

[27] S. S. Gondkar, D. B. Pardeshi and P. William, "Innovative system for water level management using IoT to prevent water wastage," 2022 International Conference on Applied Artificial Intelligence and Computing (ICAAIC), 2022, pp. 1555–1558, doi: 10.1109/ICAAIC53929.2022.9792746.

[28] S. S. Gondkar, P. William and D. B. Pardeshi, "Design of a novel IoT framework for home automation using google assistant," 2022 6th International Conference on Intelligent Computing and Control Systems (ICICCS), 2022, pp. 451–454, doi: 10.1109/ICICCS53718.2022.9788284.

[29] S. Choubey, P. William, A. B. Pawar, M. A. Jawale, K. Gupta and V. Parganiha, "Intelligent water level monitoring and water pump controlling system using IOT," 2022 3rd International Conference on Electronics and Sustainable Communication Systems (ICESC), 2022, pp. 423–427, doi: 10.1109/ICESC54411.2022.9885358.

[30] Deepak Narayan Paithankar, Abhijeet Rajendra Pabale, Rushikesh Vilas Kolhe, P. William, Prashant Madhukar Yawalkar, Framework for implementing air quality monitoring system using LPWA-based IoT technique, Measurement: Sensors, 2023, 100709, ISSN 2665-9174, https://doi.org/10.1016/j.measen.2023.100709.

[31] K. Gupta, S. Choubey, Y. N, P. William, V. T. N and C. P. Kale, "Implementation of motorist weariness detection system using a conventional object recognition technique," 2023 International Conference on Intelligent Data Communication Technologies and Internet of Things (IDCIoT), Bengaluru, India, 2023, pp. 640–646, doi: 10.1109/IDCIoT56793.2023.10052783.

[32] P. William, Y. N, V. M. Tidake, S. Sumit Gondkar, C. R and K. Vengatesan, "Framework for implementation of personality inventory model on natural language processing with personality traits analysis," 2023 International Conference on Intelligent Data Communication Technologies and Internet of Things (IDCIoT), Bengaluru, India, 2023, pp. 625–628, doi: 10.1109/IDCIoT56793.2023.10053501.

[33] E. Koukoumidis, D. Lymberopoulos, K. Strauss, J. Liu, and D. Burger, "Pocket cloudlets," *ACM SIGARCH Computer Architecture News*, vol. 39, no. 1, pp. 171–184, 2011.

[34] X. Xu, C. He, Z. Xu, L. Qi, S. Wan, and M. Z. A. Bhuiyan, "Joint optimization of offloading utility and privacy for edge computing enabled IoT," *IEEE Internet of Things Journal*, vol. 7, no. 4, pp. 2622–2629, 2020.

[35] Rushikesh Vilas Kolhe, P. William, Prashant Madhukar Yawalkar, Deepak Narayan Paithankar, Abhijeet Rajendra Pabale, Smart city implementation based on Internet

of Things integrated with optimization technology, Measurement: Sensors, vol. 27, 2023, 100789, ISSN 2665-9174, https://doi.org/10.1016/j.measen.2023.100789.

[36] M.A. Jawale, P. William, A.B. Pawar, Nikhil Marriwala, Implementation of number plate detection system for vehicle registration using IOT and recognition using CNN, Measurement: Sensors, vol. 27, 2023, 100761, ISSN 2665-9174, https://doi.org/10.1016/j.measen.2023.100761.

[37] P. William, G. R. Lanke, D. Bordoloi, A. Shrivastava, A. P. Srivastavaa and S. V. Deshmukh, "Assessment of human activity recognition based on impact of feature extraction prediction accuracy," 2023 4th International Conference on Intelligent Engineering and Management (ICIEM), London, United Kingdom, 2023, pp. 1–6, doi: 10.1109/ICIEM59379.2023.10166247.

[38] P. William, G. R. Lanke, V. N. R. Inukollu, P. Singh, A. Shrivastava and R. Kumar, "Framework for design and implementation of chat support system using natural language processing," 2023 4th International Conference on Intelligent Engineering and Management (ICIEM), London, United Kingdom, 2023, pp. 1–7, doi: 10.1109/ICIEM59379.2023.10166939.

[39] P. William, A. Shrivastava, U. S. Aswal, I. Kumar, M. Gupta and A. K. Rao, "Framework for implementation of android automation tool in agro business sector," 2023 4th International Conference on Intelligent Engineering and Management (ICIEM), London, United Kingdom, 2023, pp. 1–6, doi: 10.1109/ICIEM59379.2023.10167328.

[40] P. William, G. R. Lanke, S. Pundir, I. Kumar, M. Gupta and S. Shaw, "Implementation of hand written based signature verification technology using deep learning approach," 2023 4th International Conference on Intelligent Engineering and Management (ICIEM), London, United Kingdom, 2023, pp. 1–6, doi: 10.1109/ICIEM59379.2023.10167195.

[41] P. William, V. N. R. Inukollu, V. Ramasamy, P. Madan, A. Shrivastava and A. Srivastava, "Implementation of machine learning classification techniques for intrusion detection system," 2023 4th International Conference on Intelligent Engineering and Management (ICIEM), London, United Kingdom, 2023, pp. 1–7, doi: 10.1109/ICIEM59379.2023.10167390.

[42] Korde, S. K., Rakshe, D. S., William, P., Jawale, M. A., & Pawar, A. B. (2023). Experimental investigations on copper-based nanoparticles for energy storage applications. *Journal of Nano-and Electronic Physics*, 15(3) pp. 03002-1–03002-5.

[43] Rakshe, D. S., William, P., Jawale, M. A., Pawar, A. B., Korde, S. K., & Deshpande, N. (2023). Synthesis and characterization of graphene based nanomaterials for energy applications. *Journal of Nano-and Electronic Physics*, 15(3), pp. 03004-1–03004-6.

[44] Jawale, M. A., Pawar, A. B., Korde, S. K., Rakshe, D. S., William, P., & Deshpande, N. (2023). Energy management in electric vehicles using improved swarm optimized deep reinforcement learning algorithm. *Journal of Nano-and Electronic Physics*, 15(3).

[45] Rashmi, M., William, P., Yogeesh, N., Girija, D.K. (2023). Blockchain-based cloud storage using secure and decentralised solution. In: Chaki, N., Roy, N.D., Debnath, P., Saeed, K. (eds) Proceedings of International Conference on Data Analytics and Insights, ICDAI 2023. ICDAI 2023. Lecture Notes in Networks and Systems, vol. 727. Springer, Singapore. https://doi.org/10.1007/978-981-99-3878-0_23.

[46] Girija, D. K., Rashmi, M., William, P., Yogeesh, N. (2023). Framework for integrating the synergies of blockchain with AI and IoT for secure distributed systems. In: Chaki, N., Roy, N. D., Debnath, P., Saeed, K. (eds) Proceedings of International Conference on Data Analytics and Insights, ICDAI 2023. ICDAI 2023. Lecture Notes in Networks and Systems, vol. 727. Springer, Singapore. https://doi.org/10.1007/978-981-99-3878-0_22.

[47] G. A. Mensah, C. O. Johnson, G. Addolorato et al., "Global burden of cardiovascular diseases and risk factors, 1990–2019: update from the GBD 2019 study," *Journal of the American College of Cardiology*, vol. 34, 2020.

[48] J. Zhang, Chen , Y. Zhao, X. Cheng, and F. Hu, "Data security and privacy-preserving in edge computing paradigm: survey and open issues," *IEEE Access*, vol. 6, pp. 18209–18237, 2018.

[49] L. Chen, Z. Liu, and Z. Wang, "Research on heterogeneous terminal security access technology in edge computing scenario," *2019 11th International Conference on Measuring Technology and Mechatronics Automation (ICMTMA)*, vol. 10, p. 7, 2019.

[50] P. William, D. Jadhav, P. Cholke, M. A. Jawale and A. B. Pawar, "Framework for product anti-counterfeiting using blockchain technology," 2022 International Conference on Sustainable Computing and Data Communication Systems (ICSCDS), 2022, pp. 1254–1258, doi: 10.1109/ICSCDS53736.2022.9760916.

[51] S. S. Gondkar, D. B. Pardeshi and P. William, "Innovative system for water level management using IoT to prevent water wastage," 2022 International Conference on Applied Artificial Intelligence and Computing (ICAAIC), 2022, pp. 1555–1558, doi: 10.1109/ICAAIC53929.2022.9792746.

Chapter 9

AI-Enabled Novel Applications in Edge Computing for IoT Services

Ishita Dixit[1], Sonali Powar[1], and Kabir Kharade[2]

[1]Department of Computer Science, Vishwakarma University, Pune, India

[2]Department of Computer Science, Shivaji University, Kolhapur, India

9.1 Introduction

The Internet of Things (IoT) is a component of modern life. It is a concept that involves connecting devices to the internet and any other connected device to share information. These devices produce enormous volumes of data, which is further processed and examined to produce improved recommendations and decisions. The main drawbacks of this method are delays in results, storage problems, and bandwidth problems as data sizes grow. With traditional forms of cloud computing, which make use of constrained bandwidth and other network resources, enormous amounts of data are sent to a cloud server that is located a great distance from the end user. Because of this, there is a delay in responding. Computing in the cloud cannot fulfil the requirements of an application that needs a response in a short amount of time.

DOI: 10.1201/9781032650722-12

The majority of IoT devices have a limited amount of power, and in order to extend the lifetime of these devices, it is necessary to keep a balance in power consumption computational capabilities. This can be accomplished by allocating computation to devices that have both higher power and greater computational capabilities. Also, the processing of data in computing nodes that are positioned at the closest possible proximity to the user will cut down on the amount of time that is required for transmission, which will in turn reduce the amount of time that is required for storage. Heavy network traffic results in longer transmission times, which in turn increases the costs associated with power usage. As a result, scheduling and the allocation of processing time is a very important topic that needs to be considered.

Edge computing, on the other hand, involves the processing and storing of data at a location closer to the network's edge. The peak in the volume of traffic is reduced as a result of the fact that the nodes that make up edge computing are situated close to the end users. Devices at the network's periphery include things like routers, sensors, and other IoT hardware. These computing devices were designed to carry out certain tasks, such as remote access or monitoring equipment, and were built accordingly. They serve as the principal point of access into the network. Reaction times for IoT applications may be faster than those of the cloud-equivalent computing services. Edge nodes that have a significant amount of power resources can transfer computational and communication overhead to nodes that have a limited amount of battery life or power supply. The primary distinctions between cloud computing and edge computing are outlined in Table 9.1.

Table 9.1 Key Differences between Cloud Computing and Edge Computing

Cloud Computing	Edge Computing
Applications like big data and machine learning, which demand a lot of computer power, are good fits for cloud computing.	IoT and other applications that require real-time processing and minimal latency are good choices for edge computing.
Dependable on internet connection	Work with limited or no internet connection.
Data is processed at either a centralized data center or a distributed server farm.	Data processing occurs at or near the network's edge
Because data must be sent to a distant location for processing, cloud computing may have higher latency.	Due to data processing occurring close to the source, edge computing has low latency.
Centralized resource management and control are provided by cloud computing.	Edge computing provides for decentralized management and control that is located closer to the edge devices.

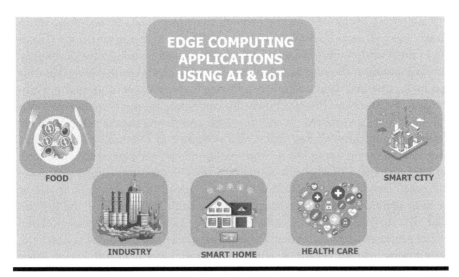

Figure 9.1 Applications of edge computing.

There are several applications where edge computing is used to improve security and performance and reduce energy consumption. Figure 9.1 shows the applications of edge computing.

9.2 Smart Cities

Edge computing is a paradigm of distributed computing that moves computation and data storage closer to the devices and sensors that generate data, as opposed to sending the data to a centralized data center. This is in contrast to traditional cloud computing, which sends the data to a remote location for processing. In contrast to this, conventional computer procedures involve sending data to a single point for processing. Fog computing and fog storage are both common names for computing that takes place on the periphery of a network. The strategic application of data to improve the performance of a variety of urban functions—such as transportation, energy, healthcare, and public safety—is a defining characteristic of smart cities. The use of AI and IoT in conjunction with edge computing has made the creation of smart cities possible. In recent years, novel applications of edge computing using AI and IoT in smart cities have emerged. In smart parking, edge computing can be used to optimize parking resources, reduce congestion, and provide real-time information about parking availability. In smart water management, edge computing is used for reducing water loss by detecting leakage and also for monitoring the quality of water. The use of edge computing in smart waste management leads to efficient waste management, requires less manpower, reduces fuel consumption, helps in planning the number of garbage collectors, and predicts the time of high waste in the city.

Computing at the edge of the network can process data in real-time, which enables users to make decisions and react quickly to changing situations. This is one of the most important benefits that may be gained by using edge computing. Also, computing at the edge can eliminate the delay that is created by transporting data to a centralized data center, which in turn makes it easier to process and analyze data more quickly. This is because edge computing reduces the amount of data that needs to be transmitted. In addition, edge computing has the potential to cut down on the quantity of data that needs to be sent to a centralized data center. This, in turn, may result in less network traffic and cheaper expenses. Nonetheless, the implementation of edge computing in smart cities presents some problems to overcome. The demand for effective data management and protection is one of the most significant challenges that must be overcome. The use of AI and IoT can make data management and security even more challenging, as edge devices and sensors generate enormous amounts of data that need to be controlled and secured. Consumption of power, network connectivity, and device compatibility are a few examples of the difficulties that might arise during the deployment and maintenance of edge devices and sensors. Edge computing, when combined with AI and the IoT, is a potentially fruitful strategy for developing smart cities that are more environmentally friendly, resource-conserving, and sensitive to the requirements of their residents. However, it requires careful planning and management to ensure that data is effectively managed and secured and that devices and sensors are deployed and maintained effectively. The various applications of edge computing in smart cities are as follows.

9.3 Smart Parks

Edge computing can be applied in parking management to improve efficiency and reduce costs. By deploying edge devices such as cameras and sensors in parking lots, data can be collected and processed locally to provide real-time information about parking availability, occupancy, and vehicle movement. This information can be used to optimize parking resources, reduce congestion, and improve the overall parking experience for drivers. For example, edge devices can be used to detect when a parking space is occupied and when it becomes vacant, and this information can be sent to a central server or mobile application for real-time updates. This reduces the need for manual monitoring and can improve the accuracy of parking data. Edge devices can also be used to automate parking payment systems, allowing drivers to pay for parking using a mobile application or digital wallet. This can reduce the need for physical payment infrastructure and can provide a more convenient and efficient parking experience for drivers. Overall, the application of edge computing in parking management can help to optimize resource utilization, reduce operational costs, and improve customer satisfaction.

The conventional parking system used so far cannot utilize the parking space efficiently. The smart parking system can overcome these drawbacks of the conventional parking system by providing immediate calculation of free parking slots and utilizing the parking space efficiently by using a variety of machine learning algorithms. The smart parking concept is made possible with the use of existing surveillance cameras and image detection systems. AI schemes like convolutional neural networks are used by image detection systems to find a free parking slot. An encouraging solution is provided by edge computing through on-demand computational resources to enable the smart parking system [1].

9.4 Smart Water Management

The identification of failures, the establishment of smart water supply networks, the monitoring of water quality, the reduction of water leaks, and the use of smart irrigation are some of the essential objectives that may be accomplished with the assistance of smart water systems. Components of the IoT are used to link the various devices that are connected through the water network. Intelligent water meters, water quality sensors, and water control actuators are a few examples of the gadgets that fall within this category. Edge nodes are responsible for supplying the smart water network with local management and monitoring capabilities. In this method, the cloud is utilized to collect the data, store the data, and utilize the data to enhance the operation of the water network and reduce the amount of water that is lost [2].

The growth of metropolitan areas, the effects of climate change, and inadequate management of the world's water resources are all reasons that can be ascribed to the rise in the demand for water around the globe. The process of assessing the quality of the water involves the utilization of sensors in addition to other IoT-based devices. After that, this information is transmitted to the edge so it may be processed. With this information, it is possible to monitor the quality and locate the source of the leak [3]. The development of a robust infrastructure that makes use of emerging technologies such as machine learning, soft computing, and blockchain is now under way. This infrastructure is being built to facilitate the effective management of water resources. A feed-forward neural network (FFNN) that was trained with the assistance of an investigation into the existence of symbiotic organisms can be found at the edge nodes. This network is in charge of generating forecasts on the amount of water used by each residence. The mixed-density network, also referred to as the MDN, is a model for neural networks that use randomized probability distribution. The objective is to ascertain a value from the past, which can afterward be compared to the value that is anticipated to be accomplished in the foreseeable future. Those homes that use significantly less water are rewarded generously, while those that use significantly more water than the historical norm are subject to a monetary fine [4].

9.5 Smart Waste Management

Edge computing can be applied in waste management to improve efficiency, reduce costs, and enhance sustainability. One application of edge computing in waste management is smart waste bin management. Smart bins can be equipped with sensors that can detect when they are full and transmit this information to a central server or mobile application for real-time updates. This can assist waste management organizations in optimizing their pickup schedules, cutting down on the number of trips that are not essential, and improving the overall efficiency of the collection process.

Edge computing can also be used to monitor the performance of waste management equipment such as garbage trucks and compactors. By deploying sensors on these machines, data can be collected and processed locally to provide insights into fuel consumption, maintenance needs, and other operational metrics. This can help companies optimize their fleet management, reduce downtime, and improve the overall sustainability of their operations. Finally, edge computing can be used to improve waste sorting and recycling efforts. By deploying sensors and cameras in sorting facilities, data can be collected and processed locally to provide real-time information about the composition of waste streams. This can help companies optimize their recycling efforts, reduce contamination, and improve the overall sustainability of their operations.

A clean and healthy environment is provided in smart cities by using emerging computing technologies. These systems provide several waste management functions like identification of places with heavy waste, providing a map that is useful for the garbage collection van, making predictions about future waste, and overall monitoring of waste management in the city. This leads to more efficient management of waste, requires fewer worker s, reduces the amount of fuel consumed, assists in the planning of the number of garbage collectors, and forecasts the times of day when there is the most waste in the city [5].

9.6 Smart Fleet Management

Edge computing can be applied in fleet management to improve operational efficiency, enhance driver safety, and reduce costs. By deploying edge devices such as sensors and cameras on vehicles, data can be collected and processed locally to provide real-time insights into vehicle performance, driver behavior, and other operational metrics. One application of edge computing in vehicle fleet management is real-time monitoring of vehicle location and status. Data from GPS trackers, telematics systems, and other sensors can be processed locally to offer real-time information on a vehicle's location, speed, fuel consumption, and other metrics if edge devices like routers and gateways are deployed in the field. This information can be put to use to increase fleet efficiency overall, as well as optimize routes, cut down on idling time, and reduce total downtime.

Another application of edge computing in vehicle fleet management is predictive maintenance. By deploying edge devices on vehicles, data can be collected and processed locally to provide insights into the health of critical components such as engines, brakes, and transmissions. This can help fleet managers identify potential issues before they become major problems, reducing downtime and maintenance costs. Edge computing can also be used to improve driver safety. By deploying cameras and sensors on vehicles, data can be collected and processed locally to provide real-time insights into driver behavior such as speeding, harsh braking, and distracted driving. This information can be used to provide immediate feedback to drivers and can help fleet managers identify and address potential safety issues. By collecting data on vehicle performance, traffic patterns, and other factors, edge devices can help fleet managers optimize routes and reduce fuel consumption. Edge computing can also complement traditional cloud computing solutions by providing faster response times and reduced latency.

9.7 Vehicular Traffic Management in Smart Cities

Mobile edge computing (MEC) is a comparatively new technology that was developed to put computing ability and the environment in which they are utilized closer to endpoints [6]. MEC is a great foundation for automotive networks because of its low response latency and real-time access to network information through a variety of applications and services. Because of the high degree of variability inherent in the vehicular environment, real-time data are required. MEC settings can deliver a speedy reaction about linked vehicles as a result of the proximity quality that they possess [7]. The following are the applications of edge computing in the vehicular environment.

9.7.1 Data Collection, Dissemination, and Analysis

The collecting of data should ultimately facilitate real-time interactions, the results of which are an increase in both convenience and safety. The utilization of smart traffic lights (STLs) is one illustration of a system that supports interaction in real-time. Location data collection, speed monitoring, and pedestrian detection are provided by STL by direct interaction with nearby sensors. When it comes to the process of managing traffic, having a group of STLs that work together to coordinate the green traffic wave plays an extremely important function [8]. When STLs are combined with the capabilities of edge computing, it is possible to improve the prediction of likely collisions through the application of real-time data analysis and learning methods. As a direct result of this, the approaching vehicles can be notified in advance so that the appropriate response can be taken [9].

9.7.2 Vehicular Control Systems

The use of a cloud-based vehicle control system allows for the periodic collection of sensor data from several cars in the surrounding area, as well as the remote operation of each of those vehicles via the cloud. In addition to that, problems with vehicles can be monitored and diagnosed with the help of this technology. The cloud-based system that controls the vehicle is complemented by an edge server that acts as a computer node and performs the same responsibilities. The controllers of the vehicles that are housed in the cloud and edge servers are referred to as the cloud controller and the edge controller, respectively. An automatic switching method is utilized in this scenario so that the edge servers and cloud servers may continue to keep a healthy load balance with one another [10].

9.7.3 Dwell Time of Vehicles

Dwell time is the period that a vehicle waits at a specific area, such as a parking lot or loading zone, without moving. It is essential to keep accurate records of dwell time to maximize the effectiveness of the utilization of available transportation resources and to make the transportation system more efficient as a whole. Research on vehicular networking is currently focusing on applications that facilitate cooperative driving and cooperative perception [11–13]. The ideas of cooperative driving and cooperative perception can be supported by the technology that is installed in modern vehicles. This technology includes sensors, processing, networking, and storage resources. The onboard sensor units collect a vast quantity of data from the surrounding environment, which is then made available for cooperative use by neighboring automobiles, bicycles, and pedestrians. As a result of the growing importance of automobiles as resources for information and communication technology (ICT), Intelligent transportation systems (ITSs) have been transformed into the infrastructure of future smart cities. When downloading data from data centers, there is a great deal of delay brought on by several variables. These issues include limitations on network bandwidth as well as the physical communication distance that exists between the cars and the data centers. The MEC architecture was developed to address issues of this nature [14]. The fundamental concept is to install processing and storage capabilities at the edge of a network, which is the portion of the network that is physically located closest to the users. Within the framework of the vehicular micro-cloud architecture, a tiny cluster is formed by cars working together to deliver computing and storage services to other adjacent vehicles, as well as to pedestrians and cyclists [15]. The idea of mobile edge computing, or MEC, is expanded in vehicular networks by vehicular micro-clouds, which function as virtual edge servers. It is possible to further classify micro-clouds produced by vehicles by splitting them into two distinct types: stationary and movable micro-clouds [16]. Computing at the edge of networks has the potential to become an invaluable instrument for enhancing the precision and effectiveness of tracking the dwell duration of cars in transportation systems. Computing at the network's edge can aid transportation authorities in improving the efficiency of the transportation system as a whole and making the most of the transportation resources that are already available. Computing at the edge has the potential to assist in the evolution of these technologies in a variety of different ways. Real-time monitoring, data analytics, predictive analytics, and integration with other systems are some of the strategies that fall under this category.

9.8 Air Monitoring System

A severe impact on human health is being caused by the ever-increasing air pollution that is a direct result of urbanization and industrialization. The respiratory system of a human being has the potential to be put in contact with a significant number of potentially harmful substances that are associated with particulate matter. Particulate matter with a diameter of less than 2.5 micrometers, also referred to as PM 2.5, is particularly dangerous since it can penetrate deeply into the lungs and lead to illnesses such as lung cancer, strokes, and heart attacks [17]. Computation capabilities located on the periphery of a network have the potential to improve the efficiency and accuracy of environmental monitoring systems. These devices are utilized to ascertain the standard of the air and locate the presence of contaminants in the ambiance. Edge computing allows for real-time monitoring and analysis of air quality data by processing the data in a location that is physically closer to the point of collection of the data. This can help to identify and minimize any health dangers that are linked to air pollution. Centralized computing duties can be distributed to more manageable nodes placed closer to the network's periphery by utilizing the technology known as edge computing [18]. The collection of data in systems that anticipate air quality often calls for the utilization of hundreds or even millions of sensory nodes [19].

9.9 Healthcare

Edge computing has the potential to change many different industries, including the healthcare business, by providing real-time data processing, remote patient monitoring, early diagnosis of health issues, and many other benefits. Because of advances in computational intelligence and the Internet of Medical Things, the conventional methods of providing medical care have given way to the delivery of "smart healthcare" services in recent years. S-health systems include services such as the automatic identification and tracking of patients, as well as rigorous real-time monitoring of crucial signs for the early detection of health issues that are deteriorating. This system requires an extremely large volume of data to be securely transmitted, processed, and stored in some form or another. The traditional paradigm for cloud computing does not provide the requisite level of scalability or responsiveness, and it also places a significant burden on the underlying communication infrastructure. These restrictions can be circumvented by utilizing a novel strategy referred to as multi-access edge computing. With the help of this technology, it is feasible to process and store the data in close vicinity to the sites at which the data was initially gathered. A shorter response time, a lower consumption of power, a more effective use of network capacity, and safe data transmission are the primary benefits that come from storing and processing data at the edge of the network.

This technology can be used to collect personal health information like ECG, heart rate, blood pressure, SpO2 level, body temperature, and pulmonary function from edge devices like personal digital assistants. The collected data can be further compressed, extracted, and classified in order to build highly responsive, low power consuming systems [20]. Edge computing can enable healthcare providers to remotely monitor patients' health in real-time, by processing data from various connected devices such as wearables, sensors, and medical equipment. This can help in early detection of health issues and enable timely intervention. It can help healthcare providers analyze patient data in real-time, enabling personalized treatment plans tailored to individual patient needs.

9.10 Smart Homes

The IoT is an umbrella phrase that refers to the billions of physical objects or things that are connected to the internet and are all capable of collecting and exchanging data with other systems and devices. This data can be accessed by other systems and devices. This information may originate from any country in the world and may be used for a wide range of different uses. The idea of a smart house can be put into practice with the assistance of IoT. The IoT is an innovative method for wireless communication. The fundamental principle that underpins this concept is that there are several objects present in our environment, including sensors, mobilephones, RFID tags, and other similar items. These things can carry out a certain activity by communicating with one another through a specific address, which allows them to be connected with one another [21]. The connected home is an important component in maintaining personal safety and peace of mind. The protection and safety features of the smart home system include, amongst other things, a smart camera, biometric lock, video door entry, smoke/fire detector, motion sensors, and so on. Further benefits of smart homes include reduced utility bills, increased comfort, and access to assisted care facilities. Several researchers have proposed a wide variety of solutions in the subject of smart homes, particularly in the areas of home automation, safety, and security. with the goal of making human life simpler. The following are features of Smart Homes.

9.10.1 Safety and Security

Fire alarms help save human life as well as loss of resources. Liquefied petroleum gas (LPG) is mostly used for cooking. Many times, gas leakage results in a blast. The gas leakage detector is a good solution to avoid such dangerous situation. The security system in homes detects motion that can help detect home invasion.

9.10.2 Energy Conservation

Not only does the smart home system offer automation and security, but it also offers effective energy management systems that allow us to utilize the electricity in our homes in the most efficient and cost-effective manner possible [22], [23]. It is not just the quick technical developments that are currently being produced in the field of "smart houses" that are having a big impact on residential electricity usage; rather, the continuously expanding global population is also having this effect. According to figures provided by the Global Business Council for Sustainable Development [24], the global energy consumption of residential buildings is between 30 and 40% less than that of commercial buildings. In addition to this, it is expected that the total amount of power that is consumed by business and residential buildings combined will increase to 53% by the year 2035 [25]. A method that is both efficient and effective for the goal of maximizing the reduction of energy consumption in residential structures is made available by the smart home system.

9.10.3 Comfort

The smart home provides comfort. For example, according to the amount of people in specific areas or in accordance with local weather forecasts, the temperature of the room can be adjusted. In order to provide a more comfortable lifestyle, the variety of home appliances can be controlled remotely using smartphones or tablets. In home automation under the cloud paradigm, the collected data gets transferred on cloud every time. Thus, cloud computing suffers from latency, storage, bandwidth, and energy consumption. Edge computing is introduced to resolve these issues. Figure 9.2 shows home automation using edge computing.

In a smart home using edge computing, the data collected via sensors are processed at the user workstation itself. This process reduces the delay, increases the speed of the process, and also increases the security. A Raspberry-Pi (RPI) device is employed in a smart home system both as a controlling unit and an edge device [26]. Home appliances can be controlled both automatically and remotely with the help

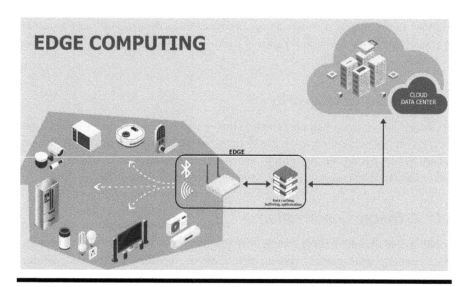

Figure 9.2   Home automation in edge paradigm.

of this method. The researcher has implemented concepts from edge computing in order to store sensitive data on local clouds in order to protect their privacy. In order to cut down on costs associated with bandwidth, computing, and storage, the sensor data is processed on the RPI device itself.

A different kind of solution for smart homes is a Vigilia system, which limits network access to various gadgets. The researcher shifts the responsibility for ensuring the safety of the system away from the companies that make the devices and onto the platform [27]. This system utilizes four apps, each of which is capable of defending the system against any and all forms of assault. The proposed system continues to function even if connectivity to the internet is lost. Also, the Raspberry Pi can run this program. The subsequent method for a smart home gives a solution that is both lightweight and secure [28]. This method introduces home automation solutions that are standardized and compatible with one another. This strategy is put into action with the assistance of an Android smartphone, a Raspberry Pi, various sensors, and actuators. NodeJs is used during the development of the edge computing platform. When home automation services are being utilized, the Raspberry Pi experiences a strain on its central processing unit (CPU) of between 14 and 20%. The Android software requires 2.89 megabytes of RAM to run, and it puts less than 5% of a typical computer's processor to work. So, in general, the implementation is both practical and unburdensome.

One more approach for smart homes recommends using a technology that is based on edge computing to improve the system's dependability and robustness [29]. Because it operates automatically dependent on the conditions of its surroundings, this technology reduces the amount of electricity that is consumed greatly. Home appliances are controlled by a total of eight distinct sensors, including light sensors, air sensors, passive infrared (PIR) sensors, smoke detector sensors, and hall effect sensors. Raspberry-Pi is responsible for transmitting the instruction to the power relay, which then turns the appliances on and off. The Raspberry Pi instructions are controlled with the help of the smartphones. A heuristic approach is utilized instead in another solution for smart homes [30]. With this method, the data collection and processing can be carried out either on a device located locally or on the cloud, depending on the significance of the data being collected. This idea reduces the amount of time needed for processing, as well as the bandwidth required, and it boosts the use of the local workstation. The priority-based task queuing mechanism used by Health Edge performs processing of emergency tasks first. A local edge workstation, a remote edge workstation, or the cloud are all examples of possible locations for the execution of a task. HealthEdge is able to predict human behavior in order to estimate the workload and available resources of these locations. It calculates the amount of time required to process the job at each location option based on its position in the queue and estimates the amount of resources that are available at each option. In conclusion, the task's execution is based on the choice that requires the least amount of processing time. On edge nodes, an intrusion detection system (also known as an IDS) is installed [31]. Convolutional neural networks can be trained using the results of this method, which involves converting network traffic into images (CNN). The UNSW-NB15 network traffic dataset is being used for the investigation. This technique can classify network traffic as either normal or abnormal, and it can obtain classification results of up to 96%.

9.10.4 Food

Obesity rates are on the rise, and unhealthy eating habits are one of the key causes of many diseases and have a substantial cost impact on the healthcare systems. Thus, some sort of food monitoring system must exist. In order for these systems to be effective in improving the overall health of the population, not only must they be able to monitor and evaluate the vast array of food options, they must also be able to provide users with the critical information they require concerning healthy food choices. Applications based on the IoT are utilized for the purposes of detecting food intake, identifying consumed food, and determining nutrition. In the case of food intake detection, studies do not attempt to identify the particular products that are ingested; rather, they focus on evaluating if user activities can be categorized as eating. This is because it is impossible to know exactly what is being eaten at any one time. By analyzing their users' day-to-day actions, systems in this field are able to recognize users' patterns and provide users with recommendations for how they should change their eating habits to improve their health [32]. Scisco et al. proposed a method in which users record their biting movement as a means of determining the amount of food they consume by wearing a sensor (a gyroscope) on their wrists. The bite detection method is utilized in this approach. Farooq and Sazonov proposed a method that might be used to identify the movement of chewing. Signals from the user's motions are gathered by a gadget the user wears on their body [33]. It comes equipped with a piezoelectric sensor, as well as an accelerometer and a hand-to-mouth sensor. Pattern recognition, using a variety of different classifiers, is the fundamental building block of data analysis [34]. In order to detect the movement of the user's throat and determine whether or not they were eating, Kalantarian et al. utilized a piezoelectric sensor that was inserted into a worn necklace. This allowed them to make their determination. The device is able to determine when and how much food is consumed, as well as provide an estimate of the overall amount of food that is consumed and classify the most fundamental types of foods [35].

The eButton may have the appearance of a decorative button, but it is actually packed with a variety of sensors, including two cameras, a UV sensor, a proximity sensor for monitoring hand or arm motion, and a GPS for determining the user's current location. In addition, the eButton also includes a microphone for the user to speak into [36]. In addition, the eButton appears to be a decorative button. This wearable device is able to detect when a user is eating and can take pictures of the food being consumed, as well as store the images. There is a risk of monitoring, as well as the collecting and storing of images without the users' knowledge, which poses privacy concerns with regard to this technology. Zhou et al. designed a system for nutritional assessment that measures the volume of foods and, with an accuracy of 80%, evaluates the type of food based on the eating habit of the user [37]. This system was established with the use of a smart tablecloth. An application known as iHearFood was proposed by Gao et al. with the intention of determining whether or not an individual is chewing food based on the sounds that are recorded by bluetooth headphones. The technology is able to determine the sort of food that consumers are consuming based on the unique sounds that are created as a result of their consumption of the meal [38]. Scientists have also developed a method for the classification of foods based on deep learning with an accuracy that ranges from 77–94% in order to achieve this goal. A system that utilizes both motion-based and acoustic-based approaches was proposed by Mirtchouk et al. as a means of detecting and identifying different types of foods. The wrist motions and chewing sounds are used as input in the proposed approach, which results in an increase in the accuracy of the meal classification. The method was accurate approximately 82.7% of the time when tested on forty distinct food products [39].

The company has developed an innovative nutrition monitoring system that is centered on food scanners. Raspberry PI is the hardware used in the implementation of the edge service. A smart scale gadget is used to measure the weight of foods, while two molecular sensors, the SCiO Sensor and the NIRONE Sensor, are utilized to detect a particular type of food item, such as raw meat or cooked meat. The serving plate is the first thing that the intelligent scanner examines. The scanning procedure begins once the user has successfully authenticated themselves through a mobile application. Edge servers immediately begin gathering sensor data after a procedure has been started by the user. In addition, the data that is captured is uploaded to the cloud, where it is stored for the long term and analyzed [40].

Liu C. et al. made use of the smartphone camera for visual sensing. In addition to using a smartphone for sensing and picture capture, edge devices (i.e., smartphones) and servers (i.e., cloud) work together for recognition. A three-layer service delivery model is represented by the [41]. At the very edge of the network, data and processing are stored locally, in close proximity to the end users. Also, the end user's equipment has the capability to passively acquire the geological position. As a consequence of this, the system may provide users with location awareness as well as low latency and reduced energy consumption. Devices located on the network's periphery and computers located in the cloud cooperate cooperatively to accomplish computations.

9.11 Industrial IoT

An expansion and application of IoT in a variety of industrial areas and applications is what is known as Industrial Internet of Things. The IIoT has the potential to revolutionize industrial and manufacturing processes because it integrates cutting-edge connectivity and automation technologies. This technology makes it possible to gather data in real time, analyze that data, and make decisions based on that data. This improves the efficiency of operations, reduces costs, and increases the level of safety. Through the use of IIoT, it is possible to continuously monitor the functioning of machinery, quality assurance, production output, and energy usage across the manufacturing environment. The use of real-time machine data analysis to spot probable issues before they happen enables predictive maintenance. Moreover, smart systems can effectively adapt to shifting situations in the operational environment thanks to machine learning algorithms. IIoT solutions are more accessible and affordable than ever, opening up chances to optimize operations that were previously impractical or expensive to complete, giving businesses a competitive edge over rivals who have not yet adopted this game-changing technology. IIoT is a computer innovation that could alter our society [42].

9.11.1 Advantages of IIoT

The IIoT provides considerable benefits to industrial enterprises by optimising operations and increasing productivity through the use of linked devices, sensors, and equipment. IIoT enables companies to monitor their assets remotely and in real time, as well as acquire profound insights into processes that were previously unobservable. This enables predictive maintenance, which can prevent unplanned downtime or system failures. This ultimately results in higher equipment availability and improved safety standards. Additionally, with the information gleaned from these systems, businesses are able to implement lean manufacturing strategies, which allow them to increase levels of performance while also cutting down on inefficiencies in the production processes. Moreover, IIoT provides businesses with valuable analytics that help identify areas for continuous improvement. This opens up new opportunities for businesses to either save money or increase their revenue. Integrating IIoT into existing industrial infrastructure has the potential to improve overall efficiency, cut down on operational costs, and enhance workforce management, all of which will lead to an increase in manufacturing operations' profitability [43].

9.11.2 Applications of IIoT

- **Predictive Quality:** Utilizing predictive quality analytics, which extracts actionable insights from a variety of sources of industrial data including production equipment, ambient variables, and human observations is one way to improve the quality of the output of a factory. This can be done to optimize the quality of the output of the factory. With the support of Amazon IoT, manufacturing companies are able to create predictive quality models, which subsequently enables them to make products of a higher quality. Improving product quality has a number of benefits, two of which are increased customer satisfaction and a reduction in the number of product recalls.
- **Asset Condition Monitoring:** Monitoring the condition of your assets, such as your machinery and equipment, can help you evaluate how well those assets are performing. You are able to record all IoT data with AWS IoT, including temperature, vibration, and error codes that indicate whether or not the equipment is functioning at its optimum level. You will be able to maximize the utilization of your asset as well as your investment in it if you boost its visibility.
- **Predictive Maintenance:** The process of using analytics to capture the state of industrial equipment in order to identify potential breakdowns before they disrupt production is known as predictive maintenance. This practice results in an increase in the lifespan of industrial equipment, an increase in worker safety, and an optimization of the supply chain. All of these benefits are a direct result of using analytics. Amazon IoT enables us to continuously monitor and infer the state, health, and performance of our equipment, which helps us to find issues in real time. Moreover, it enables us to solve issues as soon as they arise [44].

9.11.3 Risks and Challenges to IIoT

IIoT is bringing improved connection, real-time monitoring, and data analytics capabilities to the manufacturing industry, which is causing this industry to undergo a transformation. Nonetheless, the deployment of IIoT brings with it a variety of obstacles, including security concerns, restrictions on infrastructure, interoperability issues with legacy systems, and a lack of expertise among workers to handle sophisticated IIoT systems. The ever-increasing dangers posed by cyberattacks present significant challenges to the maintenance and operation of essential industrial infrastructures, such as power plants and transportation networks. In addition, existing control systems in factories frequently do not have the interoperability required by new IIoT devices, which results in integration difficulties. In addition, businesses may have a difficult time educating existing employees or recruiting new employees with the necessary skills to operate cutting-edge IIoT devices, which are needed for effective implementation. In order to address these challenges, it is necessary for manufacturers and providers of technological solutions to work together on the development of robust security protocols, the deployment of scalable infrastructure, the assurance that devices are compatible with legacy systems, and the provision of adequate training programmes to improve employees' capabilities in relation to this new technological frontier [45].

The implementation of an IIoT solution requires careful consideration to be given to three distinct aspects: availability, scalability, and security. This is due to the fact that availability and scalability may already have been second nature to industrial operations. This is due to the fact that availability and scalability make it possible for manufacturing operations to serve an increasing number of consumers. Yet, when it comes to integrating the IIoT into their operations, many businesses run into difficulties with the data security of their systems. One of the reasons for this is that many businesses are still using antiquated computer systems and business processes, which is one of the reasons why this is the case. The installation of new technology is made more difficult as a result of the fact that many of these have been in use for several decades and have not been modified since their inception [46].

Also, the proliferation of smart gadgets has resulted in an increase in security vulnerabilities, which in turn has raised concerns about accountability in the area of security. The ability of manufacturers to assure the safety of users and to provide either preventative measures or remedies in the event that security flaws are discovered is essential.

An even greater emphasis is being placed on the importance of cybersecurity as more serious security breaches come to light over the course of a number of years. If hackers were able to get access to connected systems, not only would this put the company at risk of suffering a significant data breach, but it would also put the operations at risk of coming to a halt. In order to ensure the safety of both physical and digital components, businesses and sectors that adopt the IIoT must, to some extent, organize themselves and do business in the same manner as traditional technology corporations. The appearance of threats is facilitated by voids in security, which might take the form of unprotected ports, insufficient authentication processes, or outmoded programmes. When you combine these factors with the fact that the network is directly connected to the internet, you open the door to even more potential dangers [47].

9.11.4 Comparison between IoT and IIoT

Devices that are part of the IoT include things like fitness bands, smart home appliances, and other applications that, even if something goes wrong with them, do not typically result in situations that are life-threatening. On the other hand, applications of the IIoT connect machines and devices in different industries such as manufacturing, utilities, and oil and gas. It is possible for deployments of the IIoT to experience system failures and downtime, which can lead to high-risk situations, some of which could even be life-threatening. Applications for the IIoT place a greater emphasis on enhancing productivity as well as health and safety, in contrast to the user-focused approach taken by apps for IoT [48].

9.11.5 Vendors of IIoT

Some of the vendors are:

- **ABB Ability:** A company that focuses on the IIoT that specializes in connection, software, and machine intelligence.
- **Aveva Wonderware:** A business that focuses on the creation of human-machine interfaces (HMIs) and IoT edge platforms for original equipment manufacturers (OEMs) and end users.
- **Axzon:** An IIoT company whose primary areas of concentration include intelligent vehicle production, predictive maintenance, and cold chain management.
- **Cisco IoT:** A company that specializes in networking and provides a number of different platforms for network connectivity, connectivity management, data control and sharing, as well as edge computing.
- **Fanuc Field System:** A company that has developed a framework for the interconnection of industrial IoT devices of varying ages, makers, and models.
- **Linx Global Manufacturing:** A corporation that specializes in the creation and production of products, as well as the provision of bespoke platforms for the Internet of Things, application development, and data management.
- **MindSphere by Siemens:** A solution for the IIoT that is centered on AI and advanced analytics.
- **Plataine:** An IIoT startup that specializes in applying AI to create actionable insights in the industrial industry [49]. Figure 9.3 lists well-known vendors in IIoT.

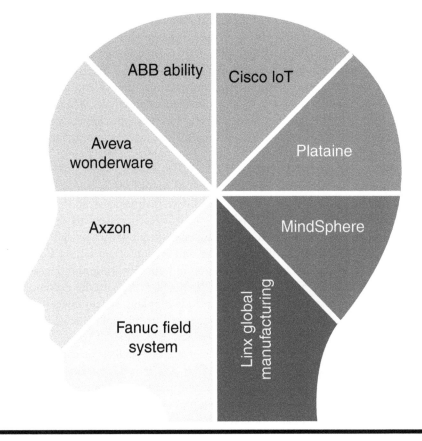

Figure 9.3 Well-known vendors in IIoT.

9.11.6 Future of IIoT

The IIoT is ushering in a revolutionary shift in the methodology that is utilized to carry out various industrial and manufacturing activities all around the world. The IIoT provides users with a variety of advantages, some of which include optimized production, analytics in real-time, and predictive maintenance. It is anticipated that the future of the IIoT will be one that is both fascinating and highly dynamic [50]. This is due to the continued development of IIoT applications as well as technology breakthroughs. As a result of this convergence, the traditional factory floor and the information technology department is brought closer together. This will make it possible to adopt IIoT in an efficient manner and on a wide scale. Nonetheless, this convergence also creates a significant number of challenges, including issues with integration and interoperability in addition to concerns around the safety of data. One further trend that will influence the future of IIoT is the development of edge computing, which will play a role in the field. The term edge computing refers to a model of distributed computing in which the computer power is moved closer to the Internet of Things devices. This brings the ability to process data, carry out analysis, and make decisions closer to the network's edge than before. Because applications for the IoT require data in real time that has minimal latency and high levels of reliability, this technology is ideal for those kinds of applications. When edge computing is used, only the data that is essential is uploaded to the cloud. This will assist to bring down the overall cost of transporting and storing data, as only the necessary data is uploaded [51].

Also necessary for the development of IIoT in the future are artificial intelligence and machine learning. The combination of AI and ML will make it possible to build intelligent factories, systems for predictive maintenance, and personalized goods. Artificial intelligence will make it possible for machines to draw lessons from their previous experiences, identify anomalies, improve quality, and maximize production. In addition, AI will assist in the automation of machine maintenance and diagnostics, which will lead to a reduction in both downtime and the expenses associated with repairs [52]. The future of IIoT will necessitate the existence of a thriving ecosystem of partners, which will include suppliers, system integrators, and service providers. An open design that promotes interoperability, scalability, and adaptability is necessary for the IIoT ecosystem. It is expected to be an exciting and extremely dynamic one, with several recurring themes like the convergence of edge computing, AI,ML, blockchain technology, and the requirement for a healthy ecosystem of partners. As IIoT develops, it will assist organizations in becoming more productive overall, as well as becoming more efficient, having fewer instances of downtime and higher-quality products.

9.11.7 Architecture and Components

The typical architecture of an IIoT system can be described using a four-layer model, which has gained widespread acceptance in the industry. As can be seen in Figure 9.4, the four layers that make up this model are the Application, Processing, Network, and perceptron layers [53].

■ **Perception Layer:** The perception layer pertains to all the sensors, actuators, devices, and physical objects used to gather data. Therefore, it is also referred to as the edge layer and device layer—a concept that also exists within IIoT. The sensors that are utilized in the IIoT are referred to as smart sensors. One of the distinguishing characteristics of smart sensors is that they communicate to the network, often via a wireless signal bypassing existing industrial networks that are typically wired. To guarantee smart sensors meet the requirements to maintain real-time data transmission successfully, the IEEE developed the 1451.4 standards [54].

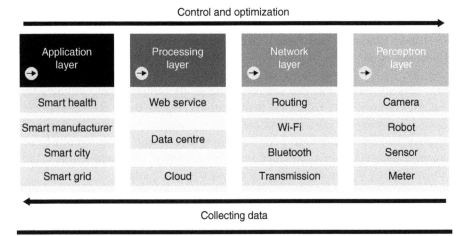

Figure 9.4 Various layers of IIoT.

■ **Network Layer:** The network layer comprises specific IIoT devices that transfer the collected data over the internet. If one follows the flow of data from bottom to top, beginning with the smart sensors and working their way up, the next device that is encountered is an IIoT Gateway. IIoT gateways, also known as edge gateways, perform the local storing and processing of the acquired data before transferring it to the next level up in the network. It is essential to keep in mind that edge gateways are not designed for process control and can only carry out the aforementioned operations on data before transmitting it to the cloud. However, they still require high processing power because of the large amounts of processed data [55].

■ **Processing Layer:** At this stage, the information has been received by a database or server located within a data centre. In order to successfully run data analytics and machine learning algorithms, typically significant quantities of processing power are required. This layer is responsible for the most crucial aspects of the data processing, as a result. In addition to the algorithms, this layer contains all of the cloud-based technologies as well as online services, which are used to assist the process. A web service describes data transfer from devices to other interfaces and programs.

■ **Application Layer:** The application layer refers to the GUIs that are deployed. These interfaces provide assistance to humans in the process of interpreting the information that was the outcome of the phase that came before it. In other words, user applications that generate reports, analyses, and statistics can be found in this layer and can be accessed through this layer. There are many application layer providers in the market today [56].

9.12 Conclusion

The chapter focused on the rapidly increasing use of edge computing along with AI and IoT in all walks of life. Edge computing complements the use of cloud computing by overcoming its limitations like increased latency, bandwidth requirement, network traffic, and reduced performance. By bringing the computing on the edge, it is possible to reduce the network traffic, reduce the load on the servers, reduce delays, provide real-time response, reduce power consumption, increase performance, and also reduce cost. Edge computing is making our lives simpler by its numerous applications in smart cities, smart homes, health care, industrial IoT, and many more such as in smart energy and mobile edge computing.

References

[1] Khan, L.U. *et al.* (2020) "Edge-computing-enabled smart cities: A comprehensive survey," *IEEE Internet of Things Journal*, 7(10), pp. 10200–10232. Available at: https://doi.org/10.1109/jiot.2020.2987070.

[2] Mohamed, N., Al-Jaroodi, J. and Jawhar, I. (2019) "Towards fault tolerant Edge computing for IOT-based smart city applications," *2019 IEEE 9th Annual Computing and Communication Workshop and Conference (CCWC)*.

[3] *Edge computing capabilities and innovations to enable value creation …* (no date). Available at: www.researchgate.net/publication/366965264_Edge_Computing_capabilities_and_innovations_to_enable_value_creation_and_sustainable_operations_in_the_different_vertical_use_cases_such_as_smart_cities_health_and_logistics_and_its_impacts_and_benefi (Accessed: March 18, 2023).

[4] Bourechak, A. *et al.* (2023) "At the confluence of Artificial Intelligence and edge computing in IOT-based applications: A review and new perspectives," *Sensors*, 23(3), p. 1639. Available at: https://doi.org/10.3390/s23031639.

[5] Pandya, S. *et al.* (2023) "Federated learning for smart cities: A comprehensive survey," *Sustainable Energy Technologies and Assessments*, 55, p. 102987. Available at: https://doi.org/10.1016/j.seta.2022.102987.

[6] Ahmed, A., Ahmed, E. A survey on mobile edge computing. In Proceedings of the 10th International Conference on Intelligent Systems and Control (ISCO), Coimbatore, India, 7–8 January 2016, pp. 1–8.

[7] O'Donnell, B. The Future of Advanced-Edge Computing Is Actually in Autonomous Cars. 2017. Available online: www.recode.net/2017/3/14/14924892/autonomous-car-self-driving-cloud-Edge-advancededge-computing.

[8] Bonomi, F., Milito, R., Zhu, J., Addepalli, S. Edge computing and its role in the internet of things. In Proceedings of the First Edition of the MCC Workshop on Mobile Cloud Computing, Helsinki, Finland, 17 August 2012, pp. 13–16.

[9] El-Sayed, H. and Chaqfeh, M. (2019) "Exploiting mobile edge computing for enhancing vehicular applications in smart cities," *Sensors*, 19(5), p. 1073. Available at: https://doi.org/10.3390/s19051073.

[10] Sasaki, K., Suzuki, N., Makido, S., Nakao, A. Vehicle control system coordinated between cloud and mobile edge computing. In Proceedings of the 55th Annual

Conference of the Society of Instrument and Control Engineers of Japan (SICE), Tsukuba, Japan, 20–23 September 2016, pp. 1122–1127.

[11] O. Altintas, S. Banerjee, F. Dressler, G. Heijenk, Executive summary–intervehicular communication towards cooperative driving, in: Dagstuhl Seminar 18202 on Inter-Vehicular Communication–Towards Cooperative Driving, Schloss Dagstuhl, Schloss Dagstuhl, Germany, 2018, pp. 31–59, http://dx.doi.org/10. 4230/DagRep.8.5.31.

[12] T. Higuchi, S. Ucar, C.-H. Wang, O. Altintas, Vehicular micro cloud as an enabler of intelligent intersection management, in: 12th IEEE Vehicular NetworkingConference (VNC 2020), Demo Session, IEEE, Virtual Conference, 2020.

[13] S. Kim, B. Qin, Z.J. Chong, X. Shen, W. Liu, M.H. Ang, E. Frazzoli, D. Rus, Multivehicle cooperative driving using cooperative perception: Design and experimental validation, IEEE Trans. Intell. Transp. Syst. (TITS) 16 (2) (2015) 663–680, http://dx.doi.org/10.1109/TITS.2014.2337316.

[14] Mobile Edge Computing (MEC), Framework and Reference Architecture, MEC 003 V1.1.1, ETSI, 2016.

[15] T. Higuchi, J. Joy, F. Dressler, M. Gerla, O. Altintas, On the feasibility of vehicular micro clouds, in: 9th IEEE Vehicular Networking Conference (VNC 2017), IEEE, Turin, Italy, 2017, pp. 179–182, http://dx.doi.org/10.1109/VNC. 2017.8275621.

[16] Pannu, G.S. *et al.* (2021) "Dwell time estimation at intersections for improved vehicular micro cloud operations," *Ad Hoc Networks*, 122, p. 102606. Available at: https://doi.org/10.1016/j.adhoc.2021.102606.

[17] Chen, C.-H., Wu, C.-D., Chiang, H.-C., Chu, D., Lee, K.-Y., Lin, W.-Y., Yeh, J.-I., Tsai, K.-W., Guo, Y.-L.L. The effects of fine and coarse particulate matter on lung function among the elderly. *Sci. Rep.* 2019, *9*, 14790.

[18] Kong, X., Tong, S., Gao, H., Shen, G., Wang, K., Collotta, M., You, I., Das, S.K. Mobile edge cooperation optimization for wearable Internet of Things: A network representation-based framework. *IEEE Trans. Ind. Inform.* 2021, *17*, 5050–5058.

[19] Sharma, V., You, I., Andersson, K., Palmieri, F., Rehmani, M.H., Lim, J. Security, Privacy and trust for smart mobile–Internet of Things (M-IoT): A survey. *IEEE Access* 2020, *8*, 167123–167163.

[20] Abdellatif, A.A. *et al.* (2019) "Edge computing for smart health: Context-aware approaches, opportunities, and challenges," *IEEE Network*, 33(3), pp. 196–203. Available at: https://doi.org/10.1109/mnet.2019.1800083.

[21] Li Jiang, Da-You Liu and Bo Yang (no date) "Smart home research," *Proceedings of 2004 International Conference on Machine Learning and Cybernetics (IEEE Cat. No.04EX826)* [Preprint]. Available at: https://doi.org/10.1109/icmlc.2004.1382266.

[22] Gazafroudi, A.S., Soares, J., Ghazvini, M.A.F., Pinto, T., Vale, Z., Corchado, J.M. Stochastic interval-based optimal offering model for residential energy management systems by household owners. Int. J. Electr. Power Energy Syst. 2019, 5, 201–219.

[23] Zhou, B., Li, W., Chan, K.W., Cao, Y., Kuang, Y., Liu, X., Wang, X. Smart home energy management systems: Concept, configurations, and scheduling strategies. Renew. Sustain. Energy Rev. 2016, 61, 30–40.

[24] Sbci, U. Buildings and climate change: Summary for decision-makers. In Sustainable Buildings and Climate Initiative: United Nations Environmental Programme: Nairobi, Kenya, 2009, pp. 1–62.

[25] Birol, F. World Energy Outlook. Available online: www.iea.org/reports/world-energy-outlook-2010 (accessed on 10 July 2021).

[26] Yar, H. *et al.* (2021) "Towards smart home automation using IOT-enabled edge-computing paradigm," *Sensors*, 21(14), p. 4932. Available at: https://doi.org/10.3390/s21144932.

[27] Trimananda, R. *et al.* (2018) "Vigilia: Securing smart home edge computing," *2018 IEEE/ACM Symposium on Edge Computing (SEC)* [Preprint]. Available at: https://doi.org/10.1109/sec.2018.00013.

[28] Chakraborty, T. and Datta, S.K. (2017) "Home automation using edge computing and internet of things," *2017 IEEE International Symposium on Consumer Electronics (ISCE)* [Preprint]. Available at: https://doi.org/10.1109/isce.2017.8355544.

[29] Sharif, Z. *et al.* (2022) "Smart home automation by internet-of-things edge computing platform," *International Journal of Advanced Computer Science and Applications*, 13(4). Available at: https://doi.org/10.14569/ijacsa.2022.0130455.

[30] Wang, H. *et al.* (2017) "HealthEdge: Task scheduling for edge computing with health emergency and human behavior consideration in smart homes," *2017 IEEE International Conference on Big Data (Big Data)* [Preprint]. Available at: https://doi.org/10.1109/bigdata.2017.8258047.

[31] Yuan, D. *et al.* (2020) "Intrusion detection for smart home security based on data augmentation with edge computing," *ICC 2020–2020 IEEE International Conference on Communications (ICC)* [Preprint]. Available at: https://doi.org/10.1109/icc40277.2020.9148632.

[32] T. Vu, F. Lin, N. Alshurafa, and W. Xu, "Wearable food intake monitoring technologies: A comprehensive review," Computers, vol. 6, no. 1, Mar 2017.

[33] J. L. Scisco, E. R. Muth, and A. W. Hoover, "Examining the utility of a bite-countbased measure of eating activity in free-living human beings," Journal of the Academy of Nutrition and Dietetics, vol. 114, no. 3, pp. 464–469, Mar 2014.

[34] M. Farooq and E. Sazonov, "Detection of chewing from piezoelectric film sensor signals using ensemble classifiers," in 2016 38th Annual International Conference of the IEEE Engineering in Medicine and Biology Society (EMBC). IEEE, 2016, pp. 4929–4932.

[35] H. Kalantarian, N. Alshurafa, and M. Sarrafzadeh, "A wearable nutrition monitoring system," in 2014 11th International Conference on Wearable and Implantable Body Sensor Networks. IEEE, 2014, pp. 75–80.

[36] M. Sun, L. E. Burke, Z.-H. Mao, Y. Chen, H.-C. Chen, Y. Bai, Y. Li, C. Li, and W. Jia, "eButton: A wearable computer for health monitoring and personal assistance," in Proceedings of the 51st Annual Design Automation Conference (DAC'14). ACM, 2014, pp. 16:1–16:6.

[37] B. Zhou, J. Cheng, M. Sundholm, A. Reiss, W. Huang, O. Amft, and P. Lukowicz, "Smart table surface: A novel approach to pervasive dining monitoring," in 2015 IEEE International Conference on Pervasive Computing and Communications (PerCom). IEEE, 2015, pp. 155–162.

[38] Y. Gao, N. Zhang, H. Wang, X. Ding, X. Ye, G. Chen, and Y. Cao, "iHear food: Eating detection using commodity bluetooth headsets," in 2016 IEEE First International Conference on Connected Health: Applications, Systems and Engineering Technologies (CHASE). IEEE, 2016, pp. 163–172.

[39] M. Mirtchouk, C. Merck, and S. Kleinberg, "Automated estimation of food type and amount consumed from body-worn audio and motion sensors," in Proceedings

of the 2016 ACM International Joint Conference on Pervasive and Ubiquitous Computing. ACM, 2016, pp. 451–462.

[40] Javadi, B. *et al.* (2020) "Smart food scanner system based on mobile edge computing," *2020 IEEE International Conference on Cloud Engineering (IC2E)* [Preprint]. Available at: https://doi.org/10.1109/ic2e48712.2020.00009.

[41] Liu, C. *et al.* (2018) "A new deep learning-based food recognition system for dietary assessment on an edge computing service infrastructure," *IEEE Transactions on Services Computing*, 11(2), pp. 249–261. Available at: https://doi.org/10.1109/tsc.2017.2662008.

[42] Chettri, L., & Bera, R. (2020). A comprehensive survey on Internet of Things (IoT) toward 5G wireless systems. *IEEE Internet of Things Journal*, 7(1), 16–32. https://doi.org/10.1109/JIOT.2019.2948888.

[43] Christou, I. T., Kefalakis, N., Soldatos, J. K., &Despotopoulou, A.-M. (2022). End-to-end industrial IoT platform for Quality 4.0 applications. *Computers in Industry*, 137, 103591.https://doi.org/10.1016/j.compind.2021.103591.

[44] Goundar, S., Bhardwaj, A., Nur, S. S., Kumar, S. S., & Harish, R. (2021). Industrial Internet of Things: Benefit, applications, and challenges. In S. Goundar, J. Avanija, G. Sunitha, K. R. Madhavi, & S. B. Bhushan (Eds.), *Advances in Computer and Electrical Engineering* (pp. 133–148). IGI Global. https://doi.org/10.4018/978-1-7998-3375-8.ch010.

[45] Hazra, A., Adhikari, M., Amgoth, T., &Srirama, S. N. (2023). A comprehensive survey on interoperability for IIoT: Taxonomy, standards, and future directions. *ACM Computing Surveys*, 55(1), 1–35. https://doi.org/10.1145/3485130.

[46] Jain, S., & Chandrasekaran, K. (2022). Industrial automation using Internet of Things: In I. R. Management Association (Ed.), *Research Anthology on Cross-Disciplinary Designs and Applications of Automation* (pp. 355–383). IGI Global. https://doi.org/10.4018/978-1-6684-3694-3.ch019.

[47] Karmakar, A., Dey, N., Baral, T., Chowdhury, M., & Rehan, Md. (2019). Industrial Internet of Things: A review. *2019 International Conference on Opto-Electronics and Applied Optics (Optronix)*, 1–6. https://doi.org/10.1109/OPTRO NIX.2019.8862436.

[48] Khan, W. Z., Rehman, M. H., Zangoti, H. M., Afzal, M. K., Armi, N., & Salah, K. (2020). Industrial internet of things: Recent advances, enabling technologies and open challenges. *Computers & Electrical Engineering*, 81, 106522. https://doi.org/10.1016/j.compeleceng.2019.106522.

[49] Madakam, S., Ramaswamy, R., & Tripathi, S. (2015). Internet of Things (IoT): A literature review.*Journal of Computer and Communications*, 03(05), 164–173.https://doi.org/10.4236/jcc.2015.35021.

[50] Patil, S., Mujawar, A., Kharade, K. G., Kharade, S. K., Katkar, S. V., &Kamat, R. K. (2022). Drowsy driver detection using OpencvAnd Raspberry Pi3. *Webology*, 19(2), 6003–6010.

[51] Posey, B., Rosencrance, L., & Shea, S. (2022, March). Industrial internet of things (IIoT). *IoT Agenda*. www.techtarget.com/iotagenda/definition/Industrial-Internet-of-Things-IIoT.

[52] Prathima, Ch., Muppalaneni, N. B., &Kharade, K. G. (2022). Deduplication of IoT data in Cloud Storage. In Ch. Satyanarayana, X.-Z. Gao, C.-Y. Ting, & N.

B. Muppalaneni (Eds.), *Machine Learning and Internet of Things for Societal Issues* (pp. 147–157). Springer Nature, Singapore. https://doi.org/10.1007/978-981-16-5090-1_13.

[53] Sun, Y., Leng, L., Jin, Z., & Kim, B.-G. (2022). Reinforced palmprint reconstruction attacks in biometric systems. *Sensors, 22*(2), 591. https://doi.org/10.3390/s22020591.

[54] Swami, A., Patil, A., & Kharade, K. G. (2019). Applications of IoT for smart agriculture or farming. *International Journal of Research and Analytical Reviews, 6*(2), 537–540.

[55] Xu, H., Yu, W., Griffith, D., & Golmie, N. (2018). A survey on industrial Internet of Things: A cyber-physical systems perspective. *IEEE Access, 6*, 78238–78259. https://doi.org/10.1109/ACCESS.2018.2884906.

[56] Xu, L. D., He, W., & Li, S. (2014). Internet of Things in industries: A survey. *IEEE Transactions on Industrial Informatics, 10*(4), 2233–2243. https://doi.org/10.1109/TII.2014.2300753.

Chapter 10

Application of Edge AI in Biomedicine

Om M. Bagade[1], Priyanka E. Doke-Bagade[2], and Krushna S. Wankhade[3]

[1]Department of Pharmaceutics, Vishwakarma University School of Pharmacy, Pune, Maharashtra, India.

[2]School of Pharmaceutical Sciences, Vels Institute of Science, Technology & Advanced Studies (VISTAS), Pallavaram, Chennai, Tamil Nadu, India·.

[3]Department of Computer Science (Data Science), D.Y.Patil College of Engineering and technology (An Autonomous Institute, Kolhapur, Maharashtra, India.

10.1 Introduction

It is challenging to define artificial intelligence (AI), in part because the term "intelligence" itself is ill-defined. At Future Advocacy, we define intelligence broadly to include "problem-solving" and define "an intelligent system" as one that acts appropriately given the circumstances [1]. The term "artificial intelligence" serves as a catch-all for a variety of methods.Up until the 1980s, "Symbolic AI," commonly referred to as "good old-fashioned AI," was the preeminent paradigm in AI research. It focuses on human-readable interpretations of issues and logic [2]. Machine learning (ML) approaches like deep learning and neural networks, whichrely on sophisticated statistical techniques to discover learn from these patterns, patterns in data, and then make predictions based on these data, are the focus of most of the present excitement surrounding AI. Predictive analytics and data analytics are further concepts that fall under the category of "artificial intelligence." Symbolic AI, which is primarily focused on expert systems, is included in the broad and straightforward classification of AI, whereas ML also includes deep learning [3].

AI and similar technologies are becoming more and more common in both society and business, and they are starting to be used in healthcare. Several facets of patient care could be changed by these technology, as well as internal administrative procedures at payer, provider, and pharmaceutical organizations. Numerous investigations have indeed demonstrated that AI can diagnose diseases as well as or superior than living beings at crucial healthcare tasks. Today, computers are already more accurate than radiologists in spotting malignant tumors and guiding scientists in the development of cohorts for pricey clinical trials. Nonetheless, we think it will be a long time before AI completely replaces humans in large medical process domains for a variety of reasons. In this essay, we discuss both the promise for automation in healthcare as well as certain obstacles that stand in the way of its quick adoption [4].

10.2 AI Milestones

The term "artificial intelligence" first appeared in print in 1956. Nonetheless, real concern and symbolic approaches have both exploited the concept of AI since 1950 [5]. In Table 10.1, significant achievements in the field of AI applications are listed.

Table 10.1 Success Steps of AI with Applications

Milestone	*Year*
The ability of neurons connected in a network to perform logical operations like "and," "or," and "not" was demonstrated by Walter Pitts and Warren McCulloch.	1943
Artificial intelligence first came into use.	1956
Perceptrons, a type of neural network invented by Frank Rosenblatt, are capable of transmitting information only in one direction.	1958
The "First AI Winter" has begun.	1974
Back propagation method design, which is frequently utilized in deep learning, was promoted by Georey Hinton.	1986
Initiation of "AI winter."	1987
IBM Deep Blue defeated Russian grandmaster Garry Kasparov.	1997
Using British technology, Google conducted effective image research.	2013
Go champion Lee Sedol was defeated by Google Deep Mind's software Alpha Go in this year.	2016

10.2 AI in Drug Delivery

Throughout the lastcouple of decades, AI has undergone noteworthy transform. Uses of AIM encompass and grown because of the prologue of ML as well as DL, allowing for personalized care as opposed to medication that relies only on computer algorithms.Prospects for anticipatory medicine may make use of predictive models for illness diagnosis, therapy response prediction, and other purposes. AI may improve patient outcomes overall, improve illness and treatment monitoring, improve procedure accuracy, and streamline clinical operations and workflow. The following timeline of the ongoing development and evolution of mobile applications in medicine is organized in accordance with significant historical turning points [5–8].

10.2.1 Evolution of AI

Modern AI sought to build machines that could make decisions or perform tasks that had previously been limited to humans. In 1961, Universal Motors introduced the Unimate, the very foremost engineering arm of robot, to the assembly line for automated diecasting. Unimate was able comply with directives stage. A few seasons back, Joseph Weizenbaum encountered Eliza for the first time (1964). He was competent to converse utilizing prototype substitution and identical techniques to simulate individual speech through natural language processing (NLP) (superficial communication). It became the template for upcoming chatbots.

Shakey, dubbed "the first electronic person," was created in 1966. This mobile robot, developed at Stanford Research Institute, was the first capable of following instructions including comprehending supplementary intricate instructions and executed the obligatory actions instead of merely subsequent one-stage instructions. This marked a significant turning point for robotics and AI. Despite these engineering advancements, AI use in medicine was gradual. But during this early stage, digitizing data was crucial since it laid the groundwork for AIM's future development and application. The National Library of Medicine (NLMcreation)'s of the Medical related Literature and its Analysis in addition to Retrieval System (MEDLARS) and the internet-based web browser "PubMed"in the 1960s served as a crucial digital source for the subsequent stepping up of biomedicine. This period saw the initial creation of health informatics databases and health record systems, which laid the groundwork for later AIM advances [9–10].

The majority of this time is known as the "AI Winter," which denotes a time of decreased financial assistance and interest and as a result less notable progress. Several people agree that there were two big winters: the initial one that occurred in the 1970s, which was caused by the claimed AI restrictions and the next in the late 1980s and early 1990s, which was due to the prohibitive charge of maintaining and creating expert digital information in order to maintain the records. Collaboration among early adopters of AI persisted throughout this time despite a widespread lack of interest in the field. This encouraged Saul Amarel to create the Equipping on Computers in Biomedicine at Rutgers University in 1971. A time-shared computer system called the "Stanford University Medical Experimental-Artificial Intelligence in Medicine (SUMEX-AIM)" was developed in 1973 to improve networking competency between clinical and biomedical researchers from various universities. The whole initial NIH-subsidized AI in delivery of drug symposium was hosted at the University of Rutgers in 1975, largely as a result of these partnerships. These occasions show the earliest instances of cooperation between AIM's founders [11].

The creation of a conference on glaucoma by means of the replica of CASNET was the best primary samples to show the viability of utilizing AI for delivery ofAPIs. A causal-combined set-up is made up of three independent approaches: sculpt-construction, consultation, as well as collaboratively created and maintained data-base.With the help of this model, doctors can learn more about a certain disease and how to treat specific patients. It was created at Rutgers University, and it made its public debut in 1976 in Las Vegas, Nevada, at the Academia of Ophthalmology convention [9–12].

Early in the 1970s, the "backward chaining" system of AI in MYCIN was created. MYCIN is defined as, it is an inventory of prospective a virulent species and afterwards proposes treatment for antibiotic alternatives accustomed correctly for the weight of the patient's as a host based on the doctor's registration of the patients information and just a technical knowledge of about 600 regulations. The subsequently developed rule-based system, EMYCIN, was built on top of MYCIN. In order to aid the chief concern physician in the case of diagnosis, INTERNIST-1 was eventually expanded utilizing the identical scaffold as EMYCIN or greater body of checkup information. A decision-support system called DXplain was introduced in 1986 mostly by the University of Massachusetts. This application creates a differential diagnosis based on the symptoms you enter. With thorough explanations of diseases and supplementary references, it also functions as an electronic health text-book. When it was first made available, it had data on about 500 different disorders. Ever since, it has grown to include more than 2400 illnesses. The resurgence of ML research in the late 1990s, particularly in the field of medicine, along with the afore-mentioned technological advancements, helped pave the way for the contemporary age of AIM [13].

10.3 Advancement in AI

Watson, an accessible question-answering system developed by IBM, competed against human contestants on the televised series Jeopardy! Unlike conventional systems, which relied onboth forward reasoning (obeying the decrees from information to findings), toward the back analysis (following rules from findings to statistics), or manually created IFTHEN rules, this new technology, known as Deep QA, analyzed data over unstructured content using natural (ordinary) language processing (NLP) and numerous studies to produce likely answers. This technology was more accessible, simpler to operate, and more affordable.

10.3.1 Classification of Artificial Intelligence [14–18]

1. According to their caliber
   a. Narrow (ANI) or Weak Intelligence
   b. General (AGI)
   c. Super (ASI)

2. According to their Presence
   a. Limited Memory System
   b. Based on Theory of Mind
   c. Reactive Machine
   d. Individuality and attentiveness

Based on their capacities, the major aspects of AI include:

- **Narrow (ANI) or Weak AI**: It is only capable of a small number of activities, including traffic signaled, chess learning, image recognition, and automotive driving.
- **General (AGI)**: Strong AI, sometimes referred to as General (AGI), is a part of AIthat is capable of carrying out all tasks at a human level. It can make human intelligence simpler and make it possible to finish difficult jobs.
- **Super (ASI)**: In terms of drawing, math, space, etc., it is considerably busier and more intelligent than people.

AI can be divided into the following categories depending on whether they are already existing or not:

- **Type I**: It serves the purpose of applications with a limited scope that cannot draw on foreknowledge since it lacks a memory system. It is referred to as a reactive machine.
- **Type II**: It has a limited memory mechanism and may make use of existing information to deal with a variety of problems. The decision-making systems in automatic cars use certain recorded observations to record subsequent actions, but these data cannot yet be stored indefinitely.

- The "Theory of Mind" is the foundation of **type III**. It means to facilitate individual judgment, objective, and desires a bearing on the choices they make. It is a hypothetical AI system.
- **Type IV**: It possesses a sense of identity and consciousness, or self-awareness. It is also artificially uncreated.

10.3.2 Neural-networks and ANNs [19–21]

Neural-networks' (since key statistics) learning algorithm primarily acquires two diverse forms.

- **Unsupervised knowledge**: Input statistics with recognized patterns are sent to the neural network and later it serves organizational needs. "Self Organizing Map" or "Kohonen" algorithm is applied in such process. Such type of modeling is regarded while being quite helpful for identifying relationships among large, complex data sets.
- **Supervised learning**: Sequences of synchronizing inputs and outputs are used to show such a type of neural network. It is employed to teach the relationships and connections between inputs and outputs.

It reveals its value in formulating a way to evaluate the cause as well as effect relationships amid key and outcome. Nearly everyone admired ANN which is artificial neural network model encompassing the mathematics along with the computations approach which imitate the processes of human brain as well as it wholly reliant on the feedforward knowledge rule. Such learning technique is regarded since the best line of attack for classification and prophecy tasks.

The primary component of the neural network is an elementary mathematical processing unit known as a neuron.

Every input has a corresponding weight that reflects its relative importance, and the output is the weighted sum of all the inputs. After being altered by a transformation function, this output is subsequently transmitted to a different neuron. The entire mechanism is referred to as a "perceptron-a feed-forward system." Many neurons in a NN are arranged in network layouts. Multilayer perceptron networks are the most well-known and successful networks. In this network architecture, identical neurons are placed so that the upshots are displayed at the top sheet and the keys are displayed in the layer below. Between the layers that provide input and output, extra covert layers may be initiated. The number of hidden layers might theoretically be attached based on individual requirements. In reality, applications with significant nonlinear behavior require numerous layers.

The (ANN) artificial neural network model which is made up of thousands of individual artificial neurons linked to the parts of the neural configuration, it become referred to as dispensation elements since it take part in structure processing.

A possible modeling strategy is presented by ANN methodology, particularly for data sets with nonlinear linkages that are frequently seen in pharmaceutical research. An analysis of the model definition using ANNs does not require knowledge of the statistics resource. Yet, they typically carry a number of weights that need to be examined. They call for bigger training sets as well. In order to tackle the issues, ANNs can also combine and merge both the literary and the investigational data [22].

ANNs have a wide range of potential applications in pharmacy, from data analysis to modeling pharmaceutical quality control. ANNs have also been shown to be useful for creating drugs, particularly for computational modeling and QSAR-Quantitative structure activity relationship which helpful to revel the relationship among structureal traits and biological activities. Additionally, they are employed in biopharmaceutical analyses including in vitro and in vivo correlation coefficient, pharmacokinetic modeling, and formulation optimization methods for creating dosage forms [23–27].

10.3.3 Differentiating Between Fuzzy and Neurofuzzy

Conventional logic states that a proposition may be true or untrue. The underlying logical hypothesis either belongs to or completely departs from the"true" set. After the assumption is part of the "true set," the involvement role is written as "1," and while it is not, it is denoted as "0." Lotfi Zadeh promoted fuzzy logic's fundamental idea in the 1960s. Unlike conventional logic, which can either be 0 or 1, fuzzy logic can be anything. Nevertheless, whichever uninterrupted assessment in the middle of these confines can be in use here. While a temperature of 20°C is considered "pleasant," temperatures of "19°C or 21°C" that fall out of such a range are "uncomfortable,"as per the common judgment. Process control can really benefit from this thinking. The automated method utilizing fuzzy logic regarding drug release has been developed and analyzed for automated circulations through the arteries and veins. Fuzzy hemodynamic management modules are currently being utilized to analyze patients' conditions and report on the control of their arterial and cardiac output. The automated system built on fuzzy logic provides a comparably quicker response and more effective hemodynamic management. Additionally, supervisory-fuzzy guideline adaptive control systems are taken into consideration as a viable means of regulating the hemodynamic process associated with various drugs.

The term "neurofuzzy logic system" refers to a fuzzy logic system that has been tightly coupled with a neural network. Fuzzy logic's capacity for naturally expressing complicated concepts and neural networks' capacity for learning from data are effectively integrated in this situation. It has the ability to mine data. Neurofuzzy networkings have been used in a study to simulate the absorption of probucol through lipid formulations. The studyshowed an effective predictive presentation, the potential for the establishment of complicated relationships, and interpolates the pharmacokinetic limitations when used in conjunction with an *in vitro* and *in vivo* correlation tool [28].

10.3.4 Principle Component Method (PCA)

Another AI-based approach called principle component method (PCA) reduces the sets of the statistics by retaining "variability"and as practicable while minimizing information loss. By creating successively more uncorrelated variables that maximize the variance, PCA modeling searches for newer variables that are linear combinations that correspond to the original dataset. The primary components speed up the resolution of an eigenvector or eigenvalue challenge by searching for such newer variables. The majority of PCA's uses are descriptive instead of inferential, and it can be predicated upon the "covariance matrix" or perhaps the "matrix of correlation" [29].

10.3.5 Machine that Supports Vectors (SVM)

The idea of a lower dimensional hyperdimensional detector serves as the foundation for this method. Most of its foundation comes from statistical learning theory (SLT). It seeks to identify a linear optimal hyperplane. The SVM approach has lately been used in numerous applications since it offers several advantages over other traditional ML techniques. The following are some of the key advantages of the SVM approach [30]:

i. The SVM approach's solution is unique, optimal, and global since an SVM is trained by resolving a quadratic problem that is linearly constrained.
ii. Just two free parameters need to be selected: the upper bound parameter and the kernel parameter.
iii. The SVM technique has strong generalization performance and high-caliber robustness.

SVM methodology has recently been used for structure-activity connection analysis, demonstrating its potential in the field of drug discovery. In a benchmark test, Burbidge et al. (2001) compared the SVM methodology to a number of ML methods currently in use in the field of drug discovery. The findings of this study illustrate that, with the exception of a manual capacity-controlled neural network, which requires much longer to guide [31].

10.3.6 Hammeistern Weiner (HW) Model

One of the AI models that have nothing to do with biology is the Hammeistern Weiner (HW) modeling approach. When compared to other approaches, itis more adaptable and flexible, andproduces a superior fitting. If two linear dynamic blocks are employed in sequence with the first straight block, the HW model is implemented. The dynamic aspects are only present in the linear block [32].

10.4 Advantages of AI [33–38]

The following are some potential benefits of AI technology:

- **Minimizing errors**: AI helps to reduce errors and boost accuracy with greater precision. Intelligent robots are used to explore space because they have durable metal bodies and can withstand the hostile atmosphere.
- **Challenging exploration**: The mining industry demonstrates the value of AI. The industry of fuel exploration also makes use of it. By overcoming the faults made by humans, AI systems have the capacity tostudy the ocean.
- **Practical use on a regular basis**: AI is incredibly helpful for our daily tasks. For instance, GPS systems are frequently utilized on long drives. AI integration in Android devices makes it possible to anticipate what someone will input. Moreover, it aids with spelling correction.
- **Digital Helpers**: The use of AI systems resembling "avatar" ("models of digital assistants") by advanced enterprises todayis reducing the necessity for human labor. The "avatar"can make the best decisions logically since they are completely impassive. Human sentiments and the doldrums interfere with effectiveness of judgment; nevertheless, it may overcome through AI.
- **Repeated activities**: Typically, humans can only focus on one task at a time. Machines can multitask and interpret data more quickly than people can. This is in contrast to how humans process information. They can change the speed and time of the machine, among other settings, to suit their needs.
- **Medical applications**: In general, doctors can evaluate patients' conditions and study the negative effects as well as other health hazards linked to a medicine with the use of AI programs. By using AI programs, like utilizing innovative surgical procedure (for instance, GIT, CVS and CNS simulation, etc.), trainee surgeons can learn new skills.
- **No breaks**: Compared to humans, who can work for 8 hours a day without taking a break, robots are programmed to be able to operate continuously for an extended amount of time without issue.
- **Increase technical expansion pace**: The majority of the world's most cutting-edge innovations involve AI technology. It strives to create newer compounds and is able to provide a variety of computer modeling programs. Moreover, the creation of delivery of drug formulations makes use of AI technology.
- **No danger**: There is a high risk of injury to the personnel working in risky environments like fire stations. If an accident occurs, the ML programs' damaged components may be reparable.
- **Provides assistance**: AI technology has served both young people and the elderly on a round-the-clock basis, fulfilling a varied purpose. It can serve as a resource for studying and teaching for everyone.
- **Endless functions**: Machines are not constrained by any bounds, which leads to endless functions. Machines without emotions are capable of performing all tasks more quickly and correctly than people.

10.5 Limitations of AI [33–38]

The following are some significant drawbacks of AI technology:

- **Costly**: The introduction of AI leads to significant financial outlays. Complicated machine designing, upkeep, and repair are very cost-effective. The research & development section needs a significant amount of time to build just one AI machine. Software for AI machines needs to be updated frequently. Reinstallations and machine recovery take a long time and cost a lot of money.
- **No human reproduction**: Robots with AI tools have the capability to behave like individuals and to be dispassionate, which gives them an edge in performing assigned tasks more correctly and without passing judgment. Robots cannot make judgments about uncharted problems or produce incorrect information.
- **Minimal advancement with experience**: Experiences can help human resources. On the other hand, AI-powered robots cannot benefit from experience. They have no ability to distinguish between those who are diligent workers and those who are not.
- **Lack of originality**: AI-powered machines lack both emotional intelligence and sensitivity. Humans are capable of hearing, seeing, feeling, and thinking. They can think and be creative at the same time. These traits are impossible to attain with this system.
- **Redundancy**: The broad applications of such technology throughout every single area may bring about a high level of redundancy. Human workers might lose their work habits and inventiveness since a result of the unfavorable unemployment has been noticed.

10.6 AI in Drug Discovery [39–42]

The drug discovery is the process of recognizing the chemical entities which shows its potential to become therapeutically active as one of the agent and which starts with the results that have been obtained from many resources, such as slightly elevated, fragment transmission models, models of computational path, and reported accessible data. Computer-assisted design methodologies can be used in the drug discovery process to examine the structural categorization of APIs either straightforwardly or ultimately before organic drug molecule synthesis is carried out. The drug molecules that have been created or the drug compounds that have been gathered are put through slightly elevated models in the prime assay, or after that, they are mitigated and assessed for systemic absorption in supplementary analysiswith effective relation between structure and activity (SAR) assessment. The effectiveness of the drug discovery process is increased by the automation of some steps in the inductive-deductive cycle, which reduces uncertainty and inaccuracy. By using deep learning software, such as "NVIDIA DGX-1," chemical and pharmaceutical producers can study and derive information from various patents as well as genetic database-based scientific research. Humans are unable to use all of the knowledge available to enhance scientific research. Supercomputers with AI are capable of absorbing and examining data in order to identify associations between compounds and provide newer drug molecules.

The usage of chemical space is a concern for AI applications in the drug discovery process.As it is possible to computationally fully utilize the required compounds, the compound gap actually provides the segment again for recognition of fresh molecules. Moreover, the identification of target-specific efficient compounds is aided by learning algorithms and related predictive techniques. Fewer molecules are processed with significantly greater confidence in their activity thanks to benevolent AI. Throughout this respect, de novo design necessitates knowledge of natural synthesis intended for the fabrication of "*in silico*" particles as well as the high throughput examining modeling, which serve as substitutes for numerous biochemical and natural tests to determine the efficacy and toxicity profiles. A variety of in silico approach for the selection of profiles, such as substituents conceptual models or molecular architecture design approaches, may be used. The next generation of AI is being developed for molecules in silico. There are several software options and suggestions available for it. This layout is not helpful in the search for new drugs, but it is related to the development of difficult-to-synthesize components [43].

Although recursive neural circuits are used in de novo design, they were first developed for the purpose of analyzing natural language. Recursive neural networks take the sequential data as input. Recursive neural networks are used in the processing a significant portion of real SMILES filaments. Newer peptide constructions also use this strategy. The synthesized chemical molecule is additionally facilitate toward the desired qualities by the application of reinforcement learning. Transfer learning is a helpful technique for creating newer chemical structures and processing appropriate biological properties. There are two steps in this method. Training the network to learn SMILES grammar makes up step 1. Step 2 entails continuing your training with substances that have the desired properties. A few further training epochs are sufficient to encourage the creation of novel compounds that can occupy the same chemical space as the active molecules [44].

The field of AI has an intriguing technique known as "Variational Autoencoder" that uses two "neural networks": (i) encoder and (ii) decoder. SMILES serves as an example of how chemical structures are translated. This depicts the dormant room and translation of vectors into real-value continuous vectors, from which encoder networks and decoder networks, respectively, translate the latent space into chemical structures. Compared to the "Variational Autoencoder," the "Adversarial Autoencoder" has a larger capacity for constructing noticeably more authentic microstructures throughout their generation mode [45].

Drug compounds can be designed using generative adversarial networks (GANs). The technique can create images that are photorealistic from text representations. Kadurin et al. (2017) used GAN in a study to findcompounds with anticancer properties. This technology also allows for the production of new data based on imagination or genuine data. The learning from massive data sets is not necessary for the development of future AI. All of the previous challenges can now be solved thanks to modern AI technology. This innovative technology aids scientists and researchers in the finding and choosing of promising different chemicals based on their efficacy, safety, and patient selection for clinical trials. As a result, AI is valuable in medication delivery since it may prioritize molecules based on how easy they are to synthesize or design practical tools that have been shown to be effective for the most advantageous synthetic technique [35–39]. Table 10.2 which provides an inventory of important intelligence techniques using computing utilized in discovery of drugs.

10.7 AI in Clinical Drug Delivery and Release [46–48]

Ingeneral, the design of drug delivery systems is fraught with several drawbacks,such as predicting the relationship involving formulation factors as well as responses.This is connected to both the treatment results and unexpected events. An on-dose adjustment or the rates of release of drug, release of APIs at exact locations, and steadiness of drug are crucial considerations in the useof various kinds of sophisticated systems for distributing drugs.

10.7.1 Solid Dispersions

Poloxamer 188 and Soluplus® were used to create solid carbamazepine dispersions utilizing ANN modeling in conjunction with experimental design. To increase the solubility and rate of dissolution of carbamazepine, solid carbamazepine dispersions were prepared. These solid dispersions of carbamazepine-Soluplus®-poloxamer 188 were created using the solvent casting method. In a study, ANN modeling (feed-forward recurrent neural network) with the sigmoid function input signal was used to analyze the relationships between various variables and the characteristics of drug dissolution in order to maximize drug dissolution rate.

10.7.2 Emulsions and Microemulsions

ANNs were additionally employed to generate stable oil-in-water emulsion formulations. In this paper, the optimizing of the fatty alcohol content to create oil/water emulsions was examined. The quantities of lauryl alcohol and duration were the unreliable variables (factors) studied in this paper. The reliable variables (responses) were conductance, viscosity, zeta potential, and droplet size. Based on

Table 10.2 An Inventory of Significant Intelligence Techniques Used in Drug Discovery

AI based computer assisted tools used in drug discovery	Websites	Descriptions
AlphaFold	https://deepmind.com/blog/alphafold	Prediction of protein 3D structure prediction
Chemputer	https://zenodo.org/record/1481731	More standardized set-up for reporting chemical synthesis
DeepChem	https://github.com/deepchem/deepchem	A python-based AI tool for drug discovery predictions
DeepNeuralNet-QSAR	https://github.com/Merck/DeepNeuralNet-QSAR	Predictions of molecular activity
DeepTox	www.bioinf.jku.at/research/DeepTox	Prediction of toxicity and biocompatibility
DeltaVina	https://github.com/chengwang88/deltavina	A scoring function for rescoring protein–ligand binding affinity
Hit Dexter	http://hitdexter2.zbh.uni-hamburg.de	Machine learning models for the prediction of molecules, which might respond to biochemical assays
Neural Graph Fingerprints	https://github.com/HIPS/neural-fingerprint	Property prediction of novel molecules
NNScore	http://rocce-vm0.ucsd.edu/data/sw/hosted/nnscore/	Analysis of neural network-based scoring function for protein–ligand interactions
ODDT	https://github.com/oddt/oddt	For use in chemo informatics and molecular modeling
ORGANIC	https://github.com/aspuru-guzik-group/ORGANIC	Molecular generation tool to create molecules with desired characteristics
PotentialNet	https://pubs.acs.org/doi/full/10.1021/ acscentsci.8b00507	Ligand-binding affinity prediction based on a graph convolutional neural network
REINVENT	https://github.com/MarcusOlivecrona/REINVENT	Molecular *de novo* design using RNN and reinforcement learning

validation testing, it was discovered that ANN-predicted values had a strong correlation to the experiment's results. It was simple to anticipate precision based on the nature of the microemulsion from the formula. Interior structural properties and the nature of the microemulsion have also been accurately predicted using a combination of genetic algorithms and evolutionary ANNs. The manufacturing of stable microemulsions containing antitubercular medications including rifampicin and isoniazid for buccal administrations waspreviously predicted using ANN modeling [38–40].

10.7.3 Use of ANNs

Stationary and dynamic ANNs were utilized during the design of matrix tablets to model the dissolution profiles of various matrix tablets. Elman dynamic neural pathways and decision trees were employed by the researcher to accurately forecast the dissolution characteristics of hydrophilic and lipid-based matrix tablets with controlled medication release patterns. Metformin HCl matrix tablets for extended release were created in a study using a multilayer perceptron and input forward back propagation approach. To get the optimal formulations, the matrix tablets' in vitro metformin HCl release pattern was optimized. For network training, the independent and dependable variables such asfactors and responses were examined. Also, the leave-one-out method was used for a number of trials during the model validation procedure. The preparation design of glipizide based discharging osmotic pump tablets uses a combination of statistical optimization and ANN-based modeling. These glipizide delivering osmotic pump tablets underwent dissolving testing in addition to having the various formulation and process variables improved and examined using ANNs. The formulation of osmotic tablets containing isradipine has been optimized using a combination of RSP and ANN modeling. The optimized radipine osmotic tablet having some difference between the predicted dissolving results and the observed dissolution results which was found to be within the experimentally generated error limitations. Additionally, the anticipated dissolution outcomes and demonstrated dissolution results did not differ based on the similarity or difference factors.

10.7.4 Multiparticulate Drug Delivery Systems

Multiparticulate pellets of verapamil were manufactured using CAD/Chem software-assisted modeling. The effects of various formulation and process factors were examined in this study. In one study, ANN modeling was used to analyze how process variables affected the amount of papain (an enzyme) that was trapped inside alginate-based beads, improving both stability and site-specific release.

Alginate-based floating microparticles as spheres of aspirin were optimized using ANN and RSM, and the quantities of excipient ingredients, drug release, and microsphere buoyancy were measured. Compared to the RSM model, the ANN additionally and accurately expected the dissolution release pattern of aspirin. In a study, polymeric verapamil HCl microspheres were created using both the prediction models and the factorial framework as multivariate approaches. Analysis was done on the interactions between the external phase pH, verapamil HCl initial loading, and polymer concentration employed on various microsphere properties. The study's findings unmistakably proved that, when compared to the factorial model, the ANN model had greater fitting capabilities and more accurate forecasting. The whole 3^2 factorial designs' anticipated values and the known outcome were closely aligned.

Using the program KinetDS 3.0 Ver. 2010, the R2 as well as "root least squared error (RMSE)" scores among these arithmetical equations were calculated to assess their accuracy and propensity for prediction. The Korsmeyer–Peppas model was discovered to be the best-fit kinetic model whenever the respective R2 was compared. The zero order models, the Weibull model, and the Baker–Lonsdale model were found to be the models that it was closest to. By comparing the RMSE values for every tested model, the Korsmeyer–Peppas model's best fitting was finally confirmed, and the lowest RMSE values (0.12–0.68) were discovered.

ANN modeling was used in a study to construct albumin-loaded chitosan nanoparticles in order to analyze the effects of numerous factors as well as responses, such as "loading efficiency and cytotoxicity characteristics." In this study, the optimal mathematical replica for prophecy was selected for preparation, investigation, and statistics validation study based on regression analysis (R2) and mean square error (MSE) values. The proportion of polymer in the formulation of the copolymer-based nanoparticles proved to be the variable that had the greatest impact out of all those tested. Verapamil HCl polymer–lipid hybrid nanoparticle formulation development was performed according to the principles of central composite design (spherical), and the effects of various formulation parameters were examined. Verapamil HCl polymer–lipid hybrid nanoparticle multi objective optimization has been carried out using (validated) ANNs and unremitting evolutionary computation, and the outcomes of the analyses showed that the ANN model had greater analytical capability [49–51]. Table 10.3 presents some recent research on the use of AI technology in the design and development of different kinds of drug delivery systems.

10.8 Contemporary Investigations and Applications [42–49]

Our literature search revealed that recent research and uses of AI in the treatment of transmittable diseases with delivery of drug for the have primarily focused on drug discovery, resistance development prediction, drug optimization, drug pharmacokinetics, clinical therapy preference, improvement of delivery system for drugs,

Table 10.3 Use of AI Technology in the Design and Development of Drug Delivery Systems over the Time

AI approaches used	Drug Delivery System
ANNs	Floating tablets of rosiglitazone maleate
ANN	Granulated pellet-containing tablets and traditional pellet-containing tablets
Adaptive neural-fuzzy inference system	Ibuprofen-sustained release from tablets based on different cellulose derivatives
ANNs	Novel granulated pellet-containing tablets and traditional pellet-containing tablets
ANN and DNN	Oral disintegrating tablet formulations
ANN and DNN	Oral disintegrating tablets
ANN, multilayer perception (MLP) algorithm and RMSE	pH-dependent mesalamine matrix tablets
ANN	Sustained release matrix formulations of salbutamol sulfate
ANNs	Ultrasonic release of drug from liposomes
Box–Behnken design, RSM and ANN	Multiple-unit pellet system of prednisone
Box–Behnken design and QbD	Voriconazole loaded nanostructured lipid carriers based topical delivery system
Central composite design and RSM	Alginate-PVP K 30 microbeads of diclofenac sodium
Central composite design and RSM	Calcium alginate-gum Arabic beads of glibenclamide
Central composite design and ANNs	Gelatin nanoparticles of diclofenac sodium
Central composite design and RSM	Modified starch (cationized)-alginate beads of aceclofenac
Central composite design and RSM	Transferosomal gel for transdermal delivery of risperidone
Genetic algorithm, ANN, and RSM	Agar nanospheres of Bupropion
Mechanistic gastrointestinal simulation and ANN	Nifedipine osmotic release tablets
Quality by Design (QbD) and 2^3 factorial design	Hydroxyapatite (HAp)-ciprofloxacin bone-implants

Table 10.3 (Continued)

AI approaches used	Drug Delivery System
RSM, ANN, and SVM modeling	Doxycycline hydroxypropyl-β-cyclodextrin inclusion complex
2^3factorial design and RSM	Emulsion-gelled floating beads of diclofenac sodium
2^3 factorial design and RSM	Transferosomal gel for transdermal insulin delivery
3^2full factorial design and RSM	Besifloxacin HCl loaded liposomal gel
3^2factorial design and RSM	Ionotropically-gelled mucoadhesive beads for oral metformin HCl delivery
3^2factorial design and RSM	Jackfruit seed starch-alginate mucoadhesive beads of metformin HCl

constructing of drug systemic delivery, portrayal of drug pharmacokinetic profile, and prognostication of treatment programs consequences. The entire subjects are crucial for conquer the difficult obstacles connected to delivery of drug for the successful cure for pathogenic diseases. It is important to note that drug resistance prediction has received the greatest attention among these issues. This is largely due to the fact that AMR is now the main barrier to the success of treating infections.

10.8.1 Development of Drug

By adopting a large research based perspective, tools learning and AI algorithms have triggered the revolution within the pharmaceutical industry that has redefined drug creation in the last ten years. Game-changing automation technologies have been widely developed and implemented throughout the entire drug research process, including drug test, drug repurposing, combinatorial chemistry and synthesis, as well as drug clinical study design and implementation. The capacity of AI models to accurately and consistently deconstruct the specific test protein's architecture, reveal the medication's physicochemical properties and toxicities, and predict drug-target interactions is particularly revolutionizing drug screening. Also, AI has begun to alter critical clinical trial processes including client batch collection and health monitoring, resulting in the main reasons for high experimental error rates and the biggest challenges in the development of novel medications. Whenever it relates to AI techniques, recognized systems (such SVM, regression trees, and exponential projection techniques) and unregulated learning algorithm (like kNN) were extensively utilized in drug discovery. The more complicated algorithms that have been suggested to increase the usefulness of AI for drug development include deep learning algorithms as a crucial component.

10.8.2 Optimization of Drug Dosing

Several AI-based strategies have been examined to enhance the delivery of drugs for communicable disease dosage design. In particular, a number of computational techniques have beencreated to forecast the antipathogenic dosage intensity or aim to accomplish the efficacy of the therapy based on characteristics of the patient or the antimicrobial substance. This model was shown to be reasonably accurate at predicting MRTD-Maximum Recommended Therapetuic Dose by external validation, and as a result, it might be utilized to help develop safer and more efficient therapies for HIV infection.

10.8.3 Drug Combinatorial Therapy

In our fight against MDR-Multidrug resistant infections, in silico methods for medication mixture design are in great demand. The amount of information that is currently available regarding the characteristics of pharmaceuticals and the biological characteristics of patients has exploded during the last several years. As a result, the development and optimization of medication combinations is receiving increasing interest from AI. In general, there are three categories that can be used to categorize the input variables an AI system used for designofdrug combinations. The first category is drug-based and typically consists of the target's andthe drug's and effectiveness profiles, as well as their substantial and compound properties in 2D as well as 3D. The second category is pathogen-based, and it largely consists of changes to the pathogen's mobility, multiplication, migration, etc., caused by drug administration and changes to the virulent genome. Patient demographics (such as weight, ethnicity, gender, height), DNA polymorphism markers, pathway of infection, microbial load, multimorbidity, duration of treatment, and laboratory factors (such as CD4+ baseline T cell number, RBCs, WBCs count, and hemoglobin threshold) generally make up the last group, known as the host-based group. The second-order quadratic model, naive Bayes, decision trees, FSC-Financial Services Council, XGBoost, fuzzy discrete event network, kNN, SVM, random forest,logistic regression, ANN, and infrastructure Laplacian regularized least square synergistic are the key AI models utilized for combination therapy design. These simulation results can be used todetermine three things: (1) whether or not combination therapy are synergistic (binary results); (2) how likely they are to be synergistic; and (3) how likely they are to result in successful microbiology or treatment, which is primarily indicated by the inhibition of microbial invasion or the slight decrease of load of virulent inside a set amount of duration.

10.8.4 Improved Drug Delivery System

Optimization of *in silico* medication systems of delivery has progressively drawn growing interest from both industry and research as information technology progresses. The creation of specialized drug delivery systems is substantially facilitated by the ability of ML, and in particular ANN, to determine the correlations involving drug technology for providing and drug release patterns. Findings have indicated that an accurate field prediction with much reduced discrepancy and a condensed preparation process is possible with the successive ensemble of classifiers. The created CCM-Cerebral cavernous malformation could be a useful instrument for evaluating medication diffusion coefficient from mucoadhesive compositions and comprehending how therapeutic compounds disperse on or after the transporters and apply their potency beneath various medical circumstances.

10.8.5 Right Choice of a Drug Delivery System

The ideal drug administration pathway can now be chosen without extensive laboratory research due to the development of AI. This feature include molecular mass/heavy tiny part, the physical properties of the APIs, logP/Silicos, which determines the APIs solubility, which is related to its lipophilicity, as well as other characteristics from medicinal chemistry.

10.8.6 Prognosis of the Treatment Schedule

Due to AI's exceptional predictive power, investigators have already been attempting to build tools for the current clinical assessment of viral diseases. The most frequently employed characteristics for the etiological agent are the applicable alterations in drug confrontation, genotype, and receptiveness testing. Client demographic data (e.g., nation, time of onset, gender, race, and socioeconomic comorbidities), clinical attributes (e.g., encircled, pathway of infection, benchmark pathogen pack, therapies record, current effective treatments, and pharmacokinetic factors, and polymorphism of a single nucleotide), and laboratory test results are the most frequently used features in general (e.g., points of mediators of systemic inflammatory), as well as radiological tests. Those AI models are primarily utilized to forecast therapeutic failure, which is shown by post-treatment microbe reduction or culture conversion. Table 10.4 lists prospective and existing uses for AI in medicine.

10.9 Future Prospects of AI in Biomedicine [50, 51]

Machine learning and AI have huge potential to change drug delivery to improve the treatment of infectious diseases. Unfortunately, there are presently few real-world uses of AI in medication distribution, especially in the clinical environment. The majority of the models related to AI have not undergone extensive testing or clinical application, demonstrating that there are significant obstacles to the practical translation of AI for drug administration in the management of virulent diseases. This

Table 10.4 List of Prospective and Existing Applications of AI in Medicine

Clinical practice	Translational research	Basic biomedical research
Automated surgery	Drug repurposing	Prediction of transcription factor binding sites
Disease diagnosis	Biomarker discovery	Automated experiments
Interpretation of patient genomes	Drug–target prioritization	Automated data collection
Patient monitoring	Prediction of chemical toxicity	Simulation of molecular dynamics
Patient risk stratification for primary prevention	Genetic variant annotation	Literature mining
Treatment selection	Drug discovery	Gene function annotation

section will therefore provide an overview of these issues, their present remedies, and potential future developments.

10.9.1 *Perspectives*

A clinical paradigm like delivery of drugs for the cure for infectious illnesses is crucial for human trust in AI. AI model has the potential to assist domain specialists in determining whether expectations are biologically possible, provide biological insight and grasp of the underlying procedures and decisions, and result in the identification of new biological processes. Yet, interpreting models is currently and significantly challenging for AI. The majority of ML techniques, including cutting-edge techniques, are "black boxes," meaning that it is challenging to understand the results. Given that there are more features than samples in genomic data, model interpretation is considerably more difficult. Genomic information about the patients or the microbes is frequently needed through AI as a decisive supply of key features to finest support the distribution of antibacterial agent(s) for a specific patient.

The analysis of the significance of various input features is one method of model interpretation. To achieve model interpretation, for instance, permutation feature significance, a metric of variations in simulation results when the information of a relevant in determining is shuffled, could be utilized. This approach was used to locate new mutations that confer resistance including all antimicrobial medications from a single chemical class. By specifying the significance of the principles in a combination or dissonance paradigm of the final predictive accuracy, one can achieve model interpretation for SCM-Supply chain management. Decision trees are often well-accepted by subject matter experts because they reflect a collection of if-then rules that are easy to comprehend and interpret.

The kNN (k-nearest neighbors algorithm) replica uses closest neighbor samples for prediction, making it simple to comprehend. During the model training phase, only one parameter needs to be adjusted. The capacity of a model to learn from complicated data is typically inversely correlated with its interpretability. In order to comprehend the complicated AI algorithms that have excellent performance, new methodologies are therefore required.

The development of a group of methods to enable interpretation though maintaining elevated concert of AI is the focus of the emerging field of explainable AI. To show the inputs and predictions, one such method uses a distributed stochastic neighborhood embedding method.

Others include 1) tree explainer, which provides tractable computation of the best local explanations; 2) particular instance reasoning, which can offer explanations and justifications in visual form; and 3) Creating visual representations of word embeddings for the term "AI replica" can provide insights into the underlying principles of AI. These visualizations can also help us gain a deeper understanding of the importance of the specific characteristics and choices made within AI models.

10.9.2 Parameters Governing the Model for Learning Algorithms and Pattern Discovery

Confronts. The process of obtaining clear and comprehensive information from either the initial input information, including antimicrobial agent structure, microorganism genotypes, and patient clinical characteristics, is known as feature extraction and is necessary for the majority of AI and ML models. Data augmentation or downsampling is typically required when the feature vector's dimension is big. The standardization and facilitation of the AI application depend on feature extraction. The effectiveness of models developed using ML is influenced by the extracted features, and the optimum features are those that are instructive and avoid duplication to maximize model learning. Yet, because feature extraction is domain-specific, various antimicrobial drugs, infections, and patients call for various approaches. In a more elaborate discussion, it becomes evident that not all artificial intelligence systems will perform tasks with equal effectiveness. This principle remains applicable when considering the utilization of AI in the context of delivering antimicrobial drugs. This assertion is supported by research that has examined the performance of over four unique neural network models in the specific task of delivering antimicrobial drugs. Consequently, the choice to employ deep learning for this particular objective continues to be a topic of ongoing debate.

Modern Techniques. The feature extraction process differs depending on the kind of incoming data. The most typical approach to selecting a model is to employ a variety of well-known ML techniques to identify the optimal model, which is based on the learning and assessment of datasets. The input features and the job are what determine the ML model optimum performance. The regulation of the feedback system is frequently employed for drug optimization. Deep convolutional neural networks are typically more effective than other ML models for picture data.

Future Outlook. The size of the dataset also affects how well ML models perform. Because of its superior performance in prediction tasks, a deeper neural network is frequently the best model when a sizable dataset is available.

10.9.3 Data Required

Creating a high-quality dataset for training an AI/ML system with consistently labeled, balanced, and sufficiently large samples becomes a formidable challenge when dealing with the administration of antimicrobial drugs. Pathogens are categorized as "drug-sensitive" or "drug-resistant" in some investigations, and "drugsensitive," "drug-intermediate," or "drug-resistant" in others. Also, the majority of research only used random batches from nearby areas, which can give the AI model a regional bias. Because the input feature material (such as pathogen AMR genes) can differ between pathogen populations, it is possible that the trained algorithm for ANN and its conclusions on specimen as of locations cannot be immediately extended to other nations or regions.

Most research relies on data from nearby hospitals that have uneven courses. Public datasets are utilized in several studies. Teams working in healthcare and research can develop trustworthy, potent, and broadly applicable ML models thanks to these open datasets. In recent times, large-scale datasets have become necessary for ML models, notably deep neural networks. To tackle contagious diseases, data sharing and global cooperation are crucial.

To summarize, the objective is to amalgamate community datasets to form a substantial dataset. This dataset will be instrumental in training a machine learning prototype algorithm aimed at assisting clinical decision-making concerning the allocation of antimicrobial medications. This is especially crucial as antimicrobial resistance (AMR) mechanisms can differ based on specific environments or niches. Moreover, to develop models capable of distinguishing between various AMR pathways, a substantial amount of data, including well-characterized strains, is essential.

10.10 Conclusion

In recent years, there has been a noticeable increase in interest in the applications of AI technology for interpreting and analyzing some key areas of pharmacy, such as regenerative medicine, therapeutic dose form design, hospital pharmacy, polypharmacology, etc. This is because AI technological approaches mimic how humans think about information, solve problems, and make decisions. It has been found to be beneficial to use analytics models and databases for efficient studies that apply AI techniques. By utilizing AI technology, it is now possible to easily, quickly, and affordably develop new assumptions, tactics, projections, and analyses of numerous connected parts.

AI is a viable technology that can be utilized to address existing problems with delivery of drug for communicable diseases, which are mostly linked to the prevalence of AMR on a global scale. To date, studies have demonstrated the transformative potential of artificial intelligence (AI) in the realm of healthcare, particularly in addressing communicable diseases. AI has proven invaluable in various aspects of pharmaceutical research, including drug delivery optimization, resistance development analysis, precise dosing recommendations, drug grouping strategies, enhancement of drug distribution systems, management of active pharmaceutical ingredients (APIs), and the characterization of dose-response relationships. Future research must concentrate on improving the interpretability of AI models, optimize feature engineering solutions, offer advice on choosing AI models, and enhance the quality of the source data in order to encourage much farther advancement and pragmatic utilization of AI in delivery of drug for the pathogenic diseases.

Acknowledgement

The authors wish to sincerely convey their appreciation and heartfelt thanks to the leadership of Vishwakarma University and D. Y. Patil International University Pune for generously providing the opportunity and platform for their endeavors.

Conflict of Interest

No conflicts of interest are disclosed by the authors.

References

1. Russell, S. J., and Norvig, P. (1995). Artificial Intelligence: A Modern Approach, Englewood Cliffs, NJ: Prentice Hall.
2. Haugeland, J. (1989). Artificial Intelligence: The Very Idea, MIT Press; New Ed edition.
3. Dasta, J. F. (1992). Application of artificial intelligence to pharmacy and medicine. *Hosp. Pharm.* 27(4), 319–22.
4. Jiang, F., Jiang, Y., Zhi, H. (2017). Artificial intelligence in healthcare: Past, present and future, *Stroke Vasc. Neurol.*, 2(4), 230–43.
5. Gobburu, J.V., Chen, E.P. (1996). Artificial neural networks as a novel approach to integrated pharmacokinetic-pharmacodynamic analysis, *J. Pharm. Sci.*, 85(5), 505–10.

6. Zupan, J, Gasteiger, J. (1993). Neural nets for mass and vibrational spectra, *J. Mol. Struct.*, 292, 141–59.

7. Achanta, A.S., Kowalski, J.G., Rhodes, C.T. (1995). Artificial neural networks: Implications for pharmaceutical sciences, *Drug Dev. Ind. Pharm.*, 21(1),119–55.

8. Sakiyama, Y. (2009). The use of machine learning and nonlinear statistical tools for ADME prediction, *Expert Opin. Drug Metab. Toxicol.*, 5(2),149–69.

9. Sutariya, V., Groshev, A., Sadana, P., Bhatia, D., Pathak, Y. (2013). Artificial neural network in drug delivery and pharmaceutical research, *Open Bioinf J.*, 7(1), 49–62.

10. Gutiérrez, P.A., Hervás-Martínez, C. (2011). Hybrid Artificial Neural Networks: Models, Algorithms and Data. Advances in Computational Intelligence, Lecture Notes in Computer Science, Berlin, Heidelberg: Springer 6692.

11. Taskinen, J., Yliruusi, J. (2003). Prediction of physicochemical properties based on neural network modeling, *Adv. Drug Deliv. Rev.*, 55(9),1163–83.

12. Husseini, G.A., Mjalli, F.S., Pitt, W.G., Bdel-Jabbar, N. (2009). Using artificial neural networks and model predictive control to optimize acoustically assisted Doxorubicin release from polymeric micelles, *Technol. Cancer Res.*, 8(6), 479–488.

13. Fleming, N. (2018).How artificial intelligence is changing drug discovery. *Nature*, 557(7706), S55-7.

14. Arulsudar, N., Subramanian, N., Murthy, R.S.R. (2005). Comparison of artificial neural network and multiple linear regression in the optimization of formulation parameters of leuprolide acetate loaded liposomes, *J. Pharm. Pharmaceut. Sci.*, 8, 243–258.

15. Sun,Y., Peng,Y., Chen,Y., Shukla, A.J. (2003). Application of artificial neural networks in the design of controlled release drug delivery systems, *Adv Drug Deliv Rev.*, 55(9), 1201–15.

16. Sakiyama, Y. (2009). The use of machine learning and nonlinear statistical tools for ADME prediction. *Expert Opin Drug Metab Toxicol.*, 5(2), 149–69.

17. Agatonovic-Kustrin, S., Beresford, R. (2000). Basic concepts of artificial neural network (ANN) modeling and its application in pharmaceutical research, *J Pharm Biomed Anal.*, 22(5), 717–27.

18. Zhang, Z. H., Wang, Y., Wu, W.F., Zhao, X., Sun, X.C., Wang, H.Q. (2012). Development of glipizide push-pull osmotic pump controlled release tablets by using expert system and artificial neural network, *Yao Xue Xue Bao.*, 47(12), 1687–95.

19. Ma, J., Sheridan, R.P., Liaw, A., Dahl, G.E., Svetnik, V. (2015). Deep neural nets as a method for quantitative structure–activity relationships. *J. Chem. Inf. Model.*, 55(2), 263–74.

20. Ruffle, J.K., Farmer, A.D., Aziz, Q. (2019). Artificial Intelligence-Assisted Gastroenterology-Promises and Pitfalls, *Am. J. Gastroenterol.*, 114, 422–428.

21. Moran, M.E. (2007). Evolution of robotic arms, *J. Robot. Surg.*, 1, 103–111.

22. Molga, E.J., Van Woezik, B.A.A., Westerterp, K.R. (2000). Neural networks for modelling of chemical reaction systems with complex kinetics: oxidation of 2-octanol with nitric acid, *Chem. Eng. Process. Process. Intensif.*, 39, 323–34.

23. Weizenbaum, J. (1996). ELIZA–a computer program for the study of natural language communication between man and machine, *Commun. ACM*, 9, 36–45.

24. Wu, T., Pan, W., Chen, J., Zhang, R. (2000). Formulation optimization technique based on artificial neural network in salbutamol sulfate osmotic pump tablets, *Drug Dev. Ind. Pharm.*, 26, 211–215.

25. Kuipers, B.F., Hart, E.A., Nilsson, P.E., Shakey, N.J. (2017). From Conception to History, *AI Mag.*, 88–103.

26. Kulikowski, C. A. (2019). Beginnings of Artificial Intelligence in Medicine (AIM): Computational Artifice Assisting Scientific Inquiry and Clinical Art–with Reflections on Present AIM Challenges, *Yearb Med. Inform.*, 28, 249–256.

27. Greenhill, A.E. (2019). A Primer of AI in Medicine. Techniques in Gastrointestinal Endoscopy, *Epub.*

28. Kalepu, S., Nekkanti, V. (2015). Insoluble drug delivery strategies: review of recent advances and business prospects, *Acta Pharm. Sin B.*, 5, 442–53.

29. Dickherber, A., Morris, S.A., Grodzinski, P. (2015). NCI investment in nanotechnology: achievements and challenges for the future, *Wiley Interdiscip. Rev. Nanomed. Nanobiotechnol.*, 7, 251–65.

30. Kulikowski, C.A. (2015). An Opening Chapter of the First Generation of Artificial Intelligence in Medicine: The First Rutgers AIM Workshop, *Yearb Med. Inform.*, 10, 227–233.

31. Weiss, S., Kulikowski, C.A., Safir, A. (1978). Glaucoma consultation by computer, *Comput. Biol. Med.*, 8, 25–40.

32. Cheng, F., Zhao, Z. (2014). Machine learning-based prediction of drug_drug interactions by integrating drug phenotypic, therapeutic, chemical, and genomic properties, *J. Am. Med. Inform. Assoc.*, 2, 278–86.

33. Takayama, K., Takahara, J., Fujikawa, M., Ichikawa, H., Nagai, T. (1999). Formula optimization based on artificial neural networks in transdermal drug delivery, *J. Control. Release*, 62, 161–170.

34. Rafienia, M., Amiri, M., Janmaleki, M., Sadeghian, A. (2010). Application of artificial neural networks in controlled drug delivery systems, *Appl. Artif. Intell*, 24, 807–20.

35. Held, C.M., Roy, R.J. (1995). Multiple drug hemodynamic control by means of a supervisory fuzzy rule-based adaptive control system: Validation on a model, *IEEE Trans. Biomed. Eng.*, 42(4), 371–85.

36. Heikamp, K., Bajorath, J. (2014). Support vector machines for drug discovery, *Expert Opin. Drug Discov.*, 9(1), 93–104.

37. Haykin, S. (1998). Neural Networks: A Comprehensive Foundation, 1st ed. Prentice–Hall PTR. NJ, United State.

38. Rode, A., Sharma, S., Hatware, K. (2017). Artificial intelligence: microchip based drug delivery through resealed erythrocytes, *Biochem. Ind. J.*, 11, 1–9.

39. Fatouros, D.G., Nielsen, F.S., Douroumis,D., Hadjileontiadis, L.J., Mullertz, A. (2008). *In vitro–in vivo* correlations of self-emulsifying drug delivery systems combining the dynamic lipolysis model and neuro-fuzzy networks, *Eur. J. Pharm. Biopharm.*, 699(3), 887–98.

40. Zadeh, L.A. (1965). Fuzzy sets, *Inform Control*, 8, 338–53.

41. Huang, J.W., Roy, R.J. (1998). Multiple-drug hemodynamic control using fuzzy decision theory, *IEEE Transact. Biomed. Eng.*, 45(2), 213–28.

42. Feng, R., Yu, F., Xu, J., Hu, X. (2021). Knowledge gaps in immune response and immunotherapy involving nanomaterials: databases and artificial intelligence for material design, *Biomaterials*, 266,120469.

43. Giuliani,A. (2017). The application of principal component analysis to drug discovery and biomedical data, *Drug Discov. Today*, 22(7), 1069–76.

44. Amisha, Malik, P., Pathania, M. (2019). Overview of artificial intelligence in medicine, *J. Family Med. Prim. Care.*, 8, 2328–2331.

45. Merk, D., Friedrich, L., Grisoni, F., Schneider, G. (2018). *De novo* Design of Bioactive Small Molecules by Artificial Intelligence Daniel, *Mol. Inform.*, 37(1–2), 201700153.

46. Jolliffe, I.T., Jorge,C. (2016). Principal component analysis: A review and recent developments, *Phil. Trans. R. Soc. A.*, 374(2065), 20150202.

47. Jolliffe, I.T. (2000). Principal Component Analysis" Springer-Verlag, (New York).

48. Heba, F.E., Darwish,A., Hassanien, A.E., Abraham, A. (2010). Principle components analysis and support vector machine based intrusion detection system, *10th International Conference on Intelligent Systems Design and Applications*, Cairo, 363–367.

49. Burges, C.J.C. (1998). A tutorial on support vector machines for pattern recognition, *Data Mining Knowledge. Discov.*, 2(2), 121–67.

50. Vyas, M., et al. (2018). Artificial intelligence: the beginning of a new era in pharmacy profession, *Asian J. Pharm*, 12, 72–76.

51. Mintz, Y., Brodie, R. (2019). Introduction to artificial intelligence in medicine, *Minim. Invasive Ther. Allied Technol.*, 28, 73–81.

COMPUTATIONAL INTELLIGENCE   IV

INTELLIGENCE

IoT Systems

Chapter 11

Artificial Intelligence and Soft Computing-Driven Evolutionary Computation Algorithms for Solving Unconstrained Nonlinear Problems

Binay Kumar[1] and Priyavada[1]

[1]Department of Mathematics, Lingaya's Vidyapeeth, Faridabad (Delhi NCR), India

11.1 Introduction

In the last few years, many evolutionary algorithms have been introduced and successfully applied to many research optimization problems. Evolutionary algorithms use the computational model of evolutionary processes as a key element and share a common concept based on the processes of selection and reproduction. These modern techniques are not static but dynamic as they can evolve over time.

DOI: 10.1201/9781032650722-15

Evolutionary algorithms can be described as a class of stochastic, population-based local search algorithms. Evolutionary algorithms are global methods used to solve nonlinear optimization problems without using derivatives. During the last 20 years most of the research has used the complex objective function without using constraints. Only unconstraint nonlinear optimization problems are solved by these algorithms. The artificial bee colony (ABC) algorithm, genetic algorithm (GA), particle swarm optimization (PSO), and ant colony optimization (ACO) algorithms are the evolutionary algorithms and nonlinear optimization problems can be easily solved using them. Both constraint and unconstraint types of problems can be solved with these algorithms. The GA was introduced by Professor Johan Holland, and is related to natural selection of Charles Darwin theory. The GA is an optimization algorithm where three operators are used with a set of chromosomes over a number of iterations. Velocity and position of every particle are measured in each iteration. It is a modern stochastic technique based on the social behaviour of particles. In 2005 Dervis Karaboga proposed the ABC algorithm inspired by the behaviour of natural bees, which uses three main phases. The main task of the bees is to find the best food place and direction with a high quantity of nectar. In this chapter, we will show the results of unconstrained optimization problems using MATLAB. Unconstrained nonlinear optimization problems use only the objective function and not the constrained one. Convergence rate and fitness value are shown by MATLAB graph and tables.

11.2 Retrospects

11.2.1 Genetic Algorithms

Chhavi Mangla et al. (2018) [1] proposed a system of nonlinear equations using the GA. Nonlinear programming problem (NLPP) changed in multiobjective problem first then a new fitness function is proposed. Amanpreet Singh et al. (2012) [2] solved a special type of unconstrained Rosenbrock optimization problem using the GA. The main focus of the GA is on the simulation of natural evolutionary processes that can be used for certain standard optimization problems. The GA is a computerized algorithm that uses natural genetics on population string structures. The global optimization technique here is used to avoid problems such as stagnation of the solution to a local minimum. The GA is a population based search method in which many solutions can be seized in the population. Punam S Mhetre et al. (2012) [3] introduced the GA to solve LLP and NLPP problems. Gauss Legendre integration method as a technique is a solution of NLPP used to get the result without changing the nonlinear equation to linear. T. Yokota et al. (1994) [4] discussed nonlinear optimization problems of integer programming and also its applications. T. Yokota also introduced a new method for the solution of NLPP for better comparison. Some methods and holding properties were discussed with the help of GA.

Chhavi Mangla et al. (2020) [5] solved the nonlinear optimization problem using the GA. In general, simultaneous nonlinear problems are used in engineering, social sciences, and medical sciences. Both types of single and multi-objective optimization problems are solved by using standard benchmark problems.

11.2.2 Particle Swarm Optimization

Raju Prajapati et al. (2017) [6] discusses the NLPP solution with the barrier method. Some improved versions of PSO are used for the solution of NLPP. Available methods for the solution of NLPP are KKT condition, subgradient method, Lagrangian multipliers and Barrier method. The Barrier method was used to transform the given nonlinear programming problems with equality constraint to unconstraint NLPP like penalty method. Then the result was compared to general PSO. Raju Prajapati et al. (2018) [7] proposed the impact of analysis with penalty constant over penalty function of NLPP using the PSO technique. Solutions of nonlinear optimization problems are difficult as compared to the Linear Programming Problem. All equality constraints are taken in the problem. The PSO improved version was used to show the result and SCILAB programming was used to show the computational results. Five NLPP problems were used for testing and to show the impact of penalty constant. The NLPP with equality constraint was changed into unconstraint NLPP by taking different constant values. Finally, it was shown that te higher penalty constant result was sharper because of the higher convexity of NLPP. W.T. Li et al. (2008) [8] discussed the MPSO algorithm applied to electromagnetic applications. To remove the limitations of PSO, improvements were made to the velocity equation; the surpassing boundary command, SQI operator global best perturbation, and global best perturbation were adopted. PSO r1 and r2 work independently. Bimal Chandra Das et al. (2009) [9] discussed different modern techniques for the solution of NLPP. A quadratic problem can be converted to LPP using Kuhn-Tucker conditions, and then Wolfe method can also be applied to LPP. Finding the optimal solution and show the result in graphical form MATLAB programming is used, then the obtained result is compared to exact solutions. Ying Dong et al. (2005) [10] discussed the application PSO. Priyavada and Dr Binay [11] reviewed a modified PSO method related to inertia weight.

11.2.3 Artificial Bee Colony Algorithm

Dervis Karaboga et al. [12] proposed the ABC algorithm for the solution of NLPP with constraints and showed the results using constrained optimization problems. A modified ABC algorithm was presented, and its results were compared to those of a state-of-the-art algorithm. The ABC algorithm was tested for real engineering problems, and it was found that it can be efficiently applied to solving constrained optimization problems. Weifeng Gao et al. (2018) [13] proposed a framework for constraint optimization problems using the novel ABC algorithm. A multi-strategy technique was used that consists of three types of strategies that play a great role in diversity and convergence. Soudeh Babaeizadeh et al. (2016) [14] introduced a constrained ABC algorithm for optimization problems. The ABC is an optimization algorithm compared to other optimization-based algorithms. There is one poor exploitation ability of the ABC algorithm. To remove this limitation of the ABC algorithm, three new search equations were introduced for three types of phases: onlooker bee, employed bee, and scout bee phases. Soudeh Babaeizadeh et al. (2015) [15] introduced an optimization problem related to the enhanced constrained ABC algorithm for optimization problems. Last few years, with fewer parameters and strong global optimization ability, ABC researchers paid attention. However, the ABC algorithm is good at exploration but poor at exploitation. Numerical examples and results have been shown with several benchmark functions. Nadezda Stanarevic et al. (2011) [16] proposed an improved ABC algorithm for the constrained optimization problem that is applicable only to unconstrained optimization problems, but later a lot of modifications in ABC were introduced for constraints problems. A modified version of ABC was introduced for the constraint optimization problem.

11.2.4 Ant Colony Optimization Algorithm

Alda Larasati Anindya et al. [17] introduced a modified ACO algorithm for the solution of the travelling salesman problem (TSP). Marco Dorigo et al. [18] proposed an ACO algorithm, which is ant-inspired algorithm, a different approach to the solution of nonlinear problems [19]. Deneubourg et al. investigated the ant pheromone level at different places and the behavior of the ants. A double-bridge experiment was used where ants were connected to a food source. Rohit Chaturvedi et al. [20] introduced a modified ACO algorithm for TSP that can handle the salesman problem and help handle complex NP problems. Few years ago, many swarm-based modern techniques [21, 22] are introduced. And these algorithms are swarm-based intelligence algorithm [23, 24]. Vittorio Maniezzo et al. [25] proposed a ACO technique for designing metaheuristic algorithms for combinatorial and NP complex optimization problems.

11.3 Evolutionary Computational Techniques

11.3.1 Genetic Algorithm

The GA is a metaheuristic population-based optimization technique based on the principal of biological theory of natural evolution. The GA also provides an extended concept survival of the fittest [26]. The GA was developed by Professor Johan Holland along with his research team at the University of Michigan during the 1960s and 1970s [27]. Dr. Holland then developed the theoretical framework for applying the GA to many complex problems. The GA gives the best and most efficient optimal solution. The GA is based on the survival of the fittest, using genetic operations found in nature. The GA starts with a group of solutions where every solution is known as a chromosome. In GA we apply three operators to find the optimal solution. The GA does not work on a single trial solution at a time but instead works on the entire population. In a special generation, the whole population comprises to the set of solution. Then select the fittest member and share some qualities, and features of both parents, proceed further, and pair them randomly.

The GA is generally used for discrete optimization problems, and is applied to find the optimum solution or near optimum solution to different problems. The GA can solve both unconstrained and constrained optimization problems [28]. The binary coding 1s and 0s are used commonly in the GA. GA algorithm has three main characteristics:

■ Population based
■ Fitness oriented
■ Variation driven

The GA has three operators, discussed as follows.

11.3.1.1 Selection Operator

The selection operator permit their genes to next generation for finding the better solution in the GA. The primary objective is to emphasize the good solution and discard the bad solution. The individual with the best fitness has a chance of selection in the next generation. There are different selection techniques in GA. Figure 11.1 shows Roulette Wheel Selection.

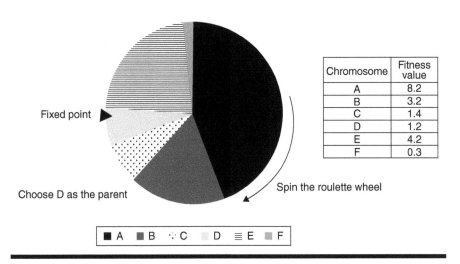

Figure 11.1   Roulette wheel selection.

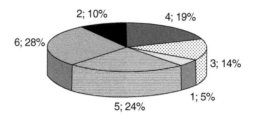

Figure 11.2　Rank-based selection.

(a) Roulette Wheel Selection

This method is used for selecting the best parents for the next generation. Relative fitness is used for each parent.

(b) Rank-Based Selection: First ranks the population then gives the fitness ranking to each chromosome. Figure 11.2 shows Rank-based Selection.

(c) Tournament Selection: In this selection a group of n particles are selected randomly and the best individual is selected from that group. Here n = size of the group; the higher n the higher the pressure to select the above-average quality individual. Many tournaments are held between the individual, and this process is repeated as often as desired.

11.3.1.2 Crossover Operator

The crossover between two parent strings produces a new population. By using swapping crossover between genes we can combine partial solutions from different candidates. Three crossover are used by the GA:

1-point crossover
2-point crossover
Uniform crossover

11.3.1.3 Mutation Operator

The GA gets better solutions by using the mutation operator. The mutation operator is used to arrange genetic heterogeneous from one generation of population to the next generation. After mutation the solution may change entirely from the last solution.

> **Bit Flip Mutation:** Select any one or more random bits and flip them to each other.

Figure 11.3 Swap mutation.

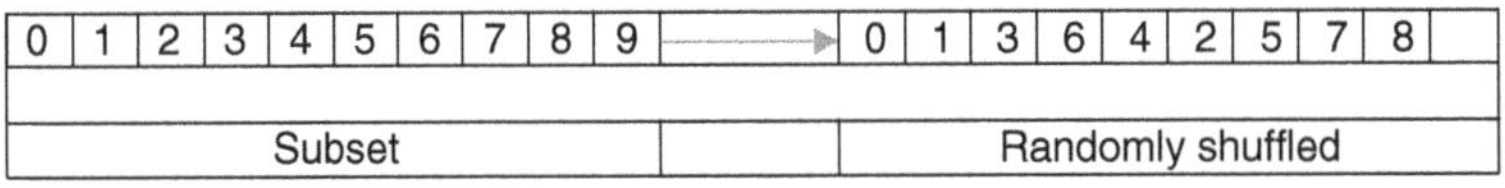

0	1	2	3	4	5	6	7	8	9	──────▶	0	1	3	6	4	2	5	7	8
			Subset										Randomly shuffled						

Figure 11.4 Scramble mutation.

Swap Mutation: Select any two chromosomes randomly and interchange their values. Figure 11.3 shows Swap Mutation.

Scramble Mutation: Select a subset of genes and shuffle their values. Figure 11.4 shows Scramble Mutation.

Inverse Mutation: In Inverse mutation, we select a subset of genes and inverse that selected subset.

11.3.2 Particle Swarm Optimization Algorithm

Gerardo Beni and Jing Wang introduced the PSO algorithm in 1989. This algorithm is based on the intelligence algorithm where a set of particles are working in the particle collective behaviour of a decentralised self-organised system. Some swarm intelligence natural examples include fish schooling, animal herding, bird flocking, and ant colonies. Eberhart and Kennedy in 1995 [29] introduced an optimization algorithm similar to PSO that closely related to the graphic animation of flocks. PSO cannot use the gradient method. After some time, PSO has been developed, modified and used for many NLPP, research problems and technical problems. Each particle in the PSO algorithm has its own velocity and position. Position and velocity change from iteration to iteration. It is an evolutionary technique inspired by the social behaviour of groups of birds. Starting in 1995, there have been many modifications of PSO with many applications in different areas. It is used in most of the areas because it is very easy to apply due to less parameter and give the output after every iteration. Pbest and Gbest are calculated in every step of PSO. Pbest is related to the cognitive part and Gbest is related the social part of this algorithm. PSO is applied for unconstraint and variable bounded optimization problem [30]. This technique simulates the behaviour of bird societies of PSO without leaders. Every bird in the PSO interfaces with other members of the bird flock and shares all the information regarding the food source. All the particles have their own language. This process is repeated many times until the best optimal solution is quickly obtained. Two main equations are updated: velocity updating equation and position updating. It is an evolutionary computational technique for updating velocity and position by which we can show all the PSO result regarding convergence rate and optimal point. The velocity updating equation is used for this purpose:

$$V_i[t+1] = V_i[t]W + c_1 {_*} r_1 {_*}(Pbest_i[t] - Xi[t]) + c_2 {_*} r_2 {_*}(Gbest_i - X_i[t]) \tag{1}$$

The position of the particles is updated by this equation:

$$X_i[t+1] = X_i[t] + V_i[t+1] \tag{2}$$

Where Vi = velocities of each particles
Xi = positions of every particle.
The velocity and position are updated for multi-particles in gbest PSO:
Pbest and Gbest are the personal best and global best value of every member of a swarm.
r1 and r2 randomly lie between 0 and 1. Two acceleration coefficients, c1 and c2, are used.

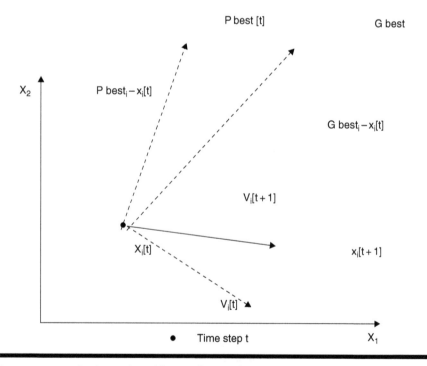

Figure 11.5 Velocity and position update at time t.

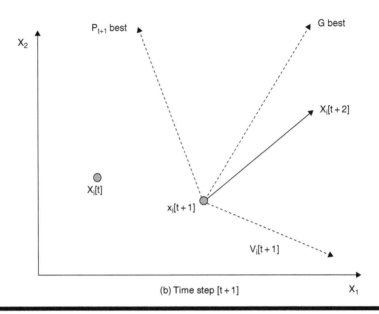

Figure 11.6   Velocity and position update at time t+1.

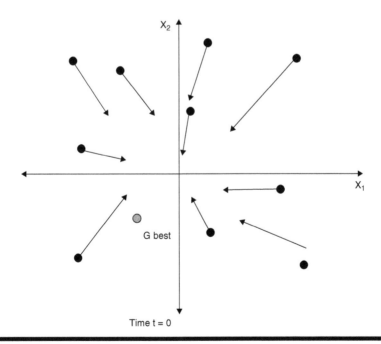

Figure 11.7   Velocity and position update for multi-particles in G best PSO at time = 0.

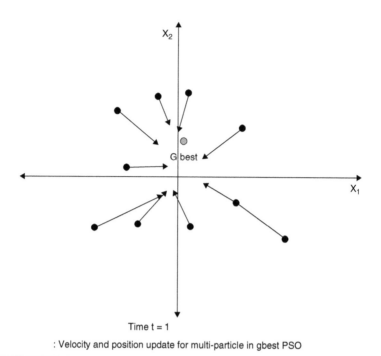

Time t = 1

: Velocity and position update for multi-particle in gbest PSO

Figure 11.8 **Velocity and position update for multi-particles in G best PSO at time = 1.**

11.3.3 Artificial Bee Colony Algorithm

Like PSO this algorithm is also an advanced metaheuristic global technique proposed by Dervis Karaboga (2005). Dervis Karaboga with his research team investigated the ABC technique and its best applications in the real world. Karaboga presented the first article of ABC in 2007 in which a comparison was done between GA and PSO. The first conference paper was published in 2006. In the ABC algorithm [31, 32], the population is categorized with three numbers of groups: (1) 50% first type of bees, (2) 50% second type of bees, and (3) 1% third type of bees. The first type of bee is working, and in the second half, the second type of bee is included. Employed and onlooker bees are equal in number. Each food source is an expected solution to the optimization problem. Here, the main aim of bees is to search food place with high amount of nectar. Fitness of bees is calculated by the best quality of the food. Initially the first group of employed bees goes to random places searching for food. At that time onlooker bees are at the beehive waiting for the employed. Employee bees return to the starting place and tell the onlooker bees all about food sources including details like quality, quantity, and distance of onlooker bees.

After receiving all the details from the first type of bee, the onlooker bees also start searching in the same direction. The solution that is abandoned is changed by the Scout Bees into a new randomly generated solution.

11.3.3.1 Behavior of Honey Bees in Nature

Bees have several qualities. They can pass on information to other bees in their own language, can memorize all the facts, and make own decisions according the facts. Using the intelligence action of bees, many researchers started to simulate foraging behaviour of the bees. The roles of these bees are:

Employed bees: These bees make use of only a single source of food and store every fact regarding that food source like richness, direction, and distance.

Unemployed bees: These bees are divided into two groups: onlooker bees and scout bees. Only these unemployed bees found and shaped all the information from the first group of bees based on a certain probability.

Foraging behaviour: This is the most important characteristic of the bees. In this process, bees go away from their hive and start finding the best food with high nectar. When the bee finds the best food source, it takes all the nectar and keeps it in their abdomen. The bee can extract nectar for 30 to 120 minutes, on the basis of nectar quantity and distance. Finally, all the bees share all the information.

11.3.3.2 Dance

Onlooker bees give all the facts to other bees who are waiting at the hive about the food source including how much nectar is present in the food source and distance and direction from the hive. These bees do a unique dance on the hive.

(1) Round dance: Bees do not get any clue on the direction of food from this dance, but they perform this type of dance only at a very short distance.

(2) Waggle dance: This dance tells the onlooker bees if the food source is far away, and if so, they perform this dance.

(3) Tremble dance: Bees do this dance only when they have spent time uploading the nectar, and by this dance, the bee tells us that she is unaware of the present position of the food point because she has taken much time uploading the nectar.

11.3.4 Phases of the ABC Algorithm

■ **Initialization Phase:** Here we select the best food place randomly with the expression:

$$x_i^j = x_{min}^j + \text{rand}(0,1) \times (x_{max}^j - x_{min}^j)$$

Here, x_{min}^j & x_{max}^j are the two bounds of the given function. The fitness function is calculated by this formula.

The fitness function of ABC is evaluated by this formula:

$$fit = \{\frac{1}{1+f}, \text{ if } f \geq 01 + fabs\,(f), \text{ if } f < 0$$

■ **Employed Bee Phase:** Three steps are mainly used in this phase:

    a) Generate a new solution
    b) Calculate new fitness
    c) Apply greedy selection

The neighbouring food source is evaluated by this equation:

$$x_{new}^j = x^j + \phi\,(x^j - x_p^j),\ \phi \in [-1,1]$$

where x = Current solution
    x_p^j = Random partner, x_{new}^j = New solution
    f = value of Objective function

■ **Onlooker Bee phase**

First, calculate the probabilities for every food source. Then generate a new solution that depends on the probability value. After that, calculate the new fitness by applying greedy selection.

$$\textbf{Probability} = \textbf{0.9} \times \frac{fit_i}{fit} + \textbf{0.1}$$

Here, fit_i = fitness function. Onlooker bees explore neighborhood food sources according to this expression.

$$x_{new}^j = x^j + \phi\,(x^j - x_p^j)$$

■ **Scout Bee Phase**

First of all, we found the abandoned solution, which was based on a limit value. Then discard that rejected solution and replace it with the new one. The new solution is randomly created by scout bees using this equation:

$$x_i^j = x_{min}^j + \text{rand}\,(0,\,1) \times (x_{max}^j - x_{min}^j)$$

11.3.5 Ant Colony Optimization Algorithm

ACO was developed in 1991 by Marco Dorigo. Goss et al. (1989) and Deneuborg et al. (1990) experimented with Argentine ants. This system mimics the behavior of real ants. ACO uses a different Max-Min system, which was introduced by Hoos and Stutzle. ACO is a probabilistic, metaheuristic, and graph-based optimization technique used to find the optimal path. It is a technique used to calculate the smallest track of the ants' journey. Ants start moving from roost to the food place and backwards to the starting point, then the ants prefers to go to the smallest track to the foodstuffs.

In computer science and operation research, this algorithm is a promising technique. Artificial ants act like multiagent methods, which are influenced by the behavior of the original ants. Ant behavior is stochastic. Ants wander randomly and explore new food sources; there is indirect communication between the ants, and every ant acts independently. The first ant navigates from nest to food source randomly until it discovers the best stock of food; after that, the ant returns to the hotbed, where it finds a different type of chemical. Then all the ants follow one of the tracks at random, leaving behind the pheromone trail. The shortest path is found through pheromone trails. A chemical substance is given away on track, and more chemical substances on track increase the chance of the smallest track being used. The pheromone trails of the longer path diminish with time.

■ **ACO construction and solution**

At the beginning when ants start searching for food, a constant amount of pheromone is assigned to all arcs. This pheromone amount helps to compute the probability from i to j node and is given by

$$P_{ij}^k = \begin{cases} \dfrac{\tau_{ij}^\alpha}{\sum_{i=0}^{N_i^k} \tau_{ij}^\alpha}, & if \ j \in N_i^k \\ 0, & if \ j \notin N_i^k \end{cases}$$

N_i^k = neighborhood of ant k when in node i.

■ **Probability equation**

The probability equation of the ant system, when an ant passes from i to j node

is $p_{ij} = \dfrac{\left(\tau_{ij}^\alpha\right)\left(\eta_{ij}^\beta\right)}{\sum \left(\tau_{ij}^\alpha\right)\left(\eta_{ij}^\beta\right)}$

where τ_{ij} = amount of pheromone from i to j node, α
α = parameter to control, η_{ij} = eligibility of i to j node.

When the ant passes from i to j node, then the value of the pheromone is changed to:

$$\tau_{ij} \leftarrow \tau_{ij} + \Delta\tau^k.$$

By using this the probability increases for the next coming ant. The pheromone evaporates when an ant moves to the next node by this equation:

$$\tau_{ij} \leftarrow (1-\rho)\,\tau_{ij}$$

where $\rho \in (0,1)$ is a parameter.

■ **ACO pheromone update equation**

$$\tau_{ij} = (1-\rho)\,\tau_{ij} + \Delta\tau_{ij}$$

Here, ρ = rate of evaporation.
The amount of pheromone deposited is given by

$$\Delta\tau_{i,j}^k = \begin{cases} \dfrac{1}{L_k} & \text{if ant } k \text{ travel on edge } i, j \\ 0 & \text{otherwise} \end{cases}$$

where L_k is the cost(length) of the kth ant tour.

11.4 Nonlinear Programming Problems

Solving NLP problems is more difficult in comparison to LP problems. Solution of LP are easy and many methods are available for the solution of these problems. But the solution of NLP is not an easy task. NLPP is a branch of Operation Reseatch (OR) and has vast application fields. There are two types of NLP problems: with constraints and without constraints. Many classical methods are accessible for the solution of NLPs. These classical techniques give the approximate result rather than accurate solutions. Different methods are available, such as the Lagrangian multiplier, penalty method, and KKT conditions, for the solution of NLP with constraints, and there are special problems of quadratic NLP that can be solved by the Beale method, the Wolfe method, etc. A special method is not available for the infusion of both LPP and NLPP. Today, there are many modern techniques (nontraditional) for NLP problems. These techniques are very easy for the solution of NLP research problems and include the PSO algorithm, ABC algorithm, the GA, ACO algorithm, artificial immune systems, and fuzzy optimization. There are other metaheuristic algorithms that can also be used to find the solutions to these problems. Nonlinear programming problems have two types of functions: convex or nonconvex. In NLPs the function may be convex or nonconvex. A convex problem sustains the properties of L3PP but a nonconvex problem keeps the properties of NLPs. The main difference between convex and nonconvex optimization is convex optimization gives only one solution, which is globally optimal while in nonconvex problem gives multiple local optimal points. So the convex problem has better efficiency than the nonconvex problem.

Suppose we are given a Non-linear programming problem with constraints

Minimize. f(x),

Subject to linear or nonlinear constraints $g(x) \leq 0$; & $h(x) = 0$;

Problem that is solved with series of unconstrained minimization

NLPP with constraints is converted to NLPP without constraints by using penalty Method.

$$P(x) = \sum_{i=1}^{m}[max\{0, g_i(x)\}]^q + \sum_{i=0}^{k}|h_i(x)|^q, q \geq 0$$

11.5 Numerical Examples of Unconstrained Optimization Problem

1. Minimize fun = $8x_1^2 + 4x_1x_2 + 5 x_2^2$

$$0 \leq x_1, x_2 \leq 10$$

2. Minimize fun = $2x_1^2 + x_2^2 - x_1x_2 - 7x_2$

$$-10 \leq x_1, x_2 \leq 10$$

Solution by the GA

1. Minimize fun = $8x_1^2 + 4x_1x_2 + 5x_2^2$

$$0 \leq x_1, x_2 \leq 10$$

Table 11.1   Solution of Problem 1 by Genetic Algorithm

SI.NO	Population Size	No. of Variable	Generation	Function Value	X1	X2
1	20	2	20	0.281616	0	0.24
2	50	2	50	0.000523447	0	0
3	100	2	100	9.38107E-05	0	0

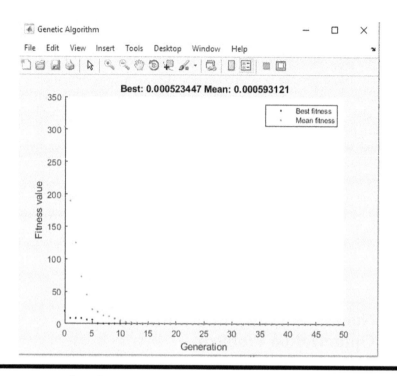

Figure 11.9   50 iterations.

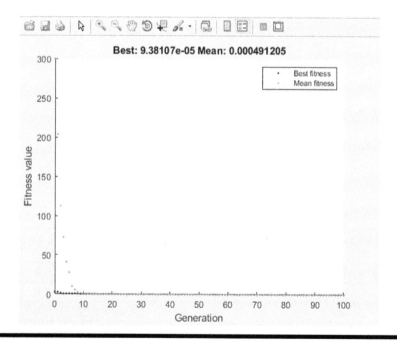

Figure 11.10   100 iterations.

2. Minimize fun = $2x_1^2 + x_2^2 - x_1x_2 - 7x_2$

$$-10 \le x_1, x_2 \le 10$$

Table 11.2   Solution of Problem 2 Genetic Algorithm

SI. NO	Population	No. of Variable	Generation	Function Value	X1	X2
1	20	2	20	-13.999999	1.01	4.01
2	50	2	50	-13.999999	1	4
3	100	2	100	-13.999999	1	4

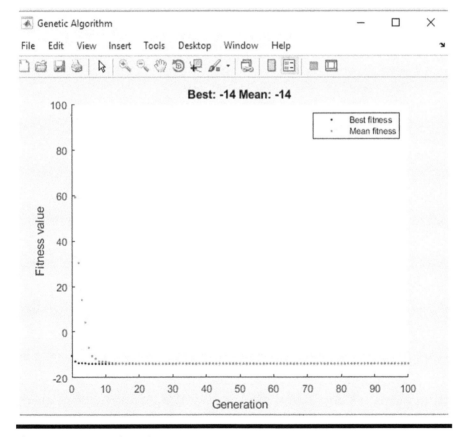

Figure 11.11   100 iterations.

Solution by ABC Algorithm

1. Minimize fun = $8x_1^2 + 4x_1x_2 + 5 \, x_2^2$

$$0 \leq x_1, x_2 \leq 10$$

Table 11.3   Solution of Problem 1 Artificial Bee Colony

Population Size	No. of Variable	Iteration	Function value	X1	X2	f New	f Value
20	2	20	0	0.036	1.6634	13.8883	0
50	2	50	0	0.2496	0	0.4984	0
100	2	100	0	4.22E-04	0	-1.42E-06	0
200	2	200	0	0	6.11E-17	1.87E-32	0
500	2	500	0	0	5.14E-40	1.32E-96	0

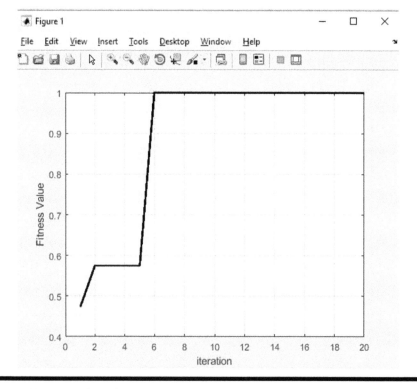

Figure 11.12   20 iterations.

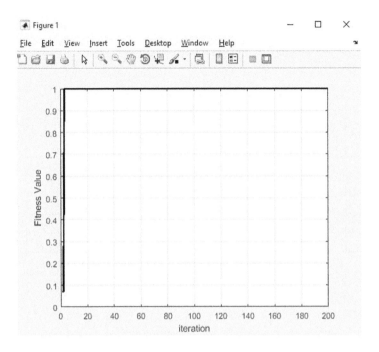

Figure 11.13   200 iterations.

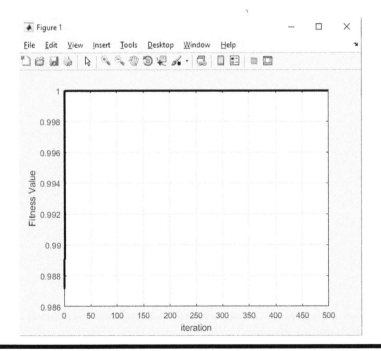

Figure 11.14   500 iterations.

2. Minimize fun = $2x_1^2 + x_2^2 - x_1 x_2 - 7x_2$

$$-10 \le x_1, x_2 \le 10$$

Table 11.4 Solution of Problem 2 Artificial Bee Colony

Population Size	No. of Variable	Iteration	Function value	X1	X2	f New	f Value
20	2	20	-14	-1.7181	1.3735	0.5351	-13.1718
50	2	50	-13.999999	-0.159	3.2866	-11.6314	-14
100	2	100	-13.999999	0.9998	3.9998	-14	-14
200	2	200	-14	1	4	-14	-14
500	2	500	-14	1	4	-14	-14

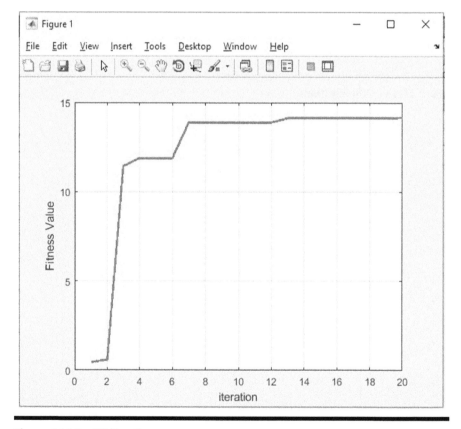

Figure 11.15   20 iterations.

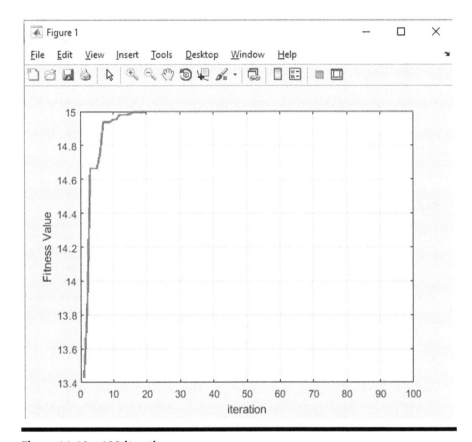

Figure 11.16   100 iterations.

11.5 Results and Discussion

From Table 11.1, we can see that the optimal point is to find out in 50 generations where x1 = x2 = 0, and in 100 generations the values of x1 and x2 again are zero. So the best result is obtained in 50 generations, and in Table 11.2, the problem function value is (0), which is the same for all generations 20, 50, and 100. Here, x1 = 1 and x2 = 4. From ABC table 11.3, the function value is zero for all iterations, and the variable values are x1 = 0.036, x2 = 1.6634, and f = 13.8883. So an optimal solution is found in 20 iterations, and from the table of ABC 11.4, the function value is -14 for all iterations 20, 50, 100, 200, and 500. In 20 iterations, our variable value for x1 is -1.7181 and x2 is 1.3735. The convergence rate and optimal solution of the ABC are faster than those of the GA.

11.6 Conclusion

In this chapter, we discussed the comparative study of evolutionary algorithms such as GA and ABC. For this comparison, unconstrained nonlinear optimization problems were taken as the solution. These algorithms are computational and efficient for solving nonlinear optimization problems. We used MATLAB® to solve the unconstrained nonlinear optimization problems. From the above tables and graph, it is concluded that ABC gives better results in fewer iterations. The optimal solution obtained from the ABC algorithm is much better than the GA.

References

[1] Chhavi Mangla, Moin Uddin and Musheer Ahmad. G.A based optimization for system of Non Linear equation. International Journal of Advanced Technology and Engineering Exploration, vol (5144), ISSN:2394,5443, IJATEE, 2018. 543009, 2018.

[2] Dr. Amanpreet Singh, Shivani Sanan, Amit Kumar. Solving Unconstrained Rosenbrock Optimization Problem Using Genetic Algorithms at High Technology Letters. ISSN NO: 1006-6748, Volume 27, Issue 3, 2021

[3] Punam S Mhetre. Genetic algorithm for linear and non-linear equation. International Journal of Advanced Engineering Technology, E-ISSN 0976-3945, IJAET/Vol.III/Issue II/April-June, 2012/114-118,2012.

[4] T.Yokota, M.Gen. Solving non-linear Integer Programming problem using Genetic algorithm. Proceeding of IEEE International Conference on System, Man and Cybernetics 5 Oct 1994.

[5] Chhavi Mangla, Moin Uddin and Musheer Ahmad. Optimization of complex Non Linear system using Genetic algorithm. International Journal of Information Technology, ISSN 2511-2104, DOI 10,1007/541870-020-00421-z, 2020.

[6] Raju Prajapati, Om Prakash Dubey and Randhir Kumar. Improved particles swarm optimization for non-linear programming problems with barrier method. Elssn: 23212543, volume 5, No 4, 2017, PP 72-80,2017.

[7] Raju Prajapati, Om Prakash Dubey. Analysing the impact of penalty constant on penalty function through PSO. Elssn: 23212543, volume 6, No 2, 2018, PP01-06,2018.

[8] W.T.Li and X.W.Shi. An improved PSO algorithm for pattern synthesis of phased arrays, proceeding in electromagnetic research, PIER 82, 319332,2008.

[9] Bimal Chandra Das. Comparative study of the methods of solving Non-Linear programming problem. Volume 4. 2009.

[10] Ying dong, Jiaeu Tang, Baodong xu and Dingwei wadg. Application of Swarm Optimization to non-linear programming. Comwa-2005, computer and Mathematics with application 49 (2005) 16551668,2005.

[11] Priyavada and Dr Binay kumar. A Review of Modified Particle Swarm Optimization Method. Computing and Optimization, Springer Proceedings in Mathematics & Statistics 404, https://doi.org/10.1007/978-981-19-6406-0_3,2023.

[12] Dervis Karaboga and Bahriye Basturk. Artificial Bee Colony (ABC) Optimization Algorithm for Solving Constrained Optimization Problems. IFSA 2007, LNAI 4529, pp. 789798, 2007. c Springer-Verlag Berlin Heidelberg 2007.

[13] Weifeng Gao, Lingling Huang & Sanyang Liu. Constrained Optimization by Artificial Bee Colony Framework. IEEE 2018.

[14] Soudeh Babaeizadeh and Rohanin Ahmad. Constrained Artificial Bee Colony Algorithm for Optimization Problems. AIP Conference Proceedings 1750, 020008 (2016); https://doi.org/10.1063/1.4954521 Published Online: 21 June 2016.

[15] Soudeh Babaeizadeh and Rohanin Ahmad. Enhanced Constrained Artificial Bee Colony Algorithm for Optimization Problems, International Arab Journal of Information Technology, Vol. 14, No. 2, 2017.

[16] Nadezda Stanarevic, Milan Tuba, and Nebojsa Bacanin. Modified artificial bee colony algorithm for constrained problems optimization A International Journal of Mathematical Models and Methods in Applied Science, issue 3, Volume 5, 2011.

[17] Alda Larasati Anindya, Ketut Bayu Yogha Bintoro, Silvester Dian Handy Permana. Modification of Ant Colony Optimization Algorithm to Solve the Traveling Salesman Problem, JISA (Jurnal Informatika dan Sains), e-ISSN: 2614-8404 Vol. 03, No. 02, December 2020.

[18] Marco Dorigo, Mauro Birattari, Thomas Stützle. Ant Colony Optimization algorithm. IEEE Computational Intelligence Magazin, December 2006, DOI: 10.1109/MCI.2006.329691. 1556-603X, IEEE, 2006.

[19] J.-L. Deneubourg, S. Aron, S. Goss, and J.-M. Pasteels. Self-organizing exploratory pattern of the Argentine ant," Journal of Insect Behavior, vol. 3, p. 159, 1990.

[20] Rohit Chaturvedi, Haider Banka. Modified Ant Colony Optimization Algorithm for Travelling Salesman Problem, International Journal of Computer Applications (09758887), Volume 97 No.10, July 2014.

[21] Dorigo, M., Maniezzo, V., and Colorni. A. The Ant System: Optimization by a Colony of Cooperating Agents, IEEE Transactions on Systems, Man Cybernetics, Part B, 1996, vol. 26, no. 1, pp. 29–41,1996.

[22] Dorigo, M., and Gambardella, L.M. Ant Colony System: A Cooperative Learning Approach to the Traveling Salesman Problem, IEEE Transactions on Evolutionary Computation, 1997, vol. 1, no. 1, pp. 53–66,1997.

[23] J. Kennedy, R. C. Eberhart, and Y. Shi, Swarm Intelligence. Morgan Kaufmann, 2001.

[24] Silva, A. R. M.; Ramalho, G. L. Ant system for the set covering problem Systems.2001 IEEE International Conference on Man and Cybernetics, 2001; Vol. 5, pp 3129–3133,2001.

[25] Vittorio Maniezzo, Luca Maria Gambardella, Fabio de Luigi in Ant Colony Optimization.

[26] JR Koza, D.Andre, F. H. Bennett and M.Keane. Genetic algorithm Programming (3) of Darwinian Invention and Problem Solving.

[27] David E. Genetic algorithms in search, optimization, and machine learning. Addison-wesley longman, USA; 1989.

[28] Dr. Amanpree Sings, Shivani Sanan, Amit Kumar. Solving Unconstrained Rosenbrock Optimization Problem Using Genetic Algorithms. ISSN NO: 1006-6748, ISSN No: 1006-6748,2021.

[29] Y. Shi and R. C. Eberhart. "Empirical study of particle swarm optimisation, "Proceedings of the IEEE Congress on Evolutionary Computation, P. J. Angeline, Z. Michalewicz, M. Schoenauer, X. Yao, and A. Zalzala, Eds., vol. 3, pp. 1945–1950, Washington USA,1999.

[30] Soniya Lalwani, Harsh Sharma, Suresh Chandra Satapathi, Kusum Deep and Jagdish Chand Bansal. A survey on Parallel particle swarm optimisation algorithm. Arabian Journal for Science and Engineering. 2018.

[31] D. Karaboga, An Idea Based on Honey Bee Swarm for Numerical Optimization, Erciyes University, Technical Report-TR06, Engineering Faculty, Computer Engineering Department, 2005.

[32] B. Basturk, D. Karaboga, An artificial bee colony (ABC) algorithm for Numeric Function Optimization, IEEE Swarm Intelligence Symposium 2006, 12–14 May 2006, Indianapolis, Indiana, USA.

Chapter 12

UAV-Enabled Mobile Edge Computing for IoT Applications

Alok Singh Kushwaha[1] and Nagendra Kumar[2]

[1]NIT Jamshedpur, India

[2]NIT Jamshedpur, India

12.1 Introduction

Unmanned aerial vehicles (UAVs) are a pilot-free flying platform. Today with the development of 5G technology, there have been a number of modifications done in UAVs to make them more useful. In the area of surveillance and military, UAVs should be efficiently integrated with IoT devices. Such a network of UAVs and IoT devices has to operate in real time and process a lot of data. Another issue related to such a network is saving of on-board battery. The mobile edge computing process analyzes data at the originating point. Applications in the field of science and engineering are highly computational. The Caihong 3 (CH-3), Caihong 4 (CH-4), Wing Loong 1, and Wing Loong 2 are the Chinese armed UAV models. America, Israel, and China are the major manufacturers and sellers of UAVs.

The global pandemic increased the use of data and proliferation of technologies like IoT and UAVs. The demand for edge computing is increasing due in part to users live streaming more and demanding content that does not lag. Akamai Technologies was founded in 1998 and deals with network, cyber security, and cloud computing services and is considered to be the largest global CDN. They have globally located servers and a wide range of products and services. Fastly, Inc. founded in 2011, is another well-known real-time CDN. In the wake of the pandemic Akamai and Fastly showed unexpected and unprecedented growth and the edge computing market continues to grow. There are also other players in the market that are providing hardware and software to deal with edge services. The category of hardware includes different types of sensors, UAVs, cameras, etc. There is different software such as PureEdgeSim and EdgeCloudSim used in edge computing. Microsoft Azure, Cisco Systems, Amazon Web Service, Dell Technologies, etc. are some of the organizations that are providing services in the field of edge computing. An open source simulator based on Java (J-sim) is used for edge computing. Taiwan-based ADLINK Technology focuses on the embedded computing sector. AirMap integrated the Microsoft Azure cloud for its UAV traffic management platform and developer ecosystem. MobiledgeX founded by Deutsche Telekom in 2018 deals with software for edges. MobiledgeX is an edge computing cloud services platform using resources contributed by mobile operators like British Telecom, Telefonica, and Deutsche Telekom. Equinix was founded in 1998 by Al Avery and Jay Adelson, an American multinational company in the co-location sector. It mainly works in co-location, where a customer puts their data in Equinix data centers. The customer does not have to maintain a data center facility. ClearBlade is another company focused on IoT and the edge. Processing of critical data at the cloud and utilizing it is a big challenge. Data processing at the edge is necessary for defense, health, and finance sectors such as stock market and crypto exchange. Big data infrastructure can handle the massive volume of data generated from crypto currency transactions. By analysis of cryptotransaction data, data science makes it possible to identify price fluctuations and prevent investors from experiencing substantial losses. Data science deals with utilizing data for proper administration. AI enables UAVs to carry out activities automatically like data capture, data transmission, data analysis, take-off, navigation, etc.

12.2 Relevance

User equipment has limited computation, storage, and limited battery lifetime. Advancements in the field of augmented reality, face recognition, animation, and online gaming requires high computation at the user side [1]. To overcome the computation issue, mobile edge computing (MEC) and wireless power transfer are suggested [2]. B. Galkin et al. discussed battery charging methods and implemented various options in a UAV-enabled cellular network. Laser power is used in UAVs to overcome battery issues [3]. Jie Ouyang et al. proposed a laser-powered UAV, proposed a UAV system acting as edge server [4]. During war UAVs are used in tactical mission, for which precise computing algorithms are used. Tri Nyugen et al. [1] suggested a unique blockchain-assisted Internet-of-Drones (IoD) architecture. The authors in Ref. [5] give a comprehensive overview of integration edge computing and blockchain technologies. Cherrueau, Ronan Alexandre et al. outlined the systematic grouping of features that administrators/DevOps expect and the requirements that edge infrastructure imposes on cloud management systems [6]. The authors of this study considered using an existing IaaS manager such as OpenStack to control the edge infrastructure and emphasized the need for effective collaboration between edge locations.

Applications that require high computation, Engineering and Science Computation–Environmental and telemetry study. Today globally countries are very conscious of changing weather conditions and global warming. Industrialization, manmade structures, cutting of trees, and vanishing of greenery are some of the activities that have had adverse effects on our environment and necessary measures have to be taken to deal with these situations. Physically monitoring everything is not possible. Thus, networks of sensors are set up in certain locations, and UAVs are used to collect and analyze data using edge computing. UAVs can easily reach remote locations and can collect data using wireless sensor nodes and instruments like tiltmeters, thermal image detectors, and volcanic gas sensors.

UAVs are used in the following areas enabled by edge computing.

- **Navigation**–GPS based, sky, land, air, and water. Measurements of 3D, radiometric, and land temporal properties is done with low cost and good accuracy using UAVs. Navigation is achieved with the help of state-of-art cameras, GPS, and edge computing. The wide range of UAVs and easy deployment make them useful in navigation.
- **Facial recognition systems**–Display devices like mobile phones, ATMs, and laptops can be secured with PIN code or by face recognition. AI-based face recognition is used in highly secured systems.
- **Geographical information system and urban planning**–Collecting spatial, spectral and temporal information related to area, color, and time can be done remotely with the help of UAV-enabled edge computing. Information is gathered by remote sensing allowing the study of trends of urban growth, morphology, and population.
- **Forestry monitoring**–Human-induced forest cutting and land requirements for agriculture have resulted in deforestation. The long-term monitoring of forests using UAVs is done by comparing the data on a regular basis.
- **Survey of agricultural land**–UAV-enabled edge computing is needed for surveying agricultural land. Identifying government land, agricultural land, village boundaries, and village pond sizes helps set up boundaries.
- **Telecommunication**–The installation of radio towers on the basis of population and usage. UAVs are used for monitoring of base station towers and for inspection of coverage areas.

- **Exploration petroleum offshore Reservoir**–Light detection and ranging techniques are used for petroleum exploration. Oil exploration is a high risk activity, thus the need for with UAVs and sensors. Sound waves are created by bursting large bubbles of compressed air. The sound waves target the rocks lying under the ocean. These waves are intercepted by sensors like hydrophones.
- **Killer UAV**–UAVs are used by defense forces in war and surveillance around the world. Lethal drones have been used by Russia and Ukraine in the war. AI-enabled UAVs have changed conventional war attacks. For example, explosive material can be loaded on UAVs and then targeted into enemy premises.

12.3 UAV-Enabled Blockchain Technology for Edge Computing

Data in a centralized network can be altered or deleted at server side. Blockchain technology shares the data in real time simultaneously with linked computer networks, which can be monitored or analyzed in a distributed manner. Blockchain is a database that stores encrypted blocks of data. Instead of generating copies or transferring of data, it is shared in-network for real-time access making it immutable. Blockchain technology finds application in sharing valuable or tamperproof data. The increased use of UAVs in the field of surveillance, disaster management, and exploration rescue mission. Decentralized approaches are adopted to minimize a single point of error. Issues like cyber-attacks, hacking of data, and crashing of hard disk/operating do not have much effect on decentralized systems. Cryptocurrency/crypto assets are based on blockchain in which each transaction is done on a smart digital platform. Privacy safety, security, and scalability are the basic features of blockchain technology. A block is a fundamental part of the blockchain and consists of the information part, hash, and block ID. If anyone tries to tamper with the block, there will be a change in the hash and the link of the blockchain will no longer exist. Transparency is maintained at every node. At every node authentication is done for new transactions. Each node holds its own copy of the entire blockchain. If anyone tries to manipulate the copy, it has to change the copy with at least 50% of the network. The more nodes the greater the security.

A decentralized consensus mechanism, known as proof of work, is used for validating transactions, processing peer-to-peer in a secure manner, and mining new tokens. A random or semi-random number called a nonce is used in cryptographic communication. The nonce ranges from 0 to 4294967296, so forecasting the output is impossible. The process of finding the valid block is called mining. Out of 21 million, 19 million bitcoin have already been mined. The task of developing a blockchain is done by Ethereum and other similar blockchain software. This technology can have a profound impact on the work of science and its open environment but that largely depends on the acceptance of technology by the scientific community and other related stakeholders.

12.3.1 Decentralization

Each member of the blockchain structure has access to the whole distributed database. The data in the blockchain is accessed in real time by the developer and user, thus leaving no room for data loss. Spatial allocation ensures the entire blockchain network is evenly distributed between different nodes in order to make full use of resources. The blockchain has demonstrated its ability to transform traditional computing with its salient features of distribution and persistence. Figures 12.1 and 12.2

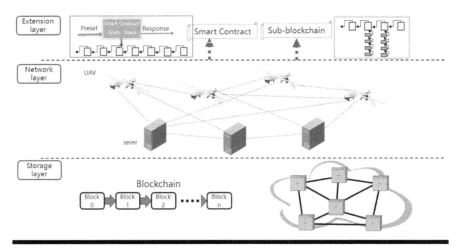

Figure 12.1   UAV-enabled blockchain MEC.

Source: [7] Guan et al.

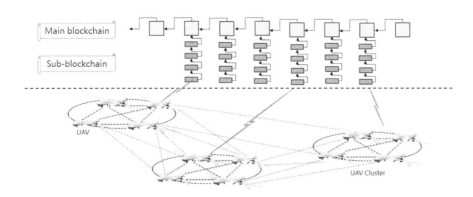

Figure 12.2   UAV-enabled sub-blockchain MEC.

Source: [7] Guan et al.

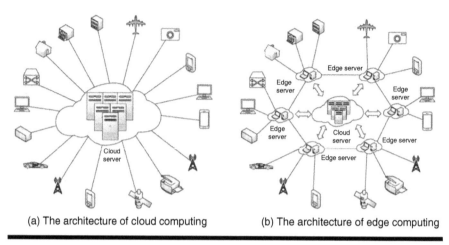

(a) The architecture of cloud computing   (b) The architecture of edge computing

Figure 12.3 Architecture for cloud and edge computing: (a) The architecture of cloud computing and (b) The architecture of edge computing.

Source: [8] Luo et al.

shows UAV-enabled blockchain MEC and sub-blockchain MEC while Figure 12.3 depicts the architecture for cloud and edge computing.

12.3.2 Immutability

Immutability refers to the ability of a blockchain to remain unchanged, unaltered, and indelible. Each of the blocks of information is carried out with the help of a hash value.

12.3.3 Anonymity

The blockchain adopts pseudonyms to conceal the information of participants. Each participant has an address, not a user identity. Due to features like transparency, security, trust, and accuracy, the blockchain can be used in industrial data computation in areas like real estate, education, donations, politics, pharmaceuticals, etc.

12.4 Cloud Computing

Cloud computing is server-based virtual technology. It is used when the client end wants to get rid of local server maintenance. Usually clients do not want to risk server failure, so the burden of data handling is transferred to data centers. To establish this type of IT system at their end is also costly. Engineers at the data center site are skilled in managing data. Thus, the risk of data load is transferred to such data centers. Cloud computing plays a major role when IT infrastructure has to deal with remotely accessing, storing, and manipulating data. A web browser is used to access the data server. With the development of 5G technology, it is required to have high and fast computation of data to fulfill the need of user.In MEC it is desired to bring cloud-loaded applications to the edge or the user. Real-time, cloud-based applications like Twitter, Facebook, and LinkedIn are social networking sites that connect millions of people globally. Mobile, laptop, and desktop are used to access these applications.

MEC deals with computing and storage at the user end. User equipment faces issues like operating system compatibility, storage, and battery life while communicating with data centers. It is predicated by *Fortune* magazine that the cloud gaming market will be 40.81 billion by the 2029. There is lot of competition in the gaming business. Traditional video games need storage as well as high processing capability of user devices. Edge computing enhances processing and storage experience of users with the help of remote servers. Gaming on-demand relies on such remote servers to reduce latency. As with remote desktop connection applications for computers, it allows users to remotely access a computer. MEC we are doing same thing while accessing number of application. Amazon prime videos, Netflix, You Tube, Zee5, etc., are some of the cloud-based video on-demand services.

Wearable handheld devices or user equipment have low computation power. It is predicted that in the coming era most devices will communicate with each other. This massive volume of data cannot be handled by cloud computing, but the MEC can. To overcome the issue of data latency in IoT devices people from academia and industry have high interest in MEC. IoT devices are the points at which data is generated. The edge devices are the located at the edge and having high computing capability. IoT devices send data to edge hardware where it is analyzed and processed in real time. In conventional methods data is sent to a data center using cloud technology where it is analyzed. Data is analyzed locally to reduce latency to get fast results of processed data. UAV- and MEC-integrated structures have gained the interest of researchers. UAVs are used for processing and analyzing in MEC.

Researchers are now focusing on UAV-assisted computing servers for user equipment. UAVs can act as:

(a) Flying platform server: In locations where UEs are unable to do fast computing, UAVs can be used as computing servers. Installed IoT or WSN are not in a position to establish a reliable communication link to transfer data. For computing by MEC server the UAV will reach to the IoT installed area, set up the link with these IoT devices, and then compute the data in real time.

(b) Flying platform relay: There are two common ways to use UAVs as relay: (i) amplify and forward and (ii) decode and forward [9]. Sometimes due to certain design limitations it is not possible to equip an MEC server on the UAV platform and the communication link between end user and base station thus fluctuates. In these cases UAVs can collect data for UE and forward to cloud computing server.

(c) Flying platform server with limited computation: In some cases UAVs use a hybrid mode where some data is processed by the UAV and some data is forwarded to the MEC server for theremaining computation. NOMA, OFDMA, TDMA multiple access techniques are used with UAVs and IoT 5G communication networks. 5G cellular technology was developed using NOMA technology. NOMA improves system throughput, reduces latency, and supports massive connectivity. The combination of NOMA and MEC in the area of UAVs has attracted a lot of researchers.

12.5 Integrating UAVs for Data Offloading in Smart Cities

In 2015, the Government of India launched the Smart City Project. The National Democratic Alliance initiated this plan to provide better quality of life to citizens. Smart drainage systems, water harvesting technology, mass transit, automating power systems, and pollution-free environment are provided by smart use of technology. The objective of these cities is to provide improved quality of life by using information and communication technology with smart data analysis. Cities enabled with smart traffic monitoring, smart parking, and smart surveillance camera, smart power supplies of public use. Figure 12.4 gives an idea of the way data is collected by UAVs in smart cities.

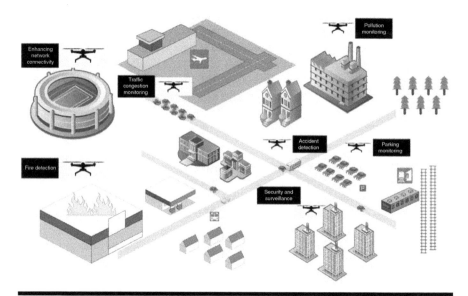

Figure 12.4   Data collection by UAVs in smart cities.

Source: [5] Luo et al.

For smooth operation in smart cities a lot of sensors and IoT devices are installed and the massive volume of data is analyzed and stored. Edge computing, cloud computing, and storage techniques are used to deal with such big data.

Liberalised Drone Rules, 2021 published by Ministry of Civil Aviation, India after feedback from academia, end users, start-ups and stakeholders increased the possibility of UAV civil uses. Green zones are identified where no permission is required for flying drones.

Integration of UAV and IoT plays a critical role in enhancing the quality of life in smart cities. Smart sensors such as biosensors are installed at various locations in smart cities and UAVs are used to collect data from these smart sensors for edge computing. An electronic sensor detects a physical parameter like heat, light, sound, or environmental activity and converts it into electrical signal. Electronic sensors such as streetlight automation, smart parking sensor, speedometer sensors, and motion sensors generate data that is processed locally by UAVs. Today sensors are equipped with AI to process data locally to reduce the use of bandwidth. These sensors use a computing algorithm to convert the data into meaningful insights. Next-generation sensors must have high computing power, integration, speed, flexibility, energy efficiency, and high sensing to pace with 6G technology. Today edge systems perform complex computing with limited processing capacity of processor, limited mounted battery power, and limited storage capacity.

12.5.1 UAV-Enabled Edge Computing for Pollution Control in Smart Cities

Computing sensor responses at measuring node is not easy. The output of sensors depends on application, site, conditions, and set-up. The signals from sensors depend on the air pollutant and combination of interfering compounds, temperature, humidity, atmospheric pressure, and instability of signal. When the concentration of air pollutant is high, sensor responses have high output signal.

An ultraviolet–visible spectrometer provides daily data of ozone, nitrogen dioxide, and other elements in the atmosphere. Satellite-based imagery is complex and requires hardware and software for processing images. UAV-based measurement systems are less complex and the network can be set up as per the requirement. Edge computing uses the following methodology:

(1) Placing of sensor in the atmosphere where pollution rate must be estimated.
(2) The system is initiated by sensing the presence of the pollutants like SO_2, NO_2, CO, and CO_2, and transmission of the real-time data to the next layer.
(3) Then, at the edge computing layer, the real-time data sent is transmitted to an Air Quality Index (AQI) checkpoint.
(4) The AQI value thus estimated is compared with the moderate AQI value 100 and then further transmission takes place accordingly.

(5) If the AQI value <= 100 then transmission of signal is abducted. If the AQI value >100 then, the data is further transmitted to the next stage such as the local cloud.

(6) Further, each local cloud gathers information from the places selected for monitoring.

(7) Then, all the local clouds transmit the data to the main database.

(8) The final analysis of all the results are displayed on the monitor.

(9) Preventive steps can be taken for increasing pollution rate.

Using an edge computing-based air pollution monitoring system, pollution levels of cities can be studied. The AQI is divided into six categories. Each category also has a specific color to quickly conclude pollution status. Each category corresponds to a different level of health issue.

(i) Dynamic re-routing: UAVs enabled with AI have re-routing and de-confliction capability. The data collected from installed sensors or WSN is collected and analyzed by UAV in real time with reduced latency.

(ii) Geospatial surveying: Information on the natural, built, social, and economic environments is collected, interpreted/analyzed, modeled, visualized, simulated, and presented. Surveying with UAV is more efficient. There is enhancement of performance and scalability of GIS systems with the use of MEC. With edge computing architecture, a theoretical model is proposed for formulating the GIS systems and quantitative analysis by Jianbing Zhang and et al. Figure 12.5 shows a flow chart for data collection.

12.5.2 Intelligent Transportation Systems

Real-time traffic monitoring system is also a major concern in smart cities. A vehicular ad-hoc network provides communication vehicle to vehicle (V2V). Every vehicle is a moving node and acts as a unique router. Data like GPS, speed, and driver/vehicle information is directly broadcasted to the ad-hoc network. Since missing data of moving vehicle is prone to accidental situation so it becomes necessary to transmit data through optimal path with any loss or noise. Trajectory design and resource allocation policies have been investigated by researchers for UAV-assisted vehicle networks. F. Zeng et al. [10] used an UAV as relay and studied the scheduling strategy to maximize the VANET throughput [11]. Considered a shared resource allocation algorithm based on maximizing the throughput of D2D communication [12]. UAV as a flying base station has been used for restoring V2V communication using joint resource allocation. Each vehicle can send or receive data from other vehicles. To ensure data security, every vehicle has a table of authenticated nodes registered under edge computing software. When a new vehicle enters the region

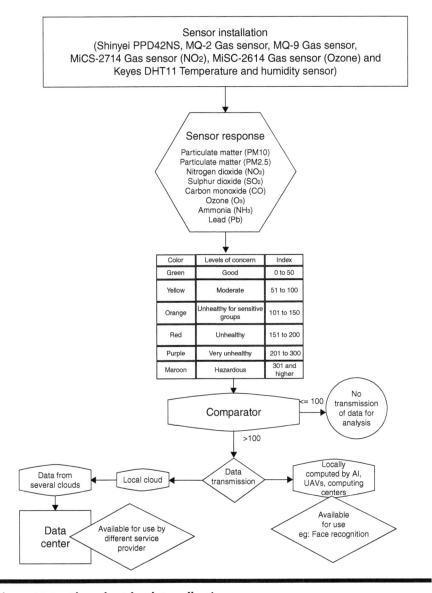

Figure 12.5   Flow chart for data collection.

of the edge node, authenticated data such as owner of vehicle, vehicle registration number, speed, and GPS will be updated by the edge node, then the required data will be shared with nearby vehicles. A space-efficient probabilistic data structure approach of quotient filter (QF) is used to check whether a particular element is a member of a particular set or not. QF has the ability to delete the element and resize

Table 12.1   AQI Basics for Ozone and Particle Pollution

Daily AQI Color	Level of Concern	Values of Index	Description of Air Quality
Green	Good	0 to 50	Satisfactory, little air pollution and no risk
Yellow	Moderate	51 to 100	Acceptatable, but there may be a risk for some people particularly those are unusually sensitive to air pollution
Orange	Unhealthy for Sensitivity Groups	101 to 150	People of sensitive groups may experience health effects ,the general public is less likely to be affected
Red	Unhealthy	151 to 200	Some members of general public may experience health effects, members of sensitive groups may experience more serious health effects
Purple	Very Unhealthy	201 to 300	Health alert: The risk of health effects is increased for everyone
Maroon	Hazardous	301 to Higher	Health warning of Emergency condition: everyone is likely to be affected

Source: [19] https://docs.airnowapi.org/webservices.

its content. When the vehicle moves away from the node and is registered with other nodes the QF algorithm updates the data of the edge node.

An intelligent transportation system (ITS) is an advanced technology enabled with AI, sensors, UAVs, data analysis and computing system, with the noble aim to help the society in the field of transportation and traffic management. An efficient ITS relies heavily on data collection and computing. In the metro cities heavy traffic is a challenging issue. The unauthorized vehicle parking on roadside, results to traffic jamming. Unorganized and manual traffic management cannot handle huge urban traffic. City roads are succumbing to the pressure of growing populations. ITS planning and deployment is in its infancy in India.

12.5.3 Architecture

ITS network design has a number of benefits:

a. Develops facilities to share required information across the network.
b. Time and cost of planning is lowered.
c. Minimizes accident rates.

d. Maintenance of roads and bridges can be done by estimating past traffic rates.

e. Improves future operational cost planning.

For proper organization and movement of vehicles in metro cities it is necessary to adopt ITS architecture. Automatic parking systems, smart toll plazas, anti-collision systems, etc., need to be organized in a systematic manner. While designing the ITS system some basic points must be taken into consideration including source of information, technology of information collection, methodology of information analysis, transmission of information to the required locations for different applications, etc. The geographical area under consideration is divided into different sectors, then each sector is divided into subsectors. In the given subsector, the number of data generation points are identified. Architecture for ITS data generation points in the form of cameras and sensors has to determine which are used for surveillance and which for traffic monitoring. The combination of IoT, AI, edge computing, and 5G technology fulfills most of the requirements of ITS architecture.

- **Roadside installation of smart sensors**. Magnetic detector inductive loop sensors and magnetometers are placed roadside,which capture road activities.
- **Sensor installed in vehicle**

Today advanced automobile manufacturing technology has made vehicles essentially moving computers. The type of electronic devices embedded on vehicles include GPS sensors, tire pressure sensors, digital fuel sensors, air conditioner sensors, infrared sensors, ultrasonic sensors, cameras, microphones, etc. There are many GPS service provider companies in India that provide services such as live location of vehicles, A/C on off alert on mobile, geofencing service, immobilizer enabled with 24 volt relay, fuel level alerts on owner's mobile, etc. Cloud-based storage systems are integrated with GPS navigators/trackers. Driver behavior can also be monitored. For example, information on abnormal body posture condition can be automatically captured by a camera and communicated to the nearest traffic monitoring station. Figures 12.6 and 12.7 show ITS architecture flow diagram and ITS subsystem and communication flow diagram, respectively.

12.6 Big Data for Smart Traffic Management

Big data has its own issues like utilization. The big data framework collects information from heterogeneous resources such as Internet of things devices CCTV. Further it is studied by big data technology through the MapReduce framework. Figure 12.8 depicts the big data framework.

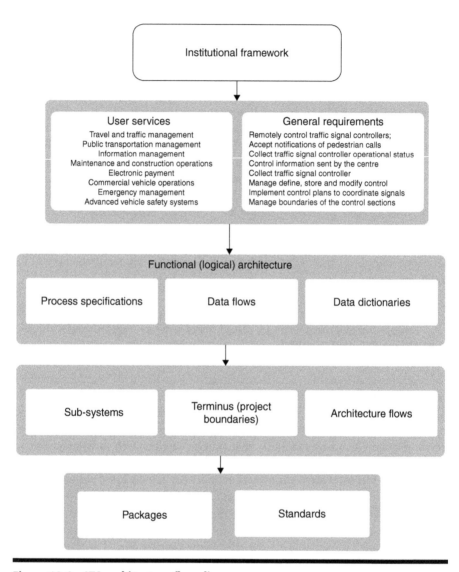

Figure 12.6   ITS architecture flow diagram.

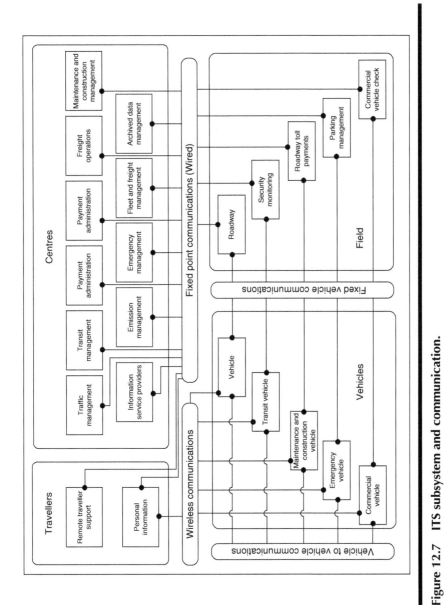

Figure 12.7 ITS subsystem and communication.

Source: [20] https://smartnet.niua.org/sites/default/files/webform/pan-1b_itms_rfp_.pdf.

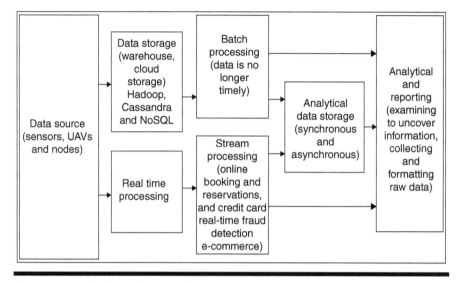

Figure 12.8   Big data framework.

12.7 Edge Computing for Energy Harvesting-Enabled IoTs

IoT devices have limited battery power supply, and the computation of data at the user end consumes a lot of battery energy. An UAV-enabled edge computing system provides flexible computation of data from mobile IoTs. Energy management in the IoT device is required for efficient data computation. The UAV acts as an edge computing server and relay station to offload data. UAVs and IoTs are powered by batteries. Due to the limited capacity of batteries energy harvesting is required at relay and user equipment side. Most of the time UEs and UAVs are mobile, which results in data failure. Some researchers [13] have proposed an energy-efficient UAV-based edge computing system with energy harvesting. H. Wu et al. [15] proposed an algorithm for computational workload and data traffic to optimize system performance of a network enabled with MEC. Integrating AI and ML with edge computing increased the possibility of accuracy in data analysis. End devices smartphone, wearable devices used for social networking and entertainment and handheld IoTs requires moderate battery life for data computation.

Karim Arabi defined edge computing in 2015 broadly as all computing outside the cloud happening at the edge of the network. Cloud computing works on big data while edge computing on instant data. Offloading of data for computation to nearby fog nodes, edge nodes, and access points increase the battery life of user equipment. Cyber foraging is used to achieve effective resource utilization in mobile cloud computing.

Table 12.2   UAV-based Edge Computing with Energy Harvesting Capability

Ref.	Proposed model/Algorithms	Results
[3]	Stochastic game model	Improved life cycle
[4]	GLOBE	MEC-enabled base stations-optimization
[13]	Lyapunov optimization	satisfactory computation performance and achieving green computing
[14]	Joint trajectory and resource allocation	energy savings demonstration
[13]	compromised offloaded information by eavesdroppers	analyzed full offloading, zero and partial

Table 12.3   UAV-based Offloading

Ref.	Challenges	Approach
[16]	offloading of videos	demonstrate the efficiency with the help of testbed
[17]	energy consumption minimization	performance is compared and
[18]	energy, delay, and cost	trade-offs between power consumption, time delay, and complexity
[15]	edge-user-allocation problem	developed MobMig, for allocating users in real-time

Different challenges of cloud computing are overcome by adopting edge computing such as scalability, latency, lack of mobility support, etc. The different features of edge computing are cloudlets, fog computing, mobile cloud computing, and multi-access node computing. Table 12.2. gives an overview of UAV-based edge computing with energy harvesting capability while Table 12.3 covers UAV-based offloading.

12.8   Challenges and Future Directions

The issue like computation capability and battery consumption during edge computing-enabled UAV for IoT. The upcoming 6G brings lot of research topics and future research opportunities related to computational offload. 3G- and 4G-enabled devices do not require much computation, as it was done by cloud but when 5G/6G will run in full-fledged, there would be need of very high local computing to minimize latency. Today MEC research is in its infancy. Yet there are many research areas on which lot of work has to be done to improve the quality of service used by IoT devices. IoT devices do not have much processing capability and even fewer security features.

- **Security**: Researchers are concerned about data security in the network. To implement proactive threat detection technologies. Securing access to edge servers by encrypted tunnels, firewalls, and access control. Edge computing-loaded applications need to be highly secured. To have pace with new security challenges more research is needed.
- **Mobility**: WSN, UE, and IoT devics face the communication link setup challenge especially during bad weather conditions. User devices such as laptops and mobiles are most of the time mobile and in time-varying positions. The movement and trajectory of users is dynamic for MEC servers, and this affects the outsourcing strategy. In addition, frequent user movements result in frequent handovers between edge servers, reducing computing power.

  iii **Data accumulation**: Data collection from the edge servers is again a hot area for researchers. Data storage and access both are critical.

  iv **Scalability**: Adding and removing IoT devices at the edge changes the network structure. This affects computation, storage, management, and security. The use of AI in edge computing resolves many issues of scalability. Yet there are many challenges to address.

12.9 Conclusion

Blockchain is a highly secured technology, but it is still in its infancy stage and lot of research has to be done to make to it applicable in different forms of data analysis. The areas of e-commerce, social networks, and search engines will be more secure with the application of blockchain concepts.

Edge computing minimizes the need for long-distance communication between user and client and server to reduce latency and bandwidth requirements. It manages the data generated by remote sensors and IoT devices.

UAV-enabled edge computing has features like easily reconfigurable but lack suitable routing algorithms and is prone to malfunctioning. A lot of research work needs to be done to deal with frequent link breakage, power requirements, situations like bad weather conditions, etc.

References

[1] T. Nguyen, R. Katila, and T. N. Gia, "A Novel Internet-of-Drones and Blockchain-based System Architecture for Search and Rescue".

[2] M. Kishk, A. Bader, and M. S. Alouini, "Aerial Base Station Deployment in 6G Cellular Networks Using Tethered Drones: The Mobility and Endurance Tradeoff," *IEEE Veh. Technol. Mag.*, vol. 15, no. 4, pp. 103–111, 2020, doi: 10.1109/MVT.2020.3017885.

[3] J. Ouyang, Y. Che, J. Xu, and K. Wu, "Throughput maximization for laser-powered UAV wireless communication systems," *2018 IEEE Int. Conf. Commun. Work. ICC Work. 2018–Proc.*, March, pp. 1–6, 2018, doi: 10.1109/ICCW.2018.8403572.

[4] K. Tian, Y. Liu, H. Chai, and B. Liu, "Deep Reinforcement Learning-Based Dynamic Offloading Management in UAV-Assisted MEC System," *Wirel. Commun. Mob. Comput.*, vol. 2022, 2022, doi: 10.1155/2022/2491389.

[5] C. Luo, L. Xu, D. Li, and W. Wu, "Edge computing integrated with blockchain technologies," *Lect. Notes Comput. Sci. (including Subser. Lect. Notes Artif. Intell. Lect. Notes Bioinformatics)*, vol. 12000 LNCS, no. February, pp. 268–288, 2020, doi: 10.1007/978-3-030-41672-0_17.

[6] R. A. Cherrueau, A. Lebre, D. Pertin, F. Wuhib, and J. M. Soares, "Edge computing resource management system: A critical building block! Initiating the debate via OpenStack," *USENIX Work. Hot Top. Edge Comput. HotEdge 2018, co-located with USENIX ATC 2018*, 2018.

[7] Z. Guan, H. Lyu, D. Li, Y. Hei, and T. Wang, "Blockchain: A distributed solution to UAVenabled mobile edge computing," *IET Commun.*, vol. 14, no. 15, pp. 2420–2426, 2020, doi: 10.1049/iet-com.2019.1131.

[8] C. Luo, L. Xu, D. Li, and W. Wu, "Edge computing integrated with blockchain technologies," *Lect. Notes Comput. Sci. (including Subser. Lect. Notes Artif. Intell. Lect. Notes Bioinformatics)*, vol. 12000 LNCS, no. March, pp. 268–288, 2020, doi: 10.1007/978-3-030-41672-0_17.

[9] N. Kumar and V. Bhatia, "Performance Analysis of Amplify-and-Forward Cooperative Networks with Best-Relay Selection Over Weibull Fading Channels," *Wirel. Pers. Commun.*, vol. 85, no. 3, pp. 641–653, 2015, doi: 10.1007/s11277-015-2799-y.

[10] F. Zeng, R. Zhang, X. Cheng, and L. Yang, "UAV-Assisted data dissemination scheduling in VANETs," *IEEE Int. Conf. Commun.*, vol. 2018-May, no. Mvc, pp. 1–6, 2018, doi: 10.1109/ICC.2018.8422219.

[11] Y. Qiu, Y. Wang, C. Tan, M. Zheng, and K. Yu, "Joint resource allocation algorithm based on throughput maximization in D2D communication," *Proc. 2015 4th Int. Conf. Comput. Sci. Netw. Technol. ICCSNT 2015*, no. Iccsnt, pp. 1074–1078, 2016, doi: 10.1109/ICCSNT.2015.7490922.

[12] L. Deng, G. Wu, J. Fu, Y. Zhang, and Y. Yang, "Joint Resource Allocation and Trajectory Control for UAV-Enabled Vehicular Communications," *IEEE Access*, vol. 7, pp. 132806–132815, 2019, doi: 10.1109/ACCESS.2019.2941727.

[13] T. Bai, J. Wang, Y. Ren, and L. Hanzo, "Energy-efficient computation offloading for secure uav-edge-computing systems," *IEEE Trans. Veh. Technol.*, vol. 68, no. 6, pp. 6074–6087, 2019, doi: 10.1109/TVT.2019.2912227.

[14] S. Jeong, O. Simeone, and J. Kang, "Mobile Edge Computing via a UAV-Mounted Cloudlet: Optimization of Bit Allocation and Path Planning," *IEEE Trans. Veh. Technol.*, vol. 67, no. 3, pp. 2049–2063, 2018, doi: 10.1109/TVT.2017.2706308.

[15] Q. Peng *et al.*, "Mobility-aware and migration-enabled online edge user allocation in mobile edge computing," *Proc.–2019 IEEE Int. Conf. Web Serv. ICWS 2019–Part 2019 IEEE World Congr. Serv.*, pp. 91–98, 2019, doi: 10.1109/ICWS.2019.00026.

[16] N. H. Motlagh, M. Bagaa, and T. Taleb, "UAV-Based IoT Platform: A Crowd Surveillance Use Case," *IEEE Commun. Mag.*, vol. 55, no. 2, pp. 128–134, 2017, doi: 10.1109/MCOM.2017.1600587CM.

[17] M. Hua, Y. Huang, Y. Wang, Q. Wu, H. Dai, and L. Yang, "Energy Optimization for Cellular-Connected Multi-UAV Mobile Edge Computing Systems with Multi-Access Schemes," *J. Commun. Inf. Networks*, vol. 3, no. 4, pp. 33–44, 2018, doi: 10.1007/s41650-018-0035-0.

[18] M. Messous *et al.*, "in an UAV Network To cite this version: HAL Id: hal-02539821 A Game Theory Based Efficient Computation Offloading in an UAV Network," pp. 0–11, 2022.

[19] https://docs.airnowapi.org/webservices.

[20] https://smartnet.niua.org/sites/default/files/webform/pan-1b_itms_rfp_.pdf.

Chapter 13

Internet of Things Enabled Software-Defined Networks

Santosh Kumar Sharma[1], Debendra Muduli[1], Sukant Kisoro Bisoy[1], Srikanta Kumar Mohapatra[2], and Prakash Kumar Sarangi[3]

[1]Department of Computer Science & Engineering, C.V. Raman Global University, Odisha, India

[2]Chitkara University Institute of Engineering and Technology, Chitkara University, Punjab, India

[3]School of Computer Science and Engineering, Lovely Professional Univeristy, Punjab, India

13.1 Introduction

Today's modern world is based on heterogeneous networks with various types of heterogeneous technologies [1, 2]. The role of the Internet of Things (IoT) is to keep track of the current ecosystem. In a smart system IoT refers to the various ways in which IoT devices and systems can operate, communicate, and interact, depending on specific use cases and requirements such that it will keep the balance between smart ecosystems and various heterogeneous technologies [3]. IoT networks connect via the internet different physical devices like wireless communication devices, RFID tags, sensors, actuators, etc. IoT refer to the

DOI: 10.1201/9781032650722-17

ecosystem of applications and services that interact with IoT devices used in the different prospectus of environments from the machine-to-machine or within the cellular network. It is also used in different embedded system applications. IoT applications now use advanced computing technologies that enable the environment to be restructured, which refers to such devices' functionality for a long time, durable based on the environment. Manufacturing and industry sectors for digital transformations, automatically process and control projects. Its major application areas are energy, cities, transportation or mobility, healthcare management, supply chain management, agriculture, building architecture, smart traffic management, industrial monitoring, designing of safety-enabled systems, and in different other sectors [4, 5, 6]. It is a smart computing technology aimed at connecting physical devices.

In day-to-day living, IoT devices are increasing rapidly; as per the Mordor Intelligence forecast, in 2026, the number will be 1.38 trillion last decades based on a statistical analysis of 761.4 billion last year [7]. So however data refer to any specific IoT devices devices are using is currently supposed to increase 500% more in upcoming years. This amount of data requires a special network. That's where software-defined network (SDN) correlated with IoT comes into play [8, 9].

SDNs generally operate on two planes: control and data planes [10, 11]. A significant amount of research has been done on the application, issues, analysis, challenges, and prediction factors of different aspects of SDN with the implementation of IoT in different domains. In recent years, SDN looks like it may be the future of integrated domains (i.e., centralized with other networks like wireless sensor networks).

13.2 Software-Defined Networks-Enabled IoT Architecture

SDN technology is uniquely specified from IoT technology. Here we focus on sensor devices used to propagate to sense, processes, transfer, manage, and store information within unbounded sensor devices. IoT methods add complexity and non-interoperability to the network landscape due to the thousands of communication protocols and billions of network-connected devices. In this context, SDN based on IoT based on the general framework for managing IoT devices intelligently SD-IoT architecture is also proposed with implementation IPV6 [12]. Research has shown how IoT devices can be managed in open flow-based networks [13, 14, 15].

IoT consists of several technologies at each layer-by-layer architecture. SDN is based on the traditional network that provides a stepping stone that overcomes the features of IoT with new services.

13.2.1 SDN Architecture and Protocol

SDN process is analysed as a group of different open software-based technologies within the computing environment of networking system along with a combination of network hardware. In SDN, APIs like open flow operates on both the forward and control planes to decouple them. Then create a transmitted link in between them for operation. SDN architecture has three layers: application layer, control layer, and infrastructure layer. The application layer consists of firewall management, balancing of loads and introductive detection system of all the associated issues [16]. The SDN uses a controller to manage the behaviour of the data plane. Architecture manages all the appliances by NAPIs and SAPIs, i.e. north side APIs and south side APIs [17,18]. The control layer is the network's nerve center, where everything is governed and coordinated. Only the key aspects are the network visualization and already specified on APIs. SDN is based on the orchestration of different technologies. The controller acts as a steppingstone that manages the overall network. All applications execute over the controller. Whatever incoming flows come from the data plane are managed by the rules that are defined by the SDN controller. The NI (Northbound Interface) and SI (Southbound Interface) APIs SDN layers communicate with each other [18]. There are different types of controllers such as FloodLight, OpenDaylight, Nox/Pox, etc., in the market.

The controller manages the data plane's flow based on predetermined statistical metrics and operational directives. So as a whole SDN is an reliable network that works along with IoT devices to manage all the demand of customers in an efficient manner with high data transmission rate. So as a conclusive part IoT in this technology objects are more connected with each other within internet than people. SDN correlated with IoT which focused on training, academic and corporate area, and several sectors that can be based on network to network with respect to people. Most of the work culture of IoT is embedded within SDN.

13.2.2 SDN–Cellular Network

Today, cellular systems not easy to accesses the desired result by getting physically intervenes in radio technologies. It provides high complexity and greater propagation in the communication system. SDN is being used to realize flexible and scalable cellular networks. It enhances mobility management in a deployed network, and increases the performance and implementation of security and backup challenges. Cellular-based SDNs consist of various rules that can be taken over different user groups of LTE network and establish the secure network communications [19, 20]. SDN–cellular network also concentrates on local agents by performing on every switch that can provide deep packet system due to decrease SDN–cellular network process of controller system.

A software-defined radio access network runs by using principles based on 4G LTE networks [21]. Today it is implemented in 5G networks [22, 23]. A centralized controller with a huge base station that processes the allocation of resources based on three-dimensional grid structure that is frequency on time. It is based on the centralized approach of control plane abstracts the entire RAN around a distributed system. This network performs the assignment of resources in the specific domains of space slots, range of frequencies, and time stamps. The public network can manage its decision upon the delay that occurs on the network. Another SDN architecture (i.e., SoftCell) also provides certain policies for LTE networks to run in the core cellular networks. This architecture has also defined the uses of switches rather than the use of gateways in traffic classification [24]. By using the gateway each local agent can access the switch on the network using User Equipment profile to control packet classification through the ISP.

UE identifiers provide assigned policies in a step-by-step manner of IP addresses and are embedded into the packet header by ignoring traffic control.

In the 5G networking application, The SDN and SDR collections provide the hybrid architecture infrastructure [23]. It implies a combined layer collection with SDN and SDR link systems that manage the frequency arrangement network system. The cross-layer of the controller handles traffic control and assigns a request frequency speed system. This layer grants access to excellent bandwidth and performs authentication. software architecture is also proposed upon the resilience networks where redundancy, diversity, and modularity of systems are measured and integrated with 5G networks along with virtualization. This architecture provides load balancing along with allocation of resources in an efficient manner [25, 26].

The aggregated control mechanism regulates the public flow of data between the SDNs and SD-core network nodes and allocates resources based on the combined demands of multiple networks. All cloud-enabled systems can be managed based on policies and proper plans based on the network using end-to-end protocols [27, 28].

The SDN architecture merges the principles of SDR as well as the principles of SDN for cellular networks.

In this case, the base station (BS) plays an important role in the radio signal used to implement by SDR. By using cognitive edges (CE), the open flow system can work on radio allocation and over all view of signals on radios. This infrastructure is focused on the controller connected to a base station and SDN associated with the IoT network by managing network architecture [29].

13.2.3 SDN in WSN for Sensor-Enabled IoT Devices

In IoT, wireless sensor networks play a crucial role in different devices, since a number of tasks can be done by them. SDN-WISE architecture is one way to manage a network of sensors. In this architecture, SDN is the core of IoT by using a WSN. It is the collection of information and provides a concrete result [30].

In WSNs, sensors are very essential and are used in each step of the network in the system-to-system interactions between systems. SDN follows a set of rules and conventions based on detailed analysis.

In IoT, the hierarchical structure of elements concentrates on base stations and focuses on several nodes. Each node can communicate to the sink node for the transfer of information to other nodes present in the network. In this environment, a network is used to share information to sink nodes through source station nodes. The source station transmits information through a set of nodes by using data propagation by network hosts. In some cases, the role injection WSN method is also used in reconfigurable WSNs [31].

In IoT, sensors can sense signals by using different devices in transmitting data by the guided or unguided medium of peer-to-peer through a different approach to the network. The objective of the compiler is depicted through the transmission of data in a directed way to control by using core units.

This proposed system for multiple application structures is based on a universal infrastructure. Every system in the network is based on a layered approach. Here, the network has common software and hardware to perform additional work in the different abstract networks.

The mechanism of the sensor-to-sensor communicated multiple times to process tasks and process instructions through a set of blocks and perform in proper order by resetting the system by coordinating nodes to communicate with sink node linearly. Also, it monitors the manufacturing environment [32, 33].

13.3 SDN-Based IoT Management

In IoT, a management system is a collection of servers interconnected in a distributed network for transmitting information. It is a type of networking system by which each node can be located in a different location and perform independently.

In some cases, heterogeneous IoT makes use of a controller architecture that spans many networks. An SDN is a network that uses a distributed, and heterogeneous. It is a self-configured collection of nodes in a layered structure that creates a difference between IoT and assign work solution in a geographical system. The main aim of this type of network is to manage the unguided flow of data transmission that access through gaining information from different nodes.

A framework like UbiFlow integrates the properties of SDN and IoT to provide effective data transmission in a structured approach that enables the network to locate a mobile system point of attachment for delivery of packets. It is also based on connection as it continues to change its structure. In this type of network, networks are furthered divided into several mini-systems and each part is assigned by a different combination of the network system in a heterogeneous system. In this structure, each part is linked with different sub-parts for information inquiries [34, 35].

Certain frameworks are also implemented in the smart environment for IoT devices. In these types of frameworks, a set of nodes are grouped to maintain services from different nodes. The infrastructure plays a vital role in the simple-to-access method for inventing new devices in the network and creating abstract knowledge about the network for different policies.

In this infrastructure, information is gathered from different nodes and collected on the ISP. The gathered information is transmitted to several networks safely by checking its validation and integrity. In this way, information is only accessible by the registered network by providing protocols for proper IP verification and about URL. Protocols are assigned according to data transmitted to proper nodes and manage regulation on the priority level. Thus, SDNs play a vital role in information propagation in IoT systems.

13.4 IoT Security Architecture Based on SDN

In this type of network, the security structure plays a vital role in managing important information by transferring each node's information to each system by ignoring the fault tolerance mechanism. In certain cases, the secure architectural mechanism for an IoT-SDN is implemented. Generally, it is based on a backup and recovery subsystem by sharing of hardware and software by the disaster recovery system [36]. In this networking, by using IoT when in a distributed network nodes are connected in a structured manner to maintain in density between the nodes deployed in the network only through security mechanism. Sensors are managed through a set of blocks where the interlink mechanism is fulfilled. If the node is valid and its features are managed by other nodes so the controller starts its transmit to other nodes. The controller plays a vital role in the case of backup and authentication for transmitting information in a secured manner with each node through a proper transmission path. In this case, the transmission control protocol (TCP) also checks how information is transmitted to different nodes without any data loss and congestion control in the data transmission [37].

The distributed intelligent firewall system (DISFIRE) depicts the step-by-step order of data transmission in a network created in a group manner to more than one node to arrange them in-network by cluster system. It implements all the data in a grid architecture IoT-based SDN. It works as the head of the SDN by providing backup and auto recovery and disaster recovery management systems. In this network architecture, many SDN controllers form a cluster, and the cluster heads are at the top of the hierarchy. Each cluster head uses a security policy. For this reason, opFlex is used instead of openFlow [38].

In this type of security system, each node shares information or messages between them for information error detection and correction mechanism by avoiding redundancy information by selected nodes by approved constraint for correcting information so that outsiders cannot easily access the information and having no access of updating data in the network. so, in the security mechanism rules and conventions must be followed by each node to access each information instantly required in the network [39].

In a security architecture the key challenge is to control all hosts in a secured manner so that there is no chance of essential information loss for distributed systems. Information technology provides a security mechanism for ignoring validation, fault tolerance, etc. It also provides guarantees based on information, accessibility, and storage in such a database so that outsiders or the subscribers who are not members of the network cannot access it. The main requirement is the propagation of data or information through either a guided or unguided medium of transmission. In this approach, each node autonomously works without depending on other nodes.

The IoT network is a vast network of servers in a virtual system correlated with several nodes interconnected by sink nodes. Each node communicates in a distributed manner in a dynamic network arrangement with proper security features. This structure allows valid users in the network in a time-sharing manner to avoid flow control mechanisms.

IoT presents the safety of an SDN with IoT network by deploying an SDSec module that makes use of NFV to generate a virtual topology for the device in question.

In a software-defined IoT architecture where the SDSec module utilizes NFV to create a virtual topology, proper security can be maintained by a backup mechanism to store the important data in the virtual database in a secured manner [40]. In some cases, the proposed security framework is divided into individual segments within the self-domain SDN controller. In IoT, nodes act as agents for list of information in proper order to maintain a proper manner for the propagation of data in a proper directed path securely.

13.5 Discussion and Open Issues

The entire structure is based on the IoT-SDN concept. It is an efficient way to understand by specifying a universal standard that gives to society for perfect solutions by fundamental aspects. The concept of SDN is based on IoT by security features which increase the growth of network data transmission safely and securely. In SDN, the structure is cellular management, sensor infrastructure, and IoT networks. This proposed model takes consternate on some current years.

Hence, this structure is not fully correlated with the SDN network. It is a comprehensive system and its structure has not so far. If we will consider the architectures like SDIoT, BlackSDN, SoftAir, SDN-WISE, etc uses a little bit of effort. But architectures like SDSec, SD system, SD storage, etc., uses embedded sensor networks and operating systems implemented within SDN. The main key point towards SDN is the infrastructure is purely the framework of IoT devices. Another problem is the addressing and service provision regarding QoS support which is open in IoT.

Today, current status comes under IoT concepts since it is a connection-oriented approach to provide services based on congestion control, which is included under the transport layer of the OSI-Indian standard organization model [41]. To transmit information or messages or frames safely and reached recipient nodes without any error by only the TCP mechanism.

Another major issue is to check flow control in-network since important data can be lost or missing frames may lead to traffic problems in network transmission theorems. But the key issue is how frames are transmitted safely based on security concepts. When a network is distributed in nature any data cannot be easily tracked by outsiders for whom data is very important. However, considerable data in an IoT network is very critical in network challenges.

13.6 Qualitative Assessment for Future Scope

Today, IoT plays an important role in smart systems used in educational, economical, and agricultural applications. It is around 6.4 billion networks upto 2016 that pays connectivity has increased by 30% since 2015, with an estimated 5.5 million devices now online. This number is increasing about 50 billion approximately in 2020. It is estimated that IoT and SDN enable devices to increase rate will be more than 90% in the year from 2020 to 2030.

By using both qualitative and quantitative assessment methods to understand how it is affected our workspace. It is a good starting point when methods can be essential for describing a point and can be accessed to your best of knowledge.

Methods of assessment are ways of gathering information that yield results that cannot easily be measured by or translated information based on results. It is also expected that in the year the total IoT devices will be more than 30 billion (i.e., four IoT devices per person on an average) [42].

It is also expected that the global SDN market size will increase by a CAGR of 19% from 2020 to 2025. If we consider this growth amount, we can expect USD32.7 billion from USD 13.7 billion in this forecast period of 5 years [43].

13.7 Conclusion

IoT is currently and will continue to be a large part of daily life. However, this technology has some drawbacks including non-secure aspects, demanding agility, and efficient data management. For this purpose, managed IoT integrated with SDN is required to overcome all the roadblocks. In this chapter, we discussed different data and control planes along with different WSN-based architectures. We also discussed other related issues. In conclusion IoT embedded with SDN is required to meet the needs of today.

References

1 Zekkori, H. and Agoujil, S., 2019. Hybrid delay tolerant network routing protocol for heterogeneous networks. *Journal of Network and Computer Applications, 148,* p.102456.

2 Chien, W.C., Lai, C.F., Hossain, M.S. and Muhammad, G., 2019. Heterogeneous space and terrestrial integrated networks for IoT: Architecture and challenges. *IEEE Network, 33*(1), pp.15–21.

3 Mumtaz, S., Alsohaily, A., Pang, Z., Rayes, A., Tsang, K.F. and Rodriguez, J., 2017. Massive Internet of Things for industrial applications: Addressing wireless IIoT connectivity challenges and ecosystem fragmentation. *IEEE Industrial Electronics Magazine, 11*(1), pp.28–33.

4 Zeinab, K.A.M. and Elmustafa, S.A.A., 2017. Internet of things applications, challenges and related future technologies. *World Scientific News, 2*(67), pp.126–148.

5 Kyriazis, D., Varvarigou, T., White, D., Rossi, A. and Cooper, J., 2013, June. Sustainable smart city IoT applications: Heat and electricity management & Eco-conscious cruise control for public transportation. In *2013 IEEE 14th International Symposium on" A World of Wireless, Mobile and Multimedia Networks"(WoWMoM)* (pp. 1–5). IEEE.

6 Kabalci, Y., Kabalci, E., Padmanaban, S., Holm-Nielsen, J.B. and Blaabjerg, F., 2019. Internet of Things applications as energy internet in Smart Grids and Smart Environments. *Electronics, 8*(9), p.972.

7 www.mordorintelligence.com/industry-reports/internet-of-things-moving-towa rds-a-smarter-tomorrow-market-industry#:~:text=The%20global%20IoT%20mar ket%20is,period%20(2021%2D2026).

8 Gheisari, M., Wang, G., Chen, S. and Seyfollahi, A., 2018, December. A Method for Privacy-Preserving in IoT-SDN Integration Environment. In *2018 IEEE Intl Conf on Parallel & Distributed Processing with Applications, Ubiquitous Computing & Communications, Big Data & Cloud Computing, Social Computing & Networking, Sustainable Computing & Communications (ISPA/IUCC/BDCloud/SocialCom/ SustainCom)* (pp. 895–902). IEEE.

9 Conti, M., Kaliyar, P. and Lal, C., 2019. CENSOR: Cloud-enabled secure IoT archi-tecture over SDN paradigm. *Concurrency and Computation: Practice and Experience, 31*(8), p.e4978.

10 Kuzniar, M., Peresini, P. and Kostic, D., 2014. *What you need to know about SDN control and data planes.*

11 Poularakis, K., Iosifidis, G. and Tassiulas, L., 2018. SDN-enabled tactical ad hoc networks: Extending programmable control to the edge. *IEEE Communications Magazine, 56*(7), pp.132–138.

12 Jararweh, Y., Al-Ayyoub, M., Benkhelifa, E., Vouk, M. and Rindos, A., 2015. SDIoT: a software defined based internet of things framework. *Journal of Ambient Intelligence and Humanized Computing, 6*(4), pp.453–461.

13 Nobakht, M., Sivaraman, V. and Boreli, R., 2016, August. A host-based intrusion detection and mitigation framework for smart home IoT using OpenFlow. In *2016 11th International Conference on Availability, Reliability and Security (ARES)* (pp. 147–156). IEEE.

14 Gonzalez, C., Charfadine, S.M., Flauzac, O. and Nolot, F., 2016, July. SDN-based security framework for the IoT in distributed grid. In *2016 International Multidisciplinary Conference on Computer and Energy Science (SpliTech)* (pp. 1–5). IEEE.

15 Cerroni, W., Buratti, C., Cerboni, S., Davoli, G., Contoli, C., Foresta, F., Callegati, F. and Verdone, R., 2017, July. Intent-based management and orchestration of heterogeneous openflow/IoT SDN domains. In *2017 IEEE Conference on Network Softwarization (NetSoft)* (pp. 1–9). IEEE.

16 Badotra, S. and Singh, J., 2019. Creating firewall in transport layer and application layer using software defined networking. In *Innovations in Computer Science and Engineering* (pp. 95–103). Springer, Singapore.

17 Lin, Y., Kozat, U.C., Kaippallimalil, J., Moradi, M., Soong, A.C. and Mao, Z.M., 2018, March. Pausing and resuming network flows using programmable buffers. In *Proceedings of the Symposium on SDN Research* (pp. 1–14).

18 Henneke, D., Wisniewski, L. and Jasperneite, J., 2016, May. Analysis of realizing a future industrial network by means of Software-Defined Networking (SDN). In *2016 IEEE World Conference on Factory Communication Systems (WFCS)* (pp. 1–4). IEEE.

19 Zhang, D., Chang, Z., Yu, F.R., Chen, X. and Hämäläinen, T., 2016, September. A double auction mechanism for virtual resource allocation in SDN-based cellular network. In *2016 IEEE 27th Annual International Symposium on Personal, Indoor, and Mobile Radio Communications (PIMRC)* (pp. 1–6). IEEE.

20 Heinonen, J., Partti, T., Kallio, M., Lappalainen, K., Flinck, H. and Hillo, J., 2014, August. Dynamic tunnel switching for SDN-based cellular core networks. In *Proceedings of the 4th workshop on All things cellular: operations, applications, & challenges* (pp. 27–32).

21 Xu, X., Zhang, H., Dai, X., Hou, Y., Tao, X. and Zhang, P., 2014. SDN based next generation mobile network with service slicing and trials. *China Communications*, *11*(2), pp.65–77.

22 Tayyaba, S.K. and Shah, M.A., 2019. Resource allocation in SDN based 5G cellular networks. *Peer-to-Peer Networking and Applications*, *12*(2), pp.514–538.

23 Yao, J., Han, Z., Sohail, M. and Wang, L., 2019. A robust security architecture for SDN-based 5G networks. *Future Internet*, *11*(4), p.85.

24 Ma, L., Wen, X., Wang, L., Lu, Z. and Knopp, R., 2018. An SDN/NFV based framework for management and deployment of service based 5G core network. *China Communications*, *15*(10), pp.86–98.

25 Tello-Oquendo, L., Lin, S.C., Akyildiz, I.F. and Pla, V., 2019. Software-defined architecture for QoS-aware IoT deployments in 5G systems. *Ad Hoc Networks*, *93*, p.101911.

26 Lin, S.C. and Akyildiz, I.F., 2017, May. Dynamic base station formation for solving NLOS problem in 5G millimeter-wave communication. In *IEEE INFOCOM 2017-IEEE Conference on Computer Communications* (pp. 1–9). IEEE.

27 Tayyaba, S.K. and Shah, M.A., 2017, March. 5G cellular network integration with SDN: Challenges, issues and beyond. In *2017 International Conference on Communication, Computing and Digital Systems (C-CODE)* (pp. 48–53). IEEE.

28 Foster, N., McKeown, N., Rexford, J., Parulkar, G., Peterson, L. and Sunay, O., 2020. Using deep programmability to put network owners in control. *ACM SIGCOMM Computer Communication Review, 50*(4), pp.82–88.

29 Tayyaba, S.K., Shah, M.A., Khan, O.A. and Ahmed, A.W., 2017, July. Software defined network (sdn) based internet of things (iot) a road ahead. In *Proceedings of the International Conference on Future Networks and Distributed Systems* (pp. 1–8).

30 Alves, R.C., Oliveira, D.A., Nez, G. and Margi, C.B., 2017, May. It-sdn: Improved architecture for sdwsn. In *XXXV Brazilian Symposium on Computer Networks and Distributed Systems*.

31 Bera, S., Misra, S., Roy, S.K. and Obaidat, M.S., 2016. Soft-WSN: Software-defined WSN management system for IoT applications. *IEEE Systems Journal, 12*(3), pp.2074–2081.

32 Amarlingam, M., Mishra, P.K., Prasad, K.D. and Rajalakshmi, P., 2016, December. Compressed sensing for different sensors: A real scenario for WSN and IoT. In *2016 IEEE 3rd World Forum on Internet of Things (WF-IoT)* (pp. 289–294). IEEE.

33 Li, W. and Kara, S., 2017. Methodology for monitoring manufacturing environment by using wireless sensor networks (WSN) and the internet of things (IoT). *Procedia CIRP, 61*, pp.323–328.

34 Desai, A., Nagegowda, K.S. and Ninikrishna, T., 2016, March. A framework for integrating IoT and SDN using proposed OF-enabled management device. In *2016 International Conference on Circuit, Power and Computing Technologies (ICCPCT)* (pp. 1–4). IEEE.

35 Molina, E. and Jacob, E., 2018. Software-defined networking in cyber-physical systems: A survey. *Computers & Electrical Engineering, 66*, pp.407–419.

36 Mishra, P., Biswal, A., Garg, S., Lu, R., Tiwary, M. and Puthal, D., 2020. Software defined internet of things security: Properties, state of the art, and future research. *IEEE Wireless Communications, 27*(3), pp.10–16.

37 Bekri, W., Jmal, R. and Chaari Fourati, L., 2020. Internet of things management based on software defined networking: a survey. *International Journal of Wireless Information Networks, 27*, pp.385–410.

38 Gonzalez, C., Charfadine, S.M., Flauzac, O. and Nolot, F., 2016, July. SDN-based security framework for the IoT in distributed grid. In *2016 International Multidisciplinary Conference on Computer and Energy Science (SpliTech)* (pp. 1–5). IEEE.

39 Yassein, M.B., Aljawarneh, S., Al-Rousan, M., Mardini, W. and Al-Rashdan, W., 2017, November. Combined software-defined network (SDN) and Internet of Things (IoT). In *2017 International Conference on Electrical and Computing Technologies and Applications (ICECTA)* (pp. 1–6). IEEE.

40 Alam, I., Sharif, K., Li, F., Latif, Z., Karim, M.M., Biswas, S., Nour, B. and Wang, Y., 2020. A survey of network virtualization techniques for internet of things using sdn and nfv. *ACM Computing Surveys (CSUR), 53*(2), pp.1–40.

41 Monteiro, T.G., do Amaral, M.A., Mota, L.T.M. and Iano, Y., 2019, October. IoT Security: A Simplified Analysis of the Literature. In *Brazilian Technology Symposium* (pp. 519–526). Springer, Cham.

42 https://content.techgig.com/iot-connections-surpass-non-iot-devices-in-2020/arti cleshow/79356013.cms.

43 www.marketsandmarkets.com/Market-Reports/software-defined-networking-sdn-market-655.html.

Chapter 14

Smart and Sustainable Energy-Efficient Wireless Sensor Networks: Design and Techniques

Dattatray G. Takale[1], Parishit N. Mahalle[2], Piyush P. Gawali[1], Gopal B. Deshmukh[1], Chitrakant O. Banchhor[1], and Pradnya S. Mehta[1]

[1]Department of Computer Engineering, Vishwakarma Institute of information Technology, SPPU Pune, India

[2]Department of Artificial intelligence and Data Science, Vishwakarma Institute of Information Technology, SPPU Pune, India

14.1 Introduction

Modern advances in computer-based technology have led to the development of numerous compressed storage systems. These systems allow for the data to be gathered, processed, and sent with a significantly reduced amount of energy consumption. A wireless network is used to connect the components of the system, and this same network is used for transmission of data. This method is easily modified to accommodate a smaller number of data. Concurrently, sensor advancements have furnished devices that can be effectively interfaced with microchips (when they are not legitimately incorporated on-chip). Because

DOI: 10.1201/9781032650722-18

of this, it is now possible to create systems of canny sensors, in which even large numbers of hubs equipped with memory, sensors, processing capacity, and a radio frequency segment work together to consequently gather data even in circumstances that can be regarded as "threatening" to human administrators or possibly are not easily reachable. These kinds of technologies provide an intriguing solution to several problems associated with data collection and distribution and it is possible to obtain a level of information that is simultaneously geographic and transient [9].

The design of applications that are dependent on wireless sensor networks (WSNs) calls for multidisciplinary skills, including phenomenological abilities such as estimations, installed frameworks, communications, programming designing, information bases, and the executive's ones, to name just a few. WSN designers need to handle in field and operational concerns such as the removal of sensors, sending and receiving difficulty, vigor and rainproof of the casing [1]. The final ones are connected with the checking the link of frameworks with nature and also the growth of life cycle of the system. The remote system study pertaining to the system of correspondence initially failed many times, but now being utilized in every field. In the following section, we provide an in-depth analysis of the WSN point by point.

14.2 Communication Network

Within an organization, information transfer is carried out according to a predetermined pattern that is known as the communication network. During communication, this network can only conduct a limited set of functions. Virtual data centers, virtual storage access networks, virtual computers, and virtual memory are just a few of the sectors where the process of virtualization is becoming significantly more pervasive. This is especially true in the information and communications technology (ICT) sector of the global economy. It is possible to reduce costs associated with management and equipment thanks to flexible management, quicker migration to more recent services and products, decoupled functionality from infrastructure, and increased hardware utilization thanks to virtualization [10]. Connecting devices using either wired or wireless media in order to communicate the necessary data can be done in any of these ways.

As a result of recent advancements in software-based technology, a method known as WSN has been experiencing growth as of late. Many studies written by a variety of authors have been conducted in this area of study with the goal of achieving energy efficiency while simultaneously lowering the cost of deployment. WSNs are used in a variety of fields including environmental monitoring, land monitoring for intelligent farming, remote healthcare, and military surveillance, amongst others. The development of protocols and algorithms for WSNs presents a number of issues, the most notable of which are the enhancement of the lifespan and the preservation of connectivity. Virtualization plays an essential function in both wired and WSNs [2,3]. It is analogous to the role that virtualization plays in wired networks. The implementation of virtualization in wireless networks, including air interface virtualization, infrastructure virtualization, and spectrum sharing, will result in significant benefits for the industry [11].

When it comes to wired networks, a great percentage of service providers will keep the physical infrastructure. Also, a number of other service providers will share this infrastructure. When it comes to the virtualization of wireless networks, the approach is very similar to the one described before. In this case as well, the physical infrastructure is maintained by a multitude of providers and shared among those providers. As can be seen, virtualization is relatively comparable whether a network is wireless or cable. In virtualization the entire network is partitioned. The operation of the virtualization of wireless networks takes on the basis of a specific admittance technology. Compared to wired networks, wireless networks have more advanced technological capabilities than wired networks. The fact that wireless networks also make use of a number of other technologies makes the process of establishing connectivity and determining coverage extremely laborious [12].

After the virtualization process, two distinct types of logical roles, such as Service Provider (SP) and Mobile Network Operator (MNO) may be possible. Core Networks (CNs), Transmission Networks (TNs), backhaul, Radio Access Networks (RANs), and licensed spectrum are some of the wireless network resources that are operated by this MNO. MNO is going to be the one in-charge of carrying out the execution of the resources that are created through physical substrate. The wireless network is used to execute the physical resources on virtual resources that already exist in the network. Based on the findings of investigation, it was discovered that this MNO will eventually transform into indium phosphide (InP). This will only help in the process of obtaining the data from the various resources and transmitting it to the SPs. SPs are responsible for the distribution of resources as well as their deployment and allocation [13]. In addition to this, they accomplish the objectives set forth by the end-to-end services. Figure 14.1 shows a wireless network.

Certain responsibilities play important role during the consideration of company strategy. In the case virtual a network, a number of tasks, such as SP, mobile virtual network operator (MVNO), mobile virtual network provider (MVNP), and Internet service provider (InP), will also be taken into account.

14.3 Wireless Sensor Network Model

14.3.1 VANET (Vehicular Ad-hoc Network)

Wireless communication between moving cars is made possible by a vehicular ad-hoc network (VANET). This network makes use of dedicated short range communication, or DSRC. The primary focus of development for DSRC has been on its

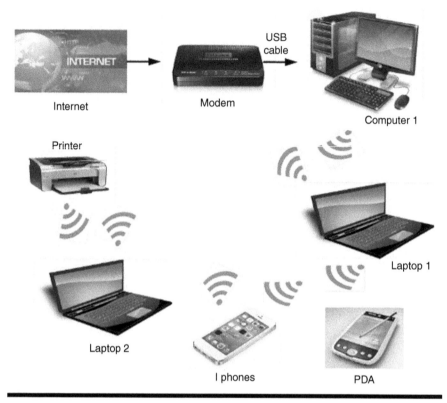

Figure 14.1   Schematic representation of wireless networks.

capacity to carry out low-power operations. The wireless access (IEEE standardization) in automotive environment is available to every type of vehicle in surrounding area. Direct communication between automobiles is possible if they are equipped with a system called vehicle-to-vehicle communication, or V2V.

Using vehicle-to-infrastructure communication, it is possible for various devices located along a roadway to communicate. A communicate is possible between the devices along the road side unit (RSU) and the car. Information pertaining to traffic bottlenecks, post-crash investigations, and accident prevention can all be shared. The architecture of VANET is shown in Figure 14.2 [14].

Everything of the information that has been mentioned so far is connected to safety information. Other individuals who use motor vehicles will also get the remaining information, which is sent to them despite the fact that it is not considered to be safety-related information [15]. The purpose of this information exchange is to warn motorists about potential dangers on the road in order to reduce the number of accidents.

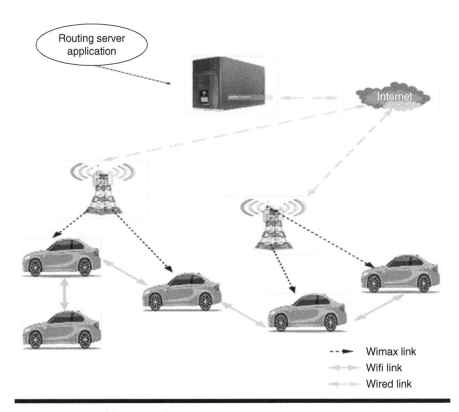

Figure 14.2   Architecture of VANET.

A growing number of researchers are beginning to concentrate their efforts in this field with the aim of developing applications based on VANET [9,10].

14.3.2 WMN (Wireless Mesh Network)

Wireless mesh networks (WMNs) are used to ensure effective delivery of coverage for wireless local area networks and access to broadband Internet. WMNs function as a communication network in some capacity. The participation of a greater number of Internet Service Providers (ISPs) is made possible by this. WMNs make it possible to cover a large portion of a network while maintaining high bandwidth. Users may be online at any time and from any location if they are connected to the internet using wireless mesh routers [17]. Figure 14.3 shows a schematic of a WMN.

Furthermore using this mesh network the connectivity among several wireless technologies like Wi Media networks, "worldwide interoperability for microwave access" (WiMAX), wireless-fidelity (Wi-Fi), wireless sensor and cellular can be achieved and the bridge can be made [17,18].

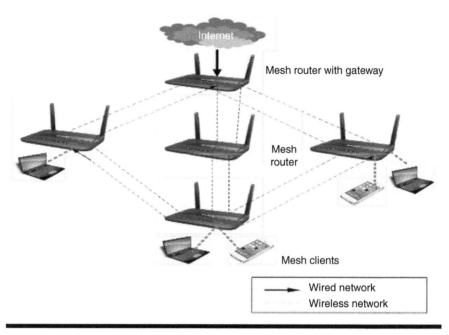

Figure 14.3   Schematic representation of WMN.

14.3.3 MANET (Mobile Ad-hoc Network)

Mobile ad-hoc networks (MANETs) are growing in popularity. As communication may be made possible via the use of this network even in the absence of any infrastructure, it has been recognized as an emerging technology in recent years. This network does not need a specific geographical location to function properly. It is referred to as an infrastructureless network since it does not have any underlying physical infrastructure [12, 13]. The remarkable rise of MANET may be attributed to the development of very effective devices that are both compact in size and affordable. One of the types of networks that may organize themselves (self-configuring, self-organizing and infrastructure-less network) is called ad-hoc network. In order to successfully carry out communication and the exchange of data inside a MANET, the identification of additional devices that may already be present is required. Internet connectivity is provided to the devices in an ad-hoc network. They are able to effortlessly initiate connections to the network as well as remove connections already made. The placement of the nodes inside these devices is constantly shifting. For this reason, the structure of the network is changed, and as a result, it continues to be unpredictable [18]. Figure 14.4 shows a diagrammatic representation of a MANET.

In a MANET the connection of the network and the transmission of messages from one system to another system must be accomplished via a decentralized

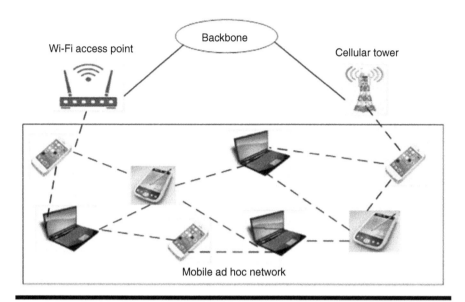

Figure 14.4   Schematic representation of MANET.

network. Whenever a message is sent across a decentralized network, there is a chance that the network's topology may be disrupted, leading to some kind of problem. Finding the most efficient route between a source and a destination using the information provided by a cost function is required. This is performed in a network that is not dynamic. The term "perfect path" refers to this particular route. Nevertheless, this might be challenging with MANET [20]. Applications of MANET range from static networks that are limited by power sources to tiny, highly dynamic networks that are mobile, ranging from large-scale, diverse applications, and so on.

14.3.4 Wireless sensor Network (WSN)

WSN-based devices have been evolving rapidly in recent years as a result of recent advancements in both embedded electronics and wireless networks. The nodes in a WSN are responsible for the most important aspects of the network. Communication may be established only with the assistance of the nodes in the network [21]. The nodes consist of several intelligent sensors, a restricted amount of processing capacity, and an integrated CPU. The sensors, also known as nodes, may be of assistance in monitoring environmental elements such as vibration, heat, pressure, and humidity via the network of nodes that connects them. The power unit, the transceiver unit, the processing unit, and the sensor interface are the fundamental components that are present in the nodes. Figure 14.5 shows the structure of a WSN.

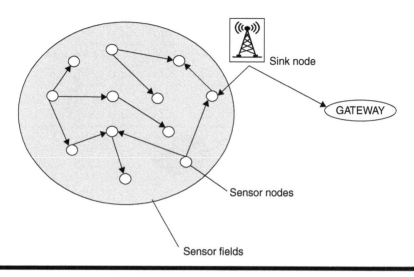

Figure 14.5   Schematic representation of WSN.

The different units that are present in nodes can be used to communicate with other and helps in transmitting the data acquired through sensors. The centralized system among nodes is necessary in order to achieve communication. The Internet of Things (IoT) concept was developed to make access to the network easily and quickly. The present work is based on WSN. A detailed discussion of the sensor nodes in a WSN, the architecture as well as application of WSN in different fields along with the issues related to WSN follows.

14.4 Historical Development of Sensor Nodes

The author named Marconi in the year 1896 developed the modem related to remote interchanges. In this remote-based telecommunication, the Morse code is used for gathering and transmitting the information. For performing this function of the radiation used was long–wave and for power high-power transmitters is used [15, 16]. The business trans-Atlantic-based remote was begun in the year 1907 in which 30 m x 100 m poles consisting of radio cable was used. The advancement were made on the field of modem which lead to the development of cryptography, catch innovation, knowledge and framework related to modem was developed along with this advancement during the first world war.

Marconi again in the year 1920 developed a transmitter based on shortwave. The wavelength for this shortwave is found to be < 100 m. In order to make transmission more effectively these waves provide ricochet, ingestion, refractions and reflections within the ionosphere. The tubes supported with vacuum were invented in the year

1906 for obtaining higher liequencies. Furthermore the development of transmitter is made to fulfil the requirement such quality, litter and little expensive. The transmitting of voice through remote among the country San Francisco and New York was established in the year 1915. The radio station with the idea of business was developed in the year 1920 at the place called Pittsburgh located in Pennsylvania.

Within the squad car, Michigan and Detroit fitted the radio which will operate through remote in the year 1921. The first communication through phone was done in the year 1935. For supporting the soldiers in war at the time of Second World War the establishment of radio was growing tremendously. Mostly in urban areas found in US the open telephone was first come into existence in the year 1946. 120 kHz present in RF transmitter was utilized and spit onto identical parts existing as duplex mode. The renovation was made in altered developed RF transmitter in the number of adaptable channels was improved and this leads to increase in capacity to around 60 kHz in the year 1950. Then again the capacity of radio transmitter was again decreased to 30 kHz. The presence of trunking was found in addition to the transmitter and further the arrangement of phone may render auto-dial and full-duplex framework.

In spite of using RF transmitter for communication AT&T in the year 1968 developed the concept of mobile phones. Within the framework named NY Bell portable the involvement of 543 clients in around 12 channels was done in the year 1976. The establishment of "Global System for Mobile Communications" (GSM) was made in the year 1982 at the country called Europe. The duplex channels around 666 that were present in radio transmitter lead to the development of Advanced Mobile Phone System (AMPS) in the year 1983. Due to some issue in the year 1984 AT&T got separated and the framework based on AMPS starts emerging. The ISM groups which were unrestricted is settled along with FCC and it was invented in the year 1985. This was carried out in order to make advancement in the LANs network.

Previously, around twelve channels were present in AMPS following that in the year 1989 around sixteen channels were included through FCC onto AMPS. The advanced cell which is established in US in the year 1991 consists of three major clients where the channel with 30 kHz was used. Further the advancement was made and transferred into six clients existing in every channel. Computerized Personal Communications System (PCS) was developed in the year 1993 which adopts 1.8GHz. Following that in the next year code division various accesses (CDMA) with IS-95 was established. While CDMA was established in that specified year around sixteen million phones was in use. Many principles involved in remote are getting advanced. So the information related to remote is considered as significant. In the year 1990 tow guidelines namely IS-95 and GSM was being developed in which for the purpose of administration the information based on remote can be utilized.

On the basis of CDMA which was already invented, the framework named third-age (3G) remote was developed. They can support the transmission of voice and information in close-fitting reconciliation. Recently it was found that traffic existing in remote is well versed on comparison with traffic found in voice. For providing the wider entrance the gadget that is controlled through remote information can be well suited in office markets and home.

In order to obtain faster remote system much number of colleges such as University of Tennessee, Georgia Tech, Camogie Mellon etc. are carrying out their research in this field. The modem WSN is developed based on the principle of remote system which is referred to as Sound Surveillance System (SOSUS). In the year 1950 this developed SOSUS was utilized as Soviet submarines through U.S. military.

It was discovered that SOSUS was being used in conjunction with hydrophones and underwater devices. Oceans in the Pacific and Atlantic are home to these instruments. The most time-consuming WSNs were created and implemented by DARPA from the United States in 1980 using the Distributed Sensing Network (DSN) idea. For academics, the DSN's potential and growth in the academic community have stuck out. These factors helped the WSN's research capacity, which has started to be examined by academics and non-military people conducting logical explorations. The sensing node is the most important part of the WSN. The following part explains the fundamental idea behind the sensing nodes used in the WSN.

14.5 Techniques in WSN

The classification of technique in WSN can be divided into two major types. One is distributed and another is centralized. In case if the ability of network in power handling depends on distinctive device then it is found to be centralized approach. The devices in a centralized network are responsible for management, coordination, and processing of the gathered information [23]. The gathered information is also transmitted to the central node. Some of the advantages of this technique are discussed here.

The technique which is developed in WSN can be divided majorly into two part called as distributed or centralized. A network that relies on a single device as a power source for processing is referred to as a centralized formation technique. The gathered information is transferred to the nodes. The main benefits of using this technique are discussed in the following.

14.5.1 Centralized WSNs

Centralized methods use a unique device to provide direction. Providing system activity management, such as hub restriction, event placement, and traffic directing, is the responsibility of this central hub. A star is a logical clever shape for this approach. The way the data is produced can be used to classify the united systems. The following are included in these united systems:

One Sink: target employed for arrangement procedure was in diminishing sending time as well as course present data to one of a kind sink. The primary downside of single sink frameworks is the absence of excess.

The principle concern that is predictable is a sensor with its job inside the system. Traffic-sending hubs have a lower inclination than completely utilitarian hubs (sense, facilitate, forward and process data). System control mechanism was carried out during various leveled technique as well as it was characterized as upheld jobs. These types of systems was ordinarily actualized utilizing certain convention. For instance, exhibits a multi-sink condition design upheld the convention referenced. It utilizes a multi-jump sending technique and addresses the sensor the restriction issue. They built up a concentrated system for assuring great portability among the sink hubs.

A method known as "Self-setup" was used to find a deserving node in order to carry out the enrollment process; a few measurements were taken in order to choose the right node, gather data effectively, etc. Each sensor hub receives all valid communications from the sink hub. They consider two scenarios: the primary one may be a closed one with obstacles and impediments, and the secondary one without such obstacles. The scenario that follows shows the greatest results because hubs produced a much better division and display.

Despite the fact that multi-leap provides a few interesting points and is also more convenient for ensuring effective fast transfer among nodes, the makers do not guarantee the full utility of the sensor inside the earth and do not present clear results. Since all nodes transmit and receive information, system submersion may occur. This approach is found to be suitable for portable situations; however a usage isn't accounted for in the introduced work. Also, vitality utilization or versatility isn't considered. In the present work, only connection superiority was taken into account, which settles on wasteful of basic leadership in picking central node. The protocol Tree-Based Routing Protocol (TBRP) in which each hub has the ability in natural detecting as well as calculation errands or else retains correspondence along with rest of the nodes within system. Hubs were portable; nodes developments were characterized succeeding an objective. A sensor is considered as principle concern predictable with its job inside the system. The Hubs that transmit traffic have a lesser slope than hubs that are only used for utility (sense, facilitate, forward and process data). A system regulating technique was carried out using different leveled methods and is known as supported work. These methods are typically implemented using a particular pattern. For instance, displays support the mentioned standard with a multi-sink condition design. It takes care of the sensor limitation problem and sends data in multiple jumps. A focused system was developed to ensure maximum mobility between sink centers.

The various stages involved in the routing algorithm are as follows: through broadcast messages the formation of tree is achieved at the first stage. Using TDMA schedule the gathering and transfer if data is achieved at the second stage. In the final stage the motion of the parent node, energy level or failure is considered. The lifespan of the nodes existing in the network can be enhanced by changing the position of node to the highest level after reaching the threshold value. This achieved through TBRP protocol. The way of approach for this algorithm is centralized. The message is transferred through node. During this process the energy consumption is not taken into account. A comparison analysis is performed with LEACH. But this algorithm is not suited for TEEN protocol and tree formation. The classification of this algorithm is achieved through Tree topology and Routing Networks.

14.5.2 Distributed WSNs

Similar to a centralized WSN the distributed WSN has specific sort of trademark and various systems additionally exist in conveyed WSN. Portions of the trademark that are particular just for conveyed WSN are given as follows. Appropriated methods are utilized when the application needs to save a few properties, to be specific, vitality sparing, the quantity of associations, memory, and proficiency, among others, or when the data handling is wasteful in a concentrated manner [25]. The circulated methods have some unique attributes:

■ **Independence**: It is available when a client is the one in particular who picks where the information is put away and when the information can be adjusted or erased. The data spared does not have any data reliance with different gadgets. The significant choices depend on the gadget information. This component offers more often than not data support by possessing one host or server gave through auxiliary organization.

■ **Reliability** concerning Additional Facilities: availability among this kind on circulated strategies does not intend to offer extreme to the honesty accessible through brought together approach.

■ **Scalability**: based on use, versatility permits including many number of hubs within system devoid of alteration in system execution that implies they does not influence remainder present in the system.

The classification of this network is shown in Figure 14.6.

In this system, the quantity of kids per hub is constrained by including some facilitator rules, and a fitting estimation of the most extreme tree profundity for a superior presentation. There are a few downsides in the revealed re-enactments: the total availability of the system is not guaranteed, results or executions are not appeared, and reconfiguration or vitality imperatives are not considered. There are different proposition in which multiple topologies are consolidated, yet the usage is troublesome. For example, three unique topologies are grown; such topologies are standard hexagon (arrangement of a nearby framework of ordinary hexagon), plane matrix (customary neighbouring quadrangle), and symmetrical triangle (normal contiguous

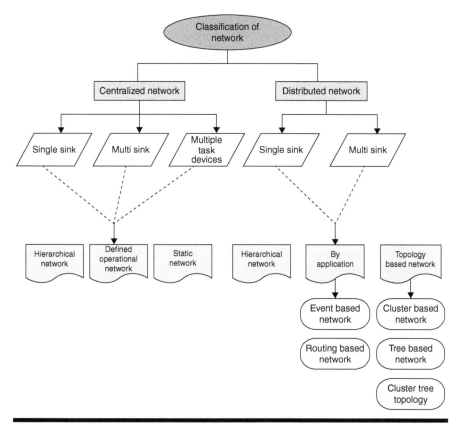

Figure 14.6   Classification of wireless sensor network.

symmetrical triangles) models. For each topology, there are distinctive arranged sensor hubs; their exercises and the execution time rely on the dynamic topology.

14.6 Protocols in WSNs

When it comes to the communication between sensor centers, protocols are important components of sensor arranging methods. The standards are broken down into levels and sub-layers, allowing users to choose how and when to obtain, send, organize, and process data on every device. The component that links information gathers and organizes the data before sending it to another sensing device. This layer provides management capabilities for information transfer and potential error corrections. Media Access Control (MAC) and Logical Link Control (LLC) are its two sub-layers.

The LLC sub-layer serves as a link between the MAC layer and system management operations; it provides flow and error control and is in charge of information transfer between devices on a system. This sub-layer employs a number of standards, including 802.3/Ethernet, 802.5, 802.11, and FDDI (Fiber Distributed Data Interface). The entry control to the earth is handled by the Macintosh sub-layer, which is also in charge of package transmission, information outline clearance, error-minding dispatches, transmission rate, stream control, message recognition, etc. This sub-layer has a direct bearing on how the center contacts the ground to obtain readily available information regarding the routes. These norms can be divided into two categories, as follows.

14.6.1 Slots Based or Slotted Protocols

The time in this WSN get classified onto intervals which may be either as slots or frames. The nodes are positioned in order to perform these operations such as turn off, receive, or transmit. Cost depends on bandwidth and energy utilization the maintenance and organization. The main protocols used are T-MAC protocols, S-MAC, IEEE 802.15.4, and TDMA.

14.6.2 Sampling-Based Protocols

In contrast to opened protocols, these conventions are typically killed and only turned on during specific timeframes, watching for movement in the channel; if some activity is noticed, at that point they start receiving information; otherwise, they turn off again for the purpose of energy conservation. These kinds of protocols are flexible and, in the majority of instances, they allow communication with any instrument that is within their range; however, occasionally, communication is impossible due to timing issues. Aloha, B-MAC, Sensible MAC, the ChipconCC2500 phone, and the Berkeley stage are examples of these standards. The open protocols are the ones most frequently used in WSNs. Some people consider newly expanded standards; examples of these are given below.

14.6.3 Time Division Multiple Access (TDMA)

The principle behind Time Division Multiple Access (TDMA) is simple. Normally the voice channels have been developed which helps in the classification of radio spectrum onto the radio frequency channels. This classification is done using duplex channel. This approach to classification is referred to as FDMA (Frequency Division Multiple Access). Within TDMA the Radio Frequency get classified into a number of channels. The formula for interval length is $T = Ti/N$. N denotes the number of frames at particular time interval. Ti represents the duration of transmission possible within frames. This implies that one channel can proceed with only one conversation at a time. But it necessary to develop RF through which many conversations can be achieved.

14.6.3.1 ZIGBEE/802.15.4

It was developed in reaction to the need for a sensing network protocol with minimal energy usage, typically in WPANs (Wireless Personal Area Networks); it is adaptable and has a narrow capacity. It has been under consideration as a standard since 2003. There are only two configurations this protocol supports.

14.6.3.2 Sensor Medium Access Control (SMAC)

The S-MAC is dependent on places and identifies phases (tune in and slumber) for each sensor in which the sensor can conserve its vitality. The following tasks can be carried out at a central location that is currently available. Currently, a sensing hub has entered a slumber period, during which it deactivates itself and programs its schedule to become active at a later point in time.

14.7 Sensor Network Design Issues

Various goal and limitation were considered based on application in designing the wireless network. The model based on architecture was found to be linked with the presentation of routing protocol. In the following section sensor network design issues are discussed in detail.

14.7.1 Network Dynamics

A sensor assemble is comprised of three fundamental components: recorded instances, sensing nodes, and sinks. The overwhelming majority of system models anticipate that sensor nodes is fixed in position, with the exception of a small number of configurations that make use of moveable sensors. The ability to support the flexibility of drains or group heads (portals), on the other hand, is regarded as fundamental in certain circumstances. In addition to factors such as liveliness, data transmission capability, and so on, directing communications from or to moving centers can be difficult; thus, the trustworthiness of the route is an important improvement factor. The application determines whether the observed occurrence is one-of-a-kind or inactive for the user experience. For instance, the event (marvel) at hand in an application for objective identification and subsequent following is a case of a dynamic occasion, whereas monitoring the forests for early fire apprehension is an example of a stagnant occasion. By checking for inactive events, the system is able to operate in a responsive manner, generating only traffic when it is actually showing. The occurrence of dynamic events in many applications necessitates the execution of intermittent outlining and, as a result, generates a significant volume of traffic that must be directed to the drain.

14.7.2 Node Deployment

The organization of node is found in certain topology. This sort of arrangement is found to be rendering effect in application ward and directing convention. There are two types of arrangements: self-sorting and deterministic. The deployment of nodes is made physically and the direction of information in sensors is done using pre-decided ways. The sensor is randomly distributed in a self-arranging framework. This will create a basis in unplanned way. The location and position of the head node or sink node is considered as vital in this framework to ensure good execution and productivity. In certain point if distribution of the node is found to be disturbed in the group there arises a problem in the network and this will lead to decrease in effectiveness of the system.

14.7.3 Energy Considerations

The deployment of the node as well as its creation of foundation greatly depend on the vitality contemplations. To remove the squared the intensity of transmission existing in node is found. In the presence of multi-jump steering, sight of hindrances less sort of effectiveness is achieved on comparison with straight communication. For execution of topology in critical upstairs as well to access the medium control the multi-bounce directing is used. If each of the sensor nodes is located nearer to sink then direct steering can be used for performing the task. If the distribution of sensor is not distributed arbitrarily then the multi-bounce steering is used unexpectedly.

14.7.4 Node Capabilities

The sensor nodes are responsible for performing different functions within the sensor organization. These nodes in earlier days were assumed to be homogenous, but they were found to have equal boundary in terms of force, correspondence, and calculation. However, it is a known fact that certain types of specified ability exists in these nodes based on application. For instance total, detecting and transferring. These three functions are considered as important in nodes. This function will constantly exhaust the vitality of the node. As of considering the progressive it mostly depends on assigning a head node that is linked with every other nodes. Based on certain parameters the group head is assigned for every application. These group heads are dominant because they are responsible for memory, transmission capacity, and vitality.

The information transmission from the sink to the rest of the member in cluster will mediated through the cluster head. Organization of the sensor node in the heterogeneous case will create a number of problems related to transmission of information. For performing certain application like video succeeding in touching articles, catching the picture, finding program over acoustic marks, mugginess of the encompassing condition, weight and detecting temperature the sensors must be linked to one another.

Sensors that are not involved in transmission will remain inactive and in case of getting any sort of request from other sensor the transmission of information through this sensor node will take place. As is known, sensor nodes transmit information at different rates, follow various conveyance models, and have different administration requirements. Mostly in heterogeneous organization many kinds of information or data is subjected to testing.

14.7.5 Data Delivery Models

Based on the organization of the sensor the model named conveyance model relating the information to sink were found to be hybrid, inquiry driven, occasion driven and nonstop. In the conveyance model information sent through the sensor node is irregular. The information transfer is triggered at the time of necessary or whenever the question is raised through the sink in models such as inquiry driven and occasion driven. Some systems use both types of models.

The conveyance model which is related to information will possess greater influence on directing convention. The use of vitality gets reduced as well as the course soundness get minimized. For the case of specified application in which the transfer of information to the sink takes place. To perform this function the directing convention is found to be more effective. The application in which the repeated information is gathered and stored on the sink and basically sparing vitality and lessening traffic.

14.7.6 Data Aggregation Fusion

Essential repeated information may be contained in the sensor nodes. So in order to decrease the rate of transmission the information gathered from various nodes can be collectively linked and set as a bundle. The data that is gathered from different sources through using its ability is linked together and this is referred to as Information collection. For instance, normal, max, min, and concealment. In every sensor node the assumed ability can be performed. The sensor node is organized in a way that reduces information.

The vitality existing in the sensor node is calculated correspondence with the particular vitality investment funds. This vitality is activated using information conglomeration. For finding the progress in traffic and effectiveness in vitality the abovementioned method can be utilized. This finding is mostly done in directing conventions. Mostly in every design the capacity is assigned for the collected node as well as to specified node. The additional technique that is added along with sign handling systems in order to perform Information accumulation. The node is fixed in a particular sight in order to gather information and transfer it to the necessary site. They will also involve in of function such as bar framing that helps in joining the signs.

14.8 Sustainable Design Techniques for Energy-Efficient WSNs

Various energy-efficient techniques have been developed by researchers in recent years. The technique is based on optimization algorithm, classifier, and clustering technique. The most widely used approaches are clustering-based and optimization algorithms. In the following section the various existing method based on optimization for achieving energy efficient is given below.

14.8.1 Energy-Efficient Model Based on Probabilistic Approach

Many researchers have focused on fault recovery in WSN due to challenges such as deployment, environment, and limitations of energy. Using utilizing fewer resources employed in network the most effective and reliable method for recovering the fault must be developed. The effective path must be selected from the sink to the node, and this is done using a certain protocol. Using selecting an alternative route the effective transmission of data can be done even in the case of failure of a previously chosen path. Many algorithms have been developed recently for controlling the utilization of energy in sensor nodes as well as to improve connectivity.

The issue of energy management is referred to as a probabilistic combinatorial optimization issue. In some cases there is presence of combinatorial optimization problem. The initial problem must be solved and further other similar problems must also be solved. When compared to the originally defined problem the copies of problem given in additional will have little changes. But this problem needed separate solutions. The technique used to solve these kinds of optimization problems is called re-optimization. There exists certain sort of limitation in this approach that is this technique is most expensive. For solving this problem different technique must be developed. One technique where the first solution obtained for a specified problem can be slightly modified and given as solution for other similar problem. This approach is called as priori strategy. Based on this priori approach the technique named Periodic, Event-driven, Query-based (PEQ) was developed for solving this

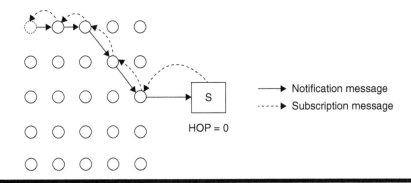

Figure 14.7   PEQ mechanism.

optimization problem. Figure 14.7 shows a diagrammatic representation of the PEQ mechanism.

Surely, the fundamental inspiration of this calculation is driven by the need to give a help to the entirety of the accompanying limitations: unwavering quality, low inactivity, vitality reserve funds and quick way recuperation within the sight of mistakes. PEQ consolidates the vitality preservation with the multipath steering by choosing, among all the accessible courses, the one that devours less vitality. Notwithstanding this preventive system which permits dependable steering, a disappointment recuperation component is executed. Subsequently, the PEQ convention covers the methodology of adaptation to internal failure by the administration of vitality utilization, choosing the best streets and their recuperation within the sight of disappointment. PEQ is a directing methodology, and is accomplished in three stages.

The initial step involves the development of a bounce tree. The sink begins the way toward building this tree is utilized as a design of the conceivable multi-bounce ways to defeat information in the sensor arrange and toward the finish of this stage simply the best defeats are spared. The subsequent advance includes the transmission of warning messages from the sensor hubs and the spread of memberships from the sink to the system. Finally, the last advance is liable for conveying occasions from the sensors to the authority hub, by utilizing the less expensive and quickest course, as far as vitality reserve funds.

The operation and efficiency of the node must be maintained when using this PEQ protocol. Failure in nodes is due to communication link errors, malicious attack, energy depletion, hardware failure, etc., which results in alignment fault and network topology changes. This fault is referred to as a probabilistic combinatorial optimization issue. The graph which denotes the WSN is $G = (V,E)$. The vertices for this graph are n. In the above equation n denotes the presence of deployed nodes as a whole in the network and represents the size of the problem; E denotes the link existing in wireless; and V denoted the number of sensor. The sensor, referred to as a functional sensor, will lie between 0 and n. The function sensor nodes that are considered in this issue is $(n - 3)$. The number of routing way that exists after the detection of failure.

The probability of a fault in a sensor node is denoted as P (absent). The delivery of data by the node to terminus in the presence of failure related to construction, proper equipment, age, etc., can be defined as a probability given as

$$p(\text{present}) = 1 - p(\text{absent}) \tag{2.1}$$

The transmission of data must be carried out in an effective way even in the presence of fault in the related element by selecting an alternative path that uses less energy. The depletion of energy in a WSN is due to positioning of sensor nodes in harsh environments that degrades network performance. The amount of energy in a small sensor node is $< 1.2\text{V}$. In most cases the battery is impossible to replaces and the lifespan of the network relies on battery life.

The topology of the network must be altered and an alternate route must be found in the case of failure. In order to maintain effective performance of network as well as to reduce the consumption of energy while broadcasting and transmitting the data to BS. By utilizing energy three significant function is followed by the node such as data processing, acquisition, and data transmission. The energy consumption formula of transmitting and receiving data between two nodes is as follows:

$$E_R(k,d) = elec * k \tag{2.2}$$

"While denotes distance among two nodes, k refer to the volume of data to be transmitted (bit), amp denotes the constant for consumption of energy engaged for expanding the wireless coverage using $nJ/(\text{bit} * \text{m}^2)$ and Elec denotes the consumption of energy for understanding data broadcast using nJ/bit. Let m_s denote the number of nodes present in the selected path represented through s. Consequently, the following function is used to compute the total spent energy of functional nodes fitting to the presented paths".

$$f(s) = \sum_{i=1}^{m_s} (m_s - 1) * E_{Ri}(k,d) + \sum_{i=2}^{m_s-1} E_{Ti}(k,d) \tag{2.3}$$

"Our goal is to determine the optimal one, between all of these possible paths, named s_{opt} and achieving this condition":

$$f(s_{opt}) = \min f(s) \tag{2.4}$$

Through the selected path the collected data from the environment can be transferred effectively towards the appropriate application with less consumption of energy. To maintain the connectivity of the network as well to perform effective data transfer even in the case of fault an effective and reliable fault recovery method must be developed, as has been shown here.

14.8.2 Energy-Efficient Model for Multiple Node Failure

For a network that has been partitioned into disconnected components, this work's primary objective is to concentrate on re-establishing connectedness while simultaneously improving network coverage in a way that minimizes wasteful use of energy. The general effectiveness of partitioned networks is something that can be improved with the help of the model that was established. The developed approach can be broken down into two distinct stages: intra-partition phase and inter-partition phase. Figure 14.8 provides a graphical representation of the segmentation network.

Every sensor node is present inside the partition in intra-partition. Each partition is represented as one or many areas where relay node is present at the center. In every partition based on inter-node detachment, the sensor nodes that are redundant are found. Certain area will denote an undiscovered area within the network. Towards this area the redundant node that was found is moved. The main aim of this phase is to achieve the best coverage and maintain the energy released from every node. Among every partition pair in inter-partition only a single relay node is present. This relay node takes part in the game along with other sensor nodes. On the basis of a theoretical technique followed in a game scenario related to cooperative game is established in this phase. A technique called zero-sum is utilized in this game. Here different players have various losses and profits. The sum of the losses and profits of the player is given as zero.

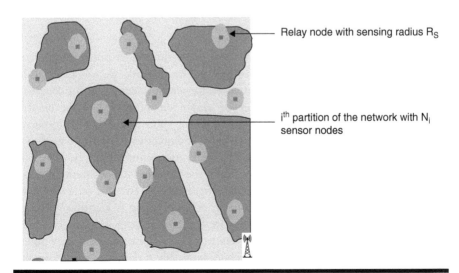

Relay node with sensing radius R_S

i^{th} partition of the network with N_i sensor nodes

Figure 14.8   Representation of partition network.

The motion of players must be done effectively to maintain connectivity in various partitions in the network. The policy in game as well as other criteria is developed based on energy utilization in this work. Within both phases the distance among the nodes is considered as minimum to attain effective operation related to energy efficiency within the network. A detailed description of the two phases is provided in the following section.

14.8.3 Intra-Partition Phase

The purpose of this phase is to develop coverage of the entire network by improving the area of coverage within every divided partition. In this phase the selection of partition is made in a dynamic manner and within every partition the developed algorithm is utilized. The finding of useless nodes is carried out in order to push them towards boundaries in the partition. The replacement of the useless nodes must be done in order to improve the coverage within every partition.

The connectivity of the network is maintained with the use of relay nodes. The jobless node must not lie in the range where the relay node is present because the connectivity is affected. In the appropriate area of transmission the coverage is maintained by keeping the relay node in place and the jobless node at the boundary surrounding it to achieve a wider coverage range. The movement of the jobless nodes is done on the basis of threshold distance. By taking into account the arrangement of the node the value for the threshold is found. The steps followed in the intra-phase are as follows:

- Initialization
- Redundant node identification
- Movement of redundant nodes

For performing these three steps in the intra-phase three algorithms were utilized which is named. Several parameters related to the network are initialized using Algorithm I. The parameters are ID employed for sensor nodes, range for collecting and transmitting the information given for relay node and sensor nodes, quantity of relay node existing as a whole, quantity of sensor nodes as a whole, within every partition the total number of sensor nodes exist, and quantity of partition necessary. The derivation utilized for deriving the average in Algorithm I is as , $(k + N_A)$. In order to find the presesnce of reductant nodes the variable such as threshold value, appropriate area for present of relay node, angle fraction etc. The reluctant node that is present along with the relay node in every partition is identified through Algorithm. The identified reluctant nodes are removed and put in a list. The communication between the relay nodes in every partition is done using the reply packet and request packet. The distance of the nodes internally is estimated using strength of signal. After calculating the distance the reluctant nodes are identified based on some drawback condition. The derivation utilized for deriving the average in Algorithm I is $\theta\left(k + N_A + N_S\right)$.

The reductant nodes that are present in appropriate area of every partition which were identified and moved is declared. Taking into account three kinds of radii the presence of reductant nodes along with relay nodes are analyzed in every partition. The reductant nodes that are identified in every partition are transferred towards the boundary of the specified partition. The reductant nodes that have the greatest enduring energy are given priority during movement. The replaced reductant nodes are removed from the reductant node list.

The derivation utilized for deriving the average in Algorithm III is $\theta\left(k + N_A + N_S\right)$. The work of the algorithm in this phase is to identify the reductant node and replace it in order to improve the area of coverage. The jobless node must not lie in the range where the relay node is present because connectivity is affected. In the appropriate area of transmission the coverage is maintained by keeping the relay nodes and the jobless nodes at the boundary surrounding it to achieve wider coverage range. Using the developed algorithm and partioning the overall connectivity of the network is enhanced.

14.8.4 Inter-Partition Phase

The connectivity in every partitioned area is maintained using the prior phase. The achieved connectivity must be maintained through this phase. The relay nodes that are present in any partition is referred to as free relay node. Using the algorithm the free relay nodes are identified and then removed from the partition. In case of most awful arrangement among every partition one free relay node is present. Based on the details gathered from the previous phase regarding the boundary of every partition the arrangement of free relay nodes is carried out. The free relay is placed so the area of coverage is overlapped. A union employing three nodes must be considered in this phase for performing game theoretic technique. The sensor nodes that are selected for union must be from various partitions and also exist within the range.

The sensor nodes with the highest energy are given priority. Based on this the arrangement are made in order to obtain effective union. The union is created to make the relay nodes perform the function of bridging among the neighbouring partitions. Through this technique communication among the nodes in the neighbouring partition can be achieved. Using the union the connectivity among the neighbouring partitions can be maintained. The calculation of partnership is made for each couple existing in neighbouring partition. Based on the free relay nodes for the sensor node that are selected as membership the calculation of pay-off is done. In case very more amount of energy is dissipated the movement is constricted.

To select a specified action the amount gain achieved by the nodes is referred to as payoff. The overall gain depends on the minimal distance between the free relay nodes and sensor nodes $\{s_i, s_j\}$. Using payoff the overall gain for the membership is estimated. In order to transfer data will less amount of energy the minimal distance is taken into account. To control the connectivity in specified partitions the sensor nodes are moved towards maximal distance. A cooperative game is carried out by three players to calculate the entire payoff. The nodes that are selected are $\{s_i, s_j, \text{relay free}\}$. Only the membership is considered in the game and not the individual players. A method called consensus decision-making is used by these players. The variables considered in this game are pay-off for each strategy, a set of strategies for players and set of players. The payoff function is expressed as

$$PO_i(s) = \begin{cases} \dfrac{E_{RES}}{(D_{freerely} - D_{parent\ relay})}, & E_{Res} \geq E_{Avg} \\ 0 & E_{Res} < E_{Avg} \end{cases} \qquad (2.5)$$

The average energy taken for the partition is represented as E_{Avg} within the position of the sensor nodes. The residual energy present within the sensor node is denoted as E_{Res}. The distance of the sensor node from the parent relay node is denoted as $D_{parent\ relay}$ and the distance of the node from the common free relay node is denoted as $D_{freerelsy}$. Sometime the present energy is larger when compared to the average energy obtained through partition. So for reducing the distance the motion of the node towards free relay node will take place. Using 2D matrix the pay-off function is determined. For instance, for $A(I,j)$ the matrix representation is given as $\{I,C_j\}$. Here C_i denotes i^{th} sensor node cost function and C_j denotes the jth sensor node cost function. The newer coordinate in the matrix of nodes can be found through the column index and row index. A certain index in the matrix possesses high value for payoff. These are selected as different location for sensor nodes. The sensor nodes are transferred to this position. The network topology is altered using this technique through which effective path altering is achieved.

14.9 Energy-Efficient Model Based on Cuckoo Optimization

As of late in WSN, grouping based vitality mindful directing conventions isolate neighbouring hubs into independent bunches and select nearby bunch heads in order to consolidate and transmit data of every one of the groups to the focal station. Right now, endeavour to keep up vitality utilization balance by the system hubs. When contrasted and different techniques, bunching strategies have had the option to accomplish the best productivity with respect to the upgrade of system lifetime. In the present work, utilizing cuckoo enhancement calculation, vitality mindful grouping-based steering convention was created in WSNs which can bunch the system and select ideal bunch heads. The created strategy considers four criteria for choosing bunch heads in the focused on cuckoo calculation, in particular the rest of the vitality of hubs, separation to the base station, inside group separations and between bunch separations. In the following we give the details on this advancement technique.

14.9.1 Developed Methodology

In this technique, estimations for deciding bunch takes are carted away in a focal control framework. The system model is a solitary jump model in which group heads straightforwardly speak with the focal station. In each round, the focal station knows about the energy level and the status of system hubs. In each round, every hub faculties and gathers encompassing data. At that point, it forms data and transmits it as an information bundle to the group head. Next, each bunch head gets information identified with all the part hubs of its group; from that point onward, it transmits the got information in the arrangement a parcel to the focal station in one bounce. There are three phases in this cuckoo advancement calculation based steering convention. The principal organize is choosing the bunch head, the second stage is setting up the group, and the third stage is transmitting the data.

There are two kinds of phases in this algorithm. The first phase is the start-up phase and the second phase is the register phase. In the initial stage the creation of clusters and finding of cluster heads is done. In the second stage the process of forecasting the program as well as achieves data transfer. The cuckoo optimization is used for selecting CH. Next, the clusters are created and register phase is done. We give a detailed description of the stages involved in this method next.

14.9.2 Start-up Phase

The CH is selected separately for every round in order to maintain energy balance. The selection of CH is done by cuckoo optimization. This CH will transfer the data to the BS. The BS will send a message regarding the work of CH in the present round in order to convey for every member of CH. Then the CH will send this message to the rest of the nodes in the cluster to explain their role. In this way, communication is maintained between the CM and CH within the network. The normal nodes are selected as CH for the proceeding round. The nodes that possess less energy for communication are chosen. As well as the distance must also be minimal. The receiving signal has the specified strength based on that the selection of CH is done.

The normal nodes make decisions regarding to which clusters they must be present in a specific round. Then they inform the corresponding CH. This communication is achieved by sending a Join-REQ message from the nodes to the CH. To avoid collision of data and to achieve effective transmission of data the CH generates TDMA, which is referred to as a scheduling program. This program is carried out considering the CM. This program created the by CH is transferred to the CM.

Through this technique it is proved that there is no possibility of collision in data. The nodes that are referred to as CM is in the state of rest in other span of time and they can be in active state in their time span. Through this approach the consumption of energy in every node can be decreased. Once the TDMA scheduling program processing is completed this phase is terminated and the next phase begins.

14.9.3 Register Phase

The network is divided into individual frames based on time in order to evaluate performance. In every frame related to time the transmission of data between the nodes in the cluster and the CH is done. The assumption is made in the developed algorithm that every node in the cluster is related to each other and the initial phase is conducted based on this assumption. The synchronizing pulses are transferred from BS to the nodes to know these criteria. The consumption of energy for the rest of the nodes that are not CH must be reduced. This is done by considering the signal strength obtained through advertisement (ADV) from CH. To maintain the power of communication, the energy and power control mechanism is utilized.

After running the scheduling program and forming the clusters the transmission of data from the nodes to CH is started. This transmission must be carried out in a specified time. The carrier scene with multiple access (CSMA) method is utilized by the normal nodes for transferring the collected data into respective the CH using distribution code. The specified distribution code exists for every cluster and every cluster will transmit the data using this code. If certain clusters need to transfer data then it must view the channel for the presence of other nodes that transmit data utilizing distribution code. In cases like this transmission is stopped for a while.

The previously mentioned two stages deal with the premise of enhancement calculation. The means engaged with enhancement calculation to accomplish compelling grouping is given in the accompanying segment. Cuckoo advancement is viewed as a populace-based and emphasis-based calculation. Right now, arbitrary introductory populace is initially delivered. At that point, in a tedious cycle, two phases identified with assessing the wellness and reasonableness of the present populace and refreshing the populace are completed continuously until the calculation end condition is met. This condition necessitates that all the pre-indicated emphases of the calculation are done.

■ **Step 1: Production of random initial population**

The binary method is used for solving the problem related to clustering of sensor nodes. The length of the binary string is denoted as N and refers to the entire sensor node number. For denoting CH "1" is used, for dead nodes "-1" is used, and for normal nodes "0" is used. Using cuckoo search optimization the search is conducted in a continuous manner and is carried out in this work. A continuous string is used for representing each member in the population. The length of the binary string is denoted as N, which refers to the entire sensor node number. The solution is expressed continuously within the interval $[0,1]$ as $(1 \le i \le N)$ i. I is the probability at which it is selected as CH. The selection of population in this algorithm is carried out in a random manner within $[0,1]$. The represented structure is continued in every stage of the algorithm. This selected random population is transferred into a typical cluster. Using this member function the fitness function is evaluated in the next section.

■ **Step 2: Evaluating the fitness function**

As indicated by the developed COARP technique, hubs with more vitality and less separation with the focal station are chosen to have more possibilities for being chosen as the group heads. Likewise, as for the between group and intra-bunch separates, an increasingly proper dissemination of the group heads is acquired in the whole system. At the end of the day, an endeavour is made in the created technique to limit the normal intra-group separations among bunch individuals and bunch heads. Simultaneously, the separations between bunch heads has to be boosted. For assessing every individual from the populace, from the start, the consistent structure of the arrangement has to be changed into the standard structure. For this, –1 is set for all the latent and dead hubs. At that point, as indicated by Eq. (3.14), the numerical estimations of all the alive hubs whose vitality levels are not exactly a threshold are changed into "0."

$$S^{new}(i) = \begin{cases} s^{old}(i) & \text{if } E(i) > \text{threshold} \times E_{avg}^{live} \\ 0 & \text{otherwise} \end{cases} \qquad (2.6)$$

In Eq. (2.6), $s^{old}(i)$ and $S^{new}(i)$ denote the solution for the node I, which are real and new values, correspondingly. $E(i)$ denotes the energy of node i in this present round and E_{avg}^{live} denotes the energy of all the alive nodes in the recent round. Moreover, the threshold values are found within the $[0,1]$ break. On the off chance that the edge esteem is viewed as zero, no confinements and changes are applied and the arrangement esteem for all the hubs stays unaltered. On the off chance that a higher worth is considered for the edge, group heads are chosen from hubs that have more vitality. Under exceptional conditions, the facts might confirm that the quantity of hubs with vitality levels higher than the edge is not exactly the absolute number of required bunch heads. In these cases, the edge level is decreased in stages with the coefficient of $\alpha=0.99$ until the quantity of hubs having vitality levels higher than the limit rises above or rises to the quantity of required bunches.

After the utilization of Eq. (2.6) on every individual from the populace, finally an answer is sorted out in a diminishing way from the most elevated likelihood to the least likelihood. C hubs with the most elevated probabilities are chosen as the bunch heads. Next, esteem "1" is set for the hubs chose as bunch heads in the arrangements and worth "0" is allotted for other alive hubs. Subsequently, every individual from the populace (each cuckoo) is changed into the standard grouping design. After each cuckoo is changed into the standard bunching design, group head hubs and non-bunch head hubs are resolved. In the following stage, each non-group head hub is apportioned to the nearest bunch head and bunches are built up. Next, the mistake level of every k individual from the populace (k cuckoos) is estimated through the created reason work.

■ **Step 3: Updating population**

After the completion of assessing the fitness of the arrangements, the best arrangement in the present cycle is chosen. At that point, it is contrasted and the best worldwide arrangement from the earliest starting point of the calculation as of recently. On the off chance that the mistake level of the best arrangement of the present emphasis is not exactly the blunder of the best worldwide arrangement, the best worldwide arrangement of the calculation is refreshed. Next, the cuckoo populace is refreshed by the conditions of the cuckoo improvement calculation. The phases of assessing arrangements and refreshing populaces are completed successively until the most extreme emphases of the calculation are done. Utilizing this strategy the vitality balance among the system can be kept up and less vitality utilization can be accomplished.

14.10 Energy Efficient Model Based on E-LFRR Algorithm

The Energy Link Failure Recovery Routing, also known as E-LFRR, is a collection of principles for two-level energy-focused routing that aims to eliminate Neighbour option put up link failures, as well as congestion in transmission, while also reducing the amount of time that traffic is held up. The E-LFRR can operate in two distinct settings, referred to respectively as Substitute Transmission modes and Monitored Transmission modes. In the event that the transmission is being monitored, the node that is neighbouring to the supply node will communicate the data regarding the signal's intensity level to the supply node after each record's transmission sequence. Within the network, the nodes that are referred to as Actuator Nodes are occupied by E-LFRR in order to disclose the multi-hop node strength levels. The actuator nodes are responsible for conveying to the parent node information regarding the amount of energy present in each of the energetic relaying nodes. In order to reduce the amount of energy needed to run the network, "sleep kingship" is used on nodes that are not in danger of being used for communication.

Actuator nodes will only disclose a single degree of the node's amount of energy, which means it will identify the concluding left lower back energy for the node once every transmission has been finished. In the event that the power of the nodes reaches 50% of its original condition, the actuator node will recommend to the supplier that the current intermediary be swapped out. When the transmission method was altered, the currently active receiving nodes were put into a slumber state, and additional nodes that were already in a sleep state were seized in order to continue developing the transmission technique. It is possible to prevent pointless communication by utilizing this strategy, which is initiated when a connection cannot be established. It is possible to cut down on the number of manipulate messages that are necessary for Neighbor discovery by using E-LFRR. This is accomplished by preserving a set of predetermined regular nodes, which are then replaced in the event that a connection fails. In addition, the new method, which makes use of advanced actuator information, will cut down on retransmissions and place existing traffic on hold within the network. It is possible to reduce overhead and postpone through the use of E-LFRR. Additionally, the number of living nodes that are present in the network can be increased, which saves a significant quantity of energy.

14.11 Energy-Efficient Model Based on (ME2PLB) Algorithm

Load balancing within WSNs requires negotiated development of power else alive nodes along the network. For decreasing the exchange-off among energy optimization and load balancing, the manner of optimization is prolonged to be utilized along three-tier routing operations incorporated along with power optimization and load-managing strategies. ME2PLB offers load balancing, data gathering, and strengthening optimization using three stages of transmitting. The routing protocol which was considered was Balanced Data Dissemination procedure, Switch over Transmission and Energy-efficient Transmission. This protocol ME2PLB will function with the assistance of monitoring nodes (MN) as well as number one and secondary aggregator nodes.

In the case of an energy-efficient transmission method, the primary aggregator begins gathering data from all of the dynamic nodes. To predict an undisturbed conscious state, the Essential Aggregator advises the inactive centers to be put into a rest state. Monitoring centers keep an eye on the viability of the primary aggregator and transmit that information to the secondary aggregators that are accessible within the MNs' communication range. MNs have a list of center data that must be replaced because they are less essential at the hour of vitality. MN recommends changing the distributor and centers based on their relative energy levels and ability to survive. When a hub is replaced by a neighbouring hub or another transmission hub, the MN spares the most recent transmission sequence. It sends clustering information to the dynamic source nodes. This prevents the same information from being duplicated and sent multiple times to the broker center. In the swapped mode transmission, MN updates the system's dynamic sending nodes with the new neighbors' and aggregator data.

The MN screens the cushion level present for aggregator hub in mode called Balanced Data Dissemination mode. As the auxiliary aggregator is unable to deal with indistinguishable measure of information from the essential aggregator, MN assumes the liability of organizing directing and information through the aggregator without misfortune. At the point when the cushion requirements are not fulfilled, MN suggests multi-way information transmission. In multipath information transmission, the essential and auxiliary aggregators play out the procedure of information gathering. In any case, the measure of information imparted to the essential aggregator in the additional opportunity is not as much as that of the information used in the primary possibility. ME2PLB guarantees anticipated information move rates and includes capacity of dynamic hubs in the system, with lower deferral and energy utilization.

14.12 Energy-Efficienct Model Based on DEOR Algorithm

Distance and Energy Optimization (DEOR) methods have consistently found as an exchange off methodology that outcomes in prior or incomplete arrangement that can't endure for quite a while. To reduce the crossing over hole between separations-based vitality preservation, DEA-OR is used. DEA-OR works in two stages: Energy and Distance Effective Path Selection and Greedy-based ease way determination. In distance-based vitality successful way choice, the source chooses neighbour with two appearances. At first, source considers separation factor for Neighbour choice and transmission. Source starts another neighbour revelation when the vitality of the present hub drops down to edge level. In the second neighbour disclosure process, the source considers vitality alongside with separation metric for neighbour determination [10].

At the moment, source processes the weight of each hub, wherein the weight is calculated as a combined determination of the distance between hubs and the amount of energy they contain. If both of these factors are taken into consideration when selecting a neighbour, the result is an imbalanced configuration [10]. The weight of each hub is communicated to its immediate neighbours, from which those neighbours choose who will serve as the hub's subsequent rebound neighbours. When it comes to transmission, a hub that has a greater weight component is preferred. When there is a course error or a connection disappointment at the time of transmission, Voracious Reduced Cost Route Selection will appear. In these types of situations, the neighbour sends a route error notification to the source, and the source immediately begins the process of re-directing from the very first node.

This helps prevent transmission interference within the source center by building up the backlog. DEA-OR searches for the guidance of covetous directing in order to avoid situations like this one. It initiates greedy guidance in the hub that is just in the opposite direction (the predecessor hub), which leads to the error hub. The predecessor hub takes every possible route to the sink hub because of its enthusiastic navigation, which takes into account all of the available options. A singular route is selected on the basis of its simplicity of use to reduce the amount of handling interference [25]. The accessibility and trustworthiness of a hub's interfaces are taken into consideration when determining a hub's cost factor over the course of communication. During the process of rerouting, the source looks for the previous transmission way, while the center of the road hub begins rerouting through a desirable easy way. The process in question is known as the neighbouring course correction technique.

14.13 Energy-Efficienct Model Based on Clustering Approach

In the present work for achieving effective selection of cluster head the swarm intelligence-based breeding artificial fish swarm algorithm is utilized. To remove faulty nodes as well as to improve energy efficiency the clustering related technique is used. The sensor nodes are arranged for the purpose of using clustering monitoring technique [12]. All sensors within the network are involved in communication and data transferring. This leads to collision of data resulting in wastage of energy. To address this issue the nodes are divided into clusters using a clustering technique. Within the cluster the nodes referred to as cluster members are present that is led through CH. The CH is referred as the controller.

In this process the data is gathered by the sensor nodes and is transferred to the CH. This CH will compress the data and further send it to the BS. Through this method the lifespan of the network can be maintained. Generally a two-level pyramid is visualized in these cluster generations in which the CH is present at the greatest level. The greater the energy required for the CH the more they perform the process of compressing and transferring of data towards the sink. The process of re-election of the CH is done in this technique in order to maintain the energy balance, but at the same if similar nodes are utilized as the CH then high energy is utilized leading to exhaustion. The CH is considered as provisional BS which will communicate with rest of the member is the cluster. The elementary step considered in this technique is selection of the CH. For prolonging the life of the network effective CH must be selected.

Group-based information collection has two stages: the arrangement stage and the relentless stage. In the set-up stage, the CH is chosen and the individuals chose.

The subsequent stage is the stage where the CH gets information from every one of its individuals and transmits it to the BS. Each procedure of the arrangement and the consistent stage is known as a round. This procedure is rehashed so that the CH is pivoted at customary interims with the end goal that all hubs disperse uniform vitality. In the determination of the CH every hub concludes whether to transform into CH or not founded on the goal work. A few hubs with increasingly remaining vitality transform into CHs and send CH data to illuminate different hubs. Different hubs with less remaining vitality transform into normal hubs, and send data about a joining group to a CH. The choice of CHs is a nondeterministic polynomial (NP)–Hard issue as existing factual procedures produce imperfect arrangements. True discrete and combinatorial issues are generally testing and require computationally serious calculations. Swarm knowledge (SI) calculations have been an intriguing option for giving acceptable arrangements where the individual qualities of the constant swarm calculations are utilized viably to address a given issue.

In this present work an SI algorithm called Artificial Fish Swarm Algorithm (AFSA) is utilized. Certain advantages are found in this algorithm that are insensitive towards initial values, tolerance of parameter setting, global search ability and robustness. This algorithm is based on the behaviour of preying in a group of fish. It is widely used for solving many optimization problems. The random solution is plotted based on the number of fish. The evaluation of fitness is carried out and further the process of initialization is done. Following the fish each iteration is performed until a better solution is found. If the solution process is not up to the requirement then starting from initialization the process is carried out. Until meeting the end criteria the process is carried out [16].

On the basis of considering the behaviour of a group of fish, four functions were developed in this algorithm. The behaviour of free movement is stated as the initial function. Basically the fish follow random movement in a group until they get attacked. The preying behaviour is stated as a second function in which the presence of victims can be found through smell, vision, or any other sensor present within their body. The sensing of prey is done through fish in a specified area. This area is considered as a neighbourhood in this algorithm. Up to the visualization the size of the radius is considered. The following behaviour is considered as a third function where particular fish identify the food, and the rest of the fish in the group follow in order to obtain the food. The grouping behaviour of fish is the final function in which the fish are present in groups all the time to protect them from predators. The solution space is taken as the living environment of fish. The amount of food present in water for fish is taken as theobjective function [17].

The initialization process is performed in these algorithms and is denoted as $X = (x_1, x_2, \dots x_n)$. In the this equation $x_1, x_2, \dots x_n$ represent the position of fish. Based on the visual length the radius of the area is fixed. $y = f(x)$ is the equation used to represent the concentration of fish existing for fish. Y is denoted as the value for the objective function. The distance exhibited among the fish is given by the equation $d_{ij} = \|x_i - x_j\|$. In this equation i and j represent the fish. The congestion factor is denoted by α. The swarm behaviour is carried out in every solution. Through event basis the choosing process of best fish is done. Then the operation of preying is started. The fish that are excellent in preying are chosen and are mated. The best which produces newer solution were considered for next iteration. The binary values are used for representing the solution and the Hamming distance is used for finding the distance among the fish [18].

14.14 Energy-Efficient Model Based on ISIRR Scheme

An immune system-inspired routing recovery (ISIRR)-based scheme was developed for achieving energy efficiency in WSNs. The immune system is a biological system. Its main function is to protect the body from disease and keep it healthy. The immune system which is found to be functioning normally can find much number of agents such as parasitic worms, viruses and bacteria. At the same time the agents present in one individual tissues and the foreign agent can be distinguished. The objective function that is performed the immune system is explained as follows. Many microorganisms exist in the environment that can attack humans. These intruded agents, referred to as antigens, cause destruction to the human body and can be identified by the immune system. Using finding the epitopes present in the layer of microbes the identification can be carried. The process of immune response is carried out on the identified agent found to be intruded upon. The microorganism is engulfed by the macrophages during this process and further they get split into pieces. On the surface layer of macrophage these dissolved pieces are found. They become antigens. For exploiting the microorganism higher quantity of antibodies is produced by the antigens. The antigen has definite binding along with B and T cells. Using this process the immune system can be protected from the entry of foreign agents.

An immune learning scheme was developed for progressing the antibodies towards higher attraction in "non-self" antigens. These antibodies have some young one which iscome as memory cells and they is long-lived. The invasion of a particular pathogen into the body of a specific person can be stored in memory cells. If a similar antigen invades the body later, a stronger immune response is generated spontaneously by these memory cells that protects the body. Energy harvesting-related wireless sensor network (EH-WSNs) was initializes at first. Definite path is followed by the node in order to each the sink. The selection of path can be done through an algorithm called DVP. In this technique the routing for recovery is considered as antibody and the fault routing is considered as antigen. If due to some issue such as depletion of energy source the recovery approach is carried out to find an alternative way within EH-WSNs. Mostly, the shortest path must be preferred from the sensor nodes to sink. Using this approach less consumption of energy can be achieved.

14.15 Energy-Efficient Model Based on SVM Classifier

Based on this SVM classifier the fault detection is achieved and further by detecting the fault and recovering the energy efficiency can be enhanced. The developed method works in two phases: anticipated time phase and real-time phase. The selection of cluster head using SVM classifier is represented in Figure 14.9.

In this figure the selection of cluster head is done using the SVM classifier. A particular set of datasets is created. Some of them are used in the training phase and the rest are used in the testing phase. For achieving effectiveness in clustering the training phase must be performed properly. Finally, using this process the cluster head is determined [19].

14.15.1 Anticipated Time

Using data learning approach the classification is carried out. Through this technique effective resolution can be taken for a problem. The transfer of data is carried as significant when WSN is considered. In the case of fault effective transmission must be achieved. Through certain researchers this learning process was carried out. Within the anticipated time this phase is recognized [20].

The major objective of this technique is to effectively solve the problem that is existing in real time through classification. On the basis of statistical learning the abovementioned data learning technique was developed. Lagrangian coefficients needed to found in learning phase. Employing this coefficient the objective

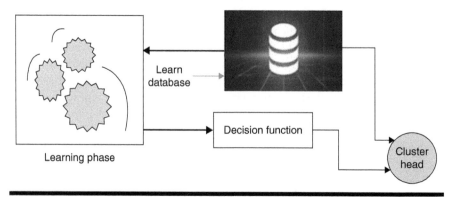

Figure 14.9 Selection of cluster head using SVM classifier.

function and support vector can be estimated. Following that the positioning of this objective function within the cluster head is carried out for classification purposes [18].

The database needed for this learning phase is taken from the labeled dataset. Within the dataset there exists both faulty and normal data [21].

14.15.2 Real Time

Through the data preparation block, a new observation vector, denoted as v_t, is created for every data estimation. The measurements relating to the last three data are provided in that observation vector $v_t; v_{t-1}; v_{t-2}$. For the purpose of fault detection the data extraction block is not necessary. Basically three successive estimations are considered for two sensors. For achieving multidimensional classification the SVM technique can be utilized.

Along with the newer observation this objective function is adopted. If the obtained result is found to be positive then it is referred as normal condition, if not then it is taken as fault. The algorithms used for finding this objective function are simple and are thus not expensive. Due to this reason this technique is considered as effective for the case of sensor nodes [22–24].

14.16 Energy-Efficient Model Based on GSA

Recently, the clustering technique has played a vital role in enhancing the efficiency of energy in WSN technology. To achieve better performance using this approach the selection of cluster head and cluster member as well as the arrangement of sensor nodes into clusters has been found to be significant. This process has greater impact on energy consumption within the network. In this present work the objective function is determined for the purpose of selection of the CH and to arrange the sensors within the cluster. For solving this objective function and for achieving better solution a modification is made in GSA (Gravitational Search Algorithm) and utilized. In this developed method the process and computation is carried out within the BS.

The implementation of the developed method is carried out in certain rounds to obtain the simulation results. Two phases are present in every round. The setup phase is considered as the first stage. In this stage the cluster head is selected and the arrangement of the cluster is achieved. The second stage is a steady state phase during which the gathered data is acquired by the cluster head and further compress it. The gathered data is transferred to the BS. The operation in this presented method is carried out within the BS. The data from the sensor node regarding the energy utilization and their position is sent to the BS. The candidates that are referred to as CH and nodes that possess higher energy level than average are considered [25].

The main objective is to enhance the quality of link and to minimize the energy consumption. The clusters present in the round are estimated by BS. The arrangement of the cluster is done in a compact manner by the BS to achieve an enhanced level of energy. The objective function is developed. For finding the best solution related to the fitness function GSA is utilized. The number of CH must be decrease to attain less consumption of energy. The objective function for saving the energy consumption is

$$f_1 = \frac{K}{S} \tag{2.7}$$

In the above equation K represents the optimal number of clusters and S denotes the size of the cluster head candidates. The arrangement of clusters in a compact manner is achieved by this method. Through this approach the energy consumption in WSNs can be minimized [26].

14.17 Challenges Faced in Fault Recovery in WSNs

Fault detection and recovery in WSNs is a challenging problem for many reasons:

1. The conventional technique is not suited for solving drawbacks existing in sensor nodes. This technique also has high computation cost [27].
2. Mostly the sensors are positioned in harsh environment where hazardous such as volcanos, highways, forest and indoor can be achieved.
3. The accuracy in detection is difficult to be achieved. The difference among the faulty and normal nodes must be detected effectively.
4. The time taken for detection must be minimal in order to reduce the loss. For instance, if incorrect data is collected from faulty nodes high energy loss will occur [28].

14.18 Conclusion

This chapter looked at concepts behind energy management in WSNs. The primary issues with energy consumption in WSNs that have an effect on load balance, node lifetimes, and network effectiveness were disucssed. The transmission of data is one of the services that uses the most power, and problems with communication, such as packet collisions, overhearing, and interference, can throw off the energy balance of the network. Innovative new solutions that are also good for the environment and save energy were developed so that the network can continue to function effectively and for as long as possible. Data-driven, task reassignment, navigation, and movement-driven are the four primary approaches that were been and characterized as ways to save energy. This topic was covered in a broad sense, with a concentration on the ways in which these techniques can consume less energy while still transferring data. Utilizing these methodologies can help reduce the amount of energy that is lost in detecting networks. However, practices like data minimization and extrapolation have the potential to have an effect on the dependability of the information that is communicated. When conducting additional research, it is important to take into consideration the effects that these techniques have on the connection quality and the reliability of the data.

This chapter also covered fault that arises in WSNs. The sources of fault were described along with the classification of fault. The classification was explained on the basis of behaviour, severity of occurrence, and time at which fault recovery action is taken. Further, the various methods for fault detection and recovery were explained. The developed methodology in various existing methods was elaborated on. Following that an introduction based on energy efficiency in WSN was given. The energy flow management in large and small WSNs was described briefly. Further the presentation was done on various existing techniques for achieving energy efficiency in WSNs. A technique based on clustering, swarm intelligence-based algorithm as well on classifiers was considered. In all these techniques there are limitations or drawbacks, which were also discussed.

References

1. Rathee, R. Singh, and A. Nandini. Wireless sensor network-challenges and possibilities. International Journal of Computer Applications, 140(2), 2016.
2. S. Khriji, D. El Houssaini, M.W. Jmal, C. Viehweger,M. Abid, and O. Kanoun. Precision irrigation based on wireless sensor network. IET Science, Measurement & Technology, 8(3):98–106, 2014.
3. A. Tzounis, Katsoulas, T. Bartzanas, and C. Kittas. Internet of things in agriculture, recent advances and future challenges. Biosystems Engineering, 164:31–48, 2017.
4. Dbibih, I. Iala, D. Aboutajdine, and O. Zytoune. Collision avoidance and service differentiation at the mac layer of wsn designed for multi-purpose applications. In Cloud Computing Technologies and Applications (CloudTech), 2016 2nd International Conference on, pages 277–282. IEEE, 2016.
5. R. Sett and I. Banerjee. An overhearing based routing scheme for wireless sensor networks. In Advances in Computing, Communications and Informatics (ICACCI), 2015 International Conference on, pages 2076–2082. IEEE, 2015.
6. A. Razaque and K.M. Elleithy. Low duty cycle, energy-efficient and mobility-based boarder node—mac hybrid protocol for wireless sensor networks. Journal of Signal Processing Systems, 81(2):265–284, 2015.

7. M. A. Kafi, J. Ben-Othman, A. Ouadjaout, M. Bagaa, and N. Badache. Refiacc: Reliable, efficient, fair and interference-aware congestion control protocol for wireless sensor networks. Computer Communications, 101:1–11, 2017.

8. W. Han, B. Zhu, N. Wang, and J. Xu. Development and evaluation of a wireless sensor network monitoring system in various agricultural environments. In 2013 Kansas City, Missouri, July 21–July 24, 2013, page 1. American Society of Agricultural and Biological Engineers, 2013.

9. Aijaz Ali Khan, R. M. (2022). A Research on Efficient Spam Detection Technique for Iot Devices Using Machine Learning. NeuroQuantology, 625–631.

10. D.G, M. (2019, January). A Review on Implementing Energy Efficient clustering protocol for Wireless sensor Network. Journal of Emerging Technologies and Innovative Research (JETIR), 6(1), 310–315.

11. D.G, T. (2019, January). A Review on QoS Aware Routing Protocols for Wireless Sensor Networks. International Journal of Emerging Technologies and Innovative Research, 6(1), 316–320.

12. D.G, T. (2019, January). A Review on Wireless Sensor Network: its Applications and challenges. Journal of Emerging Technologies and Innovative Research (JETIR), 6(1), 222–226.

13. Dattatray G. Takale, R. R. (2022). Skin Disease Classification Using Machine Learning Algorithms. NeuroQuantology, 9624–9629.

14. Dattatray G. Takale, S. D. (2022). Road Accident Prediction Model Using Data Mining Techniques (20). India, Maharashtra, India.

15. Dattatray G. Takale, S. S. (2022). Analysis Of Students Performance Prediction in Online Courses Using Machine Learning Algorithms. Neuroquantology, 13–18.

16. Dattatray G. Takale, S. U. (2022). Machine Learning Methode for Automatic Potato Disease Detection (20). India, Maharashtra, India.

17. Dr. Dattatray G. Takale, P. S. (May 2019). Load Balancing Energy Efficient Protocol for Wireless Sensor Network. International Journal of Research and Analytical Reviews (IJRAR), 153–158.

18. Dr. Dattatray G. Takale, M. A. (2014, November). A Study of Fault Management Algorithm and Recover the Faulty Node Using the FNR Algorithms for Wireless Sensor Network. International Journal of Engineering Research and General Science, 2(6), 590–595.

19. Takale D.G, D. K. (2019, January). A Review on Data Centric Routing for Wireless sensor Network. Journal of Emerging Technologies and Innovative Research (JETIR), 6(1), 304–309.

20. V. Raghunathan, S. Ganeriwal, and M. Srivastava. Emerging techniques for long lived wireless sensor networks. IEEE Communications Magazine, 44(4):108–114, 2006.

21. T. Rault, A. Bouabdallah, and Y. Challal. Energy efficiency in wireless sensor networks: A topdown survey. Computer Networks, 67:104–122, 2014.

22. J. A. Khan, H. K. Qureshi, and A. Iqbal. Energy management in wireless sensor networks: A survey. Computers & Electrical Engineering, 41:159–176, 2015.

23. C. Antonopoulos, F. Kerasiotis, C. Koulamas, G. Papadopoulos, and S. Koubias. Experimental evaluation of the waspmote platform power consumption targeting ambient sensing. In Embedded Computing (MECO), 2015 4th Mediterranean Conference on, pages 124–128. IEEE, 2015.

24. N. A. Bhatti, A. A. Syed, and M.H. Alizai. Sensors with lasers: Building a wsn power grid. In Proceedings of the 13th international symposium on Information processing in sensor networks, pages 261–272. IEEE Press, 2014.

25. M. Erol-Kantarci and H. T. Mouftah. Radio-frequency-based wireless energy transfer in lte-a heterogenous networks. In Computers and Communication (ISCC), 2014 IEEE Symposium on, pages 1–6. IEEE, 2014.

26. Q. A. Bakhtiar, K. Makki, and N. Pissinou. Data reduction in low powered wireless sensor networks. In Wireless Sensor Networks-Technology and Applications. InTech, 2012.

27. S. Lai. Duty-cycled wireless sensor networks: wakeup scheduling, routing, and broadcasting. PhD thesis, Virginia Polytechnic Institute and State University, 2010.

28. S. A. Nikolidakis, D. Kandris, D. D. Vergados, and C. Douligeris. Energy efficient routing in wireless sensor networks through balanced clustering. Algorithms, 6(1):29–42, 2013.

Index

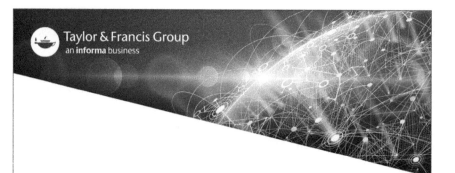